Studies in Public Opinion

Studies in Public Opinion

ATTITUDES, NONATTITUDES, MEASUREMENT ERROR, AND CHANGE

Editors

Willem E. Saris
Paul M. Sniderman

PRINCETON UNIVERSITY PRESS

PRINCETON AND OXFORD

Published by Princeton University Press, 41 William Street, Princeton, New Jersey 08540
In the United Kingdom: Princeton University Press, 3 Market Place, Woodstock,
Oxfordshire OX20 1SY

Library of Congress Cataloging-in-Publication Data

    Studies in public opinion : attitudes, nonattitudes, measurement error, and change /
editors, Willem E. Saris, Paul M. Sniderman.
       p. cm.
    Includes bibliographical references and index.
    ISBN 0-691-09254-0 (cl : alk. paper)—ISBN 0-691-11903-1 (pbk : alk. paper)
    1. Public opinion.   2. Political psychology.   3. Public opinion polls.   I. Saris,
Willem E. II. Sniderman, Paul M.

HM1236.S78 2004
303.3'8—dc22   2003064805

British Library Cataloging-in-Publication Data is available

This book has been composed in Galliard

Printed on acid free paper. ∞

pup.princeton.edu

Printed in the United States of America

10 9 8 7 6 5 4 3 2 1

Contents

PART IV: *Attitude Strength and Attitude Stability*

PART V: *An Alternative to the Standard Opinion Poll*

PART VI: *Looking Forward*

List of Contributors

MATTHEW K. BERENT is former assistant professor of psychology at Idaho State University. He is currently a project manager for Regenex Corporation.

JAAK BILLIET is professor in social methodology at the Katholieke Universiteit Leuven in Belgium. He is a member of the central coordination team of the European Social Survey. His research in methodology concerns the modeling of measurement error in social surveys. He has published longitudinal and comparative research in the domains of ethnocentrism, political attitudes, and religious orientations.

GEORGE Y. BIZER is assistant professor of psychology at Eastern Illinois University. His research, some of which has appeared in the *Journal of Personality and Social Psychology* and the *Journal of Personality*, primarily focuses on the structure and antecedents of attitude strength.

PAUL R. BREWER is assistant professor of journalism and mass communication at the University of Wisconsin-Milwaukee. His research on public opinion has appeared in such journals as the *American Journal of Political Science*, the *Journal of Politics, Public Opinion Quarterly*, and *Political Psychology.*

JOHN BULLOCK is a Ph.D. candidate in political science at Stanford University. His research, primarily in political behavior, includes articles on the measurement of political knowledge and the impact of changing civil rights attitudes. His dissertation is about the ways in which candidate evaluations are shaped by institutions and false consensus effects.

DANIELLE BÜTSCHI is a private consultant on project management and mediation in the field of technology assessment, with a special focus on issues related to the information society and the democratization of science. Previously, she worked for the Swiss government as the assistant director of the Swiss Centre for Technology Assessment (TA-SWISS). She received her doctorate from the Social Sciences and Economics Faculty of the University of Geneva, where she conducted research on the formation of public opinion and on welfare policies.

MICHAEL GUGE is a senior research analyst at Starr Litigation Services. His dissertation research at the State University of New York at Stony Brook examined the antecedents and consequences of ambivalent political attitudes.

HANSPETER KRIESI is professor of political science at the University of Zurich. He is the author of several books and articles on social movements, direct-democratic choice, and Swiss politics. Most recently, he coedited (together with David Snow and Sarah Soule) *Blackwell's Companion to Social Movements*.

JON KROSNICK is professor of psychology and political science at Ohio State University. He is the author of four books and more than one hundred articles and chapters focusing on political attitude formation, change and effects, the instigators of political behavior, and optimal design of survey questionnaires.

MILTON LODGE is a Distinguished University Professor in the Department of Political Science at the State University of New York at Stony Brook. His work on political psychology has appeared in the *American Political Science Review, American Journal of Political Science, Journal of Politics,* and *Political Analysis*.

MICHAEL F. MEFFERT is assistant professor of communication at the University of Maryland, College Park. His research focuses on political communication, persuasion and attitude change, and media effects.

PETER NEIJENS is professor in the Communication Science Department of the University of Amsterdam and scientific director of The Amsterdam School of Communications Research (ASCoR). He has published on public opinion, referenda, persuasion, and research methodology. In 1997, he was granted the Worcester Prize for the best article in the *International Journal of Public Opinion Research*.

WILLEM E. SARIS is professor of social science research methodology at the University of Amsterdam and guest professor at the Universidad Ramon Llull in Barcelona. He is the coauthor of several books, including *Causal Modelling in Nonexperimental Research* (with H. Stronkhorst) and *Foreign Policy Decision Making: A Qualitative and Quantitative Analysis of Argumentation* (with I. N. Gallhofer).

PAUL M. SNIDERMAN is Fairleigh S. Dickinson, Jr., Professor in Public Policy at Stanford University. His books include *The Outsider, Black Pride and Black Prejudice, The Clash of Rights,* and *Reasoning and Choice*. He is a Fellow of the American Academy of Arts and Sciences.

MARCO R. STEENBERGEN is associate professor of political science at the University of North Carolina at Chapel Hill. His research lies in quantitative methods and political psychology. He has published about voting behavior, public opinion, measurement, and multilevel inference. He is currently completing an edited volume about the contestation of European integration (coedited with Gary Marks), as well as a book about political deliberation (coauthored with Jürg Steiner, André Bächtiger, and Markus Spörndli).

MARC SWYNGEDOUW is research professor of political sociology at the University of Leuven (K. U. Leuven), Belgium. He is the author of numerous publications in the fields of political sociology, minority studies, and social science methodology.

SEAN M. THERIAULT is assistant professor in the Government Department at the University of Texas at Austin. His primary research focus is on the U.S. Congress. He has published articles on a variety of subjects including the Pendleton Act of 1883, the Compromise of 1850, congressional pay raises, and congressional careers.

WILLIAM VAN DER VELD is assistant professor in the Faculty of Social and Behavioral Sciences at the University of Amsterdam. He holds degrees in communication science and engineering and is writing a doctoral dissertation about models for response behavior in survey research.

PENNY S. VISSER is assistant professor in the Psychology Department at the University of Chicago. Her research focuses primarily on the structure and function of attitudes, including how attitudes influence information processing, how they motivate and guide behavior, how they are influenced by the social context in which they are held, and how they are maintained in the face of persuasive appeals. Her work has appeared in journals such as *Journal of Personality and Social Psychology, Journal of Experimental Social Psychology, Personality and Social Psychology Review, Personality and Social Psychology Bulletin, British Journal of Social Psychology, Public Opinion Quarterly, American Political Science Review,* and *American Journal of Political Science,* and in a number of edited volumes.

HANS WAEGE teaches research methodology and policy evaluation research at the University of Ghent. His actual research deals with the analysis of social networks, cultural participation, and policy analysis. He is promoter of both the Policy Research Centre Governmental Organisation in Flanders and the Research Centre on Cultural Participation. His work on the measurement of cultural participation was recently published in *Quality and Quantity.*

JOHN ZALLER is professor of political science at UCLA. He is the author of *Nature and Origins of Mass Opinion* and coauthor of *The American Ethos* (with Herb McClosky). He is attempting to finish two manuscripts, *A Theory of Media Politics: How the Interests of Politicians, Journalists, and Citizens Shape the News* and *Beating Reform: The Resurgence of Parties in Presidential Nominations* (coauthored with Marty Cohen, David Karol, and Hans Noel). He is a member of the American Academy of Arts and Sciences.

Introduction

Willem E. Saris and Paul M. Sniderman

IN THE STUDY of politics and political choice there are long-running streams of studies, proceeding along a common channel, with the later studies drawing out and testing the implications of the earlier. Broadly, these works have followed one of two opposing strategies—pushing one argument to its limit or pulling together apparently irreconcilable arguments. Mancur Olson's work on collective choice and the problem of the "free rider" exemplifies the first strategy;[1] Philip Converse's seminal work on the nature of belief systems in mass publics exemplifies the second.[2]

The first of Converse's master themes is the now famous "nonattitudes" hypothesis. Very briefly, and therefore roughly, the idea is that large numbers of the public do not hold any view on major issues of the day, but when asked their opinion, they express one anyway. These counterfeit attitudes are made up on the spot to avoid the embarrassment of appearing ignorant or the shame of seeming negligent. Converse dubbed these counterfeit responses "nonattitudes" and presented evidence suggesting that they are a pervasive feature of the political thinking of mass publics.

The second theme is the role of political sophistication. Two points have long been agreed upon. First, citizens are distributed along a gradient of awareness and understanding of politics. Second, the distribution of citizens along this gradient is skewed to the right: only a small proportion fall toward the tail of engagement with politics and political sophistication while a very high proportion fall toward the tail of political ignorance and inattentiveness. Converse drove home the lesson that the character of citizens' thinking about politics—the articulation of their positions on the major issues, their grip on fundamental political abstractions, even the stability of their opinions over time—is conditional on their level of political awareness and sophistication.

These two master themes—the pervasiveness of nonattitudes and the conditioning role of political sophistication—need not logically butt heads with one another: indeed, their conjunction yields the standard prediction that the likelihood of nonattitudes is inversely related to the level of political information and awareness. But the two themes tug in different directions. Focus on the pervasiveness of nonattitudes, and you emphasize the formlessness and incoherence of the political ideas of ordinary citizens; their indifference to matters of public concern and absorption in day-to-day concerns; the absence of deliberation or serious discussion of public affairs on their part; and an all-too-common failure to form any view whatever about central issues of the day. By contrast, focus on the structuring role of political sophistication, and you emphasize the organization of political belief systems, their crystallization, constraint, and stability, all of course conditional on political awareness and understanding. In a word, the first theme highlights the absence of political thought among citizens as a whole; the second, the conditions of their thinking coherently about politics.

Curiously, although the themes of nonattitudes and political sophistication were yoked together in Converse's original formulation, research on them proceeded independently of one another. The nonattitudes theme struck sparks first, rapidly generating a body of methodological research oriented to measurement issues.[3] The political sophistication theme took hold nearly a decade later, ultimately spawning at least as large a body of substantive and methodological studies. But a small number of honorable exceptions notwithstanding, work on the problems of nonattitudes and political sophistication have whistled down parallel rather than intersecting tracks. The mission of this book is accordingly integrative: to examine from as many vantage points as possible, in as many ways as possible, how these two master concerns—the problem of nonattitudes and the role of political sophistication—bear on one another.

This work also aims to be integrative at another level. European researchers who have done work on both problems have followed the work of their North American colleagues; North American researchers have not followed the work of their European colleagues as assiduously, to put it generously. Accordingly, a major aim has been to bring these two communities into closer contact.[4] The result is a work designed so that each can engage the other, and both their points of difference and commonality in approach to the core problems of nonattitudes and political sophistication can be brought into focus.

Each substantive chapter has a distinctive story to tell. But their cumulative contribution—the variety of ways, some obvious, others less so, in which they complement one another and so contribute to developing a theory of political choice—is our concern here. By considering the new studies reported in this book in the context of the larger bodies of research of which they are a part, we believe it is possible to develop a framework in which many—perhaps most —of the distinct models of public opinion choice can be coherently situated.

THE HISTORICAL BACKGROUND

When Converse first presented the concept of nonattitudes, he proposed an explanatory mechanism. When citizens had not given thought to an issue, yet wanted to act as though they had, he suggested that they choose a position at random. The act of choosing, so conceived, is like flipping a coin. Citizens oppose a government action if it comes up tails; support it if it lands heads. For a generation of research, the metaphor of coin flipping served as an explanatory mechanism for nonattitudes.

But it was only a metaphor and never an entirely apt one. As a choice mechanism coin flipping presumes indifference: landing heads is just as satisfying, from the point of view of the person making the choice, as landing tails. But how plausible is indifference to the outcome as a motivational postulate? On Converse's story, people act as though they have an attitude even when they don't because they want to appear as properly conscientious citizens who have given thought to the leading issues of the day even when they have not. Making a choice at random is a satisfactory way out. And it might be a satisfactory escape route if they had to answer only one question. But what is an easy way out once is onerous and duplicitous done time after time and at odds with the standard (and usually warranted) premise that respondents try to answer in good faith.

Converse's seminal study of mass belief systems triggered a landslide of research. Some minimized the nonattitude problem, attributing the largest part of response lability to measurement error (Achen 1975; Judd and Milburn 1980). Others differentiated the issue, attempting to specify who is most, and who least, susceptible to nonattitudes (see, for example, Zaller 1992 and Petty and Krosnick 1995). It is the work of Zaller that has had the greatest impact. He formulated a theory of how people can so readily change their position from one occasion to the next as to appear to be answering randomly, yet on every occasion be responding sincerely. They can do so, Zaller argued, because most of them simultaneously have reasons to say yes and no. What they do, when responding to a question, is not to look for an attitude they have already formed and stored away in a file drawer. Instead, they sample from a miscellany of positive and negative considerations that happen to be salient when they are searching for a response. Depending on the proportion of positive to negative considerations, their answer is affirmative or negative.

Viewed through the lens of sampling considerations from memory, a new theory of public opinion comes into focus. The problem with public opinions is not, as Converse suggested, that citizens have too few ideas. It is, Zaller contends, just the opposite. Most people have too many ideas and, what is more, ideas on all sides of most issues. These contradictory ideas, on this explanatory story, are stored in memory without their consistency either with one another or with other ideas that people hold being checked, particularly by those who are less politically aware and involved. Though the proportion of relevant ideas may be roughly balanced between positive and negative in total, particularities of question wording and ordering direct their attention to the one or the other. So they take one course of action as willingly, as sincerely, as its opposite.

A New Aspect: The Task

Sampling considerations from memory is thus the pivotal mechanism underlying nonattitudes according to Zaller. This mechanism can explain instability, but it does not explain why some people have more stable opinions, others less. Some researchers have argued that the choice mechanism is different for politically interested citizens; others favor a uniform mechanism. In chapter 1, following the lead of Tourangeau, Rips, and Rasinski (2000), Saris advances the argument that the theory of sampling considerations applies across the board. However, he contends that two factors cause the sampled considerations to be different for different people.

The first factor is people's political interest. Interested people collect more information and integrate this information in more fundamental considerations that can be standardly invoked across occasions. Paradigmatic examples are party identification and ideological outlook. There is thus an inverse relation between congruence of accessible considerations and political interest and awareness. The second factor conditioning the sampling process of accessible considerations is the task the people have to perform. People do not automatically recognize the relevance of a general principle they have in memory. The formulation of the task can condition the salience of deeper-lying considerations that serve as a basis for a coherent, stable response.

Van der Veld and Saris, in chapter 2, develop a tri-component formal model distinguishing stable considerations, unique considerations, and measurement error. In doing so they move away from Converse's black-and-white model, which assumes that people are either stable or not. They also move away from measurement error model of Achen, which has no separate provision for unique considerations at each specific point in time, assigning them instead to the error term, which therefore balloons, in the process giving the impression of striking stability to opinions. Van der Veld and Saris's formal model also differs from Zaller's, because it assumes that all people react in the same way, sampling considerations from memory, but differing in the amount of unique and stable considerations at their disposal. Completing the analytical story, Saris suggests, in chapter 1, that difference in amount of stable and unique considerations depends on the two parametric factors in our larger account: political interest and the task given to the people.

These two variables, interest and task, fill the gap left by Converse, Achen, and Zaller concerning the conditions that determine whether people provide stable or unstable answers and are seen as having an attitude or not. All the chapters have, of course, their own purpose and value, but in this introduction, we would like to concentrate on those aspects that speak to the plausibility of the theory concerning the two relevant factors: the task and political interest. We start with the effect of the task, then discuss the effects of political sophistication or awareness or political interest, then finally, by way of exploring further the role of political awareness and interest, consider bases of attitude stability.

THE EFFECTS OF THE TASK

The clearest case where one can see the effect of the task is the analysis of the structure of political argumentation by Sniderman and Theriault (chapter 5). A sizable body of studies on issue framing has now accumulated. Without exception, these studies report that large numbers of the general public can be moved from one side of an issue to the other depending on how the issue is framed. Sniderman and Theriault, however, observe that these studies have been confined to one-sided presentations. An argument is presented to evoke support for a policy, or opposition to it, but not both. But in real politics, of course, opposing candidates compete to put across their point of view. Sniderman and Theriault therefore add to the standard design of framing experiments a condition in which people are confronted with both pro and contra arguments. They then show that when exposed to conflicting arguments, people are significantly more likely to make a specific choice that is consonant with their general view of the matter than is the case under the one-sided situation common to framing experiments. This is a clear example that shows that the accessibility of relevant considerations is conditional on the structure of the choice.

Kriesi (chapter 8) also pays attention to the effect of characteristics of the choice options the people are presented with. He characterizes them as more or less familiar, complex, and constrained. Notice that this last element, the concept of constraint, is used in a sense quite different from its customary one in American political science. Here it refers not to the degree of connectedness between positions on an array of public policies, but instead to whether a policy measure has a direct bite on an individual or not, as, for example, the closing down of the centers of town for car traffic or the introduction of speed limits has a bite for car owners that it lacks for those who do not own a car. One would expect that the more familiar the people are with policies and the more constrained by them they are, the more stable their responses to them will be. In his analyses Kriesi indeed finds that stability is higher conditional on policy familiarity and constraint. But no comparable effect conditional on complexity is observed. This result is interesting because it confirms that the different choice options make a difference.

A third study that shows that the task plays an important role is that of Neijens (chapter 10). The Choice Questionnaire tries to tackle the problem that many people are not so interested in political problems and therefore do not have enough information. By providing them with the necessary information, the designers of the Choice Questionnaire try to fill this gap so that the choices of the people become better. In this context, "optimal" means that people make a choice in agreement with their evaluation of the consequences of different options. Accordingly, in the Choice Questionnaire, the two variables, task and effort, are manipulated to explore their contribution to more optimal choices. Neijens shows that the formulation of the task makes a substantial difference in the performance of the respondents. In the most complex form of the Choice Questionnaire people indeed make use of the necessary information. The result: a much larger group of the public makes choices consistent with their own evaluations of possible consequences.

The notions of consistency—and its conceptual rival, ambivalence—are both pivotal and elusive, as the chapters by Meffert, Guge, and Lodge (chapter 3) and by Steenbergen and Brewer (chapter 4) make plain. The former examines ambivalence toward candidates for public office; the latter, ambivalence about policy. The former study shows ambivalence to have a pair of key properties. The first corresponds to a familiar, albeit contested, claim; the second represents an original contribution. The familiar claim concerns the frequency of ambivalence. It is, they maintain, commonplace, showing up, in at least one of their estimates, in as much as 40 percent of the American electorate. The original contribution consists in establishing that the more inconsistent people's opinions and feelings toward presidential candidates, the less extreme their evaluations of them, the weaker their approval of them, and the less crisp their images of them. In a word, ambivalence is inversely related to attitude strength.

By contrast, though treating ambivalence the same conceptually, Steenbergen and Brewer seemingly reach very nearly the opposite substantive conclusions. In their view, rather than ambivalence being common, it is atypical, and rather than being inversely related to attitude strength, it is unrelated to attitude stability, constraint, or consistency, to all of which it should be negatively related, if it truly is inversely related to attitude strength.

This difference between the findings of Meffert, Guge, and Lodge on the one side and Steenbergen and Brewer on the other may turn just on a correct assessment of the facts of the matter. One may be closer to the way that things are across the board. That is not a conclusion that can be comfortably drawn either way, given the evidence on hand. It is perfectly possible there is one state of affairs for views about political candidates, another for public policies. The choice of candidates or parties in elections gets so much attention that even people with little political interest get a lot of information about the candidates or the parties. This may lead a large portion of the public to "ambivalence" as suggested by Zaller (1992), that is, an unordered set of contradictory considerations. On the other hand, for many matters of public policy, most people characteristically collect very little information. So for the most part those who make up an issue public specially focused on this matter of policy will obtain contradictory information. And given their special degree of engagement, they are in a position to integrate conflicting information. In short, they may have "ambivalence" as suggested by Alvarez and Brehm (1995), that is, an ordered set of pro and contra considerations bearing on the policy at stake. Just so far as this is so, it is yet another illustration of how the nature of the task—choices between candidates or courses of action—can shape the process of choice and thereby the stability and consistency of choices.

Political Interest and Awareness

Focusing on the gradient of political awareness, Zaller (chapter 6) comes away with a new insight into the nature of electoral dynamics. His takeoff point is the now taken-for-granted finding that the less politically informed and sophisticated that citizens are, the less likely they are to form genuine attitudes about political matters. The inference that has seemed immediately to follow is that the less politically informed and sophisticated that citizens are, the more unsound and illogical their reasoning about political choices. By viewing successive elections as a choice sequence, however, Zaller puts the issue in a quite different light. Turning the standard argument on its head, he shows that the more politically sophisticated, by virtue of having stronger, more crystallized opinions that are more consistently interlocked one with one another, are more likely to be anchored in place politically. Hence they tend to support the same party from one election to the next, even when circumstances have changed (for example, the economy has gotten worse). By contrast, the less politically sophisticated, precisely because they have not formed and committed themselves to a consistent set of political ideas, tend to be more insecurely anchored, freer to respond to changes in objective circumstances, and therefore better able to reward those responsible for government when times are good and punish them when times are bad.

The implications of this result for a theory of electoral accountability merit serious attention.[5] Zaller highlights the dependence of political accountability on citizen responsiveness to short-term factors. By virtue of being more responsive to short-term factors, it is less informed voters, not more informed voters, who enhance electoral accountability. Or more exactly, Zaller's findings show that they enhance accountability for judgments on one dimension—economic. The calculus of accountability taken as a whole involves a complex blend, with more informed voters contributing a stability component based on fundamental political orientations, less informed ones a dynamic component based on changing aspects of the political situation.

Danielle Bütschi (chapter 11) also concentrates on political interest—but with a new twist. Taking advantage of the Choice Questionnaire technique, she examines the effect of obtaining new information relevant to the choice at hand. She comes to the conclusion that it is mainly the people with less political interest, and therefore less stable opinions, who use the information in the Choice Questionnaire to reformulate their choice. This conclusion is of obvious importance on both empirical and normative grounds.

All of these studies confirm the effect of political interest and engagement on the choices the respondents make. It is all the more important, therefore, to work through the relations of a family of concepts and indicators bearing on the concept of political interest. This is the mission of the studies in part 4.

Attitude Strength and Stability

It is natural to expect that political interest and attitude strength and stability should be related. And, as one would expect, all of the contributions in part 4 that order respondents on the basis of some indicator of political interest, information, or sophistication show that the more interested and engaged respondents are much more stable in their preferences than the less sophisticated respondents. This indicates the importance of this ordering principle.

Yet there is an obvious problem. Different concepts have been used to make the same, or exceedingly similar, ordering distinction. Some scholars have suggested the use of political sophistication, others awareness, political interest, issue importance, knowledge of the issue, etc. Even more confusing is that social psychologists use all these terms as indicators for a latent concept "attitude strength" (Krosnick and Abelson 1992). One of the nice results of this book is that some general evidence to clear up this discussion about attitude strength has been brought together.

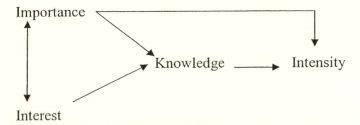

Figure 1 A simplified causal model of Bizer et al. (chapter 7 in this volume) with respect to different variables often seen as indicators of attitude strength.

Krosnick and Petty (1995) define attitude strength in terms of two parameters—stability and crystallization. On their view, strong attitudes should be stable and should have a strong impact on judgments and behavior. Krosnick and Abelson (1992), however, argue that a slew of variables are treated as indicators of attitude strength. It is accordingly of general importance that Bizer, Visser, Berent, and Krosnick (chapter 7) show that these different variables do not measure the same attribute. It follows that they cannot be equivalent indicators of attitude strength. Bizer and his colleagues then make an argument that these variables should instead be viewed as possible causes of crystallization or stability and, thus, as indirect causes of attitude strength. In a set of analyses the authors look at possible causal relationships among the different variables in the set. In doing so they show, for example, that the variables "importance of an issue" and "knowledge of the issue" have different causes and have different effects on other variables. Their analysis leads to a kind of model (Figure 7.2 of Bizer et al.), which we would like to summarize here in Figure Intro.1.

It is straightforwardly plausible to suppose that there is a strong effect of attitude intensity on the stability of the attitude. Figure 1 is interesting, then, because it suggests which of the conditional variables customarily taken to be indicators of attitude strength would be the best predictor for the stability of responses. Naturally enough, the best predictor is the variable that is closest in the causal chain to stability. The farther away a variable is in the causal sequence from the variable "stability" the less the effect will be.[6] According to this path model, then, the best predictor would be "attitude intensity." The second best would be knowledge. And trailing along would be political interest and issue importance, although a cautionary note should be sounded for issue importance since it has also a direct effect on attitude intensity.

Bizer's analysis thus provides an ordering of the conditional variables with respect to their effect on the attitude stability which, until now, has not been available. This result is also interesting because it gives an explanation for findings in two other studies on the effect of different conditional variables for attitude stability.

Taking the two in turn, Billiet, Swyngedouw, and Waege (chapter 9) advance the straightforward hypothesis that stability should be a function of political awareness: the more engaged citizens are in politics, the more stable over time their attitudes should be. They distinguish three indicators of political involvement or awareness—education, political interest, and political knowledge—and then estimate the stability of attitudes conditional on these three variables. Of the indicators of awareness that Billiet and his colleagues examine, political knowledge dominates education and political interest in predicting attitude stability. On the basis of the results of Bizer et al., we suggested that the effect of knowledge would be larger than the effect of interest. That the effect of education is also smaller is not surprising because that variable is even farther away for attitude strength. So this result of Billiet, Swyngedouw, and Waege is an interesting corroboration of the causal ordering suggested by us on the basis of the study of Bizer et al.

The second study comparing the effects of different conditional variables for stability is Kriesi's (chapter 8). Kriesi looks at the effect of political awareness, among other factors, on the stability of the responses. As we have noted, he uses a trio of variables, two familiar—knowledge and opinion strength or intensity—and one original—situational constraints, defined as the immediate relevance or "bite" of a policy for specific citizens. According to the hypothesis we have derived from the results of Bizer et al., we would expect that attitude strength or intensity would have the most effect on stability of the preferences. This is indeed what Kriesi reports on the basis of his analyses. He even shows that knowledge and constraint have no significant effect anymore in an analysis where the three variables are introduced together. In that case only the strength of the opinion has a significant effect. This does not mean that these variables have no effect at all but that the effects of these variables all go through the variable strength or intensity of the opinion. This is another corroboration of the model set out in the figure above.

All the chapters described so far show that personal characteristics have an effect on the way people generate their responses to policy questions. It becomes clear that people with more intense opinions also have more stable opinions. Whether that is a good sign or a bad one from a normative perspective is an interesting question. From an empirical standpoint, however, the studies in this book show that the conditions for opinion strength can be ordered with respect to their effect where attitude strength is the best predictor of stability, then follow knowledge and importance, then interest and other variables like education. This ordering of conditions is a new and simplifying contribution of this book to the field of nonattitude research.

LOOKING FORWARD

Three questions run through this book: When do citizens form genuine attitudes about politics? What is the impact of political awareness and interest on the formation of political ideas? And what difference does the task, the structure of the problem presented to citizens, make to the choices citizens make? The three questions are not emphasized equally, but they recur repeatedly. And intuitively, the answers to one bear on the answers to the others. The last chapter, by Sniderman and Bullock (chapter 12), presents a theoretical framework to tie them together. It is admittedly a framework that proceeds from an unusual perspective. In the study of public opinion the overwhelming emphasis descriptively has been on the inconsistency of ordinary citizens' political ideas. By contrast, Sniderman and Bullock contend that if a theory of public opinion is to go beyond the problem of nonattitudes, it must provide an account of the conditions under which citizens achieve consistency. They accordingly distinguish a trio of ways the construct of consistency commonly has been understood, singling out one—maximizing congruence between alternative ways of dealing with a particular matter with one's general view of the matter. How, they ask, can ordinary citizens achieve consistency so understood?

A number of consistency-generating mechanisms—among them, on-line processing, core values, and judgmental heuristics—have been identified. But these mechanisms cannot provide a basis for a consistency theory of any substantial scope. Quite simply, given the minimal level of attention the public pays to politics, it is difficult to see how ordinary citizens are in a position to achieve consistency in political judgments and choices making choices *on their own hook*. But that, according to Sniderman and Bullock, is just the point. Citizens do not have to do all the work on their own. Political institutions—and above all, political parties—do the heavy lifting.

They accordingly focus on the idea of menu dependence. On this hypothesis, the choices that citizens make are a function of the set, or menu, of choices on offer. This menu is organized by political parties competing for electoral support. Stated broadly, citizens can coordinate their responses to political choices insofar as the alternatives they can choose among are coordinated by political parties.

By way of draping some evidentiary clothing on this hypothesis, Sniderman and Bullock explore three aspects of menu dependence: consistency for sets of issues; for issues taken one at a time; and for variations across issues. In the process they introduce a number of distinctions, for example, between consistency within and between political domains. This is very much a venture in looking forward. The evidence on hand is indirect and incomplete. And there are obstacles that it is not obvious now how to clear, above all, on what terms consistency maximizing should be reconciled with belief updating. But with all appropriate qualifications capitalized for emphasis, there is something to be said for acknowledging that citizens do not organize politics on their own: it comes to them already organized.

Notes to Introduction

We are grateful to our respective universities for support in this project. Sniderman also has a particular debt to acknowledge—a National Science Foundation Achievement Based Award (SES-0111715), which has been of invaluable assistance for this project.

1. Olson 1965.
2. Converse 1964.
3. The classic battle citations are Achen 1975 and Judd and Milburn 1980.
4. With two exceptions only, the chapters were presented and critically evaluated at a conference titled "Non-Attitudes, Measurement Error and Change," organized by W. E. Saris and P. Neijens at the University of Amsterdam in September 1997.
5. We want to thank an anonymous reviewer for stressing this point.
6. This argument is based on the path analysis result that an indirect effect is the product of the two direct effects, and will always be smaller than either of the direct effects because normally these effects are smaller than 1.

References

Achen, Christoper H. 1975. "Mass Political Attitudes and the Survey Response." *American Political Science Review* 69:1218–31.

Alvarez, R. M., and J. Brehm. 1995. "American Ambivalence toward Abortion Policy." *American Journal of Political Science* 39:1055–82.

Converse, Philip E. 1964. "The Nature of Belief Systems in Mass Publics." In *Ideology and Discontent,* ed. David E. Apter. New York: Free Press.

Converse, Philip E., and Greg Markus. 1979. "A Dynamic Simultaneous Equation Model of Electoral Choice." *American Political Science Review* 73:1055–70.

Fiorina, Morris P. 1985. *Retrospective Voting in American National Elections.* New Haven, CT: Yale University Press.

Gamson, William, and Andre Modigliani. 1987. "The Changing Culture of Affirmative Action." *Research in Political Sociology* 3:137–77.

———. 1989. "Media Discourse and Public Opinion: A Constructionist Approach." *American Journal of Sociology* 95:1–37.

Jackman, Simon, and Paul M. Sniderman. 2000. "The Institutional Organization of Choice Spaces: A Political Conception of Political Psychology." In *Political Psychology,* ed. Kristen Renwick Monroe. Mahwah, NJ: Erlbaum.

Judd, C. M., and M. A. Milburn. 1980. "The Structure of Attitude Systems in the General Public: Comparisons of a Structural Equation Model." *American Sociological Review* 45:627–43.

Krosnick, Jon A., and Richard E. Petty. 1995. "Attitude Strength: An Overview." In *Attitude Strength: Antecedents and Consequences,* ed. Richard E. Petty and Jon A. Krosnick. Hillsdale, NJ: Lawrence Erlbaum.

Krosnick, Jon A., and Robert P. Abelson. 1992. "The Ease for Measuring Attitude Strength in Surveys." In *Questions About Questions: Inquiries into the Cognitive Bases of Surveys,* ed. Judith M. Tanur. New York: Russell Sage.

Olson, Mancur. 1965. *The Logic of Collective Action.* Cambridge, MA: Harvard University Press.

Petty, R. E., and J. A. Krosnick, eds. 1995. *Attitude Strength: Antecedents and Consequences.* Mahwah, NJ: Lawrence Erlbaum.

Sniderman, Paul M. 2000. "Taking Sides: A Fixed Choice Theory of Political Reasoning." In *Elements of Reason: Cognition, Choice, and the Bounds of Rationality,* ed. Arthur Lupia, Mathew D. McCubbins, and Samuel Popkin. New York: Cambridge University Press.

Sniderman, Paul M., Richard A. Brody, and Philip E. Tetlock. 1991. *Reasoning and Choice: Explorations in Political Psychology.* New York: Cambridge University Press.

Sniderman, Paul M., Robert Griffin, and James M. Glaser. 1990. "Information and the Psychology of Electoral Choice." In *Information and Democratic Politics,* ed. James Kuklinski and John Ferejohn, 117–35. Champagne, IL: University of Illinois Press.

Tetlock, Philip E. 1984. "Cognitive Style and Political Belief Systems in the British House of Commons." *Journal of Personality and Social Psychology* 46:365–75.

Tourangeau, Roger, Lance J. Rips, and Kenneth Rasinski. 2000. *The Psychology of Survey Response.* New York: Cambridge University Press.

Zaller, John R. 1992. *The Nature and Origins of Mass Opinion.* New York: Cambridge University Press.

PART I

A Synoptic Perspective

CHAPTER 1

Different Judgment Models for Policy Questions: Competing or Complementary?

Willem E. Saris

EVEN BEFORE the first study of public opinion, Lippmann (1925:20, 36–37) had already called it a "false ideal" to imagine that voters were inherently competent to direct public affairs. "If the voter cannot grasp the details of the problems of the day because he has not the time, the interest or the knowledge, he will not have a better public opinion because he is asked to express his opinion more often." When the first polls were subsequently held, researchers were disappointed to find that people's preferences were not so much determined by the discussion taking place but more by demographic characteristics and interpersonal influences (Lazarsfeld, Berelson, and Gaudet 1948). It was also shown that most people did not pay much attention to campaigns, even presidential campaigns, and that people seldom changed their opinion because of new information (Berelson, Lazarsfeld, and McPhee 1954). Lazarsfeld, Berelson, and Gaudet (1948) suggested that most people expressed opinions that were developed by a limited number of opinion leaders. This model has been called the two-step flow of communication model.

Campbell et al. (1960) also found that people did not know what government policies were on the most important issues. They suggested that, as an empirical matter, people make a choice for a political party not so much on the basis of knowledge of issues but rather on the basis of a longer existing identification with one of the parties.

Although these discussions on the competence of the public had been going on for a long time, Converse's work (1964) had a big impact on the debate with respect to the possible role of citizens in the democratic process. He suggested as the others did that "large portions of the electorate do not have meaningful beliefs, even on issues that have formed the basis of intense political controversy among elites for substantial periods of time" (245). His argument was based on an analysis of the stability of people's opinions on political issues. It turned out that some people easily change their opinions about certain issues even though exactly the same question is asked while others do not change their opinions at all. This change was interpreted as indicating a lack of a strong opinion on these issues, which Converse referred to as "nonattitudes." Because of the difference in reaction between different groups, this finding became known as the black-and-white model.

Nonattitudes call into question the fundamental democratic assumption that citizens can evaluate political issues and can therefore be asked to participate in the political decision-making process by voting in elections or by direct participation through referenda. If only a limited number of people have insufficient information to participate, and if these people do not participate, there is no problem. But if many people have insufficient information and nevertheless participate in the political process then there is a real problem.

Given the importance of this problem for the functioning of democracy, this issue has led to sometimes fierce discussions over the last forty years. First, several researchers argued that the situation was not as bad as Converse suggested. They argued that Converse did not take measurement error into account. By formulating models for repeated observations that took measurement error into account, they suggested that people's attitudes were stable and that the instability of their responses was almost entirely due to measurement error. By this account, the low reliability of responses to over-time batteries of questions was due to the poor quality of the questions (Achen 1975; Erikson 1978, 1979). But Converse and Markus (1979) showed that after correction for measurement error, different stability estimates were obtained for questions with exactly the same format. This difference in stability had something to do with the object and not with the form of the question. Using a different model Judd and Milburn (1980) and Judd, Milburn and Krosnick (1981) also suggested that the measurement errors caused the instability of the responses rather than unstable opinions. Their contribution is very harshly criticized by Converse (1980).

In the aftermath of this debate on both sides of the ocean, models have been developed for the responses to policy questions in survey research. Some are in line with Converse; others, following Achen, suppose that people have very detailed opinions. Most of the time these models have been discussed as competing models and have been tested as such. In this chapter I suggest that these models are not so much competing as complementary. I argue that the different models are specific cases of a more general model that applies to all people while the specific models apply to different tasks and different groups of people. In total, I briefly describe eleven different models that have been presented in the literature, and then I introduce a general judgment model and indicate how the different models connect with this general model and when the specific models describe the choice process of people in survey research.

A HISTORICAL OVERVIEW

Different models have been developed on both sides of the ocean. Some are in line with the ideas of Converse. For example, in Europe the two-stage model, originally suggested by Lazarsfeld, Berelson, and Gaudet (1948), was tested by Wiegman, de Roon, and Snijders (1981) and the party identification model was tested by Thomassen (1976). There were other researchers who believed that respondents were capable of a more rational approach, in some sense ignoring the remarks of Converse and working in the line of Achen and others. For example, Middendorp (1978) introduced choice models on the basis of ideology. Models related to the rational choice theory were also discussed and tested. For example, the Multi Attribute Utility model (MAUT) was tested by Himmelweit, Humphreys, and Jaeger (1981). And a simplified model, suggesting that choice is determined by the distance between the respondent and the parties on a left-right scale (the so-called smallest distance model) was tested by Van der Eijk and Neimöller (1983).

In the United States we see a similar development. Rational choice models in their extreme form and bounded rationality models have been discussed by several people. For an overview of the different models we refer to Taber and Steenbergen (1995). Sniderman, Brody, and Tetlock (1991) suggest that more politically sophisticated people will behave differently from less sophisticated people if they have to vote. More sophisticated people will base their choice on ideological orientations but less sophisticated voters do not use their knowledge of the ideological positions of the different candidates; rather, they use their evaluation of how much they like or dislike the persons. We will call this model the like-dislike model.

A similar kind of model has been developed by them for choices with respect to policies in favor of specific groups. It suggests that people make a choice in favor of a group if they like that group and against it if they don't. This has been called the affect-driven choice model. They claim that different groups make choices in different ways, but that their choices do not differ by degree of rationality: one group's choice is not necessarily more or less rational than the choices made by other groups.

In the same year Krosnick (1991) published an essay suggesting that when people are asked to answer questions in a survey, they do not try to give the best possible answer (optimize) but often give an answer that will cost them less effort and will be acceptable to the interviewer. He calls this the satisficing model for survey research. He distinguishes between weak and strong forms of satisficing where in the former case the respondent looks in his memory for possible information to generate an answer while in the latter case the respondents just choose an acceptable answer from the provided possibilities without any further effort.

A crucial contribution in the further debate on nonattitudes has been provided by Zaller (1992). He suggests that the instability is not so much due to respondents' lack of information but to an overload of information that is not structured by most people. As a consequence the respondents will pick up from their memory the information that is most salient at the moment they have to answer a survey question. What is salient can be different from moment to moment and from question formulation to question formulation. Zaller also makes a strong argument that political awareness plays an important role in the amount of structuring of the beliefs and therefore of the instability of the responses. We will call this the Saliency model because the saliency determines the mechanism that causes the instability in the responses.

Partially inspired by the ideas of Zaller, many so-called framing experiments have been done to show that the questions' context has a considerable effect on the responses (see, for example, Gamson and Modigliani 1987; Nelson and Kinder 1996).

In 1995 Lodge, Steenbergen, and Brau added a new model to this discussion: the on-line model. They suggest that people do not keep a record of the opinions of candidates on issues or of positive or negative acts of politicians. Instead, they propose that people forget all this information rather quickly but that they keep a tally of positive and negative events related to the candidates. These tallies are available on-line in memory and determine how they will make their choice pro or contra different candidates.

In this brief overview, I have mentioned eleven different models used to describe the way respondents generate answers when they are asked questions about political issues. These models have been discussed as alternative and competing models.

In this chapter I argue that these models are not competing but complementary because each of them has been developed with a different kind of question and/or a different group in mind. In order to show this I will first discuss a general judgment model and then argue that two basic factors determine which model will be used by respondents, namely, their interest in politics and the task presented to them. In this way I will place these different models in a general framework. The general model is formalized in Chapter 2; in subsequent chapters, the effects of the two factors are illustrated.

A GENERAL JUDGMENT MODEL

Zaller suggests that people have a lot of considerations in memory from which they select some for a response to a question. He adds that most people do not order these considerations. Therefore, each time they are asked the same question in a different context, they can select different considerations from memory to answer the question. He makes a clear distinction between the way politically sophisticated and unsophisticated people generate their answers. The sophisticated respondents might have a more stable response pattern on the basis of the ordering of their considerations.

In this volume, Van der Veld and Saris elaborate the same idea on the basis of cognitive psychological theory, as some other authors have recently done (Boynton 1995; Tourangeau, Rips, and Rasinski 2000). Tourangeau, Rips, and Rasinski (2000) call their model the belief sampling model, suggesting that the response to a question is determined by the sampling of beliefs or considerations from memory at that point in time. Zaller suggests the same basic process. The difference is that Tourangeau, Rips, and Rasinski promote this as a general model for all people. They do not distinguish between sophisticated people and others; they suggest that the model is the same for all respondents. But then the question is, of course, how can one explain the difference in stability of responses among the different groups, varying in awareness of sophistication? This is a very important question.

It is not necessary here to elaborate on the model of Tourangeau, Rips, and Rasinski but they suggest that the stability of the opinions expressed in the correlation between responses to the same question over time depends on the overlap between the considerations (stable considerations) "sampled" at the two occasions, the correlations between the new considerations and the considerations used at the first moment and the reliability of the responses given the created judgment on the basis of the "sampled" considerations at each point in time. Ignoring reliability for the moment (see chapter 2 in this volume), we could argue with Zaller that people with little interest in politics will sample different considerations each time. If these considerations are very weakly correlated, this will explain the finding of Converse that some people show no stability in their responses. But then the major question is: which considerations will be retrieved by the politically more interested people at several occasions so that their responses remain more stable? For the answer to this question we can refer to the models suggested above. Some scholars suggest that respondents will use ideological considerations over and over again, while others have suggested that identification with parties or liking or disliking specific groups are good candidates. Still others have suggested that the main consideration for some people is the number of positive and negative experiences a person has had with a party or group. Some scholars think that some people are able to retrieve complete overviews of the decision problem including the likelihood of consequences of choices.

Our point is that not all respondents will build up such fundamental considerations to be used over and over again. Only people with more than minimal interest in politics will organize their thoughts in such a way. These people organize their thoughts in the form of ideologies or party identification or even a complete overview of a choice problem with all its consequences and probabilities. Political interest will lead to a better organization of the considerations in memory and these networks of considerations provide a stable source of arguments to be used to answer survey questions. In this way we can explain why people who are politically more interested or sophisticated have more stable opinions. However, such stable considerations will not always be retrieved when a question is asked; this depends on the formulation of the question. If they get very little time and if the formulation does not give a hint as to these fundamental considerations, the less sophisticated respondents will not detect the connection between the question and the fundamental consideration and therefore will not "sample" or "activate" these considerations. These considerations will not be used in generating an answer. These changes in the formulation can have a considerable effect, as has been shown in several studies (e.g., Schuman and Presser 1981; Zaller 1992).

This brings us to the following summary of the model. We expect that people formulate responses on the basis of a sample of considerations at a point in time. Whether or not these are more fundamental considerations like ideological orientations or like/dislike of persons or groups depends on the answers to two questions:

1. Have people been sufficiently interested in the issue at hand to build connections between the issue and these fundamental considerations?
2. Is the question formulated in a way that allows the respondent to detect that the connection to these more fundamental considerations should be made?

This starting point is different from Converse's point of view because it is not a black and white model suggesting that a person is either stable or unstable, i.e., has an opinion or has no opinion. This model suggests that all respondents generate answers in the same way. But respondents may differ in the number of stable fundamental considerations and unique time-specific considerations they sample from memory to answer a question.

In this respect this model is also different from that of Achen, who suggested that measurement error was the driving force behind most perceptions of attitude instability. Here we hypothesize that in addition to stable considerations, unique considerations can be expected and that they should not necessarily be seen as measurement error. So far, we have not taken into account the problem of measurement reliability as Achen did. It would be interesting to see what would happen if we were able to separate the observed responses into stable components, unique components, and measurement error. (This is done by Van der Veld and Saris in chapter 2 in this volume.) Here we would like to discuss in more detail the basic principles that make a fundamental difference in the way people generate responses to policy questions.

Two Basic Variables

In this section we will discuss in more detail the two basic variables that play a role in determining the considerations people will sample from memory to answer survey questions concerning policy options. The two variables are the interest of the people in the choice option and the type of questions asked. We start with the most commonly accepted criterion—dividing the population into different interest groups.

Different Interest Groups

Several authors have suggested that the public is not homogeneous with respect to the way in which they generate responses to policy questions. Converse (1964) suggests a difference between more or less politically sophisticated people. Sniderman, Brody, and Tetlock (1991) uses the same criterion. Zaller (1992) uses political awareness as a criterion. Psychologists discuss attitude strength as a criterion (Krosnick and Abelson 1992). For an overview of the debate in political science we refer to Luskin (1987). This debate is, however, certainly not finished (see Bizer, Visser, Berent, and Krosnick, chapter 7 in this volume).

For the time being we will follow Zaller's argument as specified in his Reception Axiom (1992:42). With that axiom, Zaller suggests the following difference between citizens: "The greater a person's level of cognitive engagement with an issue, the more likely he or she is to be exposed to and comprehend—in a word to receive—political messages concerning that issue."

In line with this axiom, we would expect some citizens to be so interested in a specific problem that they will collect a great deal of information about it—for example, people working in a specific field or individuals participating in an action group with a special stake in the debate. These groups have been called "issue publics." We would expect them to have in memory nearly all relevant information available at that point in time for the issue at stake. Therefore, we expect that they are able to retrieve many pro and con considerations if they are asked to do so. Given the amount of information they have, these people will not be surprised by new information. If they are asked the same question again they will generate a response in the same way. We expect them to have a rather stable preference. But we also assume that only very few citizens will be so highly involved and for each problem there might be a different issue public.

We also anticipate that there are a larger number of people who are interested in political issues in general, those who pick up general information about political events, stands of politicians, parties, and other groups. They might also be oriented to some ideology and attached to a party. But they will miss detailed information concerning a specific issue. Given that these persons do not have all detailed information in memory, they have to make their choices in a different way than do members of the issue publics. If the question is clear enough they will detect the link between the specific question and the general principles they have stored in memory and use these general considerations to generate an answer to the specific question. If they can easily make these connections with their general considerations, their preference will also be rather stable because the general principles they use will be the same each time.

There are also people who are less interested in politics: still sufficiently interested to pick up the major political events from the media, but not interested enough to order this information consistently or in accordance with some ideology. Such people with limited interest and limited information will make their choice differently again from the members of the issue publics or those more interested in politics. They will use any argument that comes to mind if they are asked; their preference will not be overly stable. The stability will depend on the formulation of the question, the context of the question, and recent events. This has been shown in many framing experiments. Finally, there are people who are not interested in political problems at all. They collect almost no information, even when it is freely available. It is simplest to say that they have no opinion, as suggested by Krosnick (1991), and that if they are forced to give an answer it is most likely a random response, as suggested by Converse (1964). If these respondents know anything about politics it will concern politicians or other groups' representatives who appear very frequently in the media. These persons, uninterested in politics, probably do not store information about events or issues but only an impression of whether or not they like the politician, as suggested by Sniderman, Brody, and Tetlock (1991). Given the amount of media coverage of President Clinton's activities in 1998, it is hard to imagine that people do not have at the very least a positive or negative feeling toward him. But for politicians with less exposure, even these feelings might not exist. Zaller (1992:16) mentions George Bush Sr. as an example. Even after he had served two years as vice-president, 24 percent of the public could not identify him in a photograph. These uninterested people must also make their choices differently from members of the other three groups mentioned thus far. Sniderman, Brody, and Tetlock

(1991:165–66) suggest that these differences in interest and information have their consequences in the ways citizens argue about choices.

Summing up the argument we have made, we suggest that respondents with a lot of interest in the issue asked about will also collect more information and organize their thoughts in a number of fundamental considerations that they can use over and over again to determine their ideas concerning different policy issues. Given that they will use and reuse the same fundamental considerations, their opinions will be more stable than the opinions of people who are less interested in politics and, therefore, have less organized considerations. These differences with respect to political interest and knowledge and attitude stability have been found in different studies (MacKuen 1984; Bartels 1996; Sniderman, Brody, and Tetlock 1991; Zaller 1992). We will come back to the different effects of interest. Here we want, first of all, to stipulate that with difference in interest in the issue people will also have different considerations available in memory and, therefore, they will also retrieve different considerations from memory and make their choices on the basis of different arguments. Given the difference in considerations used, we also expect differences in stability with respect to preferences over time.

Different Tasks

The considerations people use to generate answers vary not only because of differences among respondents with respect to political involvement and information. The judgment models also differ because the tasks that respondents have to perform differ according to the questions with which they are presented.

To give an idea of what I shall discuss, I present here typical examples of questions that have been used in this debate. In later sections I will introduce the different models.

In many studies the following question has been used regarding voting:

If there were elections today which of the following candidates would you vote for?
    Candidate A
    Candidate B
    don't vote

Converse (1964) initiated the nonattitude discussion with questions like the following:

The government in Washington ought to ensure that everybody who wants to work can find a job. Do you think that the federal government ought to sponsor programs such as large public works in order to maintain full employment, or do you think that problems of economic readjustment ought to be left more to private industry or state and local government?

Sniderman, Brody, and Tetlock (1991) worded one of their questions as follows:

> Some people think that the government in Washington should increase spending for programs to help blacks. Others feel that blacks should rely only on themselves. Which makes more sense to you?

Zaller (1992:25) used the following question as an example:

> Would you strongly favor, not so strongly favor, not so strongly oppose, or strongly oppose, sending U.S. troops to Central America to stop the spread of communism?

Before discussing the differences between the questions we should draw attention to their similarity. They all ask people to choose between two or more options. Most of the time these questions present choices with respect to policy options. (Only the voting question is in this respect a bit less clear, because the choice refers to a choice between persons.) However, one can also see this task as a choice between clusters of policy options supported by the different candidates. The similarity between these questions allows us to develop criteria for the quality of the process, which generates the answer, because the respondents need some information in order to answer this type of question. This issue will be discussed in the last part of this volume.

Here we want to argue that the different questions create different tasks for the respondents and, as a consequence, the way the answers are produced will also differ. The voting question is very different from the other questions. The most important difference, besides the fact that it concerns a choice between persons, is that the two "objects of choice" often receive much more exposure in the media than any of the other choice options, even to the extent that it is impossible for any citizen interested in politics in general to store all this information. The way this choice problem is solved will, therefore, be discussed as a special case.

Another class of questions presented to respondents concerns specific policy issues related to special groups. For example, questions are often asked concerning whether or not extra support should be given to blacks, the unemployed, and so on. Another type of question concerns the division of labor between different organizations in society. An example might be whether the federal government or the local government together with local businesses should start employment programs. The question asks who should perform a certain task. Such questions are quite difficult and can lead to specific approaches. But in essence this question is about a specific issue that can be linked to specific groups. So we can place these two questions in the same class. In the absence of detailed knowledge about the consequences of the different options, people might react differently

TABLE 1.1
Available Information to Make Choices for Different Groups on the Basis of
Their Interest in the Issue

Type of Question	Interest			
	Specific Interest	General Interest	Limited Interest	No Interest
Voting	RC SD	SD PI	likes and dislikes on-line	likes and dislikes no-opinion satisficing
Options linked to specific groups	RC	ideology two-stage	on-line or saliency affect-driven	affect-driven no-opinion satisficing
General issues	RC	ideology two-stage	saliency	no-opinion satisficing

RC = rational choice model; SD = smallest distance model; PI = party identification model

to these issues than to issues that do not refer to specific groups and to voting questions.

Another kind of question concerns general issues without any reference to any specific group or person. An example might be whether or not to continue using nuclear energy. Such a question may again call for a different approach. Confronted with such tasks, the respondent cannot make the link to groups they like or dislike. Therefore, different approaches are required again. If the question is formulated in such a way that the link with general principles like ideological orientations or environmental protection can be made, the respondents will use this information. This brief overview suggests that for these tasks a different approach can be expected.

A Hypothetical Taxonomy of Judgment Models

Combining these four types of groups with the three types of questions, one gets in principle twelve possible situations. However, the judgment model is not expected to differ in all these situations. Our hypotheses in this respect have been summarized in Table 1.1, which will be discussed in the next sections using the types of respondents as the starting point. The next four sections thus will indicate what will be the most likely way for the different groups of respondents to try to formulate answers to the various types of policy questions asked in survey research. If necessary, we will make a distinction in this discussion between the different question types mentioned previously.

SPECIFIC INTEREST: ISSUE PUBLICS

As already mentioned, we expect persons with a special interest in an issue to have much information at their disposal supporting arguments for and against the different options. These respondents are expected to be able to give the reasons for their preference, comparing possible consequences of the different options. Here the rational choice (RC) model suggested by many people, for example Himmelweit, Humphreys, and Jaeger (1981), may apply.

For some of these respondents the consequences of one option are much better than those of another option and therefore they will have a clear preference. There may also be citizens for whom the advantages and disadvantages of the different options are approximately in balance. These people will not have a clear preference. Although this group has no preference or a very weak preference, the persons in this group will be able to give positive and negative arguments for all options in line with the RC model. Given that citizens know arguments in favor of and against all options, the ambivalence discussed here is an ambivalence of which the citizens will be aware. This kind of "conscious" ambivalence has been discussed by Alvarez and Brehm (1995) and should be distinguished from the unconscious ambivalence described by Zaller (1992).

In the case where the question concerns the choice of candidates, the amount of information available may be so vast that these respondents reduce it by using an ideological classification of the candidates to summarize the policies they stand for on a left-right scale and then select the candidate closest to their own position (Downs 1957; Van der Eijk and Niemöller 1983). In the table this model is denoted as the smallest distance (SD) model. Given the amount of information we expect to be present in this group, the task makes not much difference except in the case of voting, where the information may be so overwhelming that simplifying procedures may be used.

PEOPLE WITH A GENERAL INTEREST IN POLITICAL ISSUES

People who have no involvement in a specific issue but only a general interest in political issues do not have all the arguments for their choice at their fingertips. On the other hand, people with a general interest in politics might have in their mind strong connections between many specific issues and fundamental considerations, such as ideological considerations or the relevance of issues for different groups. Although they have no specific information about the particular issue they may use this more fundamental information to generate an answer to a question. Therefore, if a question is asked for which the responses can be readily interpreted as conforming to an ideology or a general principle—or conflicting with it—the respondents in this class can easily generate an answer by choosing the one that corresponds to their ideological point of view.

For example, if they are asked about sending troops to Nicaragua to stop communism, the connection with the ideological point of view will be clear to them. Agreeing with the policy means support for capitalism in its struggle with communism. Disagreeing with the policy does not indicate support for capitalism. Thus, these respondents can give an answer in favor of or against sending troops solely on the basis of the connection with their ideological considerations, without any evaluation of efficiency or other possible consequences. If the question were formulated with a reference to the recent official election in Nicaragua, others with some interest in democracy in Central America might think that the communist regime in Nicaragua has been chosen in legal and free elections and that the United States should not interfere. Therefore, a negative answer might readily be given. There are probably further possibilities for generating a response to this question on ideological grounds.

This kind of reaction has been suggested in many studies looking for ideological orientations. Converse suggested that only the elites in societies have a structured ideology (1964). This idea was confirmed in the Netherlands, for example, by Middendorp (1978), while Sniderman, Brody, and Tetlock (1991) found that people with higher education more often give answers in line with their ideological orientation than do the less educated. The formulation of the question and the political orientation of the people also determine what kind of fundamental considerations will be used in this process.

A different way of answering such questions, especially if no clear link is indicated to a general principle, is to rely on the preference of a group or person whom one believes to have more knowledge concerning the issue—so-called opinion leaders. In this case, the respondent still needs to have general knowledge because he has to know the opinion of the other person or group on this issue. If this is the case, the solution to the choice problem is rather simple and can be applied to most of the questions frequently asked. In Table 1.1 and in the literature this judgment model is denoted by the two-stage model of communication (Lazarsfeld, Berelson, and Gaudet 1948). Wiegman, de Roon, and Snijders (1981) have shown through actual experiments that such choices are indeed made by respondents.

With regard to questions concerning voting for different candidates, a variety of processes have been suggested. First of all, respondents with general interest in politics can again choose on the basis of the Smallest Distance (SD) with respect to their ideological orientation as suggested by Downs (1957) and Van der Eijk and Niemöller (1983). An alternative, however, is to make the choice on the basis of identification with one of the parties

(Campbell et al. 1960). This is denoted as the party identification model, or PI, in Table 1.1. Both variables, ideology and party identification, are related to the background variables. One can therefore also expect a relationship between voting and the background variables as suggested by Lazarsfeld, Berelson, and Gaudet (1948).

This survey shows that this group of respondents can use quite different models to generate answers to the frequently asked choice questions in survey research. This is so because they can have different salient considerations partially due to the formulation of the question or the context of the question but also due to differences in individual orientations. What these respondents with general political interest have in common, however, is fundamental considerations about ideology or relevance of the different choices for different groups: they have these considerations available in memory, and we expect that these considerations will play a role in their answers to policy questions in surveys.

PEOPLE WITH LIMITED INTEREST IN POLITICAL ISSUES

The next group also has little information about the specific issue asked and only a limited interest in politics. These people gather some information from the media or other sources but are not sufficiently interested in politics to organize this information systematically. They probably do not have fundamental considerations like ideological orientations, party identifications, and so on readily available in answering questions. They probably have to rely on unordered information to generate an answer to the usual policy questions. This information will consist of all kinds of considerations relating to specific events and stands of different people and groups. These considerations may well be inconsistent with each other. Zaller (1992) called this inconsistency *ambivalence*. We would like to reserve the term *inconsistency* for this, or call it *unconscious ambivalence,* to distinguish it from the *conscious ambivalence* discussed above. Since we expect more diversity of approach to the different types of questions, this will be discussed separately.

We start with questions concerning general issues. The respondents in this group have to construct an answer on the basis of the information they have. To illustrate, let us use as an example the question of "sending U.S. troops to Nicaragua." We assume that the respondents in this group have retained no information relating to the expected consequences of sending troops to Nicaragua (otherwise, they would belong to the first group). What kind of other information could they have available? They might remember the success, casualties, or costs of previous U.S. missions abroad.

Some respondents may try to answer the question by evaluating the efficiency of such actions in the past. Depending on their age, they may remember evaluative assertions such as "U.S. participation in World War II was positive," "the U.S. mission in Korea was a success," or "the U.S. mission in Vietnam was a failure," i.e., they would remember earlier military interventions and form a different picture of the efficiency of such actions. If they remembered a successful intervention they would probably give a positive reply; otherwise, a negative one. Other respondents would draw their conclusions on the basis of remembered information on the number of casualties or costs in such historic cases. Which specific direction the search for an answer takes will depend on the saliency of the considerations.

The processes expected for this group are the same as those suggested by Zaller (1992). For these people we also assume, as Zaller did, that the choice they make will depend very heavily on the way the question is asked or the context in which the question is formulated. For example, if earlier questions have raised the issue of the costs, they will look for an answer taking into account the costs. If earlier questions raised the issue of possible death tolls, they probably use information about this aspect more often to answer the questions. For this reason one should anticipate considerable changes in responses to approximately the same question or, let us say, a question designed to measure the same opinion (Zaller 1992). We have called this the saliency model because of the importance of saliency in generating an answer. Because this model can also be used for other choice problems and can easily be checked, it is also mentioned in connection with other questions.

With regard to voting for candidates, parties, or representatives in other organizations, even citizens who have only a limited interest in politics will get quite a bit of information. As Lodge, Steenbergen, and Brau (1995) have suggested, these persons probably do not retain the information, only a tally of the positive and negative cues they have received relating to the different candidates, parties, or representatives. With regard to questions pertaining to choices between subjects for whom respondents have kept a tally, they should then be able to give an immediate answer by deciding which candidate has the most positive tally. This is known as the on-line model.

Similarly, some people may evaluate candidates on the basis of their feelings toward them. Given the amount of information provided, it is hard to believe that they have not formed some idea about the candidates. The least they can do with this information is form an impression of whether they like or dislike a person. Such feelings cost little effort. This information can be used to choose the candidate one prefers (Sniderman, Brody, and Tetlock 1991). We have called this the likes and dislikes model in Table 1.1. In its simplest form, it is supposed to apply only to voting choices.

In deciding whether to support a particular group, a slightly more complex process is suggested by Sniderman, Brody, and Tetlock (1991:22). They suggest that respondents may not be aware of arguments for or against policies, but if asked, for example, whether blacks should get extra support from the government, they could easily answer on the basis of whether they like or dislike the group involved. If they like black people they are in favor; otherwise they are not. They call this kind of decision making "affect driven." This approach can be applied to any decision where specific groups are involved for which people have a like or dislike.[1]

In the same way, the tallies in the on-line model can be used as long as groups are involved. Therefore the on-line model is also mentioned in connection with other questions for this group of respondents.

PEOPLE WITH NO INTEREST IN POLITICS

The last group of respondents includes people who possess neither issue-specific information nor much general information about events in the past or the positions of people and parties. These respondents will have considerable difficulty making the connections described for the previous group.

Here we would like to make a distinction between questions involving people and questions concerning general problems but not involving specific people or groups. With some questions about voting for people or parties, one cannot avoid a certain amount of information, which may at any rate generate some feelings about the persons or organizations involved. In such cases, these respondents can choose candidates on the basis of their likes and dislikes (Sniderman, Brody, and Tetlock 1991). Using these likes and dislikes, respondents can also make choices with respect to support of specific groups or division of tasks in society using the Affect-Driven model discussed above.

There are also questions about relatively unknown people or groups, or questions about the division of tasks in policy or general issues where no people are involved. Some individuals will have neither knowledge nor feelings to guide them. These are certainly the respondents Converse describes (1964). The question is, how do these persons generate an answer?

One response is, "I don't know." Another possibility is, "One had better put this question to somebody else." Although these answers are just as legitimate as the behavior of a politician who relies mainly on other specialists where specific issues are concerned, they are normally not accepted by interviewers, who insist that respondents give an answer when in fact they have none.

Krosnick (1991) suggests that respondents in such cases give an answer that seems acceptable to the interviewer and costs the respondents as little effort as possible. This kind of behavior is called "strong satisficing" in contrast with the optimizing behavior described in decision-making research.[2] A satisficing response can take two forms. The first would be that the respondent says that he has no opinion. The second possibility is that he arbitrarily selects one option without further cognitive effort, as is also suggested by Converse (1964).

SUMMARY AND DISCUSSION

I have summarized my theoretical starting point as follows:

> We expect that people formulate responses on the basis of a sample of considerations at a point in time. Whether or not these considerations are fundamental considerations like ideological orientations or like/dislike of persons or groups depends on two aspects: (1) whether people have been sufficiently interested in the issue of the question to build up connections between these fundamental considerations and the issue at hand, and (2) whether the task presented to the respondents is formulated in such a way that the respondent detects that the connection to these more fundamental considerations should be made.

I have tried to indicate why we expect these two factors to have an effect on the way people will generate their responses to policy questions in surveys. The effect of political interest, knowledge, awareness, and sophistication has been discussed in other works. New in this discussion is that the task presented to the respondents will also have an effect. I have made a distinction among three different tasks, but there are probably many more types of tasks that will generate their own way of answering policy questions in surveys.

Both these factors play a role in the choice process because they cause the respondents to sample different considerations from their memory. Whether they select the same considerations each time or not is essential. The theory suggested here formulates the same model for all people but also suggests that the amount of stable (more fundamental) considerations and unique considerations will be different for different people and different tasks.

Considerations that are repeatedly selected by the respondents cause stability in their responses over time. The literature suggests a lot of different possibilities for such considerations: complete elaborate decision trees, party identification, likes and dislikes of groups and persons, on-line tallies, etc. Which of these considerations will be used depends again heavily on the task provided to the people and their political interest.

On the other hand, people with little political interest will use just those considerations that are salient to them at the moment the question is asked. These considerations can be very different or unique at different points in time and, therefore, generate a lot of variation in the responses to the same questions over time.

A side effect of this theoretical exercise has been that the different judgment models suggested for explaining choice behavior of respondents confronted with policy questions are probably not competing but complementary models. Depending on the political interest of the person and the task presented, a different model may apply.

However, this result also suggests that one should not assume homogeneous populations when studying these phenomena. One should instead look for different models for different people and different tasks.

NOTES

1. We expect them at least to have some feelings toward the persons and groups that get the most exposure in the media.
2. The satisficing model discussed here is related to the problem of how to answer a question and not how to solve the decision problem. Therefore, this is a different model than Simon's satisficing model. The similarity lies in the fact that both are based on the same principle.

REFERENCES

Achen, C. H. 1975. "Mass Political Attitudes and the Survey Response." *American Political Science Review* 69:1218–31.

Alvarez, R. M., and J. Brehm. 1995. "American Ambivalence toward Abortion Policy: A Heteroskedastic Probit Method for Assessing Conflict Values." *American Journal of Political Science* 39:1055–82.

Bartels, L. M. 1996. "Uninformed Votes: Information Effects in Presidential Elections." *American Journal of Political Science* 40:194–230.

Berelson, B. R., P. F. Lazarsfeld, and W. N. McPhee. 1954. *Voting: A Study of Opinion Formation in a Presidential Campaign.* Chicago: University of Chicago Press.

Boynton, G. R. 1995. "Computational Modelling: A Computational Model of a Survey Respondent." In *Political Judgment: Structure and Process,* ed. M. Lodge and M. McGraw, 229–49. Ann Arbor: University of Michigan Press.

Campbell, A., P. E. Converse, W. E. Miller, and D. E. Stokes. 1960. *The American Voter.* New York: Wiley.

Converse, P. E. 1964. "The Nature of Belief Systems." In *Ideology and Discontent,* ed. David E. Apter, 206–61. New York: Free Press.

———. 1980. "Comment: Rejoinder to Judd and Milburn." *American Sociological Review* 45:644–46.

Converse, P. E., and G. Markus. 1979. "A Dynamic Simultaneous Equation Model of Electoral Choice." *American Political Science Review* 73:1055–70.

Downs, A. 1957. *An Economic Theory of Democracy.* New York: Harper and Row.

Erikson, R. S. 1978. "Analysing One Variable Three Wave Panel Data: A Comparison of Two Models." *Political Methodology* 5:151–61.

———. 1979. "The SRC Panel Data and Mass Political Attitudes." *British Journal of Political Science* 9:89–114.

Gamson, W. A., and A. Modigliani. 1987. "The Changing Culture of Affirmative Action." *Research in Political Sociology* 3:137–77.

Himmelweit, H., P. Humphreys, and M. Jaeger. 1981. *How Voters Decide*. Maidenhead, UK: Open University Press.

Judd, C. M., and M. Milburn. 1980. "The Structure of Attitude Systems in the General Public: Comparisons of a Structural Equation Model." *American Sociological Review* 45:627–43.

Judd, C. M., M. Milburn, and J. Krosnick. 1981. "Political Involvement and Attitude Structure in the General Public." *American Sociological Review* 46:660–69.

Krosnick, J. A. 1991. "Response Strategies for Coping with the Cognitive Demands of Attitude Measures in Surveys." *Applied Cognitive Psychology* 5:213–36.

Krosnick, R. J., and R. P. Abelson. 1992. "The Case for Measuring Attitude Strength in Surveys." In *Questions About Survey Questions*, ed. J. Tenur, 177–203. New York: Russell Sage.

Lazarsfeld, P. F., B. Berelson, and H. Gaudet. 1948. *The People's Choice: How the Voter Makes Up His Mind in a Presidential Campaign*. New York: Columbia University Press.

Lippman, W. 1925. *The Phantom Public*. New York: MacMillan.

Lodge, M., M. R. Steenbergen, and S. Brau. 1995. "The Responsive Voter: Campaign Information and the Dynamics of Candidate Evaluation." *American Political Science Review* 89:309–26.

Luskin, R. C. 1987. "Measuring Political Sophistication." *American Journal of Political Science* 31:856–99.

Maas, C., L. J. Van Doorn, and W. E. Saris. 1991. "The Smallest Distance Hypothesis and the Explanation of the Vote Reconsidered." *Acta Politica* 1:65–84.

MacKuen, M. 1984. "Exposure to Information, Belief Integration and Individual Responsiveness to Agenda Change." *American Political Science Review* 78:371–91.

Middendorp, C. P. 1978. *Progressiveness and Conservatism: The Fundamental Dimensions of Ideological Controversy and Their Relationship to Social Class*. The Hague: Mouton Publishers.

Nelson, T. E., and D. R. Kinder. 1996. "Issue Frames and Group-Centrism in American Public Opinion." *Journal of Politics* 58:1055–78.

Schuman, H., and S. Presser. 1981. *Questions and Answers in Attitude Surveys*. New York: Wiley.

Simon, H. 1957. *Models of Man: Social and Rational*. New York: Wiley.

Sniderman, P. M., R. A. Brody, and P. E. Tetlock. 1991. *Reasoning and Choice: Explorations in Political Psychology*. Cambridge: Cambridge University Press.

Taber, C. S., and M. Steenbergen. 1995. "Computational Experiments in Electoral Behavior." In *Political Judgment: Structure and Process*, ed. M. Lodge and M. McGraw, 141–79. Ann Arbor: University of Michigan Press.

Thomassen, J. 1976. "Party Identification as a Cross Cultural Concept: Its Meaning in the Netherlands." In *Party Identification and Beyond*, ed. I. Budge, I. Crewe, and D. Farly. London: Wiley.

Tourangeau, R., L. J. Rips, and K. Rasinski. 2000. *The Psychology of Survey Response*. Cambridge: Cambridge University Press.

Van der Eijk, C., and B. Niemöller. 1983. *Electoral Change in the Netherlands: Empirical Results and Methods of Measurement*. Amsterdam: CT Press.

Wiegman, O., A. D. de Roon, and T. Snijders. 1981. *Meningen en Media: Politieke Opponenten in een Relistisch Experiment*. Deventer: Van Loghum Slaterus.

Zaller, J. R. 1992. *The Nature and Origins of Mass Opinion*. Cambridge: Cambridge University Press.

CHAPTER 2

Separation of Error, Method Effects, Instability, and Attitude Strength

William van der Veld and Willem E. Saris

IT IS WELL KNOWN that responses to survey questions, especially questions about political issues, can show a great deal of response instability across waves of panel data. Social scientists have been aware of this since Converse's work (1964) on mass belief systems. In his seminal essay, Converse comes to the conclusion that there are two types of people: those with no opinion (i.e., no consistent, stable belief system), and those with a real opinion (i.e., with a consistent, and stable belief system). The first type will randomly change their responses; the second type will always give the same responses to survey questions. The greater part of the population belongs to the first type, and this is the reason why we observe so much response instability. If the idea that most people give random (meaningless) responses is taken seriously, then the participation of people in political decision making is very questionable. However, it is hard to believe that the larger part of a population has no opinion on important issues and gives meaningless responses.

At odds with this explanation of response instability is the view that survey questions are prone to measurement error and that opinions are very stable after correction for measurement error (Achen 1975; Erikson 1978, 1979; Judd and Milburn 1980; Judd, Krosnick, and Milburn 1981). Within this frame of explanation, opinions are very stable but the random component may also be very large, especially for political issues. In such cases, we are merely measuring random error. If this explanation is taken seriously, one should really question the use of survey research to measure public opinion. It is, however, hard to believe that response instability is due solely to measurement error and that opinions are as stable as these authors suggest (Feldman 1989).

Both the measurement error model and the nonattitude model explain the same phenomenon—response instability. Underlying both explanations is the implicit assumption that people have a stack of opinions stored in memory ready for conversion to a response on a specific scale. In the measurement error model, people have problems converting their stored opinions to a response alternative and consequently generate measurement error. In the nonattitude model, people either have an opinion that perfectly matches a response alternative or they have no opinion and just pick a response alternative by chance.

Having an opinion stored in memory leads to puzzles when the implications are traced out with some care, as Zaller and Feldman (1992) have shown. Boynton (1995) makes this point very clear using an example taken from a split ballot experiment with two different but very similar questions that are intended to measure the same opinion. In Boynton's study, the issue is whether the United States should go to war against Iraq. The first question asked is whether the United States should go to war against Iraq; the second question asked is whether the United States should go to war or wait longer to see if the sanctions work.[1]

The response distributions indicate that the respondents gave very different answers to these two very similar questions: 62 percent agreed to go to war on the first question while only 49 percent agreed to go to war on the second question. The next question then, is, do people have one opinion for *each* question about going to war with Iraq or just one opinion about going to war? Given the amount of information available about this political problem at the time, it is plausible that most people had an opinion about going to war against Iraq. However, it is implausible that most people had two opinions that corresponded exactly to the wording of the two questions. If people do not have a stack of stored opinions for each question, how can they answer survey questions?

The answer can be found in cognitive science. The starting point for theorizing about answering survey questions, which is a cognitive process, is the organization of memory. Memory in cognitive science is generally understood to be a semantic, associative network that consists of associations among nodes or pieces of information stored in memory (Quillian 1966; Anderson 2000). When a question is asked, some nodes will be activated, and this activation will spread to other nodes associated with the nodes activated first. Apart from "what you know" (cognition), "what you like" (affect) also plays a role in the process of answering a question. It is assumed that cognition and affect spread in a parallel manner through the semantic, associative network. This is called "hot cognition" (Abelson 1968). This is an important point, since knowing what we like (affect) can be remembered better and longer than why we like it (cognition). Stereotyping is an example of this process.[2]

Zaller and Feldman (1992) have formulated a model that is similar in its consequences to the semantic, associative network. They base their theory on the conclusion that in many cases constructing opinions *on the spot* is a better way to understand respondents' question-answering ability than is "having" an opinion for every question. They suggest that people whose awareness of politics is rudimentary do receive and process political information, but they do not systematize this information. As a result, they may hold inconsistent or even contradictory ideas about political issues. When such people are asked questions about political issues, the context and the formulation of the question determine what considerations will become salient, leading to very different answers on different occasions, as has been found by Converse (1964), Zaller (1992), and many others.

Constructing opinions *on the spot,* however, is just a part of what the theory of semantic, associative network can explain. Using this theory one can also explain why people have an opinion stored in memory ready for conversion to a response. For this reason, the semantic, associative network theory provides a more elaborate view on the survey response process. Less clear in this literature is the way a response is generated given an activated associative, semantic network. We will come back to this issue in our theoretical framework. Ideas similar to the semantic, associative network and creating opinions *on the spot* have also been discussed under the heading of framing (Kahneman and Tversky 1984; Smith 1987; Rasinski 1989; Gamson and Modigliani 1987; Sniderman and Theriault, chapter 5 in this volume) or attitude strength (Schuman and Presser 1981; Billiet, Loosveldt, and Waterplas 1995; Petty and Krosnick 1993; Bizer et al., chapter 7 in this volume).

In sum, the nonattitude model and the measurement error model both assume that opinions are stored in memory and are measurable using survey questions, either with or without measurement error. This is in contrast to the idea of creating opinions *on the spot,* which assumes that an opinion is constructed after the survey question has been asked. Both views can be explained using the semantic, associative network theory. The nonattitude model, the creating opinions *on the spot* model, and the semantic, associative network model do not include a theory about measurement error, or they deny its existence.

Given these different and sometimes contradictory theories regarding the issue of response instability, we need a research design and model that would enable us to estimate some of the basic characteristics governing the response process and the development of opinions. We would then be able to differentiate between the unique and stable components of an opinion, and between the opinion and the measurement error component in the response. This will be the central theme of this chapter. We will show that it is possible to obtain independent estimates of measurement error and unique and stable components of an opinion using data on policies regarding ethnic minorities.

A Theoretical Framework

Our point of departure is the survey question. We define a survey question as a combination of a *question* and a measurement method. A *question* is related to the subject of the study and the concept of interest. It is the *premier* stimulus probing for an opinion, attitude, preference, or fact that we are interested in. A measurement method is related to the wording of the survey question and is determined by the choices that we make about: (1) the form of the response scale; (2) the place of the question in the questionnaire; (3) the presence of an introduction; (4) the choice of the data collection mode; and (5) all other possible choices that must be made when designing a survey question (Andrews 1984; Scherpenzeel and Saris 1997). It is important to note that the *question* and the measurement method cannot be separated completely from each other; they are not independent entities. Nevertheless, the distinction is important as shown by the following example.

Suppose we want to measure how happy the average person is on a five-point scale using the following question: "Taken all together, how happy are you these days?" We draw a sample and make two random subgroups. For one subgroup, we use face-to-face interviews and for the other, telephone interviews. Now, the wording of the survey question is the same for each subgroup; it is the method of data collection that differs. It is common knowledge that this will make a difference in the distribution of the responses due to recency or primacy effects in telephone interviews that do not occur in face-to-face interviews using a show card (Schuman and Presser 1981; Krosnick and Alwin 1987). Should we, therefore, conclude that both groups have different opinions? This is implausible because of the random assignment of the sample units to the subgroups. It is plausible, however, that the difference is caused by the different measurement methods, i.e., telephone versus face-to-face interviews. Thus, it seems that the method causes an error defined as the difference between the (created) opinion and the response. Let us now look at the opinion[3] that is constructed in or extracted from memory as a reaction to a *question*. An opinion is the result of a set of activated nodes (Boynton 1995) or, in the words of Zaller and Feldman (1992), the result of a set of considerations. This result is a function of two possible sets of considerations. First, there could be a set of unique considerations (UC_{ij}) for a specific administration of a *question*. Second, there could be a set of considerations (SC_{ij}) used at more than one administration of that *question*. This second set is, therefore, constant or stable across (at least) two consecutive administrations of that *question*. The opinion can thus be expressed in the following equation:

$$O_{ij} = f(SC_{ij} + UC_{ij}). \qquad (Eq.\ 2.1a)$$

In equation 2.1a, O_{ij} is the opinion due to a function f on a set of considerations that come to mind due to *question* i observed at time j. For our purpose, we do not need to specify the function f. However, it represents the mechanism that integrates the different considerations into an overall evaluation of the object, which we have called the opinion at time j. Anderson (1970) has suggested that the most common form is the weighted average, but several different forms can be specified for this function as suggested by Münnich (1998).

If we can assume that:

$$f(SC_{ij} + UC_{ij}) = f(SC_{ij}) + f(UC_{ij}), \qquad (Eq.\ 2.1b)$$

Then we can also write for equation 2.1a:

$$O_{ij} = S_{ij} + U_{ij}, \qquad (Eq.\ 2.1c)$$

where $S_{ij} = f(SC_{ij})$, and $U_{ij} = f(UC_{ij})$.

Here, $f(SC_{ij})$ is the result of a set of "stable" considerations (SC_{ij}) that are related to *question* i at time j. S_{ij} is stable because it is based on a set of considerations that were also present at time $j-1$ and/or present at time $j+1$. While S_{ij} is stable within a period of time, U_{ij} is unique for a specific point in time because it is the result of a set of unique considerations (UC_{ij}). In the set of "stable" considerations (SC_{ij}) we put stable in quotes because we foresee that this set can change. The set SC_{ij} can be split into two sets: SC_{ij-1}, a set of considerations also present at time $j-1$; and NSC_{ij}, a set of considerations new at time j but will remain at least till time $j+1$. With this we can formulate, in the same manner as with O_{ij}, an equation for SC_{ij}:

$$f(SC_{ij}) = f(SC_{ij-1} + NSC_{ij}). \qquad (Eq.\ 2.2a)$$

If we can assume that

$$f(SC_{ij-1} + NSC_{ij}) = f(SC_{ij-1}) + f(NSC_{ij}), \qquad (Eq.\ 2.2b)$$

then we can also write for equation 2.2a:

$$S_{ij} = S_{ij-1} + N_{ij}, \qquad (Eq.\ 2.2c)$$

where $S_{ij} = f(SC_{ij})$, $S_{ij-1} = f(SC_{ij-1})$, and $N_{ij} = f(NSC_{ij})$.

To clarify what we mean by these different sets of considerations and the function f we shall give an example. Imagine that we ask you about your satisfaction with your social contacts. Normally, your social contacts are relatives, friends, neighbors, and colleagues. Across the years, you could make new friends, switch jobs, and get to know new colleagues, get new relatives by marriage or birth, and so forth. You can also lose friends, colleagues, or relatives due to disputes, death, moving, or other reasons, and there are also contacts that exist only for a very short time, for example, during a holiday or during a party. Some of these relationships will be positive ($+1$) and others negative (-1). In the set of all positive and negative relations at a specific point in time, we can recognize the considerations that were already present at a previous point in time (SC_{ij-1}), the considerations that are new at that point in time but will continue (NSC_{ij}) and the unique considerations that existed briefly around the time of the interview (UC_{ij}).

When you are asked how satisfied you are with your social contacts, you will take into account all these—or at least the most important—relations you have at that point in time, which are the salient considerations in our model. To construct an overall evaluation, we assume that the function f is the sum of all positive relations ($+1$) and negative relations (-1). In this way, a total score is obtained. We could also apply the same function on the sets SC_{ij-1}, NSC_{ij}, and UC_{ij}, which gives respectively S_{ij-1}, N_{ij}, and U_{ij} and follows for the overall judgment $O_{ij} = S_{ij-1} + N_{ij} + U_{ij}$. This result is in agreement with the equations 2.1c and 2.2c.

The opinion O_{ij} is not the same as the response given. We have already made clear the idea that the response given can be different if different measurement methods are used, even when the opinion is the same. In cognitive approaches to the survey response process, the distinction between an opinion and a response is not made, which leads to a contradiction in those approaches. One cannot posit that it is implausible that a person has a different opinion stored in memory for each question, and at the same time posit that the differences in responses are only due to different considerations being taken into account—for what, then, is the opinion that is either constructed in or extracted from memory? We are convinced that at a specific point in time an opinion exists independent of the measurement method. We do not believe that people construct an opinion that completely fits one of the response alternatives provided in a survey question. Therefore, the opinion and the response alternatives must be matched to produce a response, and errors will be made in this matching process. For more details about such matching processes we refer to Saris (1987a, 1987b) for continuous variables and to Anderson (1982) for categorical variables. We propose here to use a description that is as simple as possible, commonly used in psychometrics (Lord and Novick 1968):

$$R_{ijk} = O_{ij} + e_{ijk}. \qquad (Eq.\ 2.3)$$

In equation 2.3, R_{ijk} is the response at time j. This response is the result of the matching process that maps the opinion O_{ij} onto a response alternative, given measurement method k. The term e_{ijk} represents the errors that are made in the mapping process using measurement method k. The measurement error term may contain systematic measurement error and random measurement error. Random measurement errors are the random mistakes connected to any measurement method. Systematic measurement errors arise due to the fact that a respondent reacts in the same (systematic) manner across different *questions* when the same measurement method is used, and that across individual respondents there is variation in these systematic manners. Responses to different *questions* observed using the same measurement method could therefore be related to the measurement method, apart from the substantial relationship. We, however, will not make the distinction between systematic and random measurement error here to keep things as simple as possible.

Given the above specified equations, we derive the following model:

$$S_{ij} = S_{ij-1} + N_{ij}$$
$$O_{ij} = S_{ij} + U_{ij} \qquad \text{(Model 2.1)}$$
$$R_{ijk} = O_{ij} + e_{ijk}$$

The first equation in model 2.1 specifies that the result of a set of stable considerations S_{ij} stems from the result of a set of stable considerations at a previous point in time and a set of new stable considerations. The second equation in model 2.1 states that the opinion is a combination of the result of a set of stable considerations and a set of unique considerations that only comes into play at that specific point in time and neither before nor after. The last equation posits that a response is the result of an opinion and measurement error.

It is assumed in model 2.1 that all e_{ijk}, U_{ij}, and N_{ij} are independent, that all N_{ij} are independent of the stable considerations (S_{ij-m}) preceding N_{ij} in the causal ordering, that U_{ij} is independent of S_{ij} and S_{ij-1}, and e_{ij} is independent of O_{ij}, S_{ij}, and S_{ij-1}. These assumptions seem plausible because the sets of considerations cannot overlap and have no connection to the measurement errors.

ESTIMATION OF DATA QUALITY, OPINION CRYSTALLIZATION, AND OPINION STABILITY

The theoretical framework (model 2.1) set out above contains all the components we are interested in—measurement error, unique considerations, and stable considerations. To estimate the size of these components, it is convenient to use the standardized version of this model. In model 2.2 the variables S_{ij}, O_{ij}, and R_{ijk} have been standardized. In doing so, the structure of the equations remains the same but the effects of these variables on each other also need to be standardized (Saris and Stronkhorst 1984). So far, they have been assumed to be 1. Now these coefficients become equal to the standard deviation of the dependent variable divided by the standard deviation of the independent variable.

$$S_{ij} = s_{j,j-1} \times S_{ij-1} + N_{ij}$$

$$O_{ij} = c_{ij} \times S_{ij} + U_{ij} \qquad (Model\ 2.2)$$

$$R_{ijk} = q_{ijk} \times O_{ij} + e_{ijk}.$$

The advantage of this formulation is that under these conditions the parameters q_{ijk}, c_{ij}, and $s_{j,j-1}$ in this model get an interpretation that can be linked with the commonly used concepts in survey research. The meaning of the standardized coefficients are:

q_{ijk} the coefficient of quality of measurement method k at wave j. The square of this coefficient is the strength of the relationship between the opinion O_{ij} and the response, and this is what we generally call the *quality* of a measurement instrument, i.e., survey question.

c_{ij} the coefficient of the crystallization of the result of the stable considerations at time j. The square of this coefficient is the strength of the relationship between the result of the stable considerations and the opinion at time j, and this is what we call the *crystallization*.

$s_{j,j-1}$ the coefficient of stability of the result of a set of stable considerations at time $j-1$. The square of this coefficient is the strength of the relationship between the result of the stable considerations at time $j-1$ and time j, and this is what we generally call the *stability*.

We can see that this model has separate parameters for (data) quality, crystallization, and stability (of an opinion). It would be attractive if these parameters could also be estimated. A design to estimate the parameters of this model contains six observations using the same *question*, in a three-wave panel. In each wave, two observations should be made.[4] This design fits the model presented in Figure 2.1.

To interpret the path model given in Figure 2.1 we will start at the bottom. People are asked to provide two responses with each wave on the same *question* using a different measurement method each time. We denote the response to survey question i at time j observed with measurement method k by R_{ijk}. Each response contains measurement errors (e_{ijk}). If the response is corrected for these measurement errors, one obtains the opinion at time j. The strength of the relationship between the observed response and the opinion is the quality (q^2_{ijk}). The opinion (O_{ij}) at time j is the effect of the result of unique considerations (U_{ij}) and stable considerations (S_{ij}). The strength of the relationship between the opinion and the result of the stable considerations is the crystallization (c^2_{ij}). The result of the stable considerations (S_{ij}) at time j is affected by the result of stable

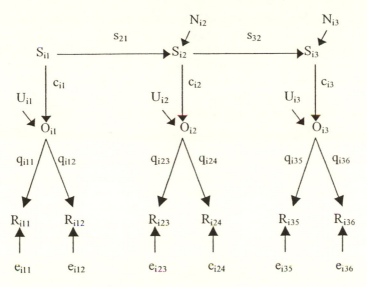

Figure 2.1 The survey response path model.

considerations at a previous point in time $(S_{i,j-1})$ and by the result of new stable considerations (N_{ij}). The latter component is different from the unique component because it will also be present at the next point in time. The strength of the relationship between the result of stable considerations at two consecutive points in time is the stability $(s^2_{j,j-1})$, although this may be a misnomer when N_{ij} becomes very large.

Without further restrictions, the model in Figure 2.1 is not identified. The reason for this is that we cannot simultaneously estimate all the variances of U_{ij} and the variances of N_{ij}. To identify the variances of U_{ij}, they are constrained such that they are equal across the waves. The meaning of this constraint is that the same variation in the result of unique considerations across the waves is present in the opinion (O_{ij}). This does not mean that for each individual the same set of unique considerations is used each year. They should deviate very much from year to year in this respect, otherwise it would be a stable consideration. Only the variation in the population should remain approximately the same.

IMPORTANT REMARKS ON THIS MODEL AND FRAMEWORK

There are several important remarks to make about this model that have to do with the way we model the response process and how we define the co-efficients in the model. We should stress that this is a theoretical framework where we explain the process of how considerations can be converted to an opinion, and how an opinion can be converted to a response. In this process, we assume that a response consists of several components that can be easily seen in the following equation: $R_{ijk} = S_{ij-1} + N_{ij} + U_{ij} + e_{ijk}$ (see model 2.1). The response is the result of the addition of four variables. Several interpretational problems could occur using this framework. First, one could make the mistake of interpreting sets of considerations as variables in the model. This is not so, because we assume that for a set of considerations, an evaluation (the function f) is made in the same dimension by all people. So, we actually model the result of a function f on considerations, which is why we preferably talk about the variables in the model as the results of a set of considerations.[5] A second mistake is to assume that the errors cannot be detected if there is no "true opinion" (Feldman 1995). However, we are measuring an evaluation of considerations (due to the function f), which we call the opinion at a specific time. This opinion really exists and does not (necessarily) have the same modality as the possible response alternatives. Therefore, the opinion is not (necessarily) the same as the response. Finally, one could make the mistake of thinking that the variables in this process must really exist. The distinction among S_{ij-1}, N_{ij}, and U_{ij} might be artificial and therefore the variables—except for the response variable and the opinion—could be purely theoretical variables. They can, however, also be real existing variables like in attitude research where S_{ij} might be the "predisposition to react systematically in a positive or negative way towards an object" (Ajzen and Fishbein 1980). This may also be true for other concepts, but the relevance of hypothesizing about what the variable S_{ij} represents should be preceded by a demonstration of its "strength" (see below).

This model also allows for the estimation of attitude strength. The combination of crystallization and stability could be interpreted as the strength of an attitude. Petty and Krosnick (1993) define attitude strength using two phenomena. They assert that a strong attitude should be stable (i.e., resistant to change and persistent over time) and crystallized (i.e., have a strong impact on thinking and behavior). In this formulation, one can recognize two components of our model. It follows from this definition that in our model a strong attitude would mean that both the stability and the crystallization coefficients should be high. Petty and Krosnick suggest that stability will be high if people think the issue at stake is important, have considerable relevant knowledge, and are certain about the attitude. The first component will produce stability by selective perception, while knowledge and certainty will produce stability because they can easily generate counterarguments. Crystallization will be higher if the accessibility of the attitude in memory is high and if the attitude components have a low degree of ambivalence. For more details on this issue, we refer to Petty and Krosnick (1993) and Bizer et al. (chapter 7 in this volume).

To get an estimate of attitude strength, Bizer et al. propose different measures that predict stability and crystallization. A difficulty with this approach is, therefore, that one needs to measure a multitude of strength-related attributes to predict the strength of the attitude for each individual. In our approach, the attitude strength is represented by just two parameters of a model: the crystallization and stability parameters. A possible drawback of our approach is that we cannot obtain individual measures of the strength of the opinion. However, we could estimate the crystallization and stability for different (homogeneous) subgroups in the population.

From model 2.2 (with standardized variables) it follows that the similarity between the response R_{ijk} and the stable considerations (S_{ij}) is equal to $(q_{ijk} \times c_{ij})^2$. It is now quite easy to see that the overlap between R_{ijk} and S_{ij} can become quite small, if the crystallization coefficient (c_{ij}) is small. For example, if c_{ij} equals 0.6, then the overlap can at most be 36 percent ($.6^2 \times q_{ijk}$), because q_{ijk} cannot be larger than 1. That the relationship between the stable considerations (S_{ij}) and the observed variable R_{ijk} can be very small has also been found by Achen (1975), Erikson (1978, 1979), and many others. They attribute this to the poor quality of the measurement instrument. We, however, also take the crystallization into account and expect that the effect of the measurement instrument on the response instability might be a lot smaller than was found by these authors. This characteristic makes this model attractive compared to the commonly used measurement models (Heise 1969; Wiley and Wiley 1970) or latent state-trait models (Steyer and Schmitt 1990) that do not make this distinction. In the same manner, we can determine the overlap between two responses at different points in time. This overlap is an indication of the response instability and is equal to $(q_{ij-1}, k \times c_{ij-1})^2 \times (s_{j,j-1})^2 \times (q_{ijk} \times c_{ij})^2$. Again, the similarity can be quite low if the crystallization coefficient is small, even when the stability ($s_{j,j-1}$) and the quality coefficients are quite large.

The limitations of our model should also be discussed here. If the correlation between the opinion (O_{ij}) across time becomes very small, which is the case when the strength of the opinion is very weak, then it is impossible to estimate the different parameters. In this limiting case, there are theoretically three possibilities: the stability coefficient is zero; the crystallization coefficient is zero; or both are very small. Under these conditions, the estimation will not work; but without this estimation it is clear that the opinion is "totally" created *on the spot*.

TABLE 2.1
Design of the Policy Data from the RUSSET Panel

Year	Wave	Observation # in wave #	Question 1	Question 2	Question 3
Autumn 1995	3	1	R_{131}	R_{231}	R_{331}
		2	R_{132}	R_{232}	R_{332}
Spring 1997	4	1	R_{143}	R_{243}	R_{343}
		2	R_{144}	R_{244}	R_{344}
Autumn 1999	7	1	R_{171}	R_{271}	R_{371}
		2	R_{175}	R_{275}	R_{375}

THE DATA AND THE METHODOLOGY

We have chosen to test the model using data on policies regarding ethnic groups. The data have been collected in three waves of the Russian Socio-Economic Transition (RUSSET) panel. The RUSSET[6] panel is a random sample of the Russian population, and the data are collected using paper and pencil face-to-face interviews. The panel originally began in 1993 with approximately 3,700 respondents (sample size, 4,000), and about 2,500 respondents participated in all seven waves, until 1999. The policy data we will use here is collected in waves 3, 4, and 7. The design of the study is presented in Table 2.1.

We will discuss shortly the design of the survey questions in this study. From Table 2.1, it follows that the design for each issue consists of six observations with the same *question* in a three-wave panel, and in each wave two observations are made. The survey questions were designed using carefully considered choices of the measurement methods. We have chosen to put survey questions in a battery of items without any change of order across the waves. The battery was always put within a constant context of other batteries addressing similar issues. Different choices were made on the length and formulation of the introduction, the number, and the wording of response labels, the number of response alternatives, the presence or absence of a "don't know" option, and so forth. So, the measurement method varied across the batteries. The *questions,* however, were kept constant across the waves in order to ensure that the same opinion was probed (Saris 1982; Saris and van den Putte, 1988; Saris and Hartman 1990). The formulations of these *questions* were as follows:

Question 1: Minorities should be allowed to receive education in their own language.

Question 2: To reduce the level of crime, we should move minorities to their own territory.

Question 3: Minority groups who live here illegally should not get free access to medical and educational facilities.

Following our design, the *question* columns in Table 2.1, we have three different data sets. Using listwise deletion on the data sets, approximately 200 respondents for each question can be used for our study. This may seem rather low compared to the 3,700 respondents in the first wave. However, these experiments were done within randomly selected subgroups of 500 respondents from the whole sample. Due to item non-response and sample attrition, there are four years between the first and the last observations. Moreover, because only ethnic Russians were allowed to respond to these questions the listwise sample size for each data set was approximately 200 respondents.

The Pearson correlations, the means, and the standard deviations of the variables in each data set are presented in Tables 2.2a, 2.2b, and 2.2c. These figures were computed using PRELIS 2 (Jöreskog and Sörbom 1996) under the assumption that all variables are continuous.

One can easily see in these three tables that the response *stability within* the waves is pretty high ($j = k$) and that the response *stability across* the waves is pretty low ($j \neq k$). The low across-wave correlations, indicative of response instability, are typically found for policy-related survey questions and are the source of the discussion around nonattitudes.

TABLE 2.2A

Correlations between Observations with Survey Question 1 across the Waves, and the Mean and Standard Deviation of These Variables

	R_{131}	R_{132}	R_{141}	R_{142}	R_{171}	R_{172}
R_{131}	1.00					
R_{132}	0.69	1.00				
R_{141}	0.28	0.16	1.00			
R_{142}	0.36	0.27	0.84	1.00		
R_{171}	0.14	0.09	0.20	0.22	1.00	
R_{172}	0.10	0.09	0.18	0.18	0.67	1.00
Mean	4.07	4.09	5.38	5.27	3.66	5.03
St. Dev.	0.98	0.97	1.87	1.87	1.07	1.80

TABLE 2.2B
Correlations between Observations with Survey Question 2 across the Waves, and the Mean and Standard Deviation of These Variables

	R_{231}	R_{232}	R_{241}	R_{242}	R_{271}	R_{272}
R_{231}	1.00					
R_{232}	0.81	1.00				
R_{241}	0.35	0.37	1.00			
R_{242}	0.36	0.36	0.87	1.00		
R_{271}	0.27	0.28	0.23	0.28	1.00	
R_{272}	0.23	0.22	0.24	0.26	0.84	1.00
Mean	3.05	3.10	4.63	4.73	3.18	4.45
St. Dev.	1.45	1.44	2.05	2.11	1.28	1.97

The analyses were done using Quasi Maximum Likelihood estimators available in LISREL 8 (Jöreskog and Sörbom 1993). Within waves 3 and 4, we made the assumption that the variances of the measurement errors (e_{ijk}) are equal.[7] This is a plausible assumption, since the measurement procedures are very similar.[8]

The topic of policies on ethnic groups could give rise to problems with respect to the heterogeneity of the population, for example, that there are subgroups in the population that differ with respect to the opinion strength. Analysis of subgroups would be a good alternative in this case. However,

TABLE 2.2C
Correlations between Observations with Survey Question 3 across the Waves, and the Mean and Standard Deviation of These Variables.

	R_{331}	R_{332}	R_{341}	R_{342}	R_{371}	R_{372}
R_{331}	1.00					
R_{332}	0.79	1.00				
R_{341}	0.17	0.15	1.00			
R_{342}	0.21	0.21	0.88	1.00		
R_{371}	0.17	0.14	0.18	0.16	1.00	
R_{372}	0.19	0.19	0.24	0.25	0.70	1.00
Mean	2.62	2.58	3.93	3.91	2.64	3.30
St. Dev.	1.36	1.40	2.43	2.46	1.25	2.08

we expected that the greater part of the population would have a pretty low opinion strength on this issue and would be homogenous with respect to the specified relationships. In additiion, the sample sizes for the different questions do not allow for further subdivision of the samples.

THE RESULTS

Table 2.3 shows the results of the analyses with the three data sets on policies regarding ethnic minorities using model 2.2. We can observe that the model is capable of providing a variety of estimates for the issues at stake. The models fit well at a 5 percent level for all policy items, even though some parameters have been fixed or constrained. Furthermore, all estimates were significant.

The quality of most measurement instruments is quite good, which could not be expected on the basis of the high response instability across the waves (Tables 2.2a–2.2c). The explained variance (the square of the quality) of time-specific opinion O_{ij} on the response R_{ijk} ranges from 52 percent to 94 percent. An explained variance of 52 percent (wave 7, M1) is, of course, not good, and is a reason to search for a better instrument, which is available in the form of the measurement method used in wave 7,

TABLE 2.3

Completely Standardized Estimates of the Quality, Crystallization, and Stability Coefficients from Model 2.

Domain	Fit		Quality		Crystallization		Stability
	χ^2	df	q_{ijk} (M1)	q_{ijk} (M2)	c_{ij}	var(u_{ij})	$s_{j,j-1}$
Q1 (n = 223)							
Wave 3 (R_{13k})	14.71	8	.83	.83	.71	.49	.64
Wave 4 (R_{14k})			.91	.91	.77	.41	.52
Wave 7 (R_{17k})			.89	.76	.64	.59	
Q2 (n = 199)							
Wave 3 (R_{23k})	4.41	9	.90	.90	.64	.59	
Wave 4 (R_{24k})			.93	.93	.67	.56	1.0
Wave 7 (R_{27k})			.97	.87	.60	.64	.76
Q3 (n = 17)							
Wave 3 (R_{33k})	5.89	8	.89	.89	.44	.81	.97
Wave 4 (R_{34k})			.94	.94	.52	.73	.92
Wave 7 (R_{37k})			.72	.97	.56	.68	

[a] The variance of the resultant of the new "stable" considerations (N_{22}) is fixed to zero in this case, because this variance was negative (which is unacceptable for a variance), but statistically not significant.

M2 (q_{372} = 0.97, R^2 = 94%). Furthermore, it follows from the results that the measurement methods used in wave 4 are better for these three different questions than the methods used in wave 3. For more detailed information on why one measurement method is better than the other, we refer to Andrews (1984) and Scherpenzeel and Saris (1997).

The stability coefficients are close to perfect for question 3. Still, for this question the effects of the result of the unique considerations (U_{ij}) are the largest of the three questions. This means that although the result of the stable considerations is really stable, it does not have a large impact on the opinion (O_{ij}). In the case of question 1, the situation is rather different. Here the crystallization coefficients are larger, but the stability coefficients are smaller. We could conclude here that result of the stable considerations has a larger impact than for question 3, but it is more prone to change. All in all, the crystallization coefficients are low for all the policy issues studied here, which indicates that Russians come up with very different (unique) considerations each time a question about a policy on ethnic minorities is asked.

Finally, we want to show the differences among opinion stability, opinion strength, and response stability. It follows from our model that by definition response stability is at most equal (when q_{ijk} = 1) but usually smaller than opinion strength. In addition, by definition, opinion strength is at most equal (when c_{ij} = 1) but usually smaller than opinion stability. From these definitions it also follows that response stability is at most equal (when c_{ij} = 1 and q_{ijk} = 1) but usually smaller than opinion (attitude) stability.

We will clarify this using survey question 2 of our data. Opinion stability is defined as the parameter $s_{j,j-1}$ in model 2.2. Opinion strength has been defined as the product of the crystallization and stability parameters between two time-specific opinions (O_{ij-1}, O_{ij}). For example, opinion strength between waves 3 and 4 for question 2 is equal to $0.64 \times 1.0 \times 0.67 = 0.43$. For response stability, we will use the fitted correlation between two observed variables as an indicator. The fitted correlation is defined as the product of the crystallization, the stability, and the quality parameters between two observed variables. For example, the fitted correlation between R_{231} (wave 3) and R_{241} (wave 4) is equal to $0.90 \times 0.64 \times 1.0 \times 0.67 \times 0.93 = 0.36$. This fitted correlation is actually very close to the observed correlation between R_{231} and R_{241}, which is 0.35.

Table 2.4 clearly shows the differences among stability, opinion strength, and response stability. The first row, for example, shows that stability is very large (s_{43} = 1). This is in sharp contrast with opinion strength (0.43) and response stability (0.36). The difference between the high stability on the one hand and the low opinion strength and response stability on the other is due to the relatively small size of the crystallization coefficients (0.64, 0.67, 0.60). In contrast is the large size of the quality coefficients. Because of this, there is only a small difference between opinion

TABLE 2.4
Computations of Stability, Opinion Strength, and Response Instability

Stability		Opinion Strength			Response Instability		
between		between	$c_{ij21} \times c_{ij}$		between	$q_{ij21}, k \times q_{ijk}$	
$S_{23} \bullet S_{24}$	1.00	$O_{23} \bullet O_{24}$	0.43	.43	$R_{231} \bullet R_{241}$	.84	.36
$S_{23} \bullet S_{24}$	1.00	$O_{23} \bullet O_{24}$	0.43	.43	$R_{232} \bullet R_{241}$	.84	.36
$S_{23} \bullet S_{24}$	1.00	$O_{23} \bullet O_{24}$	0.43	.43	$R_{231} \bullet R_{242}$	.84	.36
$S_{23} \bullet S_{24}$	1.00	$O_{23} \bullet O_{24}$	0.43	.43	$R_{232} \bullet R_{242}$	.84	.36
$S_{24} \bullet S_{27}$	0.76	$O_{24} \bullet O_{27}$	0.38	.29	$R_{241} \bullet R_{271}$	.90	.28
$S_{24} \bullet S_{27}$	0.76	$O_{24} \bullet O_{27}$	0.38	.29	$R_{242} \bullet R_{271}$	.90	.28
$S_{24} \bullet S_{27}$	0.76	$O_{24} \bullet O_{27}$	0.38	.29	$R_{241} \bullet R_{272}$	.81	.25
$S_{24} \bullet S_{27}$	0.76	$O_{24} \bullet O_{27}$	0.38	.29	$R_{242} \bullet R_{272}$	.81	.25
$S_{23} \bullet S_{27}$	0.76	$O_{23} \bullet O_{27}$	0.40	.31	$R_{231} \bullet R_{271}$	.87	.25
$S_{23} \bullet S_{27}$	0.76	$O_{23} \bullet O_{27}$	0.40	.31	$R_{232} \bullet R_{271}$	.87	.25
$S_{23} \bullet S_{27}$	0.76	$O_{23} \bullet O_{27}$	0.40	.31	$R_{231} \bullet R_{272}$	.78	.23
$S_{23} \bullet S_{27}$	0.76	$O_{23} \bullet O_{27}$	0.40	.31	$R_{232} \bullet R_{272}$	.78	.23

strength and response stability. Consequently, quality has only a small effect on response stability compared to crystallization, at least for these policy-related issues in Russia.

DISCUSSION AND CONCLUSION

In conclusion, the example shows that although response instability is high across the waves (Tables 2.2a–2.2c), the quality of the measurement instruments can still be quite good. This could not be expected using the work of Achen (1975) and other authors on measurement error. We also showed that opinion stability will be larger than response stability due to the crystallization and quality of the survey question. This could not be expected with Converse 1964 as a basis. In our example, the crystalliza-tion, or the unique considerations, played a major role in the explanation of response instability, as suggested in the recent models of Zaller (1992), Lodge (1995), and Boynton (1995). Therefore, it makes sense to simul-taneously obtain information about the important characteristics—quality, crystallization, and stability—of a survey question to get an impression of their effects on the response. We have shown that this is possible with the approach put forward here. This approach is rather complex, but there are alternative designs available that are simpler. For details of these alternative designs and an evaluation of their efficiency, we refer to Van der Veld and Saris (1999).

It should be clear by now that the relation between observed variables could be distorted by measurement error, unique considerations, and new stable considerations. However, so far we have only discussed the relation between observations of the same opinion. Suppose now that we are interested in the relation between two different opinions, one from question a and one from question b. We have the choice to use the relation between the observed variables, or the relation between the opinions, or the relation between the result of the stable considerations. The choice we make can have large consequences, as shown below.

As an example we take the relation between R_{141} (*Minorities should be allowed to receive education in their own language*) and R_{241} (*To reduce the level of crime, we should move minorities to their own territory*), which are the first observations of questions 1 and 2 in wave 4. The observed correlation between the two variables is -0.29.[9] The correlation between O_{23} and O_{24} is equal to -0.34 ($0.77 \times -0.66 \times 0.67$), which is somewhat higher than the correlation between the observed variables. The relation between S_{14} and S_{24} is much higher and equals -0.66. Therefore, the relation between the stable considerations *seems* to be preferable because it shows that these latent variables have the strongest relation.

There are, however, two reasons why this may not be such a good choice. First, if we are interested in the opinion at a specific moment, including both the result of the stable considerations and the result of the unique considerations, we should use the variable O_{ij}. Second, the explained variance of the observed variable by the result of the stable considerations can become quite small when measurement error and unique considerations are present. For example, the result of the stable considerations S_{24} explains 45 percent ($.67^2 \times 100\%$) of the variance in O_{24}, and only 39 percent ($.67^2 \times .93^2 \times 100\%$) of the variance in R_{241}. So, even though the quality of the measurement is rather high (.93) and the crystallization is not extremely low (.67), the explained variance of R_{241} by S_{24} is still pretty poor. This is probably not an uncommon result for issues about politics. It should be obvious that the impact of the unique considerations on a response variable could be so large that the use of such a variable will be questionable. Consequently, such variables are best not used in (long-term) prediction equations. It should also be obvious that the larger the impact of the unique considerations, the lower the observed relation between the same opinion across time will be, and the lower the observed relation between different opinions across time or on a specific point in time will be.

The former has been assumed to be indicative for nonattitudes (Converse 1964) or lack of opinion. We must dispute this idea for two reasons. First, when the response stability is large and when the opinion is not crystallized, there can still be considerations that are stable in the opinion. Second, and more important, lack of opinion cannot be based on the instability of responses, and not even on the presumably "logically" contradictory responses that people seem to provide for certain issues (Converse 1964). The opinion is the result of all considerations that come to mind at a specific point in time; that these may not be stable over time has nothing to do with "lack of opinion."

We have concluded that the result of the stable considerations (S_{ij}) is not always the right variable to use when one is interested in the relation between two different opinions. But what about the opinion (O_{ij})? This opinion contains, as we said above, all considerations that come to mind at a specific point in time, and we should attach value to this opinion. In addition, the opinion contains no measurement error. For these reasons, the relation between (different) opinions is always preferable to the observed relation. In other words, one should always correct for measurement error to obtain the error-free opinion. After correction for measurement error, the correlation between opinions a and b will be equal to $\rho_{ab} = cor_{ab} / (q_a \times q_b)$. See also the example above about the relation between R_{141} and R_{241}.

It can be easily seen here that the difference between ρ_{ab} and cor_{ab} will be larger if the quality of the survey questions (q_a and/or q_b) gets worse, i.e., there is more measurement error. What happens if the quality becomes so poor that the opinion (O_{ij}) can hardly explain the variance in the observed variable? Is the use of O_{ij} in this case also questionable in the same way as the use of S_{ij}, becoming questionable when the crystallization gets worse? Yes and no. Yes, because we should not work with latent variables that explain so little. No, because the quality is an attribute of the measurement method and the population, and we could try to improve our measurement method to obtain a fair amount of explained variance of the variable O_{ij}. Improving the measurement instruments might, however, be an endless task if we do not know the determinants of the quality of our survey questions. There is, for this purpose, a fair amount of knowledge about the ex ante improvement of the quality of our survey questions (Andrews 1984; Alwin and Krosnick 1991; Saris and Andrews 1991; Költringer 1995; Scherpenzeel and Saris 1997; Van der Veld, Saris, and Gallhofer 2001; Zouwen et al. 2001; Krosnick and Fabrigar 1996). So the measurement procedure can be adjusted to get higher quality, but crystallization is an attribute of the population and of the issue asked, and we cannot change both the issue and the population, as this would be a different study.

NOTES

1. The wording of the first question was: "As you may know, the United Nations Security Council has authorized the use of force against Iraq if it doesn't withdraw from Kuwait by Jan. 15. If Iraq does not withdraw from Kuwait, should the United States go to war against Iraq to force it out of Kuwait at some point after Jan. 15 or not?" The wording of the second question was: "The United Nations has passed a resolution authorizing the use of military force against Iraq if they do not withdraw from Kuwait by Jan. 15. If Iraq does not withdraw from Kuwait by then, do you think the United States should start military actions against Iraq, or should the United States wait longer to see if the trade embargo and other economic sanctions work?"

2. For an interesting description of the memory process when a question is asked, we refer to Lodge and McGraw (1995), and especially to Lodge (1995) and Boynton (1995).

3. We will use the word *opinion* in this chapter; however, one could replace this with *attitude, preference, fact,* etc.

4. A design with repeated observations within the wave can lead to a practical problem concerning the independence of the repeated observations. When memory effects play a role in the second observation, then the observations are said to be dependent. To prevent these memory effects one should make the time between the repeated observations as long as possible. However, the time between the observations cannot be too long, because then the opinion (O_{ij}) may change. Van Meurs and Saris (1990) have shown that memory effects are virtually gone after twenty minutes if similar questions have been asked in between the two observations and the respondents have no extreme opinions. In this study the first measure is always observed at the very beginning of the interview and the second observation at the end. The total length of the questionnaires was around fifty minutes. Therefore, we think that there is no problem with memory effects.

5. We will, however, use "the result of a set of considerations" and "considerations" alternately. It should be clear from the context whether we talk about a variable (the result) or the set of considerations.

6. Visit the RUSSET Web site at http://home.pscw.uva.nl/saris.

7. The reason for this is that the estimates were in some cases unacceptable, i.e., negative error variances, though statistically not significant.

8. If the assumptions are not plausible then the models would be rejected, but this is not the case.

9. This correlation (-0.29) was computed using PRELIS 2, assuming the both variables are continuous. With this correlation we can predict the correlation (ρ_{21}) between S_{14} and S_{24} using the equation derived from the structural model: $r_{21} = q_{141} \times c_{14} \times \rho_{21} \times c_{24} \times q_{241}$. So, $\rho_{21} = r_{21}/(q_{141} \times c_{14} \times c_{24} \times q_{241}) = -0.29/(0.91 \times 0.77 \times 0.67 \times 0.93) = -0.66$.

REFERENCES

Abelson, R. P. 1968. "Simulation of Social Behavior." In *The Handbook of Social Psychology,* ed. L. Gardner and E. Aronson. 2nd ed. Vol. 2. Reading, MA: Addison-Wesley.

Achen, C. H. 1975. "Mass Political Attitudes and the Survey Response." *American Political Science Review* 69:1218–31.

Ajzen, I., and M. Fishbein. 1980. *Understanding Attitudes and Predicting Social Behavior.* London: Prentice Hall.

Alwin, D. F., and J. A. Krosnick. 1991. "The Reliability of Survey Attitude Measurement: The Influence of Question and Respondent Attributes." *Sociological Methods and Research* 20(1):139–81.

Anderson, J. R. 2000. *Cognitive Psychology and Its Implications.* 5th ed. New York: Worth Publishers.

Anderson, N. H. 1970. "Functional Measurement and Psychophysical Judgment." *Psychological Review* 77:153–70.

———. 1982. "Cognitive Algebra and Social Psychophysics." In *Social Attitudes and Psychophysical Measurement,* ed. B. Wegener. Hillsdale, NJ: Lawrence Erlbaum.

Andrews, F. M. 1984. "Construct Validity and Error Components of Survey Measures: A Structural Modeling Approach." *Public Opinion Quarterly* 48(2):409–42.

Billiet, J., G. Loosveldt, and L. Waterplas. 1995. *Het Survey-Interview Onderzocht. Effecten van Het Ontwerp en Gebruik van Vragenlijsten op de Kwaliteit van de Antwoorden.* 4th ed. K. U. Leuven: Sociologisch Onderzoeksinstituut.

Boynton, G. R. 1995. "Computational Modeling: A Computational Model of a Survey Respondent." In *Political Judgment: Structure and Process,* ed. M. Lodge and K. M. McGraw, 229–48. Ann Arbor: University of Michigan Press.

Converse, P. E. 1964. "The Nature of Belief Systems." In *Ideology and Discontent,* ed. David E. Apter, 206–61. New York: Free Press.

Erikson, R. S. 1978. "Analyzing One Variable Three Wave Panel Data: A Comparison of Two Models." *Political Methodology* 2:151–66.

———. "The SRC Panel Data and Mass Political Attitudes." *British Journal of Political Science* 9:89–114.

Feldman, S. 1989. "Measuring Issue Preferences: The Problem of Response Instability." *Political Analysis* 1:25–60.

———. 1995. "Answering Survey Questions: The Measurement and the Meaning of Public Opinion." In *Political Judgment: Structure and Process,* ed. M. Lodge and K. M. McGraw, 246–70. Ann Arbor: University of Michigan Press.

Gamson, W. A., and A. Modigliani. 1987. "The Changing Culture of Affirmative Action." *Research in Political Sociology* 3:139–77.

Heise, D. R. 1969. "Separating Reliability and Stability in Test-Retest Correlation." *American Sociological Review* 34:93–101.

Jöreskog, K. G., and D. Sörbom. 1993. *LISREL® 8 User's Reference Guide.* Chicago: Scientific Software International.

———. 1996. *PRELIS® 2 User's Reference Guide.* Chicago: Scientific Software International.

Judd, C. M., and M. A. Milburn. 1980. "The Structure of Attitude Systems in the General Public: Comparisons of a Structural Equation Model." *American Sociological Review* 45:627–43.

Judd, C. M., J. A. Krosnick, and M. A. Milburn. 1981. "Political Involvement and Attitude Structure in the General Public." *American Sociological Review* 46:660–69.

Kahneman, D., and A. Tversky. 1984. "Choices, Values, and Frames." American Psychologist *39:341–50.*

Költringer, R. 1995. "Measurement Quality in Austrian Personal Interview Surveys." In *The Multitrait-Multimethod Approach to Evaluate Measurement Instruments,* ed. W. E. Saris and Á. Münnich, 207–24. Budapest: Eötvös University Press.

Krosnick, J. A., and D. F. Alwin. 1987. "An Evaluation of a Cognitive Theory of Response-Order Effects in Survey Measurement." *Public Opinion Quarterly* 51:201–19.

Krosnick, J. A., and L. R. Fabrigar. 1996. *Designing Good Questionnaires: Insights from Cognitive and Social Psychology.* New York: Oxford University Press.

Lodge, M. 1995. "Towards a Procedural Model of Candidate Evaluation." In *Political Judgment: Structure and Process,* ed. M. Lodge and K. M. McGraw, 111–41. Ann Arbor: University of Michigan Press.

Lodge, M. and K. M. McGraw, eds. 1995. *Political Judgment: Structure and Process.* Ann Arbor: University of Michigan Press.

Lord, L. M., and M. R. Novick. 1968. *Statistical Theories of Mental Test Scores.* Reading, MA: Addison-Wesley.

Münnich, Á. 1998. "Judgment and Choice." PhD diss., University of Amsterdam.

Petty, R. E,. and J. A. Krosnick. 1993. *Attitude Strength: Antecedents and Consequences.* Hillsdale, NJ: Lawrence Erlbaum.

Quillian, M. R. 1966. *Semantic Memory.* Cambridge, MA: Bolt, Beranak, and Newman.

Rasinski, K. A. 1989. "The Effect of Question Wording on Public Support for Government Spending." *Public Opinion Quarterly* 53(3):388–94.

Saris, W. E. 1982. "Different Questions, Different Variables." In *A Second Generation of Multivariate Analysis,* ed. C. Fornell. Vol. 2: *Measurement and Evaluation.* New York: Praeger.

———. 1987a. *Variation in Response Functions: A Source of Measurement Error.* Amsterdam: Sociometric Research Foundation.

———. 1987b. "Individual Response Functions and Correlations Between Judgments." In *Sociometric Research Data Collection and Scaling,* ed. W. E. Saris and I. N. Gallhofer. Vol. 1. London: MacMillan.

Saris, W. E., and F. M. Andrews. 1991. "Evaluation of Measurement Instruments Using a Structural Modeling Approach." In *Measurement Errors in Surveys,* ed. P. P. Biemer, R. M. Groves, L. E. Lyberg, Nancy A. Mathiowetz, and Seymour Sudman, 575–99. New York: Wiley.

Saris, W. E., and H. Hartman. 1990. "Common Factors Can Always Be Found But Can They Also Be Rejected?" *Quality and Quantity* 24:471–90.

Saris, W. E., and H. Stronkhorst. 1984. *Causal Modeling in Non-Experimental Research: An* Introduction to the LISREL Approach. *Amsterdam: Sociometric Research Foundation.*

Saris, W. E., and B. van den Putte. 1988. "Tests of Measurement Models: A Secondary Analysis of the ALLBUS-Test-Retest Data." *Sociological Methods and Research* 16:123–57.

Scherpenzeel, A. C., and W. E. Saris. 1997. "The Validity and Reliability of Survey Questions: a Meta-Analysis of MTMM Studies." *Sociological Methods and Research* 25(3):341–83.

Schuman, H., and S. Presser. 1981. *Questions and Answers in Attitude Surveys: Experiments on Question Form, Wording, and Context.* New York: Wiley.

Smith, T. W. 1987. "That Which We Call Welfare by Any Other Name Would Smell Sweeter: An Analysis of the Impact of Question Wording on Response Patterns." *Public Opinion Quarterly* 51(1):75–83.

Steyer, R., and M. J. Schmitt. 1990. "Latent State-Trait Models in Attitude Research." *Quality and Quantity* 24(4):427–45.

Van Meurs, A., and W. E. Saris. 1990. "Memory Effects in Multi-Trait Multi-Method Studies." In *Evaluation of Measurement Instruments by Meta-Analysis of Multitrait Multimethod Studies,* ed. A. van Meurs and W. E. Saris. Amsterdam: Elsevier.

———. "Memory Effects in MTMM Studies." In *The Multitrait-Multimethod Approach to Evaluate Measurement,* ed. W. E. Saris and A. Münnich, 89–102. Budapest: Eötvös University Press.

Van der Veld, W. M., and W. E. Saris. 1999. "Different Designs to Separate Measurement Error and the Crystallization and Stability of an Opinion." The Netherlands: University of Amsterdam.

Van der Veld, W. M., W. E. Saris, and I. N. Gallhofer. 2001. "Prediction of Quality of Survey Questions before Data Are Collected." In *Proceedings of the Fifth International Conference on Logic and Methodology,* ed. J. Blasius, J. Hox, E. de Leeuw, and P. Schmidt. 2nd ed. Leverkusen, Germany: Verlag Leske + Budrich.

Van der Zouwen, J., W. E. Saris, S. Draisma, and W. M. van der Veld. 2001. "Assessing the Quality of Questionnaires: A Comparison of Three Methods for the 'Ex Ante' Evaluation of Survey Questions." *Proceedings of the International Conference Q2001 on Quality in Official Statistics.* Stockholm, Sweden.

Wiley, D. E., and J. A. Wiley. 1970. "The Estimation of Measurement Error in Panel Data." *American Sociological Review* 35:112–17.

Zaller, J. R. 1992. *The Nature and Origins of Mass Opinion.* Cambridge: Cambridge University Press.

Zaller, J., and S. Feldman. 1992. "A Simple Theory of the Survey Response: Answering Questions versus Revealing Preferences." *American Journal of Political Science* 36(3):579–16.

PART II

The Problem of Ambivalence

CHAPTER 3

Good, Bad, and Ambivalent:
The Consequences of Multidimensional
Political Attitudes

Michael F. Meffert, Michael Guge, and Milton Lodge

CONVENTIONAL WAYS of measuring political attitudes assume a tradeoff between the polar opposite ends of evaluative scales. Focusing on the evaluation of presidential candidates, the more positive a person feels about a candidate, the less negative he must be about the candidate. Or, to use another example, the more conservative an individual is on a policy position, the less liberal she must be. This unidimensional perspective on individual attitudes is prevalent in research on political behavior. However, there is increasing evidence that many individual attitudes do not fit so easily into this unidimensional framework. There is renewed recognition in social psychology (e.g., Cacioppo, Gardner, and Berntson 1997; Jonas, Diehl, and Brömer 1997; Lavine et al. 1998; Tesser and Martin 1996; Thompson, Zanna, and Griffin 1995) and among a growing number of researchers in political science (e.g., Zaller and Feldman 1992; Alvarez and Brehm 1997, 1995; Steenbergen and Brewer, chapter 4 in this volume) that ambivalence may be a characteristic of individual attitudes. Attitudinal ambivalence suggests that positive reactions toward a presidential candidate do not necessarily mean a lack of negative evaluations of the same candidate. Or, in terms of policy attitudes about an issue such as abortion, the number of "liberal" ideas that an individual might have about abortion policy does not necessarily discount the possibility that the same individual has a number of "conservative" ideas about abortion policy. That is, people may simultaneously possess opposing ideas, considerations, or reactions about a given policy or politician. Despite the intuitive nature of such a conclusion, the presence of ambivalence has not received the attention it deserves in the dominant, unidimensional treatment of political attitudes.

We define attitudes as evaluative reactions associated with a target object, a definition that is well established in social psychology (Eagly and Chaiken 1993; Fazio et al. 1986; Fiske and Taylor 1991; Petty and Cacioppo 1986). The mere mentioning or presentation of an attitude object like a presidential candidate can elicit "hot" (emotional) and "cold" (cognitive) evaluative reactions that are then, consciously or unconsciously, processed in memory and result in the expression of an overall attitude (Fazio et al. 1986). Following this definition, we do not consider expectancy-value models of attitudes used in behavioral decision making (i.e., Fishbein and Ajzen 1975) in the present study. While also based on evaluative reactions, these attitudes are oriented toward a given course of action or behavioral intention (Ajzen 1996). Our focus is on how ambivalent evaluative reactions lead to qualitatively different attitudes.

We will start with a short review of the research on attitudinal ambivalence and present some evidence that ambivalence toward presidential candidates is indeed common among the public. We postulate three major consequences of attitudinal ambivalence: a decrease in attitudinal extremity, lower confidence in judgments, and, perhaps most intriguing, the greater aptitude of ambivalent citizens as compared to nonambivalent citizens to make more balanced or accurate political judgments. These hypotheses find supporting evidence in our analysis of recent American National Election Studies.

THE RESURGENCE OF AMBIVALENCE

The notion that individual attitudes are composed of competing ideas is one that dates back several decades in psychology (e.g., Allport 1935; Lewin 1951; Scott 1966, 1968; Kaplan 1972). For instance, Lewin's (1951) field theory, one of the most influential theories in social psychology, argues that there are distinct and independent forces pulling on individuals, producing psychological tension. Cognitive consistency theory (Festinger 1957), the dominant social psychological perspective throughout the 1960s and 1970s, is also based on the notion of multiple and contrary attitude forces. It posits that individuals will resolve the contradictory elements in their attitudes and strive for attitude consistency, thus minimizing the presence of ambivalence.

Yet, more recent theoretical perspectives suggest that individuals do not necessarily resolve the conflicts between attitude elements. They may even incorporate this conflict as an inherent characteristic of their attitudes. This notion of intra-attitude conflict or ambivalence has experienced a resurgence in attitude research following several important theoretical and empirical contributions (e.g., Cacioppo and Bernston 1994; Cacioppo, Gardner, and Berntson 1997; Thompson, Zanna, and Griffin 1995; Priester and Petty 1996). We take as our starting point the recent work by Cacioppo and colleagues. They propose a multidimensional representation of attitudes characterized by two distinct and independent attitudinal dimensions—positivity and negativity—which represent the evaluative reactions to an attitude object. Both dimensions define an evaluative space for individual attitudes

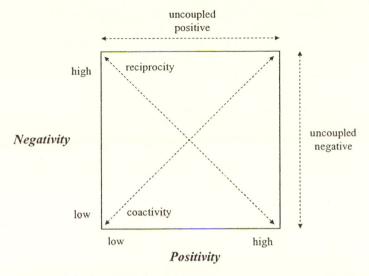

Figure 3.1 Bidimensional evaluative space. *Source:* Adapted from Cacioppo, Gardner, and Berntson 1997.

(Figure 3.1). Under this multidimensional conceptualization of attitudes it is possible for an individual to become more positive about an object of evaluation without necessarily becoming less negative. A person can experience positive *and* negative (or neither) dispositions simultaneously toward a particular attitude object. Both positivity and negativity can either increase or decrease independently of each other ("uncoupled"), they can move in opposite directions along the reciprocity axis, or they can increase simultaneously along the coactivity axis. The lower left corner of the evaluative space represents a state of indifference, the upper right corner the highest degree of ambivalence.

The critical feature of this theoretical framework is that an ambivalent individual will very likely be represented at the same position on a unidimensional scale as someone who has an indifferent attitude. Bipolar, unidimensional attitude measures such as Likert scales and feeling thermometers cannot represent, either conceptually or operationally, the process of attitude formation as posited by Cacioppo and colleagues. If the dimensions representing the endpoints of bipolar scales are independent under a multidimensional conceptualization, individuals who have a varying amount of balanced pro and con considerations are difficult to place in any meaningful way on such a single continuum. Ambivalent individuals may sort through their competing considerations and eventually fall somewhere in the middle of the scale, but so do indifferent individuals who possess no affiliation with the positions representing the polar extremes of the scale.

Thus, even though ambivalent and indifferent individuals may look similar when measured on bipolar attitude scales, the nature of their attitudes is very different. Or in other words, the same overall attitude might have very different consequences. In short, this critical distinction between dissimilar multidimensional attitude constellations is neglected in the common bipolar, unidimensional representations of attitudes.

Much of the existing research on competing beliefs explores the consequences of value conflict, a concept that is very similar to attitudinal ambivalence and thus requires a careful distinction. Both concepts represent the notion of competing ideas within a single attitude, but the exact nature of both types of ambivalence is different. Value conflict deals more specifically with the clash of antecedent core beliefs that are all-important to an individual. For instance, one may believe in the values of egalitarianism and individualism, but for issues like affirmative action these values may clash and pull the individual attitude in opposite directions (especially for white respondents). A belief in egalitarianism may lead to support for such policies (as "remedial action") while the value of individualism would pull in the opposite direction ("unfair advantage").

Attitudinal ambivalence, on the other hand, is concerned with the incongruency between positive and negative ideas and feelings toward a single attitude object. According to this definition, a person is ambivalent if he or she simultaneously possesses both positive and negative evaluations of a particular entity. These evaluative ideas and feelings are not necessarily derivative of deeply held beliefs; rather, they are specific evaluations of a particular attitude object. For instance, an individual who is ambivalent toward President Clinton would possess both positive (e.g., he has a firm grasp of policy details) and negative (e.g., he is untrustworthy) evaluations of him. While we are interested in the topic of attitudinal ambivalence, we also draw on the value conflict literature to inform our analyses since there are many similarities between the two concepts and their attitudinal consequences.[1]

AMBIVALENCE IN POLITICAL SCIENCE

To be sure, the political science literature has not ignored this idea. A number of studies suggest that conflict and ambivalence are central features of citizens' attitudes about political issues. Hochschild (1981, 1993), for instance, has found in a series of in-depth interviews numerous inconsistencies and contradictions in political attitudes on redistributive justice. Her respondents vacillated and expressed uncertainty when confronted by the full range of their own attitudes. In-depth studies like Hochschild's expose the complexities and contradictions that lie beneath the surface of many individual issue attitudes.

At the same time, uncovering citizens' ambivalence on political issues does not necessarily require in-depth probing. Zaller and Feldman's (1992; Zaller 1992) model of the survey response, which rests on the notion that citizens possess competing considerations on issues, is tested with survey data based on minimal probing by interviewers. Although ambivalence is an essential feature of the Zaller and Feldman theory of the survey response, this theory still treats attitudes as unidimensional constructs, which is antithetical to the multidimensional conceptualization discussed earlier (e.g., Cacioppo, Gardner, and Berntson 1997). In general, the process specified by the Zaller-Feldman survey response model is one of "averaging over" the host of recounted considerations on an issue. An individual will make use of the salient or accessible thoughts or ideas at the moment of forming an opinion on an issue. And when these considerations represent different points along the issue continuum, the individual will take a quasi-average of the multiple considerations. Although the process of averaging over salient competing considerations offers an appealing explanation for the instability of survey attitudes and their susceptibility to change, the theory still assumes that the attitude construct falls on a single continuum. Attitudes are temporary, yet they are still unidimensional constructs (Zaller 1992; Zaller and Feldman 1992). Consequently, there is no difference between an attitude based on the average of one "liberal" consideration and one "conservative" consideration and an attitude based on five "liberal" and five "conservative" considerations. The average is the same, only the reliability of the second attitude might be higher due to the larger sampling of considerations. There is very little difference, then, between a person with a rather indifferent attitude (none or very few considerations) and a person with a highly ambivalent attitude (many considerations on each side of the issue). This is a common assumption of unidimensional representations of attitudes and inconsistent with a multidimensional framework.

Alvarez and Brehm (1995, 1997) offer further evidence of the inherent ambivalence in citizens' issue attitudes. Their analyses find ambivalence to be a significant predictor of response variability in citizens' responses about abortion policy (1995) but conclude that Americans are not ambivalent on matters of racial policy (1997). Regardless of Alvarez and Brehm's mixed results with respect to ambivalence, the theoretical premise of their work rests on the notion that on many matters of public policy, citizens' opinions are composed of competing ideas and considerations. (Note, however, that Steenbergen and Brewer [chapter 4 in this volume] find only relatively mild levels of ambivalence among the American public.)

In sum, the work by Hochschild (1981, 1993), Zaller and Feldman (1992; Zaller 1992), and Alvarez and Brehm (1995, 1997) is instrumental in establishing the importance of ambivalence for researchers interested in political attitudes and behavior. But these initial efforts require further conceptual and empirical development.

AMBIVALENCE IN THE AMERICAN ELECTORATE

Even the sympathetic reader might ask whether all this really matters. Given the well-known fact that most people do not care very much about politics, can they really become highly ambivalent about political objects? To answer this question, we present some evidence that political ambivalence is indeed quite prevalent. A substantial portion of the citizenry is ambivalent when faced with political choices, and these ambivalent individuals cannot be accurately characterized as indifferent toward the political options before them, although they may appear to be with unidimensional measures. We use National Election Study (NES) data to examine the simultaneous presence of positive and negative considerations about presidential candidates as well as the positive and negative emotions experienced by individuals toward these candidates. For the time being, we define ambivalence as the simultaneous presence of both positive and negative emotion toward a single candidate and as the psychological state of having both positive and negative cognitive reactions to a candidate.

For emotional reactions, the NES assesses the respondents' reactions toward a presidential candidate by asking them whether they ever experienced anger, fear, pride, and hope toward the candidate. The syntax of these NES emotion questions is as follows:

> Now we would like to know something about the feelings you have toward <presidential candidate>. Has <presidential candidate>—because of the kind of person he is, or because of something he has done—made you feel <emotion>?

Respondents can respond with "yes," "no," or "don't know" to each emotion for each of the major party candidates. Because they are asked about positive and negative emotions separately, it is possible to identify individuals who experience a combination of both positive and negative emotion toward a candidate.

The same applies to cognitive (mostly affective) reactions toward the presidential candidates. NES respondents are asked whether "there is anything in particular about [candidate] that might make you want to vote [FOR or AGAINST] him?" with up to four follow-up "Anything else?" probes. Since the respondents report their positive reactions about the candidates separately from their negative reactions, this offers again the opportunity to identify the multiple dimensions of an individual's overall attitude about a particular presidential candidate.

TABLE 3.1
The Prevalence of Indifference and Ambivalence

Democrats	1980 Carter	1984 Mondale	1988 Dukakis	1992 Clinton	1996 Clinton
Considerations	N = 1570	N = 2257	N = 2040	N = 2485	N = 1714
One-sided	58.3%	58.1%	54.0%	55.2%	58.8%
Indifferent	9.2%	22.2%	23.6%	18.4%	14.2%
Ambivalent	32.5%	23.6%	22.5%	26.5%	27.0%
Emotions	N = 1548	N = 2210	N = 1995	N = 2438	N = 1706
One-sided	53.6%	59.3%	57.8%	60.6%	54.4%
Indifferent	7.2%	28.9%	29.1%	25.1%	9.7%
Ambivalent	39.2%	11.8%	13.0%	14.3%	35.6%
Combined	N = 1548	N = 2210	N = 1995	N = 2438	N = 1706
One-sided	43.4%	58.2%	54.4%	55.5%	46.7%
Indifferent	2.5%	12.5%	14.0%	10.3%	4.4%
Ambivalent	54.1%	29.2%	31.6%	34.2%	48.9%
Republicans	Reagan	Reagan	Bush	Bush	Dole
Considerations	N = 1570	N = 2257	N = 2040	N = 2485	N = 1714
One-sided	51.1%	55.2%	50.2%	54.1%	53.4%
Indifferent	18.0%	14.1%	25.4%	14.4%	23.7%
Ambivalent	30.9%	30.7%	24.4%	31.5%	22.8%
Emotions	N = 1551	N = 2227	N = 2010	N = 2456	N = 1696
One-sided	60.7%	58.9%	58.2%	50.6%	55.8%
Indifferent	23.3%	9.8%	32.0%	17.9%	25.7%
Ambivalent	15.9%	31.3%	9.8%	39.4%	17.6%
Combined	N = 1551	N = 2227	N = 2010	N = 2456	N = 1696
One-sided	50.4%	45.1%	54.5%	38.5%	53.2%
Indifferent	9.1%	4.5%	13.7%	4.8%	12.4%
Ambivalent	40.5%	50.3%	31.8%	56.9%	34.4%

Source: NES 1980–1996

Table 3.1 reports a simple classification of respondents in the last five presidential elections according to their attitudinal state: one-sided, indifferent, or ambivalent. "One-sided" refers to citizen reactions that are either all positive or all negative; "indifferent" represents respondents with no reactions at all; while "ambivalent" represents respondents who voice both positive *and* negative reactions toward a certain candidate. These simple classifications are reported separately for the positive and negative cognitive reactions or considerations, the emotional reactions, and in combined form. In the combined classification, ambivalent people might experience, for example, positive emotions and negative considerations.

Looking at the number of respondents in each of these groupings suggests that a considerable proportion of Americans were ambivalent toward the presidential candidates in each of the elections from 1980 to 1996. Although a majority of respondents experienced either consistent emotions or considerations toward the presidential candidates, a substantial number of respondents in each sample experienced some form of ambivalence toward the candidates. This phenomenon is most consistent in the realm of cognitive reactions where approximately 25 percent of all respondents across election years and candidates expressed both positive and negative considerations about a candidate. Although less consistent for emotions, sizable portions of the samples experienced some degree of mixed emotional responses toward the presidential candidates here as well. In addition, the combined indicator of mixed cognitive and emotional responses toward the candidates shows that approximately 40 percent of the sampled respondents, on average, express some form of ambivalence toward the presidential candidates.[2]

These frequencies suggest that many citizens possess rather complex attitudes about the candidates they are asked to consider in presidential elections. The failure to adequately represent the positive and negative reactions of these respondents in a multidimensional framework might have serious consequences. The simultaneous presence of positivity and negativity is likely to be consequential for *how* citizens eventually come to judge the political figures before them.

THE CONSEQUENCES OF ATTITUDINAL AMBIVALENCE FOR JUDGMENTS ABOUT POLITICAL CANDIDATES

If we accept our contention that ambivalence is quite prevalent among the public, the next logical question concerns the attitudinal consequences of this ambivalence. The psychological and political literature points to three possible consequences: attitudinal moderation, attitudinal uncertainty, and more balanced information processing.

The literature reviewed above points to the first two of these consequences: attitudinal moderation and attitudinal uncertainty. The idea of moderation becomes very clear in the Zaller and Feldman (1992) model of the survey response. If ambivalent people have considerations both for and against some position, or, more generally, if they have both positive and negative reactions, the idea of averaging across considerations or cognitive reactions should produce attitude expressions whose "mean" evaluation falls near the middle of a unidimensional scale. Ambivalent individuals are "pulled" toward the middle by their contradictory dispositions. The same prediction is made by the value-conflict research (e.g., Liberman and

Chaiken 1991). If driven by conflicting values, the resulting attitude is likely to fall in a moderate region.[3]

The second effect, attitudinal uncertainty, is suggested by Hochschild (1981), who finds conflicted respondents to be highly uncertain about their expressed attitudes. The value-conflict research by Tetlock (1986) also finds that high value conflict leads respondents to have less confidence in the correctness of their issue stands. In short, these previous studies suggest ambivalence leads to more moderate and uncertain political attitudes.[4]

Tetlock furthermore argues that value conflict leads to higher integrative complexity, the idea that conflicted people consider more information (cognitive differentiation) when stating their policy preferences and draw more connections among the different pieces of information (conceptual integration) than nonconflicted people do. This is a demanding cognitive process since effortful tradeoffs are necessary. But at the same time, a more careful and balanced information processing strategy is suggested under integrative complexity, due for example to "increased vigilance" (826). A similar process is postulated by cognitive response theories in the form of "central" (Petty and Cacioppo 1986) or "systematic" (Chaiken, Liberman, and Eagly 1989; Eagly and Chaiken 1993) information processing. Two recent studies by Maio, Bell, and Esses (1996) and by Jonas, Diehl, and Brömer (1997) in particular support the argument that ambivalence leads to systematic processing. Given the basic motivation to hold "correct" attitudes, systematic processing should usually lead to more "objective" processing. While systematic processing does not automatically lead to unbiased processing, given, for example, a motivation to defend a preexisting attitude (Eagly and Chaiken 1993; Lodge and Taber 1998), it is important to keep in mind that someone who holds a moderate attitude is not thought to have as strong a motivation for biased information processing. In short, a final and more tentative hypothesis to be drawn from this literature suggests that ambivalent people hold more balanced and less biased attitudes or, in other, very tentative words, more "accurate" attitudes.

THE MEASUREMENT OF AMBIVALENCE

The challenge in measuring attitudinal ambivalence is twofold. First, it is necessary to identify the types of attitudinal reactions that can lead to ambivalence. Second, the problem of operationalizing ambivalence needs to be addressed.

We propose three types of ambivalence: cognitive, emotional, and trait-based. The first two types have already been introduced earlier in the section on the prevalence of ambivalence. *Cognitive* ambivalence, in short, can be characterized as an affective, evaluative reaction to a specific target, in this case a presidential candidate. The open-ended NES questions eliciting reasons to vote for or against a candidate (often called "likes" and "dislikes") are an adequate source of information on which to base our measure of cognitive ambivalence. Positivity (likes) and negativity (dislikes) can comprise up to five reactions of each type and, most important, can do so independently from each other. Our measures of *emotional* ambivalence are constructed from the NES questions inquiring about respondents' emotional reactions toward the presidential candidates (see discussion above). In this case, positivity and negativity can comprise up to two reactions of each type.

The third postulated type of ambivalence is *trait-based* ambivalence. Good and bad trait judgments are common attributions in the evaluation of political candidates (Kinder 1986). According to the bidimensional framework, individuals may ascribe both positive and negative qualities to presidential candidates. Bill Clinton, for instance, might be seen as both intelligent and dishonest. The NES typically includes a battery of variables that ask respondents whether certain personality traits describe each of the major party presidential candidates. However, these NES variables, unlike the emotion words and "like/dislike" questions, are not amenable for the construction of ambivalence indicators since the candidate traits in the NES are exclusively positive in nature (intelligent, compassionate, decent, inspiring, knowledgeable, moral, strong leader, caring). Hence, they do not offer the opportunity to tap *both* positive and negative dimensions of an individual attitude. One notable exception, which we take advantage of here, is the 1983 NES Pilot Study that includes both good and bad trait judgments of candidates.

In the 1983 Pilot Study, the respondents were presented with a list of thirty personality traits, each followed by the question:

> How much would you say <trait> fits your impression of <candidate>: a great deal, somewhat, a little, or not at all?

Respondents who could not decide on one of the four given options were coded as such and placed in the middle of a 5-point scale, ranging from 1 (fits "not at all") to 5 (fits "a great deal"). Consequently, the positivity and negativity scales for traits are not just based on a count of the 15 positive and 15 negative trait ratings, respectively. Instead, they are additive scales based on the exact ratings for each trait.[5]

Now turning to the actual creation of the ambivalence measures, the numerical operationalization of ambivalence poses a considerable challenge as the extensive discussion in the psychology literature demonstrates. Many scales have been proposed over the years, and most have serious shortcomings and are less than perfect indicators of ambivalence. We rely on the Griffin ambivalence measure developed by Thompson, Zanna, and

Griffin (1995). In a series of comparative tests the Griffin formula proved to be the most satisfactory numerical index for both conceptual and empirical reasons. Thompson, Zanna, and Griffin (1995), Breckler (1994), and Glathar (1996) review the prominent indicators of ambivalence in relation to the Griffin formula on a number of empirical and conceptual criteria, and all studies concur on the superiority of the Griffin ambivalence formula. More specifically, the Griffin formula is an attractive measure of ambivalence as it captures two fundamental components of attitude conflict: the *similarity* in magnitude between the positive and negative dimensions of an attitude, and the *intensity* or overall importance of these multiple dimensions. The Griffin measure of ambivalence takes into account both the number of positive responses (P) and the number of negative responses (N) toward a particular attitude object and incorporates similarity and intensity directly into the formula:

$$\text{Ambivalence} = \frac{P + N}{2} - \left| P - N \right|.$$

Intensity is captured in the first term as the average of the intensity of the two dimensions, and the similarity in magnitude of the dimensions is captured in the second term as the absolute value of the difference between the two dimensions.

It is useful to compare this operationalization with other indicators. The indicators of ambivalence used in most studies fail to treat attitudes as multidimensional constructs. Multiplicative indicators ($P \times N$) and indicators based on the absolute value of the difference of the two dimensions ($|P - N|$), which Alvarez and Brehm (1995, 1997) exclusively rely on, do not adequately capture the conceptual and empirical range of ambivalence inherent in attitudes composed of multiple dimensions (Breckler 1994; Thompson, Zanna, and Griffin 1995). First, simple multiplicative indicators of ambivalence produce counterintuitive ambivalence scores. In particular, individuals with two conflicting considerations are considered as *less* ambivalent ($1 \times 1 = 1$) than individuals who have several considerations for one side but only one consideration for the other side ($4 \times 1 = 4$). Second, the indicator of the absolute value of the difference between two dimensions does not allow for important theoretical distinctions within the multidimensional framework; chief among them is the identical treatment of high ambivalence ($|4 - 4| = 0$) and indifference ($|0 - 0| = 0$). The central ambivalence dimension, as represented by the coactivity axis in Figure 3.1, is left out by sole reliance on the $|P - N|$ operationalization.

We construct ambivalence indicators for the cognitive, emotional, and trait types of ambivalence specified above by using the Griffin formula. The two dimensions, positivity and negativity, are based on the number of

TABLE 3.2
Values of the Griffin Ambivalence Scale

			Positive Reactions				
	(N)	0	1	2	3	4	5
	0	0	-0.5	-1	-1.5	-2	-2.5
	1	-0.5	1	0.5	0	-0.5	-1
Negative	2	-1	0.5	2	1.5	1	0.5
Reactions	3	-1.5	0	1.5	3	2.5	2
	4	-2	-0.5	1	2.5	4	3.5
	5	-2.5	-1	0.5	2	3.5	5

Note: The ambivalence values are calculated with the following formula: $(P + N)/2 - |P - N|$.

positive and negative considerations about a specific candidate (cognitive ambivalence), the number of positive and negative emotions (emotional ambivalence), and the additive scales of the positive and negative trait ratings (trait ambivalence). Table 3.2 shows the calculated ambivalence scores using the Griffin formula for up to five positive and negative evaluative responses.

In the subsequent analyses, we utilize cognitive, emotional, and trait ambivalence measures to test the three predicted consequences of attitudinal ambivalence using NES data from the last five presidential elections as well as the 1983 Pilot Study. First, we examine the moderation effect in terms of the extremity of candidate evaluations and the strength of presidential approval. Second, we examine the certainty and accuracy hypotheses using candidate placements on issue scales in the 1996 NES.

THE EXTREMITY OF CANDIDATE EVALUATIONS

The first major expectation about the consequences of ambivalence is the moderation effect, the presence of less extreme global attitudes. This prediction can be tested with the global evaluations of presidential candidates, or more precisely, the extremity of these candidate evaluations. For this purpose, we construct our dependent variable by folding the 100-point feeling thermometer scores for each of the candidates at the theoretical scale midpoint (50).[6] The folded measure is bounded on the low end by "neutral" or moderate evaluations of the candidates (0) and at the upper end by extreme "warm" or "cool" evaluations (50). We regressed the extremity variable on our ambivalence indicators, as well as on the separate emotional and cognitive measures that formed the ambivalence indicators to distinguish the inherent impact of ambivalence on the expressed global attitude from the effects produced by the ambivalence indicators' constituent components. To control for potentially confounding effects of political sophistication, we also include ideological extremity, strength of partisanship, and education in the models when these measures were available. Ideological extremity and strength of partisanship are also constructed by folding the standard seven-point ideological identification and seven-point party identification variables at their midpoint. The resulting scales consist of four points ranging from moderate (independent) to extremely ideological (strongly partisan). Education is measured as the standard six-point NES education variable, which breaks down the number of years of education achieved into meaningful levels. All predictor variables are recoded into the 0–1 range to facilitate a comparison of the unstandardized regression coefficients. Thus, each of the coefficients can be interpreted as the amount of change in the dependent variable going from the lowest to the highest value on the independent variable. The results of our individual regressions for each of the last five presidential elections are reported in Table 3.3a and for the 1983 Pilot Study in Table 3.3b.[7]

The performance of the ambivalence indicators is striking, especially when compared to the directional affect and emotion variables and the other non-directional variables. Across the seven presidential candidates in Table 3.3a, there is a strong effect of both cognitive and emotional ambivalence on the extremity of the evaluation of the presidential candidates. These coefficients are all significant and range approximately between -11 "degrees" for Dole in 1996 and -22 for Carter in 1980, indicating in the latter case that there is a 22-point drop in the extremity of the evaluation of Carter from the least to highest amount of cognitive ambivalence. The comparison of emotional and trait ambivalence in 1983 shows even more dramatic effects (Table 3.3b). Trait ambivalence reduces the extremity of candidate evaluations from 27 points for Kennedy, over 34 points for Mondale, to 48 points for Reagan. Trait-based ambivalence seems to be the most powerful measure of ambivalence, attenuating the effect of emotional ambivalence markedly.

More generally, the consistency of the negatively signed ambivalence coefficients indicates that ambivalent individuals gravitate toward luke-warm overall evaluations of the candidates. The presence of a moderating effect discussed above (Tetlock 1986; Liberman and Chaiken 1991) is powerfully present for the evaluation of presidential candidates. Moreover, the results reported in Tables 3.3a and 3.3b show that this effect is robust even after controlling for ideology, partisanship, education, and the directional (main) effects of the various evaluative reactions. With the exception of education, which is most often statistically insignificant, these control variables lead to more extreme evaluations of the candidates, while ambivalence works in the opposite direction toward more moderation. In

TABLE 3.3A
Attitudinal Ambivalence and the Extremity of Candidate Evaluations

Democrats	1980 Carter	1984 Mondale	1988 Dukakis	1992 Clinton	1996 Clinton
Cognitive ambivalence	-22.38 (2.37)**	-20.32 (2.20)**	-19.90 (2.43)**	-20.93 (1.88)**	-20.77 (1.95)**
Emotional ambivalence	-20.40 (1.44)**	-17.78 (1.55)**	-15.07 (1.80)**	-14.06 (1.37)**	-18.45 (1.35)**
Positive considerations	12.97 (1.61)**	9.31 (1.16)**	9.48 (1.35)**	4.58 (0.98)**	6.28 (1.12)**
Negative considerations	-.96 (1.37)	.88 (1.27)	.32 (1.47)	2.79 (1.26)*	2.21 (1.26)+
Positive emotions	5.73 (1.00)**	9.19 (0.88)**	8.60 (1.03)**	6.77 (0.84)**	8.43 (0.94)**
Negative emotions	9.13 (1.20)**	6.00 (0.97)**	7.14 (1.13)**	6.02 (0.89)**	7.30 (1.07)**
Ideology (Extremity)	.45 (1.18)	3.18 (1.04)**	.98 (1.05)	2.63 (0.92)**	1.41 (1.17)
PID (Strength)	4.46 (1.04)**	6.74 (0.91)**	4.67 (1.05)**	6.47 (0.83)**	8.43 (1.07)**
Education	-2.68 (1.56)*	-5.24 (1.00)**	-2.02 (1.13)+	-1.65 (0.94)+	-4.08 (1.25)**
Constant	24.52 (1.17)**	20.78 (1.08)**	20.41 (1.20)**	18.87 (0.95)**	23.83 (1.16)**
Adj. R^2	.25	.32	.22	.24	.28
N	1540	2171	1952	2363	1686

Republicans	1980 Reagan	1984 Reagan	1988 Bush	1992 Bush	1996 Dole
Cognitive ambivalence	-18.69 (2.62)**	-16.86 (1.75)**	-20.45 (2.35)**	-21.24 (1.75)**	-20.45 (2.07)**
Emotional ambivalence	-18.63 (1.77)**	-19.02 (1.27)**	-13.70 (1.93)**	-12.71 (1.16)**	-11.19 (1.48)**
Positive considerations	6.65 (1.75)**	9.00 (1.13)**	11.54 (1.35)**	11.41 (1.21)**	7.88 (1.37)**
Negative considerations	.76 (1.57)	-.12 (1.08)	.30 (1.36)	-.53 (0.97)	1.10 (1.21)
Positive emotions	8.54 (1.08)**	6.76 (0.90)**	10.30 (0.97)**	2.75 (0.85)**	5.51 (0.99)**
Negative emotions	6.28 (1.17)**	6.34 (1.03)**	5.81 (1.19)**	6.85 (0.90)**	5.97 (0.96)**
Ideology (Extremity)	3.72 (1.27)**	4.93 (1.04)**	1.68 (1.15)	4.87 (0.97)**	3.32 (1.16)**
PID (Strength)	1.31 (1.08)	4.41 (0.91)**	3.20 (1.02)**	5.92 (0.87)**	2.64 (1.06)**
Education	.261 (1.23)	2.60 (1.02)*	-1.03 (1.12)	.39 (1.00)	-1.19 (1.27)
Constant	21.65 (1.24)**	20.86 (0.99)**	22.33 (1.23)**	18.92 (0.97)**	18.68 (1.14)**
Adj. R^2	.21	.28	.25	.20	.20
N	1543	2186	1966	2381	1676

Source: NES 1980–1996

Note: Coefficients are ordinary least squares estimates, standard errors in parentheses. $^+ p < .10$; $^* p < .05$; $^{**} p < .01$

TABLE 3.3B
Ambivalence and the Extremity of Candidate Evaluations

	Reagan		Kennedy		Mondale	
Trait ambivalence	-47.782	(5.914)**	-26.523	(7.128)**	-34.424	(8.920)**
Emotional ambivalence	-6.4727	(3.485)+	-8.702	(5.758)	-20.172	(6.754)**
Positive traits	7.245	(5.825)	8.462	(7.731)	5.678	(7.129)
Negative traits	33.116	(7.082)**	19.956	(8.926)*	34.989	(10.266)**
Positive emotions	2.158	(2.601)	-1.2082	(3.756)	5.857	(3.311)+
Negative emotions	-1.788	(2.837)	7.904	(3.425)*	4.403	(3.749)
Strength of PID	.662	(2.837)	12.022	(3.613)**	5.832	(3.514)+
Constant	29.731	(2.837)	10.169	(6.942)	15.453	(6.685)*
Adj. R^2	.2823		.1836		.2535	
N	306		151		133	

Source: NES 1983
Note: Coefficients are ordinary least squares estimates, standard errors in parentheses.
+ p < .10; * p < .05; ** p < .01

fact, the ambivalence coefficients are greater in absolute magnitude than the coefficients for any other variables in the model, including ideological extremity and strength of partisanship. Scores ranging from least ambivalent to most ambivalent result in a substantially greater change in the extremity of the evaluation of the candidates than do scores ranging from least ideological to most ideological or from least partisan to most partisan. In short, the moderation effect finds initial and strong support.

AMBIVALENCE AND STRENGTH OF PRESIDENTIAL APPROVAL

We now move beyond the extremity of general affective evaluations of presidential candidates to other more specific evaluations of political figures, in particular the strength of the performance evaluations of the president.

Our analysis focuses on the 1983 NES Pilot Study and the 1996 NES. These data sets allow us to probe the effects for all three ambivalence measures and to analyze different types of presidential approval in more depth.

The dependent variable is the follow-up question to the initial approval/disapproval question: "Do you (dis)approve strongly or not strongly?" The dependent strength-of-approval variable is dichotomous and coded as 0 = not strongly, and 1 = strongly. For 1996, we consider approval for President Clinton's job performance in terms of his overall handling of his job as president within four domain-specific policy areas: the economy, foreign relations, the environment, and health care. Dichotomous variables for each of these five areas of presidential performance were regressed on the ambivalence indicators, the number of positive and negative cognitive reactions toward Clinton (likes/dislikes), the number of positive and negative emotional reactions toward Clinton, extremity of ideological self-placement, strength of party identification, education, and political knowledge.

Political knowledge is a new independent variable. We use the objective sophistication measure proposed by Zaller (1992). The respondents are asked to identify the job or office of four American and foreign political figures (Gore, Rehnquist, Yeltsin, Gingrich), resulting in a five-point scale. The inclusion of the political knowledge variable provides some assurance that any effects of the ambivalence measures, especially ambivalence based on considerations, cannot be attributed to a mere sophistication effect. Greater political knowledge may carry with it the ability to report more reactions to the candidates (positive as well as negative), an ability that does not necessarily represent heightened ambivalence. Logistic regressions of the strength of approval variables on these independent variables are reported in Table 3.4a.

The hypothesis of attitude moderation again finds strong support. The negative signs on the coefficients for ambivalence indicate that the strength of (dis)approval of Clinton's job performance is attenuated by higher levels of ambivalence toward the president. This result is consistent across the different domains of presidential approval and is maintained in the face of controls for ideological extremity, strength of party identification, education, and knowledge.

The effect of ambivalence is quite dramatic. Individuals who are not ambivalent toward the president tend to make quite strong (dis)approval ratings of the president, while ambivalent individuals make much weaker (dis)approval ratings. This effect is strongest for the overall ratings of presidential approval but still quite pronounced for strength of (dis)approval in the specific policy areas. In numerical terms, the probability of strong (dis)approval drops between 34 to 81 percentage points (see Table 3.4c below).

TABLE 3.4A
Ambivalence and Strength of Presidential Approval

Clinton 1996	Overall	Economy	Foreign Relations	Environment	Health Care
Cognitive ambivalence	-3.36 (.38)**	-1.20 (.33)**	-1.07 (.34)**	-1.14 (.33)**	-1.40 (.34)**
Emotional ambivalence	-2.14 (.25)**	-.89 (.23)**	-.67 (.24)**	-1.17 (.23)**	-1.04 (.24)**
Positive considerations	.51 (.21)*	.61 (.20)**	.47 (.20)*	-.36 (.19)+	-.32 (.20)+
Negative considerations	.03 (.23)	.07 (.21)	-.34 (.22)	.35 (.22)	.25 (.22)
Positive emotions	.83 (.17)**	.48 (.16)**	.49 (.17)**	.74 (.16)**	.43 (.16)**
Negative emotions	.94 (.20)**	.28 (.18)	.32 (.19)+	.55 (.18)**	.77 (.19)**
Ideology (Extremity)	.12 (.22)	.23 (.20)	-.03 (.21)	-.01 (.20)	.03 (.21)
PID (Strength)	1.29 (.20)**	.71 (.19)**	.43 (.19)*	.10 (.19)	.52 (.19)**
Education	-.81 (.24)*	-.98 (.23)*	-.80 (.23)*	-.89 (.22)*	-.48 (.23)*

Source: NES 1996

The especially strong effect for overall strength of approval can be explained by its close association with the diffuse cognitive and emotional reactions toward the president. The ambivalence scales for the latter are based on questions that do not inquire about what one likes or feels about President Clinton's health care policies or other specific policy domains but rather focus on Clinton's performance overall.

Turning to the 1983 Pilot Study and the strength of Ronald Reagan's approval ratings, the powerful effect of ambivalence is again confirmed in Table 3.4b. As before, trait ambivalence has by far the largest effect and attenuates the effect of emotional ambivalence, which nevertheless remains significant. Together, the two ambivalence scales lower the probability of strong approval by 38 percentage points, as shown in Table 3.4c. Overall, the moderation hypothesis has found further support.

TABLE 3.4B
Ambivalence and Strength of Presidential Approval

	Reagan	
	B	SE
Trait ambivalence	-5.003	(1.115)**
Emotional ambivalence	-1.368	(.587)*
Positive traits	1.369	(.997)
Negative traits	3.291	(1.298)*
Positive emotions	-.060	(.430)
Negative emotions	1.260	(.482)**
PID (Strength)	.699	(.418)+
Constant	-.0156	(.848)
Log likelihood	-177.271	
$\chi^2(7)$	54.14	
Correctly predicted (%)	69.49	
N	295	

Source: NES 1983   *Note:* Coefficients are logit estimates, standard errors in parentheses.
+ p < .10; * p < .05; ** p < .01

AMBIVALENCE AND THE PLACEMENT OF CANDIDATES ON ISSUE SCALES

The second and third hypothesized consequences of ambivalence posit less certain yet more even-handed political judgments. The 1996 NES offers a long battery of questions concerning the placement of candidates on multiple issues as well as asking respondents how certain they are about their placements. This data set provides an opportunity to probe in more detail the effects of attitudinal ambivalence on the certainty and accuracy of candidate placements.

TABLE 3.4C
The Effect of Ambivalence: Simulated Change in Probabilities

	Clinton 1996					Reagan 1983
Type of Approval	Overall	Economy	Foreign Relations	Environment	Health Care	Overall
Change	-.81	-.40	-.41	-.34	-.34	-.38

Source: Coefficient estimates from tables 3.4a and 3.4b.

Note: The entries represent the change in predicted approval strength when both ambivalence scales are varied from lowest to highest value. At the highest degree of ambivalence, the main effects are also set to their highest values, and at the lowest degree of ambivalence (or high polarization), the positive main effects are set to their highest and the negative main effects to their lowest value. The other variables are held constant at their mean.

The operationalization of certainty in the placement of the candidates on various issue scales is straightforward and based on the "meta-attitudinal" follow-up question to the initial placement of how certain the respondents felt in their placements. The certainty scale ranges from 1 to 3: 1 (not very certain), 2 (pretty certain), and 3 (very certain).

The third hypothesis, predicting more accurate candidate placements, is based on the assumption that ambivalent people, perhaps by dint of processing information more systematically, should be able to place political candidates more accurately on various issue scales. We expect this to happen at the same time as the moderation effect with less certain candidate placements. Baseline information about the "correct" candidate issue positions is necessary for determining how accurate citizens are in their placements of the candidates on the issues. This task of delineating the "correct" candidate positions on the issues is, of course, impossible to determine in an objective sense, especially since political campaign messages are often ambiguous. Yet, we follow previous analyses that have used the sample mean of the placement of the candidates as a plausible approximation to the "true" or "correct" candidate issue positions (e.g., Alvarez and Nagler 1995; Alvarez 1997). The sample mean placement of candidates' issue positions will serve as a benchmark from which we can judge the accuracy of citizen issue placements. Accordingly, we operationalize accuracy in candidate placements as the individual respondent's deviation from the sample mean placement of the candidate. Specifically, the larger the deviation between a respondent's placement of a candidate on an issue scale and the sample mean placement, the more inaccurate is the respondent's placement of the candidate's position.

We examine the accuracy of candidate placements and individual confidence in these judgments on four different issues in detail (aid to blacks, defense spending, jobs and the environment, and government spending and services). We also present an analysis with a cumulative accuracy index based on nine different issue placements (as the five additional issues do not have a follow-up question about the certainty of the judgment). This cumulative index is operationalized as the sum of the deviations on all nine separate issue scales. All accuracy scales can range from 0 when respondents place the candidates at the sample mean, our benchmark of correct placement, to an unspecified higher value the more the individual judgment deviates from this benchmark. Given the direction from more to less accurate, these measures should be considered as indicators of inaccuracy.

The inaccuracy and certainty variables for the four issue scales as well as the cumulative inaccuracy index are regressed on the same set of independent variables as in the previous analyses. Ordinary least squares was used for the inaccuracy regressions and ordered logit was used for the trichotomous certainty dependent variable.

TABLE 3.5A
Placement of Clinton on Policy Scales—Accuracy

Inaccuracy	Aid to Blacks	Defense	Jobs and Environment	Services and Spending	Cumulative Index
Cognitive ambivalence	-.26 (.13)*	-.40 (.14)**	-.27 (.13)*	-.55 (.13)**	-3.36 (.75)**
Emotional ambivalence	-.25 (.09)**	-.42 (.10)**	-.37 (.09)**	-.24 (.09)*	-2.62 (.55)**
Positive considerations	-.05 (.08)	-.30 (.08)**	.07 (.08)	-.12 (.08)	-.80 (.45)
Negative considerations	.17 (.09)+	.21 (.09)*	.15 (.09)+	.25 (.09)**	1.87 (.51)**
Positive emotions	.01 (.07)	.07 (.07)	.06 (.08)	.09 (.07)	.48 (.39)
Negative emotions	.05 (.08)	.37 (.08)**	.15 (.07)*	.37 (.07)**	1.26 (.44)**
Ideology (Extremity)	14 .(.08)+	.08 (.08)	.06 (.08)	-.13 (.08)	.04 (.48)**
PID (Strength)	.06 (.07)	.26 (.08)**	.23 (.07)**	.09 (.07)	1.31 (.45)**
Education	-.35 (.09)**	-.38 (.09)**	-.40 (.09)**	-.22 (.09)*	-3.47 (.53)**
Knowledge	-.43 (.09)**	-.68 (.09)**	-.59 (.09)**	-.49 (.09)**	-4.76 (.53)**
Constant	1.57 (.09)**	1.61 (.09)**	1.58 (.08)**	1.53 (.08)**	14.78 (.51)**
Adj R^2	.06	.14	.09	.11	.21
N	1365	1404	1379	1459	1130

Source: NES 1996
Note: Coefficients are ordinary least squares estimates, standard errors in parentheses.
+ p < .10; * p < .05; ** p < .01

The results of these regressions for Clinton are reported in Tables 3.5a and 3.5b, and the results for Dole are reported in Tables 3.5c and 3.5d. Across the four tables we see that ambivalent individuals are more accurate in their placements of the candidates on the issue scales than are nonambivalent respondents, and at the same time, they are less certain than are nonambivalent people about their placements. The negatively signed coefficients on the cognitive and emotional ambivalence variables in Tables 3.5a and 3.5c indicate that as one becomes more ambivalent the placement of the candidate comes closer to the sample mean. This is true for the cumulative indexes as well as for each of the separate issue scales. The results are more

TABLE 3.5B
Placement of Clinton on Policy Scales—Certainty

Certainty	Aid to Blacks	Defense	Jobs and Environment	Services and Spending
Cognitive ambivalence	-.45 (.30)	-.69 (.31)*	-.36 (.31)	-1.07 (.30)**
Emotional ambivalence	-.88 (.22)**	-.98 (.22)**	-.85 (.22)**	-.79 (.22)**
Positive considerations	.11 (.18)	-.23 (.18)	.36 (.18)*	-.13 (.18)
Negative considerations	.60 (.20)**	.54 (.20)**	.68 (.21)**	.74 (.20)**
Positive emotions	.31 (.16)*	.44 (.16)**	.54 (.16)**	.27 (.15)+
Negative emotions	.52 (.18)**	.48 (.17)**	.15 (.18)	.68 (.17)**
Ideology (Extremity)	.34 (.19)+	.20 (.19)	.43 (.20)*	.54 (.19)**
PID (Strength)	.52 (.18)**	.41 (.17)*	.37 (.18)*	.52 (.17)**
Education	-.07 (.21)	-.34 (.21)	-.42 (.21)*	-.23 (.21)
Knowledge	-.55 (.21)*	-.37 (.21)+	.07 (.21)	-.06 (.21)
Threshold 1	-.55 (.20)	-1.01 (.20)	-.40 (.20)	-.89 (.20)
Threshold 2	1.72 (.21)	1.38 (.20)	1.99 (.21)	1.62 (.20)
Log likelihood	-1377.77	-1400.11	-1372.85	-1419.36
$\chi_2(10)$	69.68	74.09	66.01	129.67
N	1362	1402	1377	1457

Source: NES 1996.
Note: Coefficients are ordered logit estimates, standard errors in parentheses.
+ p < .10; * p < .05; ** p < .01

robust for Clinton than they are for Dole on the individual issue scales (where only two of the eight ambivalence coefficients for Dole reach standard levels of statistical significance); however, the consistent negative sign on the ambivalence coefficients strongly confirms that higher levels of ambivalence are associated with more accurate placements, even after controlling for level of education and political knowledge.

TABLE 3.5C
Placement of Dole on Policy Scales—Accuracy

Inaccuracy	Aid to Blacks	Defense	Jobs and Environment	Services and Spending	Cumulative Index
Cognitive ambivalence	-.14 (.14)	-.29 (.09)⁺	-.17 (.12)	-.16 (.13)	-1.63 -(.74)*
Emotional ambivalence	-.11 (.10)	-.25 (.13)**	-.13 (.09)	-.14 (.09)	-1.12 (.54)*
Positive considerations	-.09 (.09)	.06 (.09)	.06 (.08)	-.32 (.09)**	-.14 (.51)
Negative considerations	.10 (.08)	.08 (.08)	.28 (.08)**	.05 (.08)	1.37 (.46)**
Positive emotions	-.10 (.07)	-.11 (.06)⁺	-.06 (.06)	.08 (.06)	-.35 (.37)
Negative emotions	.22 (.07)**	.27 (.06)**	.13 (.06)*	.23 (.06)**	1.58 (.36)**
Ideology (Extremity)	.03 (.08)	-.12 (.08)	-.02 (.07)	-.02 (.07)	-.34 (.45)
PID (Strength)	.14 (.08)⁺	.12 (.07)⁺	.19 (.07)**	-.02 (.07)	.85 (.41)*
Education	-.30 (.09)**	-.38 (.08)**	-.10 (.08)	-.20 (.08)*	-2.27 (.50)**
Knowledge	-.33 (.09)**	-.28 (.09)**	-.34 (.08)**	-.24 (.08)**	-2.35 (.51)**
Constant	1.26 (.09)**	1.41 (.08)**	1.11 (.08)**	1.34 (.08)**	11.77 (.46)**
Adj R^2	.05	.07	.04	.05	.11
N	1295	1316	1301	1389	1014

Source: NES 1996.
Note: Coefficients are ordinary least squares estimates, standard errors in parentheses.
⁺ p < .10; * p < .05; ** p < .01

But these accurate placements by ambivalent individuals—assumed to be the result of more "systematic" processing—do not result in more confident placements. Turning to Tables 3.5b and 3.5d we see that ambivalence is closely associated with lower levels of certainty. Again the effects are more obvious for Clinton, but across both candidates the negatively signed and significant coefficients for both forms of ambivalence suggest that as ambivalence increases, one's level of certainty in placing the candidates on the issue diminishes. The directional cognitive and emotion variables have, as far as they are significant, a chiefly positive effect on both the ac-

TABLE 3.5D
Placement of Dole on Policy Scales—Certainty

Certainty	Aid to Blacks	Defense	Jobs and Environment	Services and Spending
Cognitive ambivalence	-.51 (.33)	-.98 (.33)**	.18 (.33)	-.79 (.32)*
Emotional ambivalence	-.85 (.24)**	-.50 (.24)*	-.89 (.24)**	-.56 (.23)*
Positive considerations	.19 (.22)	.85 (.22)**	.23 (.22)	.47 (.22)*
Negative considerations	.46 (.20)*	.28 (.20)	.31 (.20)	.21 (.20)
Positive emotions	.19 (.16)	.42 (.16)**	.09 (.16)	.18 (.16)
Negative emotions	.44 (.16)**	.32 (.16)*	.55 (.16)**	.50 (.15)**
Ideology (Extremity)	.58 (.19)**	.45 (.19)*	.28 (.20)	.57 (.19)**
PID (Strength)	.54 (.18)**	.36 (.18)*	.21 (.19)	.52 (.18)**
Education	-.34 (.22)	-.59 (.22)**	-.10 (.22)	-.00 (.21)
Knowledge	-.06 (.22)	.60 (.22)**	.42 (.23)+	.82 (.22)**
Threshold 1	-.20 (.21)	-.16 (.20)	.13 (.21)	.04 (.20)
Threshold 2	2.06 (.21)	2.26 (.21)	2.67 (.22)	2.47 (.21)
Log likelihood	-1280.05	-1277.89	-1232.00	-1364.27
$\chi^2(10)$	69.23	117.60	47.44	118.07
N	1292	1313	1299	1387

Source: NES 1996
Note: Coefficients are ordered logit estimates, standard errors in parentheses.
+ p < .10; * p < .05; ** p < .01

curacy and certainty ratings. This suggests that strong, one-sided feelings about a candidate lead to more biased perceptions of the candidates as well as to higher confidence in these less than optimal placements, a finding consistent with the notion of motivated reasoning (Kunda 1990). Ambivalent citizens are perhaps less prone than nonambivalent citizens to this form of biased information processing.

These results suggest that attitudinal ambivalence about political candidates has far-reaching implications. Not only are the global candidate evaluations affected, the consequences of ambivalence seem to extend to such candidate-related attitudes as performance ratings and issue placements. Ambivalence appears to facilitate a more balanced and more objective processing of information about presidential candidates. This conjecture is in line with Tetlock's (1986) concept of integrative complexity as well as evidence of systematic processing collected by Maio, Bell, and Esses (1996).

DISCUSSION AND CONCLUSION

Our findings point to a distinct and consequential influence of political attitude ambivalence on a number of political opinions and evaluations. On the most basic level, we have shown that ambivalence is a distinct and independent element of political attitudes (Cacioppo, Gardner, and Berntson 1997). Moreover, the notion that attitudes are multidimensional constructs is directly suggested by the fact that both positive and negative reactions, whether cognitive or emotional, have separate effects on the dependent variables (Abelson et al. 1982; Lavine et al. 1998; Ottati, Steenbergen, and Riggle 1992) and that the influences of ambivalence occur independently from these constituent main effects. In all of our multivariate models, the effects of ambivalence are quite strong not only after controlling for the emotional, cognitive, and trait main effects, but also after controlling for party identification, ideology, education, and political knowledge.

Furthermore, we find the attitudinal property of ambivalence to be consequential for political attitudes. First, cognitive, emotional, and trait-based ambivalence toward presidential candidates in various election years leads to substantially and consistently more moderate evaluations of these candidates on feeling thermometer scores. In addition, ambivalence variables are also consistent predictors of how strongly citizens approve or disapprove of the president. These effects are robust across many data sets and presidential candidates.

Second, the influence of ambivalence extends to how confident respondents are in judging candidate characteristics. Compared to nonambivalent people, ambivalent individuals in the 1996 NES survey are less certain in their placements of Clinton and Dole on the issue scales even though they are more accurate than nonambivalent individuals in their placements. The association between diminished attitude certainty and ambivalence is well documented (e.g., Hochschild 1981; Tetlock 1986). The association between accuracy and ambivalence is suggested to be a result of integrated and systematic processing (Maio, Bell, and Esses 1996; Jonas, Diehl, and Brömer 1997).

Regardless of the findings, the present study possesses notable limitations. First, our measures of cognitive, emotional, and trait reactions toward the candidates may not adequately represent the building blocks of larger attitudes about the candidates as we assume here. At the most extreme, they may simply be rationalizations of existing global attitudes (Rahn, Krosnick, and Breuning 1994). One way to address this problem would be to study designs that utilize reaction time measures as more reliable indicators of affective reactions. With better indicators, such studies could address the consequences of ambivalence, especially the hypothesis of slower reaction times for global attitudes under conditions of ambivalence (Bassili and Fletcher 1991; Huckfeldt and Sprague 1998).

In addition, our measure of ambivalence, the Griffin scale, may not be sensitive to the distinction between ambivalence and indifference. The state of indifference on this scale is treated as an intermediate state between the polarized (one-sided) and ambivalent extremes. Indifference might even be a dimension in its own right. Breckler (1994), for example, raises the possibility that people might not only have favorable and unfavorable reactions toward a topic but may be deliberately neutral toward some aspects of the topic as well. If such "multivalent attitudes" (Breckler 1994:364) exist, our current measurement techniques fall short and need further development. Indeed, on both conceptual and methodological grounds, more research is needed to further establish the distinction between ambivalent and indifferent political attitudes.

Notwithstanding, our work contributes to the growing recognition that ambivalence matters for the study of political attitudes. Given that ambivalence is a central feature of our everyday lives and is gaining prominence among attitude researchers in psychology (e.g., Cacioppo, Gardner, and Berntson 1997; Lavine et al. 1998), its regular omission in treatments of political attitudes deserves remedy. Some important previous work does address the prominence and consequences of political ambivalence (e.g., Zaller and Feldman 1992; Alvarez and Brehm 1995, 1997; Steenbergen and Brewer, chapter 4 in this volume); however, this research needs to be further applied and extended to a wide array of political attitudes.

Moreover, ambivalence may also be consequential for individual behavior and behavioral intentions. From a decision-making perspective, Ajzen (1996), for example, suggests that decisional conflict (ambivalence) might induce "defensive avoidance" (310) in decision makers. This could lead to difficulties in choosing among alternatives, an avoidance tendency such as shifting responsibility for a decision to others, and an exaggeration of the desirability of the status quo. Or more simply, individuals might find themselves in a state of panic and paralysis. In sum, many opportunities exist for future research to address the attitudinal and behavioral consequences of ambivalence.

The fact that a substantial number of individuals possess emotional and cognitive ambivalence toward politicians and presidential candidates with meaningful consequences for evaluations of these political figures captures something important. Ambivalence can be seen as a result of a political process in which countervailing forces and ideas are in an ongoing clash. It is thus only appropriate and natural to acknowledge a larger role for ambivalence within the study of political attitudes and behavior. Ambivalence, whether experienced toward a candidate, a party, or an issue, might very well represent the essence of politics for many citizens.

NOTES

1. Theories of behavioral decision making also deal with the pros and cons of various courses of action or probabilistic decisions to engage in certain behaviors (Fishbein and Ajzen 1975; Ajzen 1996). This is very similar to our two-dimensional evaluative space. However, a major difference should be noted. Studies of decision making deal with choices or decisions to engage in a certain behavior, while evaluative attitudes can be simply statements of liking or evaluative judgments.

2. It should be noted that the question ordering of the NES studies may underestimate the extent to which ambivalent reactions exist. By eliciting positive and negative reactions in immediate sequence, respondents are induced to answer "consistently" by contrasting positive and negative reactions. Otherwise, they might feel that they contradict themselves.

3. One notable exception to this moderation effect is the research on racial ambivalence (e.g., Katz, Hass, and Wackenhut 1986; McConahay 1986). Instead of moderating the attitude, an "amplification effect" might lead to more extreme attitudes. However, since we are more interested in political candidate evaluations and other policy attitudes, racial stereotypes and social desirability effects are of less concern.

4. Other consequences of value conflict are a tendency to answer with "don't know" to survey items (e.g., McGraw and Glathar 1994) and slower reaction times on response measures (e.g., Bassili and Fletcher 1991). See McGraw (1995) for a full review of the behavioral and attitudinal manifestations of value conflict.

5. The reliability of the positivity and negativity scales is very high. The alphas range between .88 and .92 for the three candidates. This high reliability may reflect a response-set bias in the long battery of trait ratings.

6. The global evaluation of the candidates measured by feeling thermometer scores certainly includes a considerable amount of affect. Thus the question naturally arises whether or not our independent cognitive (likes/dislikes) and emotional response variables, as well as the emotional ambivalence indicators that are based on them, are really predicting something that is meaningfully distinct from themselves. Though it would be ideal to treat the relationship between candidate evaluations and emotional/cognitive reactions toward the candidates with an instrumental variables approach, measures of exogenous factors to create such instruments are not available in these data sets. However, there is previous work, at least in terms of emotional reactions, to indicate that the causal arrow runs from emotional reaction to global evaluation, rather than the other way around. Marcus and MacKuen (1993) argue that emotional responses toward presidential candi-

dates begin a cognitive process of learning about and considering the candidates in more depth, which eventually leads to an ultimate global evaluation of the candidates. On the other hand, Lodge, Steenbergen, and Brau (1995) find evidence suggesting that global evaluations of politicians drive specific responses about the politicians, such as emotional reactions and considerations. We assume the former process of attitude formation in this paper, where specific reactions to candidates are, to some degree, instrumental in the formation of the expressed global attitude.

7. The 1983 Pilot Study also allows for the construction of an indicator of emotional ambivalence using the same battery of emotion words as in the presidential election years (anger, fear, pride, and hope). Unfortunately, the lack of open-ended questions about reasons to vote for or against the candidates in this study prevents the construction of a measure of cognitive ambivalence.

REFERENCES

Abelson, Robert P., Donald R. Kinder, Mark D. Peters, and Susan T. Fiske. 1982. "Affective and Semantic Components in Political Person Perception." *Journal of Personality and Social Psychology* 42:619–30.

Ajzen, Icek. 1996. "The Social Psychology of Decision Making." In *Social Psychology: Handbook of Basic Principles,* ed. E. Tory Higgins and Arie W. Kruglanski. New York: Guilford Press.

Allport, Gordon W. 1935. "Attitudes." In *Handbook of Social Psychology,* ed. Carl A. Murchison. Worcester, MA: Clark University Press.

Alvarez, R. Michael. 1997. *Information and Elections.* Ann Arbor: University of Michigan Press.

Alvarez, R. Michael, and John Brehm. 1995. "American Ambivalence toward Abortion Policy: A Heteroskedastic Probit Method for Assessing Conflicting Values." *American Journal of Political Science* 39:1055–82.

———. 1997. "Are Americans Ambivalent towards Racial Policies?" *American Journal of Political Science* 41:345–74.

Alvarez, R. Michael, and Jonathan Nagler, 1995. "Economics, Issues and the Perot Candidacy: Voter Choice in the 1992 Presidential Election." *American Journal of Political Science* 39:714–44.

Bartels, Larry M. 1996. "Uninformed Votes: Information Effects in Presidential Elections." *American Journal of Political Science* 40:194–230.

Bassili, John N., and Joseph F. Fletcher. 1991. "Response-Time Measurement in Survey Research: A Method for CATI and a New Look at Nonattitudes." *Public Opinion Quarterly* 55:331–46.

Breckler, Steven J. 1994. "A Comparison of Numerical Indexes for Measuring Attitude Ambivalence." *Educational and Psychological Measurement* 54:350–65.

Cacioppo, John T., and Gary G. Berntson. 1994. "Relationship between Attitudes and Evaluative Space: A Critical Review, with Emphasis on the Separability of Positive and Negative Substrates." *Psychological Bulletin* 115:401–23.

Cacioppo, John T., Wendi L. Gardner, and Gary G. Berntson. 1997. "Beyond Bipolar Conceptualizations and Measures: The Case of Attitudes and Evaluative Space." *Personality and Social Psychology Review* 1:3–25.

Chaiken, Shelly, Akiva Liberman, and Alice H. Eagly. 1989. "Heuristic and Systematic Information Processing within and beyond the Persuasion Context." In *Unintended Thought,* ed. James S. Uleman and John A. Bargh. New York: Guilford Press.

Eagly, Alice H., and Shelly Chaiken. 1993. *The Psychology of Attitudes.* Fort Worth: Harcourt Brace Jovanovich.

Fazio, Russell H., David M. Sanbonmatsu, Martha C. Powell, and Frank R. Kardes. 1986. "On the Automatic Activation of Attitudes." *Journal of Personality and Social Psychology* 50:229–38.

Festinger, Leon. 1957. *A Theory of Cognitive Dissonance.* Stanford: Stanford University Press.

Fishbein, Martin, and Icek Ajzen. 1975. *Belief, Attitude, Intention, and Behavior: An Introduction to Theory and Research.* Reading, MA: Addison-Wesley.

Fiske, Susan T., and Shelley E. Taylor. 1991. *Social Cognition.* New York: McGraw-Hill.

Glathar, Jilliann. 1996. *Between a Rock and a Hard Place: Exploring Alternative Measures of Value Conflict.* Paper presented at the annual meeting of the Midwest Political Science Association, Chicago, April 18–20.

Hochschild, Jennifer L. 1981. *What's Fair? American Beliefs about Distributive Justice.* Cambridge, MA: Harvard University Press.

———. 1993. "Disjunction and Ambivalence in Citizens' Political Outlooks." In *Reconsidering the Democratic Public,* ed. George E. Marcus and Russell L. Hanson. University Park: Pennsylvania State University Press.

Huckfeldt, Robert, and John Sprague. 1998. *Extremity, Accessibility, and Certainty: The Role of Ambivalence Regarding Abortion Rights.* Paper presented at the annual meeting of the Midwest Political Science Association, Chicago, April 23–25.

Jonas, Klaus, Michael Diehl, and Philip Brömer. 1997. "Effects of Attitudinal Ambivalence on Information Processing and Attitude-Intention Consistency." *Journal of Experimental Social Psychology* 33:190–210.

Kaplan, Kalman J. 1972. "On the Ambivalence-Indifference Problem in Attitude Theory and Measurement: A Suggested Modification of the Semantic Differential Technique." *Psychological Bulletin* 77:361–72.

Katz, Irwin, R. Glen Hass, and Joyce Wackenhut. 1986. "Racial Ambivalence, Value Duality, and Behavior." In *Prejudice, Discrimination, and Racism,* ed. John F. Dovidio and Samuel L. Gaertner. Orlando: Academic Press.

Kinder, Donald R. 1986. "Presidential Character Revisited." In *Political Cognition,* ed. Richard R. Lau and David O. Sears. Hillsdale, NJ: Lawrence Erlbaum.

Kunda, Ziva. 1990. "The Case for Motivated Reasoning." *Psychological Bulletin* 108:480–98.

Lavine, Howard, Cynthia J. Thomsen, Mark P. Zanna, and Eugene Borgida. 1998. "On the Primacy of Affect in the Determination of Attitudes and Behavior: The Moderating Role of Affective-Cognitive Ambivalence." *Journal of Experimental Social Psychology* 34:398–421.

Lewin, Kurt. 1951. *Field Theory in Social Science: Selected Theoretical Papers.* Ed. Dorwin Cartwright. New York: Harper and Row.

Liberman, Akiva, and Shelley Chaiken. 1991. "Value Conflict and Thought-Induced Attitude Change." *Journal of Experimental Social Psychology* 27:203–16.

Lodge, Milton, and Charles S. Taber. 1998. "Three Steps toward a Theory of Motivated Reasoning." In *Elements of Political Reason: Understanding and Expanding the Limits of Rationality,* ed. Arthur Lupia, Mathew D. McCubbins, and Samuel L. Popkin. Cambridge: Cambridge University Press.

Lodge, Milton, Kathleen M. McGraw, and Patrick Stroh. 1989. "An Impression-Driven Model of Candidate Evaluation." *American Political Science Review* 83:399–419.

Lodge, Milton, Marco R. Steenbergen, and Shawn Brau. 1995. "The Responsive Voter: Campaign Information and the Dynamics of Candidate Evaluation." *American Political Science Review* 89:309–26.

Maio, Gregory R., David W. Bell, and Victoria M. Esses. 1996. "Ambivalence and Persuasion: The Processing of Messages about Immigrant Groups." *Journal of Experimental Social Psychology* 32:513–36.

Marcus, George E., and Michael B. MacKuen. 1993. "Anxiety, Enthusiasm, and the Vote: The Emotional Underpinnings of Learning and Involvement during Presidential Campaigns." *American Political Science Review* 87:672–85.

McConahay, John B. 1986. "Modern Racism, Ambivalence, and the Modern Racism Scale." In *Prejudice, Discrimination, and Racism,* ed. John F. Dovidio and Samuel L. Gaertner. Orlando: Academic Press.

McGraw, Kathleen M. 1995. *Value Conflict and Susceptibility to Persuasion: The Impact of Value-Justified Survey Questions.* Paper presented at the 1995 annual meeting of the American Political Science Association, Chicago.

McGraw, Kathleen M., and Jill Glathar. 1994. *Value Conflict and Susceptibility to Persuasion.* Paper presented at the 1994 annual meeting of the American Political Science Association, Chicago.

Ottati, Victor C., Marco R. Steenbergen, and Ellen Riggle. 1992. "The Cognitive and Affective Components of Political Attitudes: Measuring the Determinants of Candidate Evaluations." *Political Behavior* 14:423–42.

Petty, Richard E. and John T. Cacioppo. 1986. *Communication and Persuasion: Central and Peripheral Routes to Attitude Change.* New York: Springer-Verlag.

Priester, Joseph R., and Richard E. Petty. 1996. "The Gradual Threshold Model of Ambivalence: Relating the Positive and Negative Bases of Attitudes to Subjective Ambivalence." *Journal of Personality and Social Psychology* 71:431–49.

Rahn, Wendy M., Jon A. Krosnick, and Marijke Breuning. 1994. "Rationalization and Derivation Processes in Survey Studies of Political Candidate Evaluation." *American Journal of Political Science* 38:582–600.

Scott, William A. 1966. "Measures of Cognitive Structure." *Multivariate Behavior Research* 1:391–95.

———. 1968. "Attitude Measurement." In *The Handbook of Social Psychology,* ed. Gardner Lindsey and Elliot Aronson. Vol. 2. Reading, MA: Addison-Wesley.

Tesser, Abraham, and Leonard Martin. 1996. "The Psychology of Evaluation." In *Social Psychology: Handbook of Basic Principles,* ed. E. Tory Higgins and Arie W. Kruglanski. New York: Guilford Press.

Tetlock, Philip E. 1986. "A Value Pluralism Model of Ideological Reasoning." *Journal of Personality and Social Psychology* 50:819–827.

Thompson, Megan M., Mark P. Zanna, and Dale W. Griffin. 1995. "Let's Not Be Indifferent about (Attitudinal) Ambivalence." In *Attitude Strength: Antecedents and Consequences,* ed. Richard E. Petty and Jon A. Krosnick. Hillsdale, NJ: Lawrence Erlbaum.

Zaller, John. 1992. *The Nature and Origins of Mass Opinion.* New York: Cambridge University Press.

Zaller, John, and Stanley Feldman. 1992. "A Simple Theory of the Survey Response: Answering Questions versus Revealing Preferences." *American Journal of Political Science* 36:579–616.

CHAPTER 4

The Not-So-Ambivalent Public:
Policy Attitudes in the Political Culture
of Ambivalence

Marco R. Steenbergen and Paul R. Brewer

THE WORLD OF politics is one of value conflict, as Lasswell's (1958) famous definition of politics makes very clear. Different policies cater to different goals and it is rare indeed to find situations in which a tradeoff between values is not required. Politicians and the media are usually keenly aware of these tradeoffs. The question is whether ordinary citizens are as well. A sizable literature in political science and social psychology answers this question in the affirmative (for instance, Feldman and Zaller 1992; Glathar 1996; Hochschild 1981; Katz and Hass 1988; McClosky and Zaller 1984; McGraw and Glathar 1994; Reinarman 1987; Schnell 1993; Sniderman et al. 1996; Sniderman and Tetlock 1986; Tetlock, 1986; Zaller 1992; Zaller and Feldman 1992). Focusing mostly on the American context, this literature claims not only that Americans are conflicted about numerous issues but also that their ambivalence has important implications for the nature of public opinion. Indeed, if we believe some, an understanding of ambivalence is essential for understanding American public opinion.

In this chapter, we provide new evidence about these claims. Examining numerous forms of ambivalence and several potential consequences, we analyze American public opinion data in four policy domains that have dominated political debate in the United States in recent decades—affirmative action, gay rights, social welfare, and abortion. Unlike past studies, we find little evidence of ambivalence in the American mass public. Quite the contrary, not ambivalence but the relative lack of it appears to be the outstanding feature of American public opinion. This finding puts the American mass public in a very different light than has been portrayed in past studies.[1]

This paper is organized as follows. In section 1, we provide an overview of the ambivalence literature and its limitations to date. In section 2, we develop our conceptualization of ambivalence and its consequences, and tie it to recent (and not-so-recent) insights in social psychology. Section 3 presents the four policy domains that we investigate, focusing both on the nature of political discourse in each domain and on what is known about public opinion. Section 4 describes our study, while section 5 discusses our findings. Finally, section 6 draws out the implications of our results.

AMBIVALENCE IN AMERICA—PAST EVIDENCE

By comparative standards, Americans live in a relatively homogenous political culture that is dominated by a liberal tradition (Hartz 1955; Santayana 1920). Nonetheless, this culture has not been spared from ideological conflict. On the contrary, there has always been a great deal of controversy about which liberal principles should be emphasized. On the one hand, the American political culture embraces equality (at least, equality of opportunity). On the other hand, it also embraces limited government, freedom (Rokeach 1973), capitalism (McClosky and Zaller 1984), and achievement (Lipset 1979). To promote equality these latter principles sometimes have to be sacrificed and vice versa. For any given issue different values of the liberal creed can pull in different directions. This situation is further complicated by the fact that these values often also conflict with other goals such as the protection of the moral order. Despite its façade of homogeneity (core values are widely shared), the American political culture is quite torn (value priorities differ considerably). The American political culture, then, is a political culture of ambivalence.

Since American citizens live and breathe this political culture, many scholars argue that the mass public has internalized the value conflicts inherent in American politics. For instance, Feldman and Zaller (1992:272) note that "nearly all Americans have absorbed the principal elements of their political culture, and . . . they are highly sensitive to its characteristic fault lines." In a similar vein, Tetlock and his colleagues argue that public opinion is characterized by "value pluralism": people tend to embrace multiple values that are often in stark conflict (Sniderman et al. 1996; Sniderman and Tetlock 1986; Tetlock 1986).

Numerous studies have investigated ambivalence in American public opinion. For instance, Alvarez and Brehm (1995) and Schnell (1993) analyze ambivalence about abortion. McGraw and Glathar (1994; Glathar 1996) describe ambivalence effects in connection with attitudes toward capital punishment. Katz and Hass (1988) discuss the role of ambivalence in the domain of affirmative action (for conflicting evidence, see Alvarez and Brehm 1997). Discussions of ambivalence about social welfare policies can be found in work by Feldman and Zaller (1992), Glathar (1996), Hochschild (1981), McClosky and Zaller (1984), Reinarman (1987), and Sniderman et al. (1996).

Taken together, these studies provide interesting evidence that ambivalence is a prevalent aspect of American public opinion. A problem with these studies, however, is that they do not present a unified conceptual or methodological approach. Studies in one policy domain often rely on different measures of ambivalence and its effects than studies in another domain. Similarly, the samples used in the studies vary greatly, ranging from undergraduate students to representative samples of the American public. This not only makes it problematic to compare results; it also makes it difficult to piece together a comprehensive picture of ambivalence. Indeed, we would argue that past studies present us with a patchwork of evidence but not yet a global image of ambivalence in the United States.

Moreover, the existing literature presents us with a very narrow view of the nature of ambivalence. This literature has focused almost exclusively on conflicts between abstract values (but see Hochschild 1981). While such conflict is of interest because of the important role that values play in politics and in public opinion, it ignores other sources of ambivalence. Political conflict is not only about values—it is also about perceptions, beliefs, and emotions. We know that these factors play an important role in public opinion. Thus, ignoring them may well lead to an incomplete—and possibly distorted—picture of ambivalence.

To remedy these problems it is necessary to develop a broad conception of ambivalence, operationalize it uniformly, study it in the same sample, assess the same effects, and do all of this across several policy domains. In this chapter we present evidence from such a research effort. Its goal is to obtain comparable results across different policy domains so that it becomes easier—and less dangerous—to form a global impression of ambivalence in American public opinion.

Such an image does not necessarily have to reproduce past findings—if it did, this study would be redundant. We believe that by using a consistent approach across policy domains, patterns may emerge that would otherwise remain obscure. Indeed, the predominant pattern in the data that we shall discuss is at odds with most past studies: we do *not* find widespread ambivalence in the American public. Before making this point, we now turn to the way we conceptualize ambivalence and its effects.

SOURCES AND CONSEQUENCES OF AMBIVALENCE

Conceptualizing Ambivalence

Policy attitudes are usually determined by myriad factors—or, as we shall call them, *orientations*—including values (Feldman 1988; Rokeach 1973), other core beliefs, and affect toward the groups that policies target (Sniderman,

Brody, and Tetlock 1991). When these forces pull a person in different directions this creates ambivalence. In this case, an individual has some grounds to favor a policy and other grounds to oppose it.

Defined in these terms, ambivalence arises always in relation to a policy attitude. In philosophical terms it is possible to argue that two orientations are incompatible—for instance, that egalitarians cannot also favor achievement. In psychological terms, however, clashes between different orientations probably manifest themselves only in relationship to a particular attitude object. That is, most people probably do not care about abstract conflicts between different orientations, until they realize that these orientations imply very different things for their opinions about a particular policy or other attitude object. In this case, people become ambivalent to the extent that they place equal weight on the two conflicting orientations that they embrace (Tetlock 1986).

Most studies to date consider a narrow version of this conceptualization of ambivalence. In these studies, ambivalence is synonymous with value conflict. The implicit or explicit assumption is that values are the most important sources of ambivalence. There is, however, precedent for considering a broader definition of ambivalence. For instance, Lavine et al. (1998) consider the impact of cognitive-affective ambivalence, a form of ambivalence in which cognitive and affective orientations clash. Hochschild (1981), too, uncovers various forms of ambivalence in her interviews, as do Meffert, Guge, and Lodge (chapter 3 in this volume) in their analysis of candidate evaluation. Because attitudes are rooted in so many different orientations, it makes sense to cast our net broadly and to define ambivalence in terms of multiple dimensions. Thus, we analyze traditional value conflict along with other forms of cognitive-cognitive conflict, as well as cognitive-affective conflict and affective-affective conflict.[2]

The Political Psychology of Ambivalence

The psychological literature makes different predictions about the extent to which one should expect ambivalence. Cognitive consistency theories (Festinger 1957; Heider 1946) predict that ambivalence should be rare because people are motivated to resolve conflicts between different orientations. They stress that ambivalence creates an incentive to resolve itself quickly and effectively. Abelson (1959) describes various strategies that people can use to this effect.

On the other hand, several other theories argue that people are not always successful in resolving conflicts between their orientations. For example, Zaller and Feldman's (1992; Zaller 1992) model of the survey response is premised on the notion that people carry conflicting considerations in their heads about most issues. Recent work by Cacioppo and his colleagues as well finds that ambivalence cannot always be resolved, and when it is not, it may manifest itself in the attitudes that people hold (Cacioppo and Berntson 1994; Cacioppo, Gardner, and Berntson 1997). That is, conflict between the determinants of attitudes transforms itself into intra-attitude conflict.

These psychological theories have very different ramifications for public opinion. Cognitive consistency theories predict consistent attitudes: a person who has resolved all conflict about an issue probably has established a coherent view of that issue. If cognitive consistency mechanisms are imperfect, however, then it is not clear that a coherent view of the issue exists. In this case, one would expect attitudes to be much more volatile (among other things).

Where to Look for Consequences

Ambivalence can manifest itself in numerous ways (McGraw and Glathar 1994). We cannot study all of these manifestations here. Thus, we focus on four manifestations—response predictability, response stability, horizontal constraint, and vertical constraint. These four manifestations tap into different facets of the structure (or lack thereof) of public opinion. The structure theme has preoccupied public opinion researchers like no other over the past five decades. Therefore, we believe this is the best place to look for ambivalence effects.

In keeping with recent work by Alvarez and Brehm (1995, 1997), we first consider implications of ambivalence for the predictability of responses to survey questions about policy attitudes. Because ambivalent individuals are pulled in different directions their survey responses should be more difficult to predict, either because their attitudes are more variable or because there is greater error variance in their responses. Predictability is one indicator of the volatility of public opinion.

Second, we consider the response stability of survey responses. This stability should be weaker for ambivalent individuals (Bargh et al. 1992; Zaller 1992; Zaller and Feldman 1992). To the extent that different orientations prevail in conflicts at different times, we would expect there to be a great deal of fluctuation in the way people answer policy attitude questions over time. An important question is the extent to which this fluctuation is due to measurement error or instability of the attitudes underlying the survey responses.

We consider two more outcomes of ambivalence. Ever since Converse's (1964) seminal work, political scientists have been interested in the question of constraint in belief systems. Such constraint can take two forms. First, constraint can be defined in terms of the relationships among attitudes across different policies—horizontal constraint. To the extent that attitudes toward related policies are more or less consistent with one another, horizontal constraint is stronger or weaker. Second, constraint can be defined in terms of the linkages among specific policy attitudes and more general orientations—vertical constraint. To the extent that specific attitudes are driven by more general orientations, there is weaker or stronger vertical constraint.

Horizontal and vertical constraint has not been widely studied in the ambivalence literature. One might predict, however, that the structure of belief systems is at least partially a function of ambivalence. If it is true that individuals cannot always successfully resolve conflict among different orientations, one possibility is that ambivalent people do not root their policy attitudes in general orientations (but see Feldman and Zaller 1992). Moreover, to the extent that different orientations prevail in conflicts for different attitude objects, horizontal constraint may also suffer from ambivalence (Brewer 1998). With these predictions in mind, let us now consider the nature of ambivalence in our four policy domains.

AMBIVALENCE IN FOUR POLICY DOMAINS

To study the predictions made by the political science and social psychology literatures we consider American public opinion data in four policy domains—affirmative action, gay rights, social welfare, and abortion. We focus on these four policy domains because policy debates in each domain have typically been cast in terms of multiple conflicting orientations. Thus, we should expect a great deal of ambivalence in these domains, making them a perfect place to study the predictions discussed in the previous section. We shall now briefly discuss each policy domain and summarize the sources of ambivalence in each (see Table 4.1 for an overview).

Affirmative Action

One of the most contentious issues on the American political landscape is affirmative action. The public debate over the subject contains appeals to a wide variety of orientations that citizens might use to form opinions (Gamson and Modigliani 1987; Kinder and Sanders 1996; Nelson and Kinder 1996). For example, the rhetoric on affirmative action frames the issue in terms of the two traditions that compose the "American ethos" (McClosky and Zaller 1984): the tradition of equality, on the one hand, and the tradition of individualism and limited government, on the other. At the same time, the debate also invokes Americans' beliefs about race, their racial stereotypes, and their feelings toward African Americans.

An extensive body of research suggests that citizens rely on all of these orientations when forming attitudes toward affirmative action policies. In

TABLE 4.1
Dimensions of Ambivalence

Affirmative Action:
Equality–Limited Government; Equality–Racial Stereotyping; Equality–Modern
Racism; Equality–Black Affect; Limited Government–Racial Stereotyping;
Limited Government–Modern Racism; Limited Government–Black Affect;
Racial Stereotyping–Modern Racism; Racial Stereotyping–Black Affect;
Modern Racism–Black Affect

Gay Rights:
Equality–Limited Government; Equality–Moral Traditionalism; Equality–Gay
Affect; Limited Government–Moral Traditionalism; Limited Government–Gay
Affect; Moral Traditionalism–Gay Affect

Social Welfare:
Equality–Limited Government; Equality–Poor Affect; Equality–Welfare Affect;
Limited Government–Poor Affect; Limited Government–Welfare Affect; Poor
Affect–Welfare Affect

Abortion:
Gender Equality–Moral Traditionalism

part Americans judge this issue on the basis of their core values (Alvarez
and Brehm 1997; Katz and Hass 1988; Kinder and Sanders 1996; Sniderman
and Piazza 1993). However, there is also strong evidence for claims that
"modern racism," anti-black stereotypes, and anti-black affect exert substantial influences on public support for affirmative action (Alvarez and
Brehm 1997; Kinder and Sanders 1996; Kinder and Sears 1981; McConahay 1986; Nelson and Kinder 1996). The relative weights of these criteria
may vary depending on the particular frames that citizens receive (Kinder
and Sanders 1996; Nelson and Kinder 1996), but a full account of public
opinion in this domain must attend to the full range of standards available
to citizens.

While Americans are obviously divided over the desirability of affirmative
action, studies disagree on whether or not individual citizens feel ambivalent about the issue. Thus far, this scholarly dispute has revolved around
one potential source of ambivalence: the tension in this domain between beliefs about equality and beliefs about individualism. Katz and Hass (1988)
argue that white Americans who hold conflicting beliefs about individualism and equality suffer from ambivalence toward racial policies; Alvarez
and Brehm (1997) conclude otherwise.

In this study, we suggest that both sides have framed the terms of this
dispute too narrowly. While Americans' beliefs about these two principles
may be sources of ambivalence toward affirmative action, so too may modern
racism, racial stereotypes, and affect toward blacks. Though the existing

literature examines the potential for conflict among *values* in this domain, it has not explored the possibility that citizens may be ambivalent because their values are incompatible with their racial beliefs (equality–modern racism conflict; limited government–modern racism conflict), their stereotypes (equality–racial stereotyping conflict; limited government–racial stereotyping conflict), or their feelings toward the intended beneficiaries of affirmative action (equality–black affect conflict; limited government–black affect conflict). Nor does the existing literature examine the potential consequences of inconsistencies within Americans' racial attitudes and beliefs. Individual citizens may hold racial stereotypes that conflict with their emotions toward blacks (racial stereotyping–black affect conflict) or their racial ideology (racial stereotyping–modern racism conflict); similarly, their affect toward African Americans may not necessarily be consonant with their level of "modern racism" (modern racism–black affect conflict). At present, then, we have yet to establish (1) to what degree citizens suffer from these forms of conflict, and (2) whether such conflicts produce ambivalence toward affirmative action.

Gay Rights

In many ways, the story of gay rights parallels the story of affirmative action. Here, too, political elites have cast the debate in terms of a variety of orientations that citizens might use as standards for judgment (Brewer 1999; Gallagher and Bull 1996; Wilcox and Wolpert 1996). Some of these orientations are values. For example, proponents of "family values" have argued that gay rights laws will undermine traditional morality, while proponents of limited government have argued that such laws constitute a new wave of "big government" meddling on the behalf of a special interest group. On the other side of the issue, gay rights supporters have claimed that gay rights policies are needed to uphold the notion of equal rights. Other portions of the public discourse invoke citizens' feelings toward the group targeted by the policies—namely, gays and lesbians. Again, public opinion research suggests that while the exact mix of orientations may vary under different frames, both values and feelings toward gays have the potential to shape mass preferences regarding gay rights (Brewer 1999; Nelson and Kinder 1996; Strand 1996; Wilcox and Wolpert 1996).

As in the domain of affirmative action, efforts to identify ambivalence toward gay rights have focused on ambivalence produced by conflict between two values. And as before, the conclusions scholars reach are mixed (Brewer 1999; Sniderman et al. 1996). More important for our purposes, the empirical record thus far does not address the possibility that ambivalence toward gay rights may arise from multiple sources. While the values of moral traditionalism and egalitarianism may clash with one another in this domain, so, too, may they clash with beliefs about the appropriate scope of government action (equality–limited government conflict; limited government–moral traditionalism conflict). Furthermore, each of these three values may come into conflict with feelings toward gays and lesbians (equality–gay affect conflict; limited government–gay affect conflict; moral traditionalism–gay affect conflict). For example, some Americans who believe in the notion of equality may dislike gays and lesbians; by the same token, individuals who believe that equal rights have been pushed too far may nonetheless feel positively (or at least neutrally) toward gays and lesbians.

Social Welfare

The domain of welfare policy follows the same patterns described above: public debate and public opinion in this domain revolve around a wide range of orientations, but the ambivalence literature restricts its attention to a narrow definition of ambivalence.

Appeals to core values pervade the public debate over broad social welfare objectives (e.g., providing more or less government services, providing a guaranteed job or standard of living) and specific social welfare programs (e.g., food stamps, welfare, and Social Security). Not surprisingly, both egalitarianism and limited government play especially prominent roles in the rhetoric on such issues (Feldman and Zaller 1992; McClosky and Zaller 1984). Yet that is hardly the sum of the orientations invoked by elites here. The debate over welfare also invokes feelings of sympathy and antipathy toward the targets of welfare programs: specifically, people on welfare and, more generically, poor people. The empirical record shows that both values and emotions shape American public opinion toward such programs (Feldman and Zaller 1992; McClosky and Zaller 1984; Sniderman, Brody, and Tetlock 1991).

Once more, though, studies of ambivalence in this domain have focused only on the potential for tension between beliefs about equality, on one side, and beliefs about individualism and limited government, on the other (Feldman and Zaller 1992; Glathar 1996). Missing from this picture are the forms of ambivalence that might arise from Americans' feelings toward the beneficiaries of the welfare state. One might plausibly argue that citizens' values could clash with their feelings toward poor people (equality–poor affect conflict; limited government–poor affect conflict) and people on welfare (equality–welfare affect; limited government–welfare affect conflict). Ambivalence springing from conflict between emotions seems possible here as well, given that Americans do not necessarily feel the same way toward "poor people" as they do toward "welfare recipients."

Abortion

The last of the issue domains we examine is abortion. In truth, we could hardly omit this issue: as Alvarez and Brehm (1995) observe, it is one of the most conflictual issues on the current American political scene. The current debate centers on not only the legality of abortion itself but also various restrictions on its availability (e.g., parental and spousal notification laws).

Here, our opportunity to examine the scope of ambivalence is limited by the narrow range of orientations we can measure. Even so, we are able to address what previous research (Schnell 1993) identifies as a crucial source of public ambivalence toward abortion: conflict between moral traditionalism, on one side, and beliefs about equality between the sexes, on the other. These two core values have served as focal points in the public debate over abortion. Elite advocates of "family values" have typically condemned abortion, while proponents of equality between men and women have defended the right to legal abortion. Moreover, the structure of mass opinion reflects the same divisions. Moral traditionalists tend to oppose legal abortion, while moral liberals tend to support it; similarly, supporters of equal sex roles tend to support abortion rights, while opponents of equal sex roles tend to oppose abortion rights.

Previous research suggests that tensions between moral beliefs and beliefs about sex roles influence public opinion toward abortion. In particular, Schnell (1993) finds that conflict between these orientations produces weaker abortion attitudes (see also Alvarez and Brehm 1995). So while we may not be able to "expand the scope" of ambivalence in the domain of abortion, we can at least test whether the most likely source of ambivalence produces substantial consequences for public opinion.

STUDY

Data

We used the 1992 American National Election Studies (ANES) as our primary data source in this study. This survey included a single question about affirmative action and multiple questions about abortion, gay rights, and social welfare policies. The survey also asked about a wide range of values, feelings, and other orientations that influence policy attitudes. The 1992 ANES forms the basis of our analyses of predictability, horizontal constraint, and vertical constraint of policy attitudes. To assess the stability of policy attitudes over time we use the 1992-93-96 and 1992-94-96 ANES panel studies.

Measuring Ambivalence

The literature provides no unified measurement strategy for ambivalence. The approach we take is to infer ambivalence from responses on scales that measure different orientations. This is an exceedingly common way of defining ambivalence (e.g., Alvarez and Brehm 1997; Glathar 1996; Schnell 1993). It has an important advantage: ambivalence is defined at the appropriate level of the determinants of policy attitudes. There is an important disadvantage as well: the measure is rather indirect.[3] We shall revisit this potential problem in our discussion of the results.

Just as there is no consensus about the general measurement strategy for ambivalence, so there has been little consensus about the exact formula that should be used to generate ambivalence scores. Recent research in social psychology, however, suggests that Griffin's ambivalence formula has the most desirable properties among the various scoring procedures. Meffert, Guge, and Lodge (chapter 3 in this volume) used this formula, and we shall use it here as well, albeit in modified form.

To define Griffin's ambivalence score, let A and B denote scale scores on two conflicting orientations. Then

$$Ambivalence = \frac{A + B}{2} - \left| A - B \right|.$$

As Meffert, Guge, and Lodge show, this formula can be applied successfully when A and B are counts of positive and negative reactions toward an attitude object. Glathar (1996) argues that the formula also performs well when A and B are measured via rating scales. To this effect she assigns the lowest rating to disagreement with a particular orientation. In many cases, however, this procedure leads to counterintuitive results. For example, imagine that A and B are both measured on 7-point scales, where low scores indicate strong disagreement. If a person would strongly agree with both items (e.g., pro-equality and pro-limited government), her ambivalence score would be at the maximum of 7. If that same person would strongly disagree with both items (e.g., anti-equality and anti-limited government), her score would only be 1 (the minimum). A priori it is not clear, however, that the person would be any less ambivalent in the second situation than in the first.

To resolve this asymmetry in the treatment of agreement and disagreement scores we make two modifications to the Griffin formula. First, we rescale orientation scales to a range from –1 to 1, where –1 represents strong disagreement, 1 represents strong agreement, and 0 is the neutral point. Second, we alter Griffin's formula by taking absolute values in both terms:

$$Ambivalence = \frac{|A| + |B|}{2} - \left|A - B\right|.$$

the first term of this expression gives the average extremity of two orientations, while the second term expresses their compatibility.[4]

Using the same example as before, a person who strongly disagrees with two items would receive a score of -1 on both. Her average extremity would be 1 and her compatibility would be 0, making for an ambivalence score of 1. A person who strongly agrees with both items would receive the same ambivalence score, so that the asymmetry in the original Griffin measure disappears.

The modified Griffin formula produces scores that range between -1 and 1. In our analysis, we rescale this so that the minimum is 0 and the maximum is 1. The behavior of this formula is clearly visible from Table 4.2, which shows that it reaches its maximum when a person strongly agrees or strongly disagrees with two conflicting items, and reaches its minimum when the person strongly agrees with one item and strongly disagrees with the other.[5]

RESULTS

Incidence of Ambivalence

We start our analysis of ambivalence by considering the question of how common ambivalence is. Table 4.3 provides summary statistics of the modified Griffin ambivalence measure for each of the ambivalence dimensions listed in Table 4.1. This table reveals a number of interesting patterns. First, there

TABLE 4.2
Values of the Modified Griffin Ambivalence Measure

			B		
	Strongly Disagree (-1)	Disagree (-.5)	Neutral (0)	Agree (.5)	Strongly Agree (1)
Strongly disagree	1.000	0.625	0.250	0.125	0.000
Disagree	0.625	0.750	0.375	0.250	0.125
A Neutral	0.250	0.375	0.500	0.375	0.250
Agree	0.125	0.250	0.375	0.750	0.625
Strongly agree	0.000	0.125	0.250	0.625	1.000

Note: A and B are assumed to be in conflict.

TABLE 4.3
Incidence of Ambivalence

Ambivalence Dimension	Mean	Median	Variance	% Incompatible
Equality–Limited Government	0.29	0.25	0.035	37.7
Equality–Moral Traditionalism	0.42	0.42	0.024	47.2
Limited Government– Moral Traditionalism	0.36	0.34	0.042	33.2
Equality–Racial Stereotyping[a]	0.45	0.45	0.012	58.4
Equality–Modern Racism[a]	0.41	0.42	0.027	48.5
Limited Government– Racial Stereotyping[a]	0.39	0.38	0.022	39.4
Limited Government–Modern Racism[a]	0.40	0.38	0.049	36.6
Gender Equality–Moral Traditionalism	0.39	0.34	0.050	49.1
Equality–Black Affect[a]	0.37	0.38	0.018	13.3
Equality–Gay Affect	0.39	0.39	0.029	28.1
Equality–Poor Affect	0.33	0.32	0.022	14.5
Equality–Welfare Affect	0.39	0.40	0.020	22.7
Limited Government–Black Affect[a]	0.33	0.25	0.036	35.4
Limited Government–Gay Affect	0.39	0.33	0.069	46.0
Limited Government–Poor Affect	0.30	0.25	0.043	36.6
Limited Government–Welfare Affect	0.34	0.32	0.034	39.8
Moral Traditionalism–Gay Affect	0.34	0.37	0.026	28.2
Racial Stereotyping–Black Affect[a]	0.46	0.46	0.012	52.9
Modern Racism–Black Affect[a]	0.42	0.42	0.025	43.9
Poor Affect–Welfare Affect	0.38	0.40	0.026	18.6

[a] White respondents only

is considerable variation in the level of ambivalence. The mean ambivalence scores range from a low of .29 to a high of .46. It is interesting to note where these extremes occur. The lowest level of ambivalence exists between egalitarianism and limited government. While the conflict between these values usually receives much attention (McClosky and Zaller 1984), our results suggest that ambivalence is relatively mild here. On the other hand, Americans appear to experience a great deal of ambivalence between their feelings toward African Americans and the racial stereotypes that they hold; quite a few whites state that they like blacks while admitting to negative stereotypes. In general, the highest levels of ambivalence are registered for racial orientations, reinforcing the conclusion of many that racial issues have yet to be sorted out in the minds of most Americans (Alvarez and Brehm 1997; Sniderman and Piazza 1993). Given this variation in ambivalence, one might expect different effects across the four policy domains that we study.

More important than the differences, however, is the convergence between the ambivalence scores: none is very high. To be sure, there are few respondents who, by our measure, experience, no ambivalence at all (looking across all of the ambivalence dimensions the maximum percentage of respondents who score 0 is never greater than 7.6; the latter percentage arises for the conflict between limited government and poor affect). On the other hand, as the medians show, only rarely do we find distributions that are lopsided to the high ambivalence end of the modified Griffin scale.

Another way to tell this story is to consider the average ambivalence score across all dimensions. This score is .38, which corresponds to an individual who feels neutral on one orientation and mildly agrees (or mildly disagrees) with another. Such a configuration of orientations hardly possesses the severity and intensity of conflict that is often suggested by studies of ambivalence in public opinion.

A similar picture emerges when we consider the percentage of respondents who simultaneously hold two incompatible orientations (regardless of the strength of commitment to these orientations). Such people should experience the most conflict between their orientations. But only in two cases does this group make up a majority of the respondents. Both of these cases occur among whites with respect to racial orientations (equality vs. racial stereotyping and racial stereotyping vs. black affect), the domain in which one would expect a great deal of ambivalence. In other domains, however, the percentages of respondents with incompatible orientations are generally considerably lower. Here we find sometimes sizable minorities with incompatible orientations. But for a majority of Americans there appears to be surprisingly little dissonance in their belief systems.

Nonetheless, variation in ambivalence does occur and this raises the question of who is most likely to be ambivalent. We regress the ambivalence scores on race (1 = black; 0 = white), gender (1 = female; 0 = male), age, income, religious fundamentalism, education, political knowledge, partisanship, ideology, and strength of ideology.[6] Table 4.4 summarizes the results of these analyses.[7] In terms of statistical significance, the strongest predictors of ambivalence are race, age, political knowledge, ideology, strength of ideology, and partisanship. Of these ideology and strength of ideology always have a negative sign, while race, political knowledge, and

TABLE 4.4
Predictors of Ambivalence

Predictor	% Significant at p = .05	Range of Significant Estimates	
Black	58	−0.101	0.053
Female	43	−0.039	0.026
Age	62	−0.078	0.097
Income	24	0.000	0.000
Religious fundamentalism	33	−0.111	0.045
Education	43	−0.104	0.035
Political knowledge	57	−0.156	0.080
Partisanship	57	−0.056	0.024
Ideology	67	−0.069	−0.021
Strength of ideology	81	−0.121	−0.031

Note: Results across the 21 ambivalence dimensions

partisanship usually have a negative sign, and age usually has a positive sign. Thus, it appears that strong ideologues, African Americans, sophisticates, and Democrats are less ambivalent. Moreover, contrary to what has sometimes been argued (Feldman and Zaller 1992), we find that liberals are less ambivalent than conservatives, a result that is probably partially due to the broad conceptualization of ambivalence that we use here. On the other hand, older people tend to be more ambivalent.

Despite the fact that different ambivalence dimensions can be predicted consistently with the same predictors, it does not appear to be the case that the ambivalence dimensions are highly correlated. The average correlation of the ambivalence dimensions is only .126 in the domain of affirmative action (for white respondents), .152 in the domain of gay rights, and .305 in the domain of social welfare. This suggests that individuals experience ambivalence in specific areas, instead of in a wholesale manner. An important implication of this result is that our ambivalence dimensions are not redundant with each other. Rather, these dimensions appear to tap into relatively specific clashes of orientations.

In sum, there is considerable variation in the level of ambivalence experienced by citizens. On the whole, however, most citizens do not appear to hold wildly incompatible orientations. The typical citizen experiences only mild to moderate levels of ambivalence. There are, of course, Americans who experience severe ambivalence. But more impressive than this ambivalence, in our mind, is the fact that it is not more prevalent. For people who live in a political culture of ambivalence, Americans appear to be remarkably nonambivalent.

Predictability of Policy Attitudes

Ambivalence is not as widespread as one might have expected, but what little there is may still have dramatic consequences for public opinion. As we discussed earlier, one of the predictions in the literature is that ambivalence causes greater variability in responses to attitude questions, making them more unpredictable. To what extent does this effect emerge for policy attitudes in the three domains that we study?

To answer this question we rely on heteroskedastic probit models (Alvarez and Brehm 1995, 1997), which simultaneously estimate a choice model (in favor or opposed to a policy) and a variance model with multiplicative heteroskedasticity. By including various covariates in the variance model we may detect the sources of the unpredictability of attitude questions. Covariates with significant positive effects in the variance model weaken predictability, while covariates with significant negative effects improve predictability.[8]

We perform separate analyses for each ambivalence dimension, using several specifications of the variance model in each analysis. The most basic model specification includes only ambivalence as a predictor. To this model we add in successive steps political knowledge, the orientations that enter the ambivalence measures, and ideology and strength of ideology. We use these different models because the results from heteroskedastic probit analysis can be very sensitive to model specification. In the tables below we list the range of parameter estimates across different specifications of the variance model, as well as the number of times (out of four specifications) that ambivalence was statistically significant. We shall first discuss the results by policy domain and then comment on the overall patterns in the heteroskedastic probit analyses.

AFFIRMATIVE ACTION

As we saw earlier, racial orientations produce the greatest levels of ambivalence as indicated by the modified Griffin measure. Hence, we would expect racial policy attitudes to be influenced particularly strongly by this ambivalence. The results in Table 4.5, however, show this is only partially the case.[9]

An analysis of responses to affirmative action reveals that only one type of ambivalence consistently increases response variability, to wit, ambivalence between equality and black affect.[10] In three more cases, ambivalence emerges as a significant inflator of response variation in some of the model specifications. Specifically, ambivalence between equality and racial stereotyping is significant in one of the model specifications, while ambivalence between limited government and modern racism and between

TABLE 4.5
Unpredictability Affirmative Action

Ambivalence Dimension	Number Significant at p = .05[a]	Range of Estimates[b]	
Equality–Racial Stereotyping	1	0.657	0.815
Equality–Black Affect	4	1.171	1.378
Limited Government–Modern Racism	2	0.440	0.762
Modern Racism–Black Affect	2	-0.097	0.902

Notes: White respondents only
[a] out of 4 model specifications
[b] table entries are ML estimates of the ambivalence parameter of the variance model in heteroskedastic probit analysis

modern racism and black affect are significant in two of the model specifications. The parameter estimates for these ambivalence dimensions, however, are considerably smaller than for equality–black affect. These results differ from those of Alvarez and Brehm (1997), who conclude that ambivalence plays little role in racial attitudes. We find that in some cases, ambivalence matters a great deal, but those cases involve different types of ambivalence than those studied by Alvarez and Brehm.

The remaining ambivalence dimensions (not reported in Table 4.5) reveal no impact on response variability. Thus, of ten ambivalence dimensions that we consider in the context of affirmative action, a majority never attain statistical significance. From this perspective, evidence for decreased predictability of racial attitudes due to ambivalence is rather weak.

GAY RIGHTS

When we consider the domain of gay rights, we find even weaker evidence for ambivalence effects on response predictability. In this domain, we consider three specific policy attitudes pertaining to (1) laws protecting homosexuals from job discrimination, (2) inclusion of homosexuals in the United States Armed Forces, and (3) the legal right of homosexual couples to adopt children.[11] Significant results of these analyses are reported in Table 4.6.

In only one instance do we obtain a fairly robust ambivalence effect in the heteroskedastic probit models. Respondents who experience conflict between the values of equality and moral traditionalism display greater response variability than those who do not experience such conflict (in three of four specifications of the variance model). In only one other case do we

TABLE 4.6
Unpredictability Gay Rights

Ambivalence Dimension	Number Significant at p = .05[a]	Range of Estimates[b]	
Job Discrimination:			
Equality–Moral Traditionalism	3	0.758	0.960
Adoption: Limited			
Government–Gay Affect	1	0.029	0.331

Notes: No significant results for gays in the military.
[a] out of 4 model specifications
[b] table entries are ML estimates of the ambivalence parameter of the variance model in heteroskedastic probit analysis.

see a hint of ambivalence effects (in one of the specifications, ambivalence between limited government and gay affect increases response variability for the gay adoption policy), but it is weak and not robust. In the overwhelming number of cases, however, there is no evidence whatsoever that ambivalence makes it more difficult to predict attitudes on gay rights policies. Public opinion on these policies appears to be remarkably unaffected by ambivalence, at least as far as response variability is concerned.

SOCIAL WELFARE

In the domain of social welfare policies, too, the impact of ambivalence on response variability is quite limited. In this domain we consider opinions about federal spending in six areas (welfare, food stamps, poor people, the homeless, Social Security, and unemployment benefits), as well as people's attitudes toward government services more generally and toward the idea that government should see to it that everyone should have a job and a decent standard of living.[12] The significant results for the heteroskedastic probit models for these policy attitudes are summarized in Table 4.7.

Again, we observe that in most cases no relationship exists between ambivalence and the predictability of policy responses. For three of the spending items (homeless, Social Security, and unemployment benefits) ambivalence is never a significant predictor of response variability. The same result holds for government services. Ambivalence effects appear sporadically for two other spending items (poor people and food stamps), but these effects are generally not robust, weak, and in the wrong direction.

Stronger ambivalence effects emerge for government job provision, where the value conflict between equality and limited government and the conflict between limited government and affect toward people on welfare exercise fairly robust effects. In both instances, respondents who experience these types of conflict have less predictable opinions than those who are not conflicted.

TABLE 4.7
Unpredictability and Social Welfare

Ambivalence Dimension	Number Significant at $p = .05$[a]	Range of Estimates[b]	
Spending on Welfare:			
Equality–Welfare Affect	4	−1.045	−0.883
Spending on Poor:			
Equality–Poor Affect	1	−0.926	−0.757
Spending on Food Stamps:			
Equality–Poor Affect	1	−1.163	−0.965
Limited Government–Welfare Affect	1	−0.532	−0.141
Government Jobs:			
Equality–Limited Government	3	0.084	1.075
Equality–Poor Affect	1	−0.831	0.185
Limited Government–Poor Affect	1	−0.481	0.626
Limited Government–Welfare Affect	3	0.410	0.658

Note: No significant results for government services, spending on homeless, spending on social security, and spending on unemployment benefits.

[a] out of 4 model specifications

[b] table entries are ML estimates of the ambivalence parameter of the variance model in heteroskedastic probit analysis.

Only in one instance do we observe significant ambivalence effects across all specifications of the variance model. In the context of attitudes toward welfare spending the conflict between equality and feelings toward people on welfare is always statistically significant. If we believe the parameter estimates, however, this conflict serves to *reduce* response variability. We find it difficult to interpret this effect, but its robustness leads us to believe that it is real. Obviously, this result is at odds with the predictions derived from social psychology.

ABORTION

Finally, we consider abortion. Here we look at general opinions about the conditions under which abortion should be allowed, as well as responses to questions about proposed state laws to (1) require parental consent to abortions by teenagers, (2) provide funding for abortion for women who need it, and (3) require notification of the spouse in the case of an abortion by a married woman.[13] We assess the extent to which conflict between gender equality and moral traditionalism makes responses to these questions less predictable.

The results are unequivocal. There is no evidence that ambivalence makes the responses to the abortion questions less predictable. No matter which specification of the variance model we take, ambivalence comes out as a statistically insignificant predictor.

Our findings for abortion contrast markedly with those of Alvarez and Brehm (1995), who claim evidence that abortion responses for ambivalent respondents are harder to predict. However, they define ambivalence not in terms of the conflict between gender equality and moral traditionalism, but in terms of conflicting considerations that respondents give for the abortion issue. To the extent that these considerations all pertain to the conflict we consider here, we should have found identical results. Our suspicion, however, is that many of the conflicting considerations have nothing to do with gender equality and moral traditionalism. This would explain the different findings.

Even though our analysis may capture only a small number of the forces that can pull people in different directions about abortion, we think our findings are telling. Earlier work has singled out the conflict between gender equality and moral traditionalism as one of the most important ambivalence dimensions (Schnell 1993). Yet we do not find much evidence that this dimension has many implications for public opinion. As we shall see, this is a refrain that is repeated for most of the analyses.

CONCLUSIONS

The idea that ambivalence makes policy attitudes less predictable has received considerable attention in recent work by Alvarez and Brehm (1995, 1997), who find mixed support for it. The present results undermine this idea even further. Considering a wider range of policy domains and policies than Alvarez and Brehm (1995, 1997) and a larger set of ambivalence dimensions, we find that ambivalence only rarely increases response variability. In a majority of cases, people who experience ambivalence are no less predictable in their responses to policy questions than those who do not suffer from such ambivalence. This suggests that an ambivalent mass public—such as it is—is not necessarily an unpredictable mass public.

Attitude Stability

Response unpredictability is not the only place to trace the consequences of ambivalence, nor is it the best place. Simply because responses are harder to predict for some individuals does not mean that public opinion is less structured. If our interest is in structure we should look at different diagnostics. We begin by considering the structure of attitudes over time, looking at the stability of policy attitudes across three waves of the ANES panel study as a function of ambivalence.

A common vehicle for estimating stability coefficients in three-wave panels is the model developed by Wiley and Wiley (1970). This model assumes that the responses to each policy are the manifestation of a true policy attitude and random measurement error. Stability is defined in terms of the predictability of the true attitude in one wave from the true attitude in the wave immediately preceding it (a lag-1 autoregressive model). To identify the model it is assumed that error variance remains constant across the three waves of the panel. If the Wiley model is analyzed with correlational data, as we do here, this implies that the item reliabilities are constant across waves, a rather stringent assumption that parallels Heise's (1969) work.

The expectation at stake here is that the stability coefficients for ambivalent individuals are lower. We put this prediction to the test by splitting panel respondents into low and high ambivalence groups on the basis of a median split of their 1992 scores on the modified Griffin ambivalence measure. We then estimate stability coefficients for each group using multigroup covariance structure analysis and compare them. Not all policy attitudes were measured in the requisite number of three waves. Consequently, stability analyses can only be conducted for affirmative action, laws protecting homosexuals against job discrimination, gays in the military, welfare spending, spending on food stamps, spending on Social Security, government services, government job provision, and the general abortion question. The data sources for the analyses are the 1992, 1994, and 1996 waves of the ANES panel study, with the exception of the gay rights items for which the 1992, 1993, and 1996 waves are used.[14]

Table 4.8 summarizes the stability coefficients for all policy items by listing the range of stability estimates across all ambivalence dimensions that are relevant in a particular policy domain (see Table 4.1). The patterns across the various issue domains are quite similar, so that it suffices to discuss the table as a whole. The most striking feature of this table is perhaps the high level of stability for each of the policy attitudes. This stability never drops below .63 and is frequently unity, suggesting a much greater level of stability in public opinion than suggested by Converse (1964, 1970).[15] Indeed with stability coefficients that are this high it seems difficult to argue that sizable portions of the American public have nonattitudes.

Of more immediate interest for our analysis are the differences in the stability coefficients between low and high ambivalence groups. Table 4.8 suggests no compelling evidence that ambivalent individuals hold more volatile attitudes than their less ambivalent peers. Indeed, in quite a few cases the stability estimates for the high ambivalence group exceed those for the low ambivalence group, a pattern that would surely not be predicted from the literature. We should not make too much of this pattern,

TABLE 4.8
Stability in Policy Attitudes

Policy Attitude	Period	Range of Stability Estimates			
		Low Ambivalence		High Ambivalence	
Affirmative action[a]	1992–94	0.82	0.99	0.63	0.97
	1994–96	0.85	0.97	0.76	1.00
Gay job discrimination	1992–93	0.83	1.00	0.97	1.00
	1993–96	0.88	1.00	0.87	1.00
Gays in military	1992–93	0.81	0.93	0.83	1.00
	1993–96	0.91	1.00	0.84	0.90
Welfare spending	1992–94	0.76	0.94	0.88	1.00
	1994–96	0.94	1.00	0.87	1.00
Spending on food stamps	1992–94	0.73	1.00	0.74	1.00
	1994–96	0.86	1.00	0.80	1.00
Spending on Social security	1992–94	0.86	0.95	0.74	0.95
	1994–96	0.88	0.93	0.74	0.90
Government services	1992–94	0.74	1.00	0.66	0.96
	1994–96	0.82	1.00	0.76	1.00
Government job provision	1992–94	0.98	1.00	0.91	1.00
	1994–96	0.75	0.90	0.73	0.81
Abortion	1992–94	0.97	0.97	0.95	0.95
	1994–96	.96	0.96	.96	.96

Note: Table entries are WLS estimates of stability coefficients.
[a] white respondents only

however, because in reality the stability coefficients for the low and high ambivalence groups are statistically indistinguishable. When we estimate the Wiley model imposing the constraint that the stability coefficients are identical in both groups the fit is deteriorated only slightly. In no case is this statistically significant (the minimum value of the χ^2 test statistic is .002, while the maximum value is 2.170; with 2 degrees of freedom this produces p-values well above .10).[16]

In sum, ambivalence exerts little influence over attitude stability in the three policy domains that we focus on. Attitudes appear to be very stable, both for ambivalent and nonambivalent citizens. These results are at odds with past predictions and findings concerning value conflict (Zaller 1992; Zaller and Feldman 1992). They suggest that citizens hold real attitudes, regardless of the conflicts between the orientations that they hold.

Horizontal Constraint

So far we have demonstrated that the opinions of ambivalent people are generally no more unpredictable or unstable than the opinions of others. The question remains, however, if those opinions also form a coherent whole. Perhaps ambivalence causes a conflict between attitudes toward different policies within the same domain. We now turn to this question about horizontal constraint in the three domains where we consider multiple policy attitudes—gay rights, social welfare, and abortion.

We use two methods for assessing horizontal consistency. In the first method we compute an agreement score across all policy attitudes in a domain for each respondent. For example, if a citizen agrees with three out of three policies her agreement score would be 3. If she agrees with two out of three policies her agreement score would be 2. It would also be 2, however, if she disagrees with two out of three policies. This agreement score serves as an indicator of horizontal constraint. It can be used as the response variable in a statistical analysis where it can be related to the ambivalence scores of a particular respondent. This approach has the advantage that it is relatively easy to include control variables in addition to the ambivalence measures. The disadvantage of using disagreement scores is that it is not possible to distinguish between true inconsistencies among policy attitudes and inconsistencies that are the by-product of random measurement error.

Our second approach is to formulate measurement models in which each policy attitude in a domain is considered to be an indicator of a broader underlying latent dimension (a "meta-attitude," so to speak). Each indicator has a unique component (which consists of measurement error as well as idiosyncratic features of a policy to which respondents respond) in addition to the common component that it shares with the other indicators. This makes it possible to control (albeit crudely) for random sources of inconsistency between responses to different policies. To consider the impact of ambivalence the measurement model can be analyzed in low and high ambivalence groups, and the loading of each policy on the underlying factor can be compared across the groups using multigroup covariance structure models. The theoretical prediction is that these loadings are weaker for ambivalent respondents than for others. A limitation of this method is that it is difficult to include control variables as this produces a proliferation of groups with small sample sizes. We now apply these methods to each policy domain.

TABLE 4.9
Horizontal Constraint Gay Rights

Ambivalence Dimension	Probit Estimate[a]	Average Factor Loading[b]	
		Low Ambivalence	High Ambivalence
Equality–Moral Traditionalism	-1.380	0.850	0.710
Equality–Gay Affect	-1.305	0.843	0.700
Limited Government– Moral Traditionalism	-0.636	0.827	0.763
Moral Traditionalism–Gay Affect	-1.300	0.857	0.677

[a] Table entries are ML probit estimates.
[b] Table entries are WLS estimates of factor loadings.

GAY RIGHTS

Table 4.9 summarizes the significant results obtained from a probit analysis of the agreement scores across the three gay rights policy issues.[17] These results suggest that agreement scores tend to be lower for ambivalent individuals for four of the ambivalence dimensions (see also Brewer 1998). This finding is particularly pronounced for the value conflict between equality and moral traditionalism, but it is also powerful for the ambivalence dimensions involving equality and gay affect and moral traditionalism and gay affect. In the domain of gay rights, then, the tendency for horizontal constraint declines as ambivalence increases.

These results also emerge when we consider the measurement model. The average factor loadings for the three gay rights policies are higher for the low ambivalence than for the high ambivalence groups on the equality–moral traditionalism, equality–gay affect, limited government–moral traditionalism, and moral traditionalism–gay affect ambivalence dimensions (last two columns in Table 4.9). In each case the model fit deteriorates significantly when the factor loadings are constrained to be equal across groups (the χ^2 test statistic values range between a minimum of 44.67 and a maximum of 79.42; with 3 degrees of freedom the corresponding p-values are all well below .01). Thus, the measurement model, too, suggests decreased horizontal constraint for ambivalent individuals.

These results should be placed in context, however. While horizontal constraint decreases as a function of ambivalence, there is little evidence that ambivalent individuals have hopelessly loose belief systems. The factor loadings in the high ambivalence group are substantial and there is no evidence of dramatic inconsistencies in the attitudes across different gay rights policies in this group. Less horizontal constraint does not imply poor horizontal constraint.

Social Welfare

The results for gay rights policies do not transfer to the domain of social welfare policies. In this domain, there is no evidence at all that ambivalence causes a decrease in horizontal constraint, at least when we focus on constraints among public assistance policies (spending on welfare, poor people, food stamps, and unemployment benefits).

An ordered probit analysis of the agreement scores between these policies shows only one instance in which ambivalence decreases agreement.[18] Those who experience conflict between limited government and their feelings toward poor people tend to show less constraint than those who do not experience such conflict ($b = -.789, p < .01$). None of the other ambivalence dimensions has a statistically significant impact on the agreement scores.

This result for the limited government–poor affect ambivalence dimension disappears in the analysis of the measurement model. There is no evidence in this model that the factor loadings for the four welfare policies are different in the low and high ambivalence groups. Indeed, when the factor loadings are constrained to be equal across the groups the resulting models have a very good fit (the χ^2 test statistic values range between .82 and 6.97; with 4 degrees of freedom this results in p-values that lie well above .10). Thus, in the domain of social welfare policies, horizontal constraint appears to be unaffected by ambivalence.

Abortion

A very similar pattern emerges for abortion. An ordered probit analysis of agreement scores reveals a decreased horizontal constraint as the conflict between gender equality and moral traditionalism becomes more intense ($b = -.603, p < .01$).[19] An analysis of the measurement model, however, shows no evidence that the factor loadings for the low and high ambivalence groups are significantly different (a model that constrains these loadings to be equal across the two groups fits the data about as well as an unconstrained model: difference in $\chi^2 = 6.98$, *ns*).

Conclusions

Taken together, the results for the gay rights, social welfare, and abortion policy domains lend only mixed support to the notion that the belief systems of ambivalent individuals display less horizontal constraint. This notion is supported for some issues, some of the time, but as a general statement about the consequences of ambivalence it is invalid. Moreover, even in those instances where ambivalence erodes horizontal constraint, the erosion appears to be rather mild. Our results suggest that Americans can hold remarkably coherent opinions in a particular policy domain, even in the face of ambivalence. This is a rather different picture than that presented to us by Converse (1964), but it is a picture that is consistent with what others have shown (Hurwitz and Peffley 1987).

Vertical Constraint

Our final analysis concerns the extent to which ambivalence impacts vertical constraint in belief systems. Here we define vertical constraint broadly as the degree to which specific attitudes are driven by more general orientations. These orientations include abstract principles such as ideology and values, which have typically been used to define vertical constraint (e.g., Converse 1964; Feldman 1988; Feldman and Zaller 1992; Hurwitz and Peffley 1987; McClosky and Zaller 1984). However, they also include affective responses to target groups (Sniderman, Brody, and Tetlock 1991) and racial beliefs (e.g., Alvarez and Brehm 1997; Kinder and Sanders 1996; Kinder and Sears 1981; McConahay 1986; Nelson and Kinder 1996). These orientations, too, affect a large number of attitudes and can thus be deemed as more general than any specific attitude, making them potential elements of vertical constraint.[20]

With this definition of vertical constraint in hand, we use the following analytic approach. As before, we used a median split to divide the sample into low and high ambivalence groups. In each group we estimate models predicting the various policy attitudes that include the following vertical constraint elements: partisanship, ideology, target group evaluations, values, and, in the case of affirmative action, racial beliefs (the target group evaluations and values appropriate for each policy domain are listed in Table 4.1). We then simply count the number of statistically significant vertical constraint elements (at the .05 level) and compare this across the two ambivalence groups. Since the number of potentially constraining elements differs slightly across policy domains, we standardize by using this number to divide the count of significant elements. The resulting score is treated as an indicator of vertical constraint.[21]

To determine to what extent vertical constraint is affected by ambivalence, we can conduct a t-test of the constraint scores. This test shows no evidence of diminished vertical constraint in the high ambivalence group (difference in means = .028, t = .841, *ns*).[22] Apparently, ambivalent individuals rely as much on general orientations to shape their attitudes as their less ambivalent brethren.

The lack of statistically significant differences in the vertical constraint scores does not mean that the low and high ambivalence groups use the same vertical constraint elements. One would expect ambivalent individuals to place less emphasis on the orientations that cause their ambivalence in structuring policy attitudes. There is evidence that this indeed is the case. In only 17.5 percent of the analyses involving the low ambivalence group was neither of two conflicting orientations statistically significant in the prediction of policy attitudes. For the high ambivalence group, this percentage is double, a statistically significant difference (Pearson $\chi^2 = 6.33$, $p < .05$). Note, however, that it is not the case that ambivalent individuals abandon the use of conflicting orientations in a wholesale manner. The difference between the low and high ambivalence group in using such orientations is one more of degree than of nature. In this regard, our results are consistent with those reported by Feldman and Zaller (1992), who argue that even in a political culture of ambivalence citizens can and do rely on the principles that are the very subject of controversy and conflict.

Do ambivalent individuals rely more on other orientations to anchor their opinions (a form of bolstering; see Abelson 1959)? The answer appears to be no. The mean proportion of significant other orientations is almost the same in both ambivalence groups (at around half of the other considerations on average being significant in both groups). This is further evidence that ambivalence has little effect on vertical constraint.

DISCUSSION

The results of the analyses tell a clear story. There is evidence neither of widespread ambivalence nor of massive implications of ambivalence for policy attitudes. Rather, we find mild levels of ambivalence and few effects, which are only occasionally very powerful. The story of this chapter is for the most part one of non-results.

This places our work in sharp contrast with many of the studies discussed earlier, which document both high levels and profound effects of ambivalence. To account for this discrepancy we should consider several factors. First, it may be that we have chosen the wrong policy domains. Perhaps we have picked exactly those domains in which ambivalence played a small role, at least at the time the ANES collected the survey data that we use. We do not find this a very plausible explanation, however. We selected the policy domains precisely because they are characterized by so much conflict. This conflict was particularly pronounced around the 1992 elections for at least two of the issue domains—gay rights and social welfare (see Brewer 1999). If anywhere, then, we would expect ambivalence to play a major role in these domains, making it all the more telling that we find so few effects.

Another possibility is that our conceptualization of ambivalence is unduly broad. Specifically, we may have included ambivalence dimensions that do not really reflect ambivalence, so that one should expect them to generate null results. This possibility, too, seems implausible. First, as we argued earlier, there are good theoretical reasons to include so many ambivalence dimensions. More important, however, even if we were to limit our attention to traditional value conflict, the lack of results is impressive. For instance, the conflict between equality and limited government that has received so much attention is impressive in its mildness and the weak effects it exerts. The conflict between equality and moral traditionalism that plays in the domain of gay rights is more impressive, but even in this case, the results are not very robust.

Yet a third possibility is that our conceptualization of ambivalence is not broad enough. We have undoubtedly missed important dimensions of ambivalence, such as conflicts involving the role of economic individualism and compassion, primarily because good survey instruments are not available. Perhaps such dimensions would show considerably stronger effects. Still, by the standards of earlier research efforts, our catalog of ambivalence dimensions is remarkably comprehensive. In our view, this adds a great deal of significance to the findings.

Fourth, our measure of ambivalence—the modified Griffin measure—can be held responsible for our different findings. We do not find this very plausible, however, because the measure correlates rather strongly with alternative measures that have been used in the literature. Moreover, we replicated all of the analyses using the multiplicative measure of Alvarez and Brehm (1997) and found only slight differences in the results.

Nonetheless, measurement is an issue. In this study, we have inferred ambivalence from responses to scales that measure different orientations. At no point in the interview were respondents asked to connect their responses concerning different orientations. When respondents are forced to make these connections, their ambivalence may come much more in focus and it may exert a much stronger influence on their response behavior. This would explain why Hochschild (1981) and Sniderman et al. (1996) find so much more ambivalence than we do, since these authors pushed their interviewees hard on possible inconsistencies in their views.

Another measurement approach that may enhance ambivalence effects is to ask respondents to list considerations before answering a question probing a specific policy attitude (Alvarez and Brehm 1995; Feldman and Zaller 1992; Zaller and Feldman 1992).[23] By bringing multiple considerations into working memory, respondents may experience a higher level of ambivalence than they ordinarily would by just answering a survey question. In the latter case, conflicting considerations may never come into play.

There are good arguments for using these alternative measurement strategies. At the same time, one should be cautious in interpreting them. Whereas our inferences from unrelated survey items may understate the level and consequences of ambivalence, these alternative approaches may well overstate them. In any case, a lot can be said for the argument that if Americans are truly ambivalent it should show up in their survey responses even without prodding them. In this regard, our measurement approach may be appropriately conservative in its assessment of ambivalence.

We conclude, then, by saying that our results present compelling evidence about the role of ambivalence in policy attitudes. This evidence has major ramifications for our assessment of public opinion in the United States. We now turn to this issue in the conclusion.

Conclusions

Our analyses sketch a remarkably consistent picture of public opinion in America. It appears that Americans experience only relatively mild levels of ambivalence and that this ambivalence does not influence public opinion dramatically. Thus, the evidence suggests a not-so-ambivalent American mass public. The implications of this finding for assessments of the quality of public opinion are important.

A recurring theme in much of the literature is that American public opinion is rather volatile, i.e., full of inconsistencies. Pessimists claim that these inconsistencies indicate a profound lack of political understanding on the part of ordinary citizens. More optimistic accounts state that public opinion simply reflects the tensions that are inherent in the political culture of ambivalence (Feldman and Zaller 1992; Sniderman et al. 1996).

Our results suggest an even more optimistic picture, namely that ambivalence does not have to breed volatility. While it would be reasonable to expect that ambivalent individuals hold volatile opinions, thus leaving an imprint on the quality of public opinion as a whole, we find quite the opposite. On the whole, those who score high on ambivalence hold opinions that are no less stable and coherent than those who score low, and their responses to survey questions are no less predictable.

Indeed, in the face of conflicting orientations, people seem to do a remarkable job in piecing together consistent opinions. This does not mean that ambivalent citizens will be consistent under all circumstances. When they are pushed hard on the conflicts between different orientations, people will undoubtedly waver more in their views and their opinions may become more volatile. Likewise, when exposed to media frames that play up conflicting orientations, ambivalent individuals may feel hard-pressed to ignore the tensions among their beliefs, values, and feelings.

We have not examined these situations here. Instead, what we have done is to analyze the influence of public opinion when people are not reminded of the incompatibilities in their orientations. In our view, this situation mimics everyday life quite well, in that we very much doubt that there are many citizens who will spend much time reminding themselves of the conflicts among their political orientations. In this situation, in which ambivalence is latent rather than manifest, we find little evidence that ambivalent citizens behave any differently than anyone else.

The political culture of ambivalence provides plenty of opportunity for piecing together incoherent views about policy issues—what Free and Cantril (1968:30) once called a "schizoid" combination of beliefs. It is striking, however, how little incoherence exists, even among the most ambivalent Americans. Not volatility but structure and consistency characterize the opinions of ambivalent citizens.

NOTES

1. We are concerned solely with the role that ambivalence plays in policy attitudes. For a discussion of the role of ambivalence in candidate evaluations we refer to Meffert, Guge, and Lodge, chapter 3 in this volume.

2. In the next section, we shall give these dimensions more specific content in each of the policy domains that we consider.

3. In addition, the measure also does not take into consideration measurement error in the assessment of orientations.

4. If agreement with A and B reflects a situation in which there is no dissonance, then the scale of one of the items should be reversed before applying this formula.

5. The modified Griffin measure shows a high correlation with the multiplicative ambivalence measure, $A \times B$, that Alvarez and Brehm (1997) use: across all ambivalence dimensions that we consider the average correlation between both measures is .87 (minimum is .69, maximum is .94). Nonetheless, we prefer the Griffin measure because the multiplicative measure has the undesirable property, at least with our coding of items, that ambivalence is always 0 once one of the items receives a neutral score, no matter what the score on the other item is. In any case, the results obtained from analyses of the modified Griffin ambivalence measure yield results that are very consistent with those obtained with the multiplicative ambivalence measure.

6. Race is not entered as a covariate in the analyses of ambivalence involving racial orientations, as only white respondents are considered in these analyses. Religious fundamentalism is a composite of items measuring how much guidance a person takes from religion in daily life (ANES variable number V923821), how literally she interprets the Bible (V923824), whether she considers herself a fundamentalist (V923846), and whether she considers herself a born-again Christian (V923847). High scores on the scale imply a more fundamentalist religious orientation (Cronbach's alpha is .89). The political knowledge scale consists of six items

that ask respondents to identify the positions of four political figures and to answer two questions about constitutional law (V925916 through V925921). High scores on the scale imply better political knowledge (Mokken coefficient of scalability is .59, reliability is .76). Partisanship is the standard ANES partisan identification question (-1 = strong Republican; 1 = strong Democrat), while ideology is the ANES question about ideological self-placement (-1 = strong conservative; 1 = strong liberal). (Because the ideology variable has many missing cases, we imputed them by assigning them to the middle category.) Finally, strength of ideology is a folded version of the ideological self-placement measure.

7. Because of the large number of analyses that were conducted, this and other tables can only present summaries of the results. More detailed reports of the analyses are available upon request.

8. We should note an important limitation of heteroskedastic models. While such models can provide us with estimates of the response variability at different levels of a covariate, they cannot tell us whether variability is due to greater measurement error or to greater variability in the underlying attitude.

9. Because we obtain many "null results" in the analyses of predictability we report only significant effects in this and following tables and comment on the insignificant effects in the text.

10. Details about the response variables in this and subsequent analyses can be found in the appendix. For purposes of this analysis the response variable is dichotomized (pro- vs. con-affirmative action). The choice model includes the following predictors: gender (1 = female; 0 = male), age, income, education, religious fundamentalism, partisanship, ideology, modern racism, racial stereotyping, equality, limited government, and black affect. Only white respondents are included in the analysis.

11. The response variable for each policy is dichotomous (1 = favor policy; 0 = oppose policy). The choice model for each policy attitude includes the following predictors: race (1 = black; 0 = white), gender (1 = female; 0 = male), age, income, education, religious fundamentalism, partisanship, ideology, equality, limited government, moral traditionalism, and gay affect. The model for homosexuals in the military also includes affect toward the military as a control variable.

12. The spending variables are dichotomous (1 = increase spending; 0 = decrease spending or keep the same), while orientations toward government services and job provision are measured on 7-point scales. The choice model includes the following predictors: race (1 = black; 0 = white), gender (1 = female; 0 = male), age, income, education, religious fundamentalism, partisanship, ideology, equality, limited government, feelings toward people on welfare, and feelings toward poor people. In addition, the models for spending on food stamps, Social Security, and unemployment contain dummy predictors for whether a respondent is a beneficiary of these programs.

13. The questions concerning state laws are dichotomous. We dichotomize the general abortion question, distinguishing between those who believe women should always have the right to an abortion versus everyone else. The choice model includes the following predictors: race (1 = black; 0 = white), gender (1 = female, 0 = male), age, income, education, religious fundamentalism, partisanship, ideology,

equality, limited government, gender equality, moral traditionalism, and feelings toward feminists.

14. For this analysis, the spending items are dichotomized (1 = increase spending; 0 = decrease spending or keep the same). Since all items in the analysis are categorical in nature, the Wiley model is estimated on the basis of the polychoric correlation matrix using weighted least squares. All estimates are obtained using LISREL.

15. These high stability values are consistent with the results obtained by Achen (1975) and Feldman (1990) (see also Judd and Milburn 1980). Feldman's (1990) analysis is particularly interesting because he uses a five-wave panel in which some of the stringent assumptions of the Wiley model can be relaxed.

16. The biggest differences between the low and high ambivalence groups occur in the estimates of the error variance. There is a tendency for this variance to be greater for ambivalent individuals than for nonambivalent individuals.

17. The agreement scores are dichotomized in this analysis: 1 indicates that a respondent favors or opposes all three policies, while 0 indicates that a respondent favors or opposes two of the three policies. The predictors in this analysis include race (1 = black; 0 = white), gender (1 = female; 0 = male), age, income, education, religious fundamentalism, partisanship, ideology, strength of ideology, political knowledge, and ambivalence.

18. The agreement score is trichotomous and rescaled so that 0 indicates support for two policies (and opposition to the remaining two), 1 indicates support for three policies (or opposition to three policies), and 2 indicates support for all policies or opposition to all. The model specification is similar to that for gay rights policies.

19. The structure of this analysis is identical to that for the assistance policy items.

20. It could be argued that we employ too broad a definition of vertical constraint by including target group evaluations and racial beliefs, making it too easy to find vertical constraint. By restricting ourselves only to abstract principles, however, we may stack the deck against less sophisticated individuals who may find it more difficult to use those principles to guide opinions. A broader conceptualization if vertical constraint alleviates this problem.

21. A total of 160 vertical constraint scores were created. This is the sample size for the ensuing analyses.

22. We also conducted a more complex analysis considering the impact of issue domain, ambivalence class (cognitive–cognitive conflict, cognitive–affective conflict, affective–affective conflict). An ANOVA shows that only domain is significant ($F[3,144] = 35.93$, $p < .01$). The latter result is due to the much smaller number of vertical constraint elements in the affirmative action and abortion domains.

23. Probes to list "likes" and "dislikes," which are commonly used in candidate evaluation questions (see Meffert, Guge, and Lodge, chapter 3 in this volume), are similar in nature.

APPENDIX: MEASURES

Policy Attitudes

AFFIRMATIVE ACTION

Some people say that because of past discrimination, blacks should be given preference in hiring and promotion. Others say that such preference in hiring and promotion of blacks is wrong because it gives blacks advantages that they haven't earned. What about your opinion . . . (1) favor strongly; (2) favor not strongly; (3) oppose not strongly; (4) oppose strongly.

GAY RIGHTS

- Do you favor or oppose laws to protect homosexuals against job discrimination? (1) favor strongly; (2) favor not strongly; (3) oppose not strongly; (4) oppose strongly.
- Do you think homosexuals should be allowed to serve in the United States Armed Forces or don't you think so? (1) feel strongly should be allowed; (2) feel not strongly should be allowed; (3) feel not strongly should not be allowed; (4) feel strongly should not be allowed.
- Do you think gay or lesbian couples, in other words, homosexual couples, should be legally permitted to adopt children? (1) feel strongly should be permitted; (2) feel not strongly should be permitted; (3) feel not strongly should not be permitted; (4) feel strongly should not be permitted.

SOCIAL WELFARE

- If you had a say in making up the federal budget this year, for which of the following programs would you like to see spending increased and for which would you like to see spending decreased? Should spending on food stamps be increased, decreased, or kept about the same?
- Should federal spending on welfare programs be increased, decreased, or kept about the same?
- Should federal spending be increased, decreased, or kept about the same on solving the problem of the homeless?
- Should federal spending on Social Security be increased, decreased, or kept about the same?
- Should federal spending be increased, decreased, or kept about the same on government assistance to the unemployed?
- Should federal spending be increased, decreased, or kept about the same on poor people?
- Some people think the government should provide fewer services, even in areas such as health and education, in order to reduce spending. Suppose these people are at one end of the scale at point 1. Other people feel it is important for the government to provide many more services even if it means

an increase in spending. Suppose these people are at the other end, at point 7. And of course, some other people have opinions somewhere in between at points 2, 3, 4, 5, or 6. Where would you place yourself on this scale, or haven't you thought much about this?

- Some people feel the government in Washington should see to it that every person has a job and a good standard of living. Others think the government should just let each person get ahead on their own. Where would you place yourself on this scale, or haven't you thought much about this? (7-point scale)

ABORTION

- There has been some discussion about abortion during recent years. Which one of the opinions on this page best agrees with your view . . . ? (1) by law, abortion should never be permitted; (2) the law should permit abortion only in case of rape, incest, or when the woman's life is in danger; (3) the law should permit abortion for reasons other than rape, incest, or danger to the woman's life, but only after the need for the abortion has been clearly established; (4) by law, a woman should always be able to obtain an abortion as a matter of personal choice.
- Would you favor or oppose a law in your state that would require parental consent before a teenager under eighteen can have an abortion?
- Would you favor or oppose a law in your state that would allow the use of government funds to help pay for the costs of abortion for women who cannot afford them?
- Would you favor or oppose a law in your state that would require a married woman to notify her husband before she can have an abortion?

Orientations in Ambivalence Dimensions

Equality: Scale consisting of ANES items V926024 through V926029. High scores are pro-equality. Cronbach's alpha = .77.

Feelings toward black people: ANES item V925323. High scores imply warm feelings toward African Americans.

Feelings toward gays and homosexuals: ANES item V925335. High scores imply warm feelings toward homosexuals.

Feelings toward poor people: ANES item V925320. High scores imply warm feelings toward the poor.

Feelings toward people on welfare: ANES item V925318. High scores imply warm feelings toward people on welfare.

Gender equality: ANES item V923801. High scores are pro-equality between the sexes.

Limited government: Scale consisting of ANES items V925729 through V925731. High scores are pro–limited government. Cronbach's alpha = .85.

Modern racism: Scale consisting of ANES items V926126 through V926129. High scores imply modern racism. Cronbach's alpha = .81.

Moral traditionalism: Scale consisting of ANES items V926115 though V926118. High scores are pro–traditional values. Cronbach's alpha = .71.

Racial stereotyping: Scale consisting of difference scores between ANES items V926222 and V926221, V926225 and V926226, and V926229 and V926230. High scores imply negative racial stereotyping. Cronbach's alpha = .74.

REFERENCES

Abelson, Robert P. 1959. "Models of Resolution of Belief Dilemmas." *Journal of Conflict Resolution* 3(2):343–52.

Achen, Christopher H. 1975. "Mass Political Attitudes and the Survey Response." *American Political Science Review* 69(4):1218–31.

Alvarez, R. Michael, and John Brehm. 1995. "American Ambivalence towards Abortion Policy: Development of a Heteroskedastic Probit Model of Competing Values." *American Journal of Political Science* 39(4):1055–82.

———. 1997. "Are Americans Ambivalent toward Racial Policies?" *American Journal of Political Science* 41(2):345–74.

Bargh, John A., Shelly Chaiken, Rajen Govender, and Felicia Pratto. 1992. "The Generality of the Automatic Attitude Activation Effect." *Journal of Personality and Social Psychology* 62(6):893–912.

Brewer, Paul R. 1998. "Values, Information, and Consistency among Gay Rights Policy Attitudes." Chicago.

———. 1999. "Values, Public Debate, and Policy Opinions." Chapel Hill, NC.

Cacioppo, John T., and Gary G. Berntson. 1994. "Relationship between Attitudes and Evaluative Space: A Critical Review, with Emphasis on the Separability of Positive and Negative Substrates." *Psychological Bulletin* 115(3):401–23.

Cacioppo, John T., Wendi L. Gardner, and Gary G. Berntson. 1997. "Beyond Bipolar Conceptualizations and Measures: The Case of Attitudes and Evaluative Space." *Personality and Social Psychology Review* 1(1):3–25.

Converse, Philip E. 1964. "The Nature of Belief Systems in Mass Publics." In *Ideology and Discontent,* ed. David E. Apter. New York: Free Press.

———. 1970. "Attitudes and Non-Attitudes: Continuation of a Dialogue." In *The Quantitative Analysis of Social Problems,* ed. Edward R. Tufte. Reading, MA: Addison-Wesley.

Feldman, Stanley. 1988. "Structure and Consistency in Public Opinion: The Role of Core Beliefs and Values." *American Journal of Political Science* 32(2):416–40.

———. 1990. "Measuring Issue Preferences: The Problem of Response Instability." *Political Analysis* 1:25–60.

Feldman, Stanley, and John Zaller. 1992. "The Political Culture of Ambivalence: Ideological Responses to the Welfare State." *American Journal of Political Science* 36(1):268–307.

Festinger, Leon. 1957. *A Theory of Cognitive Dissonance*. Stanford: Stanford University Press.

Free, Lloyd A., and Hadley Cantril. 1968. *The Political Beliefs of Americans: A Study of Public Opinion*. New York: Simon and Schuster.

Gallagher, John, and Chris Bull. 1996. *Perfect Enemies: The Religious Right, the Gay Movement, and the Politics of the 1990s*. New York: Crown.

Gamson, William A., and Andre Modigliani. 1987. "The Changing Political Culture of Affirmative Action." In *Research in Political Sociology*, ed. Richard D. Braungart. Vol. 3. Greenwich, CT: JAI Press.

Glathar, Jill. 1996. "Between a Rock and a Hard Place: Exploring Alternative Measures of Value Conflict." Paper presented at the Annual Meeting of the Midwest Political Science Association, Chicago.

Hartz, Louis. 1955. *The Liberal Tradition in America*. San Diego: Harcourt Brace.

Heider, Fritz. 1946. "Attitudes and Cognitive Organization." *Journal of Psychology* 21(1):107–12.

Heise, David R. 1969. "Separating Reliability and Stability in Test-Retest Correlation." *American Sociological Review* 34(1):93–101.

Hochschild, Jennifer L. 1981. *What's Fair? American Beliefs about Distributive Justice*. Cambridge, MA: Harvard University Press.

Hurwitz, Jon, and Mark Peffley. 1987. "How Are Foreign Policy Attitudes Structured? A Hierarchical Model." *American Political Science Review* 81(4): 1099–1120.

Judd, Charles M., and Michael A. Milburn. 1980. "The Structure of Attitude Systems in the General Public: Comparisons of a Structural Equation Model." *American Sociological Review* 45(3):627–43.

Katz, Irwin, and R. Glen Hass. 1988. "Racial Ambivalence and American Value Conflict: Correlational and Priming Studies of Dual Cognitive Structures." *Journal of Personality and Social Psychology* 55(6):893–905.

Kinder, Donald R., and Lynn M. Sanders. 1996. *Divided by Color: Racial Politics and Democratic Ideals*. Chicago: University of Chicago Press.

Kinder, Donald R., and David O. Sears. 1981. "Prejudice and Politics: Symbolic Racism versus Racial Threats to the Good Life." *Journal of Personality and Social Psychology* 40(3):414–31.

Lasswell, Harold D. 1958. *Politics: Who Gets What, When, and How*. New York: Meridian Books.

Lavine, Howard, Cynthia J. Thomsen, Mark P. Zanna, and Eugene Borgida. 1998. "On the Primacy of Affect in the Determination of Attitudes and Behavior: The Moderating Role of Affective-Cognitive Ambivalence." *Journal of Experimental Social Psychology* 34(4):398–421.

Lipset, Seymour M. 1979. *The First New Nation: The United States in Historical and Comparative Perspective*. New York: W. W. Norton.

McClosky, Herbert, and John Zaller. 1984. *The American Ethos: Public Attitudes toward Capitalism and Democracy*. Cambridge, MA: Harvard University Press.

McConahay, John B. 1986. "Modern Racism, Ambivalence, and the Modern Racism Scale." In *Prejudice, Discrimination, and Racism,* ed. John F. Dovidio and Samuel L. Gaertner. New York: Academic Press.

McGraw, Kathleen M., and Jill Glathar. 1994. "Value Conflict and Susceptibility to Persuasion." Paper presented at Annual Meeting of the American Political Science Association, New York.

Nelson, Thomas E., and Donald R. Kinder. 1996. "Issue Frames and Group-Centrism in American Public Opinion." *Journal of Politics* 58(4):1055–78.

Reinarman, Craig. 1987. *American States of Mind: Political Beliefs and Behavior among Private and Public Workers.* New Haven: Yale University Press.

Rokeach, Milton. 1973. *The Nature of Human Values.* New York: Free Press.

Santayana, George. 1920. *Character and Opinion in the United States.* New York: Scribner.

Schnell, Frauke. 1993. "The Foundations of Abortion Attitudes: The Role of Values and Value Conflict." In *Understanding the New Politics of Abortion,* ed. Malcolm L. Coggin. Newbury Park, CA: Sage.

Sniderman, Paul M., and Thomas Piazza. 1993. *The Scar of Race.* Cambridge, MA: Harvard University Press.

Sniderman, Paul M., and Philip E. Tetlock. 1986. "Interrelationship of Political Ideology and Public Opinion." In *Political Psychology: Contemporary Problems and Issues,* ed. Margaret G. Hermann. San Francisco: Jossey-Bass Publishers.

Sniderman, Paul M., Richard A. Brody, and Philip E. Tetlock. 1991. *Reasoning and Choice: Explorations in Political Psychology.* Cambridge: Cambridge University Press.

Sniderman, Paul M., Joseph F. Fletcher, Peter H. Russell, and Philip E. Tetlock. 1996. *The Clash of Rights: Liberty, Equality, and Legitimacy in Pluralist Democracy.* New Haven: Yale University Press.

Strand, Douglass Alan. 1996. "The Political Responses to Stigma: Lessons from Voter Attitudes and Behavior in Gay Rights Disputes." Chicago.

Tetlock, Philip E. 1986. "A Value Pluralism Model of Ideological Reasoning." *Journal of Personality and Social Psychology* 50(4):819–27.

Wilcox, Clyde, and Robin M. Wolpert. 1996. "President Clinton, Public Opinion, and Gays in the Military." In *Gay Rights, Military Wrongs: Political Perspectives on Lesbians and Gays in the Military,* ed. Craig A. Zimmerman. New York: Garland.

Wiley, David E., and James A. Wiley. 1970. "The Estimation of Measurement Error in Panel Data." *American Sociological Review* 35(1):112–17.

Zaller, John. 1992. *The Nature and Origins of Mass Opinion.* Cambridge: Cambridge University Press.

Zaller, John, and Stanley Feldman. 1992. "A Simple Theory of the Survey Response: Answering Questions versus Revealing Preferences." *American Journal of Political Science* 36(3):579–616.

PART III

Politics and Nonattitudes

CHAPTER 5

The Structure of Political Argument and the Logic of Issue Framing

Paul M. Sniderman and Sean M. Theriault

DEMOCRACY HAS never been so universally esteemed. Governments, it is true, continue to be headed by kings and the religious elect; the army, the church, landowners, and business still have their hands on the levers of power; and citizens in wide swathes of the world are regularly drowned in waves of despotism, corruption, civil war, and ethnic, religious, and ideological slaughter. Even so, no other pattern of government—monarchical, ecclesiastical, military—now can challenge the legitimacy of democracy as a form of governance. And what is more, the achievement of democracy is not pyrrhic, a triumph of a word or political slogan. A half century ago totalitarian regimes wished to enjoy its prestige and attempted to pass off, particularly on the left, a murderous combination of twentieth-century efficiency and eighteenth-century absolutism as democracy rightly understood. With the collapse of Soviet Russia, this Orwellian inversion has been bleached away. Democracy, it now is near universally agreed, entails a distinctive set of institutions as well as a distinct set of principles—freedom of speech, competition among political parties, constitutional or common law assurances of due process, and equality of citizens under the law, among others.

Yet there is a paradox. At the very time that democracy has won preeminent status as a form of governance, some of its closest students have concluded that citizens are incapable of playing the role assigned them under the modern theory of democracy. To be sure, the limitations of citizens, particularly in exercising informed, principled political judgment, is a well-rubbed theme. But as we mean to make plain, contemporary studies have sharpened, even radicalized, the critique of democratic citizenship.

We begin, therefore, by distinguishing from older and more familiar concerns the new grounds for skepticism that have sprung up from recent research on framing effects. The principal elements of the framing theory of public opinion have been accepted by a remarkable number and range of scholars (e.g., Gamson and Modigliani 1987, 1989; Nelson and Kinder 1996; Zaller 1992) and arguably now constitute the standard position in the study of public opinion. In particular, it now is widely agreed that citizens in large numbers can be readily blown from one side of an issue to the very opposite depending on how the issue is specifically framed. In turn, the ease with which they can be blown from one side of an issue to the other suggests that the positions they take are far from securely anchored in underlying, enduring principles.

To the best of our knowledge, the validity of framing studies has gone unexamined. It has instead been taken for granted that the logic of these experiments is correct. As we demonstrate, however, the standard design of framing studies is methodologically flawed at its core when applied to politics. And as we also show, when what is wrong methodologically is put right, the substantive conclusion that emerges is very nearly the inverse of the one customarily drawn.

ISSUE FRAMING AND CITIZEN REASONING

The principal lines of the modern critique of citizen reasoning were laid down by Walter Lippmann in his classic work, *Public Opinion* (1922). Citizens, he contended, spend the largest part of their time and energy engaged with concerns about their work, their families, the quality of life in their neighborhoods, the whir of activities of the social, recreational, and charitable groups to which they devote so much time, caught up and carried along by the currents of daily life. The world of public affairs is, by contrast, remote, complex, recondite, and of secondary interest compared to the real and pressing concerns of family, work, and religion. Certainly politics can command their attention, but as a rule only under unusual circumstances—scandals at home, crises abroad—and then only for comparatively brief periods of time. In light of the intermittent and superficial attention that citizens typically pay to politics, it is only natural, Lippmann reasoned, that the ideas that they form of it—the "pictures in their mind"—tend to be crude, oversimplified, and stereotypical.

The first wave of the systematic study of public opinion further reinforced Lippmann's debunking of public opinion. Citizens, as the classic analysis of Berelson and his colleagues drove home,[1] do not follow with attention developments in the world of public affairs, and in any case have only a thin and often unreliable fund of information about politics on which to draw. The foundations for their judgments about politics, it followed, are shallow, and their judgments, in turn, often impulsive, oversimplified, intemperate, ill-considered, and ill-informed, excessively tuned to the immediate and the emotional aspects of public controversies and insufficiently attentive, when attentive at all, to longer-run consequences.

The terms of argument, however, recently have been expanded. On first hearing, this expansion may appear merely to be wringing yet another chord on a familiar theme; on close examination it will become apparent that the contemporary critique of citizenship has been strikingly sharpened, even radicalized. The thrust of criticism, initially, was that the judgment of citizens on political matters often is ill-considered. But the question that now is under consideration is not whether citizens are judging political matters badly, but instead whether they are capable of political judgment at all—good or bad.

The challenge to citizens' capacity for judgment got underway indirectly. Over a decade ago Gamson and Modigliani introduced a constructionist perspective to the study of media discourse and public opinion.[2] Media discourse, they suggested, consists in interpretive packages, each with an internal structure, each giving meaning to an issue or event in the public domain. At the center of each package, they asserted, "is a central organizing idea, or frame."[3] A frame, by incorporating and condensing a set of "metaphors, catchphrases, visual images, moral appeals, and other symbolic devices," supplies a readily comprehensible basis suggesting both how to think about the issue at hand and how to justify what should be done about it.[4] Gamson and Modigliani go on to present a rich and complex account of the development of media frames as well as the role of frames in shaping public opinion.

It was, however, their conception of "framing effects" in public opinion specifically that sparked interest. In less than a decade a large body of research on framing has been accomplished,[5] and the studies that have been accumulated show a rare degree of agreement with respect to both causal reasoning and empirical results. How citizens think about a public issue, it now is widely if not universally agreed, depends on how it is framed. The notion of framing itself is widely, although not perhaps precisely, agreed on. It can, and frequently is, used in two distinguishable senses that are not, however, always clearly distinguished one from another. Framing effects, in the strict sense, refer to semantically distinct conceptions of exactly the same course of action that induce preference reversals. A classic example is an experiment by Kahneman and Tversky (1984) on the impact of framing on patients' decisions whether to undergo a surgical procedure. They show that experimental subjects are markedly more likely to agree to a surgery if they are told that ninety-five out of a hundred patients survive the procedure as opposed to being told that five out of a hundred die from it. It is worth emphasizing that what is crucial, from this perspective, is that people will make strikingly different decisions whether to follow one course of action even if the alternative characterizations of the choice before them are strictly equivalent in terms of expected utility.

It is difficult to satisfy this requirement of interchangeability of alternatives outside of a narrow range of choices. Certainly when it comes to the form in which alternatives are presented to citizens making political choices, it rarely is possible to establish ex ante that the gains (or losses) of alternative characterizations of a course of action are strictly equivalent. It accordingly should not be surprising that the concept of framing, for the study of political choices, typically refers to characterizations of a course of action in terms of an alternative "central organizing idea or story line that provides meaning to an unfolding strip of events."[6]

What does it mean to refer to a "central organizing idea or story line" that gives meaning to a political issue? An example from the studies of Zaller will make this plain. How citizens think about the issue of oil drilling, he observes, varies depending on whether they confront the issue in the context of a concern over American dependency on foreign energy sources or, alternatively, the economic costs of a failure to develop new energy sources—higher gas prices and unemployment, for example.[7] The relaxed conception of a "framing" effect is thus distinguished from the strict by the elision of the requirement of strict interchangeability of the expected utility of alternative characterizations of a course of action.

Based on the last decade of research on framing effects on public opinion, there now is a consensus that the way an issue is framed matters for how citizens think about political issues. As Nelson and Kinder observe, "[F]rames are constructions of the issue: they spell out the essence of the problem."[8] Frames are thus not reducible simply to an argument on one or another side of an issue. They are broader, suggesting, as Nelson and Kinder go on to remark, "[h]ow it should be thought about, and may go so far as to recommend what (if anything) should be done."[9] What is more, a frame characteristically is not narrowly tied to a unique course of action but, as Gamson and Modigliani stipulate at the outset, "typically implies a range of positions, rather than any single one."[10]

The framing of political choice, it is further agreed, may matter in either of two quite different ways. Citizens may, depending on how an issue is framed, take a position for different reasons. Or they may, again depending on how it is framed, take different positions. The first kind of framing effect may be of importance from a social psychological perspective, but it is of secondary interest from a political perspective, since it does not alter the balance of opinion on an issue. By contrast, the second kind of framing effect results in preference reversals, altering the political balance of opinion on an issue, even (and to judge from previous research, not infrequently) converting the minority position on an issue into the majority one.[11] Accordingly, when we speak of framing effects we shall have in mind situations when the position that citizens take on an issue and the reasons they take it vary as a function of the characterization of the alternatives open for choice.

A final point is important to spell out. Not only is there agreement that how an issue is framed affects how citizens think about it, but there is also consensus on how the framing of an issue affects how they think about it. Ambivalence is the key. Just so far as citizens simultaneously have reasons both to support a course of action and to oppose it, that is, just so far as they are ambivalent, they will be susceptible to framing effects. The reasoning is straightforward. In making a choice about a public policy issue—in deciding, for example, whether government spending should do more to help blacks overcome problems of poverty and discrimination or, alternatively, blacks should do more to help themselves—citizens take account of relevant reasons: "considerations" in the lingo. Citizens, on this view, have a store of considerations that they can take account of in making up their mind whether to support or oppose a possible course of action. As a long string of scholars have argued,[12] the more consistent their stock of considerations, the more likely they are to make a choice consistent with them. At the limit, if every consideration that they could take account of favors government action, they should in all circumstances support it, and vice versa. On the other hand, the more evenly balanced their considerations, the less likely they are to offer a univocal guide for making a choice. Indeed, at the limit, when citizens' considerations are evenly balanced, as many arguing against government action as for it, they will find themselves up in the air, unable on their own to choose between alternatives, in the position of Baalim's ass, caught equidistant between two bales of equally attractive hay, starving because he is unable to decide which to eat.

How do people make choices about matters of public affairs when they find themselves in this kind of fix, more or less equally divided in the number and strength of reasons to favor and to oppose a policy? How do they decide to rely on one set of reasons rather than the other? From the perspective of framing studies, attention and salience are pivotal. Whether people attend to considerations that favor a policy or oppose it, when they have both on hand, is a function of where their attention is directed just before they choose; and where their attention is directed just before they choose is a function of their immediate circumstances, particularly (in public opinion interviews, which have been the principal theater for studies of issue framing) the wording and sequencing of the questions put to them. Just so far as their attention is directed to the positive considerations they hold on a given matter of public policy, people will be inclined to give a thumbs up. However, as long as their attention is directed to the negative considerations they also hold about it, they will be inclined to give a thumbs down. As Zaller puts it, "Which of a person's attitudes is expressed at different times depends on which has been made most immediately salient by chance and the details of questionnaire construction, especially the order and framing of questions."[13] Or, as Nelson and Kinder, citing Chong and Hochschild for support, put the point: just so far as citizens hold considerations that contradict one another, it leaves them "confused and conflicted about where to stand. . . . Frames help to resolve this confusion by declaring which of the many considerations is relevant and important, and which should be given less attention."[14] In short, the weaker the consistency of the pool of considerations that citizens take account of in making a choice about an issue in politics, the stronger the framing effect. We call this the "consistency" premise.

This is the logic, briefly rehearsed, of the framing theory of public opinion. By itself the reasoning seems to us unexceptionable. But taken just by itself, it leaves the framing theory underidentified in two crucial respects. When are citizens likely to find themselves divided in their own mind about the policy alternative to support? Does this happen principally, perhaps even exclusively, for political concerns—say, the right policy to strike with respect to a little-known country—that tend to be transient, remote, unfamiliar, of negligible interest to the larger public? Or do citizens find themselves up in the air, caught between equally persuasive policy alternatives, even when it comes to the major issues of the day? And who is likely to find themselves in this situation? A relatively small portion of the public, perhaps those who are least engaged by public affairs and therefore least well-informed about them? Or a larger, more politically consequential segment?

The answer to all of these questions, according to proponents of the framing theory of public opinion, is: most of the public are up in the air about most political issues. As Zaller and Feldman put it, "[M]ost people possess opposing considerations on most issues that might lead them to decide the issue either way."[15] Not everyone, Zaller acknowledges, "[i]s ambivalent to the same degree,"[16] but the "majority of persons on the majority of issues"[17] "possess numerous, frequently inconsistent considerations,"[18] and their views on most questions of public interest accordingly are "unfocused and contradictory.[19] These two distributional assumptions— that the ideas of the "majority of persons on the majority of issues" are contradictory—coupled with the logic of the framing hypothesis have produced a transformation in the standard representation of political reasoning of the ordinary citizen. A generation ago, Converse supposed that the problem was that citizens, having given political issues little thought, often had no real thoughts about them. According to the new critique of citizenship, however, the difficulty is not that people have too few ideas to call upon, but that they have too many and they point in opposing directions rather than pointing to none. To borrow the formulation of Nelson and Kinder, the idea that "citizens are almost always in possession of a variety of considerations that might all plausibly bear on any particular issue" and that "many of these considerations may contradict one another, leaving citizens often confused and conflicted about where to stand" is now a—perhaps even *the*—standard position in the study of public opinion.[20]

Why do so many citizens find themselves, on so many issues, armed with reasons to both favor and oppose any given course of action? On the classic line of reasoning advanced by Lippmann and others, their views on politics so often are muddled, rigid, and formulaic to an excess because they are prone to oversimplify, because they find it difficult to see the connections among ideas and to make out the larger patterns of political argument; in a word, because they "morselize," to borrow Robert Lane's classic characterization.[21] The new line of argument is externalist, not internalist, focusing on the characteristics of political communication, not those of citizens. So Zaller argues that citizens wind up with reasons to favor and to oppose policies not because they have failed to attend to politics, but precisely because they have, and "in an environment that carries roughly evenly balanced communications on both sides of issues, people are likely to internalize many contradictory arguments, which is to say, they are likely to form considerations that induce them both to favor and to oppose the same issues."[22] Let us call this the "communication premise."

Given the consistency and communication premises, only one more step is necessary to complete the framing theory of public opinion—the role of elites. Just so far as citizens find themselves up in the air, ready to vote thumbs up or thumbs down, the intervention of elites is pivotal. As Nelson and Kinder declare, "[E]lites wage a war of frames because they know that if their frame becomes the dominant way of thinking about a particular problem, then the battle for public opinion has been won."[23] There is a deep irony in this elite-driven account of public opinion. Gamson and Modigliani, the originators of framing theory, deliberately proposed a two-track account of the media and of public opinion, expressly disavowing a media-driven account of public opinion.[24] The unfolding logic of the framing theory of public opinion, however, has turned their position nearly on its head. It is now an unqualifiedly externalist account of political choice. The established views, sentiments, political orientations, or values of citizens count for little; the role of elites in defining the meaning of an issue, in imposing "the dominant way of thinking about a particular problem," counts for all. This is the claim, both empirical and normative, that we want to examine.

For data we shall rely on the second wave of the Multi-Investigator Survey. The Multi-Investigator is specifically designed to offer a general purpose platform, accessible to investigators and research teams across the country who wish to combine the internal validity strengths of randomized experimentation with the external validity strengths of random sampling. The sample is a random digit dial (RDD) selection of the adult population of the country as a whole.[25]

To work through the logic of the framing theory of public opinion, we shall proceed in two steps. First, we shall show that our procedures and data reproduce the classic framing effect. Then, taking advantage of computer-assisted interviewing to break out of the excessively restrictive corset of the classic split-ballot design, we shall show that analysis of an appropriately designed experiment reverses nearly completely both the causal and normative conclusions to draw on the efficacy of citizen reasoning about contested political issues (n = 1,056).

CONTESTABILITY AND THE DYNAMICS OF ISSUE FRAMING:
A THEORETICAL PERSPECTIVE

To understand how citizens make political choices about matters on the public agenda, we shall argue that it is necessary to take account of the distinctive feature of politics as the domain of choice.

Politics in a democratic society is distinctively the domain in which choices are contestable legitimately. Some of the reasons that political choices are contestable are common to choices generally.[26] There are, for example, limits on information at hand and hence disagreement over the considerations to take into account; or even where there is agreement over the considerations to take into account, there may be disagreement over the weight to attach to them; or even where there is agreement on the principles and standards to be applied, disagreement may follow from their inherent vagueness; or even where there is agreement on the interpretation of standards, there may be disagreements over assessment and interpretation of the "facts of the matter" because of differences in people's life experiences and circumstances. But, above and beyond all of these sources of disagreement, in democratic politics political preferences are contestable because choices necessarily must be made between competing values. Previous work has traced out the implications of the inherent contestability of political choices for (i) systematic cleavages between political elites (as opposed to between elites and mass publics) for issues of civil liberties and civil rights (Sniderman et al. 1996); (ii) openings for new coalitions in the contemporary politics of race (Sniderman and Carmines 1997); (iii) the ecology of issue argumentation (Sniderman and Gould 1997; Sniderman, Crosby, and Howell 2000); and (iv) the institutional organization of choice spaces (Sniderman 1999; Jackman and Sniderman 1999). Here we wish to take another step and consider the link between the logic of issue framing and the dynamics of political argument.

Again our starting point is value conflict. The substance of political problems, by their very nature, requires choices be made between competing values—between, to cite an off-the-rack example, strengthening order and broadening the area of individual freedom. To have more of one means to have less of the other. But it also is the nature of politics that choices between colliding values are not made merely at the individual level. Given the logic of electoral competition and the substance of political problems, political parties and the candidates who run under their banner tend to commit themselves to one or the other of opposing values (Jackman and Sniderman 2002).

Just so far as political parties distinguish themselves by publicly pledging themselves to opposing values, three implications follow from the logic of electoral competition. First, political parties and candidates are not free to frame issues however they would wish. The party that puts itself forward as the guardian of order is constrained to make use of electoral appeals that are consistent with its commitment to order; the party that puts itself forward as the advocate of civil liberties is similarly constrained by its commitment to civil rights. It follows that frames, alternative ways of defining the meaning of issues, are not exogenous to political competition; they are endogenous to it. Second, just so far as it is in the interest of political parties to frame issues in a way that will appeal to established points of view with a wide following, citizens will tend to have preferences about the right way that an issue should be framed for exactly the same reasons that they tend to have preferences about how issues should be dealt with. Third, just so far as political parties contest an issue, citizens are exposed to alternative ways of defining its meaning and therefore have, thanks to electoral competition, a choice as to how they may think about it.

All three are necessary premises of a properly political theory of public opinion, but it is the second and third that bear most directly on the study of framing effects. In the first instance, any particular frame is not equally persuasive to all citizens. Some will find the particular metaphors and moral appeals invoked more compelling, others less, depending on their point of view. A person who attaches a higher priority to equality than to individual achievement will find the framing of affirmative action as "leveling the playing field" more compelling than one who has the reverse set of priorities. And in the second instance, citizens are not exposed to just one set of "metaphors, catchphrases, visual images, moral appeals, and other symbolic devices," suggesting how to think about the issue at hand and how to justify what should be done about it. Just so far as there is political competition over the issue, there will be public competition over which frame is most appropriate. But framing studies, to our knowledge without exception, have neglected the fact that frames are themselves contestable. They have instead restricted attention to situations in which citizens are artificially sequestered, restricted to hearing only one way of thinking about a political issue. But if our argument is correct, it is essential to consider how citizens will react when they are exposed, as in real politics they characteristically are, to opposing ways to think about an issue. What our findings will show is that when the logical limitation of the standard design of framing experiments is corrected, rather than citizens' being easily blown off course by political debate, the clash of political argument increases the chances that they will anchor their specific choices in underlying principles.

The "Government Spending" Experiment

Our concern is whether, and under what conditions, citizens can make principled judgments as to what government should and shouldn't do in the face of efforts to constrain their choices by framing issues in dispute. But which issues should we examine?

In the study of framing effects, the selection of issues has been higgledy-piggledy, without consideration ex ante of the principles properly governing the choice of issues to examine. There have, for example, been studies of attitudes toward the Contras in Nicaragua (Zaller 1992) and attitudes toward affirmative action (Kinder and Sanders 1990), but manifestly the former is an example of a political issue that is uncommonly obscure, and hence raises the suspicion that framing effects are too easy to demonstrate, while the latter obviously is an example of an issue that is exceptionally charged, and hence raises the opposing suspicion that framing effects may be too hard to demonstrate.[27] We shall instead concentrate on issues with three characteristics. They are (1) of major importance; (2) longstanding; and (3) competitively contested.

A paradigmatic example is government activism on behalf of those who are badly off. This is an issue contested in all contemporary democracies, and candidates and parties competing for public office attempt to frame it to their advantage. The terrain is well explored. The opposing sides have worked through the inventory of formulations of the issue, learning through trial and error the appeals and organizing ideas that best work to their advantage. On one side there is the appeal to opportunity and compassion, the idea that what is at stake is taking advantage of the government to see that those who are badly off get opportunities to become better off. On the other side there is the appeal to the costs that social welfare policies impose and the idea that what is at stake is that those who have worked hard and made their own way will be worse off so that those who have not should be better off.

ALTERNATIVE FRAMES: THE STANDARD DESIGN

The design of the "government spending" experiment is more complex than we initially are going to suggest, but we wish to begin with two of its core conditions, which match exactly the standard design of framing experiments. In one of the two, a randomly selected set of respondents were asked:

> Are you in favor of or opposed to a big increase in government spending to increase opportunities for poor people *so they can have a better chance of getting ahead in life?*

We shall call this the "getting ahead" frame. In the other, a randomly selected set of respondents were asked:

> Are you in favor of or opposed to a big increase in government spending to increase opportunities for poor people, *even if it means higher taxes?*

We shall call this the "higher taxes" frame.

Notice that in both conditions the issue is the same: whether government spending should be increased to increase opportunities for the poor. All that is varied is the symbolic appeal in terms of which the issue is framed. In addition, we measured respondents' commitment to a relevant principle that they would bring to bear if, in making a decision about governmental efforts on behalf of the poor, they were to make a judgment on the basis of principle. And if citizens were to choose their position on the issue of government spending on behalf of the poor on the basis of principle, what would serve as a point of anchorage? Equality surely is a relevant principle. The more importance that people attach to those who are badly off becoming better off, the more likely they should be to support increased government spending to increase opportunities for the poor. But how can one tell how much importance people attach to the value of equality, since nearly all principles or values, very much including equality, are of importance to most people?

It is better, we suggest, to assess how they feel about a value not in isolation from other values, but in direct competition with them. Specifically, the way to tell whether people truly hold to a value like equality is to see whether, if they are forced to make a choice between it and a rival value, they choose it. Accordingly, we said to respondents:

> Now here are some values that everyone agrees are important. But sometimes we have to choose one value over another. If you absolutely had to choose between each of the following two values, which is more important.

Then, as one of the set of competing values, we asked:

How about narrowing the gap between the rich and the poor OR increasing economic growth.

If policy choices about government activism on behalf of the poor are grounded in underlying political principles, then those who choose the value of narrowing the gap between the rich and poor should be more likely to support activist government on behalf of the poor; those who instead choose the value of economic growth should be more likely to oppose it.

Table 5.1 summarizes the choices respondents make as to whether government should increase opportunities for the poor under the pressure of the standard "alternative framing" design. Since the purpose of these experiments is to determine whether, if the organizing idea attached to an issue is systematically varied, the positions that citizens tend to take will correspondingly vary, in one condition the issue is "framed" in a way to increase support in favor of a course of government action; in the other, to reduce it. The first column of Table 5.1 accordingly reports the levels of support for government action on behalf of the poor. For simplicity, opposition to government action is scored 0, support for it 1. Since the choice is dichotomous, the mean equals the proportion.

The impact of framing, Table 5.1 suggests, is dramatic. Look at the responses of those who, if required to choose, judge that equality is more important than economic growth. When the issue of government action is framed in a way congruent with their general orientation, to call attention to increasing opportunity to get ahead, an overwhelming majority— 87 percent—support increased government spending to help the poor, just as they logically should given their preference for equality. However, when the very same matter of policy is framed in a way counter to their general orientation, to call attention to the consequence of higher taxes, the overwhelming majority in support of government action evaporates, and a majority—albeit a bare majority of 52 percent, oppose increased government spending to help the poor.

The story is the same for those whose general view is just the other way around—that is, those who, if required to choose, judge that economic growth is more important than equality. When the issue of government action is framed in a way congruent with their general orientation, to call attention to the consequence of higher taxes, a majority of them—58 percent—oppose the policy, just as they logically should given their preference for economic growth. However, when the policy is framed in a way counter to their general orientation, to call attention to increasing opportunities to get ahead, this majority melts away and the larger number of them—64 percent—support rather than oppose increased government

TABLE 5.1
Support for Government Spending on the Poor as a Function of "Standard
Alternative" Framing and Commitment to Equality or to Economic Growth

	"Higher Taxes" Frame	*"Getting Ahead" Frame*
Egalitarians (n = 191)	.48	.87[a]
Economic growth proponents (n = 343)	.42	.64[a]

[a] The difference between the two frames is statistically significant ($p < .05$).
Data from the Multi-Investigator II

spending for the poor. It appears that whoever controls how an issue is framed controls its outcome, with a majority voting thumbs up or down on greater government spending to assist the poor depending on whether the issue is framed in terms of enlarging opportunity or imposing higher taxes. In a word, a classic framing effect.

COMPETING FRAME

Our results thus reproduce the results of previous studies, and just because of this convergence, we are in a position to extend the analysis of framing beyond them. For the pivotal question is not the reality of "framing effects"—they have too often been confirmed—but their meaning. How should the apparent variability of opinion as a function of the framing of an issue be understood?

One way of searching for an answer is take the problem to be primarily a psychological one. On this approach, the step to take is to identify a psychological mechanism or property that makes intelligible the choice behavior of citizens. Historically, this is the path framing studies have taken, focusing on ambivalence in particular, accounting for the observed variability of choices by invoking a state of simultaneous commitment to opposing lines of public policy. What we are trying to understand, however, is political behavior, and without discounting the value of a psychological approach, we think a political one takes priority.

Consider, then, the problem of framing from a political perspective. In real politics opposing sides contest issues, and part of that contest is competing to frame issues, to define their meaning, to establish how they should be thought about. So one side insists that assuring equal treatment, for example, requires establishing a level playing field and therefore affirmatively assisting minorities, while the other side maintains that assuring equal treatment means, on the contrary, treating everybody the same. And both sides barrage the public, so far as they have the means to do so, to accept their way of framing the issue as the right way of framing it.

This process of argumentation, however, is just what is missing from framing studies. In the established design, respondents are presented with either one organizing idea or its rival, but they never confront both at the same time. Yet in real politics, just so far as issues are contested, voters cannot be sequestered and their attention cannot be restricted to one, and only one, view of how the issues in dispute should be thought about. On the contrary, just so far as competing sides contend to win public support for their position, citizens are exposed to opposing views—indeed, their attention often is caught by the clash of argument—and are in a position to evaluate the merits of alternative ways of framing an issue.

To capture what actually happens in politics, it is necessary to have an additional condition in framing experiments, in which opposing frames are presented together. The "government spending" experiment was accordingly designed to have not only the standard two conditions, in which either a frame designed to invoke a positive response or one designed to invoke a negative one is presented, but also a third condition, in which both positive and negative frames ("getting ahead" and "higher taxes") are presented.

The crucial question politically is how readily citizens can be deflected from their political principles by a counterargument when they encounter it not in isolation but in the course of political debate when the contentions of opposing sides are being voiced. Table 5.2 therefore contrasts the reactions of respondents in the "dual frame" condition and in the "counterframe" condition. In addition, because persuasability can be a function of political sophistication, Table 5.2 also presents responses in the counterframe and dual frame conditions as a function of levels of political knowledge.[28]

Two points stand out. First, and consistent with previous research, the better informed citizens are about politics, the more likely their choices are to be consistent with their underlying principles; this is true regardless of the experimental condition they find themselves in. For example, in the counterframe condition, among those judging equality to be more important than economic growth, support for increased government spending to assist the poor marches up from 37 percent among the least informed, to 54 percent among the middle, to 62 percent among the most informed; in the dual frame condition, among those judging economic growth to be more important than equality, opposition to increased government spending correspondingly and all together appropriately drops from 67 percent among the least informed, to 51 percent among the middle, to 39 percent among the most informed. Second, and notwithstanding the first result, the effect of hearing opposing sides of a political argument is to increase, not decrease, the likelihood that specific choices will be consistent with vot-

TABLE 5.2
Support for Government Spending on the Poor as a Function of Counter and
Dual Framing, Political Information, and Commitment to Equality or to
Economic Growth

	Egalitarian				
	Political Information				
	Low	Medium	High	Total	
Counterframe	.37[a]	.54	.62[a]	.48	(n = 94)
Dual frame	.66[a]	.71	.85a	.72	(n = 80)
	Economic Growth Proponents				
	Political Information				
	Low	Medium	High	Total	
Counterframe	.86[a]	.60	.49[a]	.64	(n = 174)
Dual frame	.67[a]	.51	.39[a]	.54	(n = 173)

[a] The difference between the low political information respondents and the high political information respondents is statistically significant (p < .05).

Data from the Multi-Investigator II

ers' underlying principles. This is especially so for those who favor equality: in the counterframe condition, they divide approximately fifty-fifty over increased government spending for the poor; by contrast, in the dual frame condition, they support it by approximately three in every four. In short, being exposed to opposing sides of an argument increases consistency among decisions taken on specific policies and underlying principles.

Consistency comes in many forms, and it is important here to distinguish between absolute and relative conceptions. Relatively, even the least informed are more consistent in the dual frame condition than in the contrary frame; absolutely, the position of those who favor economic growth is indistinguishable from that of those who favor equality. Indeed, an absolute majority of those whose general orientation is conservative, favoring economic growth over narrowing the gap between rich and poor, favor a liberal position on the issue of government spending for the poor. It would be a mistake, however, to make too much of absolute levels of consistency in policy positions. Measurement is at the ordinal level; and in any case the magnitude of effects observed is tied to the specific manipulations. Certainly, it has proven costly politically for liberals to underestimate the strength of arguments on the conservative side of the issue of government spending.

And there is a potentially far-reaching implication to draw from the results in Table 5.2. The lesson regularly drawn from the framing studies is that whoever controls the framing of an issue controls the political outcome. Frame a policy so as to favor a positive response and a majority of the public is likely to favor it; frame it so as to favor a negative response and a majority is likely to oppose it. The results in Table 5.2 suggest a different lesson. When citizens are exposed to a complete rather than an edited version of political debate, they do not succumb to ambivalence or fall into confusion. On the contrary, even though as part of the process of debate they are exposed to an argument at odds with their general orientation, they tend "to go home," to pick out the side of the issue that fits their deeper-lying political principles. This suggests that political argument, when it takes its full form rather than the stilted one of standard framing experiments, may facilitate rather than distort consistency in political reasoning, and it may facilitate political reasoning, the "government spending" experiment suggests, whether citizens are well-informed or not about politics.

CONGRUENT ARGUMENTS AND THE ABSENCE OF ARGUMENTS

In order to draw up a complete balance sheet, identifying the costs as well as the benefits when opposing sides directly clash, it is necessary to explore more fully the logical space of possibilities. To this point we have contrasted the impact of counterarguments presented in isolation and accompanied by a congruent argument. But what characterizes the daily lives of many citizens is the absence of challenges to their political beliefs and practices. Similarity of belief, according to classical studies of social life (e.g., Berelson 1964), marks a number of domains of belief, very much including politics. To borrow American examples, a Republican husband is more likely to have a Republican spouse, a Democratic wife to have a Democratic spouse, and both couples to have politically consonant friends than the other way around.

A tendency to like-mindedness in politics is only a tendency. Most people are exposed, in some aspect of their social lives, to some differences of view, if not in their homes then at their jobs. In any case all are at risk of having their established opinions challenged by dissonant opinions just so far as they are exposed to the mass media. Still, so far as the streams of opinion to which people are exposed in their everyday encounters are biased, the bias is in favor of their own outlook. It follows that to gauge the costs and benefits of political argument, it is necessary to estimate the likelihood that citizens can make issue choices consistent with their general orientation when they find themselves exposed only to arguments congruent with it.

If exposure to a congruent argument makes a difference, it is perfectly obvious that the difference it makes is to increase the consistency of issue choices. It is, however, very far from obvious how much of an advantage people gain from a homogenous political environment, or differently put, how much of a disadvantage they suffer from being exposed to genuine political argument, where opposing sides of an issue get a hearing. And we should be left with quite different impressions of the costs of political argument depending on whether the difference between the two circumstances is large or small.

Encountering only arguments you already agree with is one benchmark to gauge the impact of hearing opposing sides being voiced in political debate. And we should like to suggest another. If we are to gauge the impact of political argument on the capacity of citizens to make issue choices consistent with their political principles, it is necessary to consider the consistency of their issue choices when there is no effort to frame an issue. If they are no less capable of picking out the side of the issue that matches their political principles when they are exposed to a full debate, which necessarily involves their being exposed to arguments at odds with their general views, than if they are not exposed to any arguments whatever, they would show themselves to be capable of holding their course even in the crosswinds of political argument.

The "government spending" experiment was designed to encompass the full quartet of possibilities—positive argument, negative argument, both positive and negative arguments—and, what is relevant here, a default condition where neither positive nor negative arguments are presented. Table 5.3 accordingly summarizes responses to the issue of government spending as a function of whether respondents get to hear both sides of an argument, only the side that fits their general view of the matter, or no argument whatever, pro or con.

How much of an advantage is it to hear only arguments you already agree with as opposed to being exposed to opposing sides of a policy debate? Table 5.3 shows there plainly is an advantage judged by belief system

TABLE 5.3
Support for Government Spending on the Poor as a Function of Alternative Framing Forms and Commitment to Equality or to Economic Growth

	Congruent Frame	Dual Frame	Default
Egalitarians (n = 264)	.87[a]	.72	.83[a]
Economic growth proponents (n = 501)	.42[a]	.54	.62[b]

[a] The difference from the dual frame is significant (p < .05).
[b] The difference from the dual frame is insignificant (p > .05).
Data from the Multi-Investigator II

constraint.[29] Hearing only their side of the issue, those who favor equality over economic growth are more likely to support increased government spending for the poor; equivalently, hearing only *their* side of the issue, those who favor economic growth over equality are more likely to oppose increased government spending. But of course it cannot be a surprise that citizens are more consistent in the choices they make if they are not exposed to dissonant information. What is a surprise—certainly it was to us— is the comparative modesty of the difference between the congruent and the dual frame conditions: for those who favor equality, it is .15; for those who favor economic growth, .12—a statistically significant effect, but not a politically transforming one. And if it is suggested that a ceiling effect may constrain the difference between the two conditions for those who favor equality, it is clear that no comparable floor effect is constraining the magnitude of change for those who favor economic growth.

Meshing issue choices with underlying principles is only one aspect of political competence, and a democratic polity where citizens never find their established ideas challenged would undercut the openness of argument and exchange of views that a democratic politics demands. But if the objective is to gauge how far citizens are deflected off course politically by the presentation of opposing points of view, the standard that gives the largest estimates of the costs of debate are the choices citizens would make if exposed only to a congruent argument. Yet even measured against that standard, although a price is paid for political debate, the "government spending" experiment shows that it is very far from disabling. And how do the costs and benefits of political debate appear when assessed against the absence of argumentation altogether? Just so far as the process of debate necessarily entails the airing of opposing views, it has the potential to deflect ordinary citizens. It seemed to us, accordingly, that consistency of underlying principles and issue choices should be higher in the default condition than in the dual frame condition.

As Table 5.3 shows, the differences in consistency levels are neither large in size nor themselves consistent in direction. Those who favor equality do appear to be more consistent in the default condition. However, just the opposite is the case for those who favor economic growth: they are more, not less, likely to pick the side of the issue of government spending congruent with their general orientation when opposing frames are presented than when neither the positive nor the negative frame is presented.

These apparently inconsistent results suggest, we believe, an interesting conclusion. In designing the "government spending" experiment, we conceived of the default condition, where neither frame is presented, as involving an absence of argumentation altogether. But this patently is not the case. As the means in the default condition testify, the policy so characterized elicits support of the overwhelming number of those who favor equality and, still more tellingly, the support of the largest number of those who favor economic growth. A frame can be a sufficient condition to define the meaning of an issue. But it is not a necessary one. Issues can be meaningful even in the absence of a "frame." To put the issue of government spending before respondents, as it is formulated, as an effort "to increase opportunities for poor people," is to put an argument to them.

The "government spending" experiment thus suggests a number of lessons, above all, that citizens not only can stand up and hold to their values in the face of political argument but that the voicing of opposing arguments may even assist them in translating their political attitudes into positions on specific issues. This is a lesson which, if true, is worth learning. But only a limited amount of weight can be put on the results of one experiment. Replication is the strongest test of the reliability of a result.

THE "RALLY" EXPERIMENT

Given the importance we attach to testing ideas using observations independent of the ones that suggested them, we committed ourselves in advance to designing and carrying out a parallel experiment to test the results of the first experiment. Accordingly a replication experiment was deliberately built in to the Multi-Investigator study.

The second experiment explores citizens' judgments about freedom of expression. Specifically, the purpose of the "rally" experiment is to see how citizens respond to the competing claims of maintaining order and safety on the one side and of supporting free speech on the other. Accordingly, in one condition, a randomly selected set of respondents were told:

> This question is about a group that has very extreme political views. Suppose they wanted to hold a public rally to express their ideas. *Given the importance of free speech* would you be in favor of or opposed to allowing this group to hold the rally?

We shall call this the "free speech" condition.

In another experimental condition, a randomly selected set of respondents were told:

> This question is about a group that has very extreme political views. Suppose they wanted to hold a public rally to express their ideas. *Given the risk of violence* would you be in favor of or opposed to allowing this group to hold the rally?

We shall call this the "violent risk" condition. Since the issue deals with the collision between promoting freedom of expression and avoiding violence, to assess respondents' general orientation we presented them with a choice between, on the one side, "guaranteeing law and order in society," and,

TABLE 5.4

Support for Public Rally of an Extreme Group as a Function of "Standard Alternative" Framing and Commitment to Individual Freedom or to Law and Order

	"Violent Risk" Frame	"Free Speech" Frame
Individual freedom adherents (n = 210)	.53	.89[a]
Law and order adherents (n = 317)	.37	.81[a]

[a] The difference between the two frames is statistically significant (p < .05).
Data from the Multi-Investigator II

on the other, "guaranteeing individual freedom." If policy choices about permitting public rallies are grounded in deeper political values, then those who are in favor of guaranteeing individual freedom should be more likely to allow a group with extreme political views to hold a public rally, while those who are in favor of guaranteeing law and order in society should be more likely to oppose it.

Again we begin with the standard design of framing experiments, in which randomly selected sets of respondents are presented with an issue deliberately framed in a way either to increase support for a possible course of action or, alternatively, to reduce it. The first column of Table 5.4 accordingly reports the levels of support for a group with extreme views being allowed to hold a public rally treated as a dichotomous choice and scored 0 or 1—the "violent risk" condition is in the first column; the second column shows the level of support in the "free speech" condition similarly scaled.

Finally, since we are interested in the extent to which citizens draw on their general orientations or political values in making specific choices, the table reports the extent to which a willingness to approve a public rally is conditional on whether respondents attach greater importance to the value of individual freedom or to guaranteeing law and order in society.

The analysis here deliberately parallels the standard design of framing studies, contrasting reactions when the issue in dispute is presented as framed in a way either to evoke support or, alternatively, to provoke opposition. And as Table 5.4 shows, the results of the "rally" experiment match the standard results of framing experiments. When the issue of allowing a rally is framed in terms of the importance of free speech, an overwhelming majority—four out of every five—is in favor. What is more, a decisive majority is in favor whether they attach greater importance to guaranteeing law and order in society or guaranteeing individual freedom, though the majority is slightly larger among the latter than the former. By contrast, when the issue of permitting a rally for a group with very extreme views is framed in terms of "the risk of violence," the balance of opinion changes: among those who attach a greater priority to guaranteeing law and order, 63 percent are opposed to allowing the rally, while among those who attach a greater priority to individual freedom, support drops from nearly 90 percent to no better than approximately fifty-fifty.

It again appears that you can get large numbers of ordinary citizens to swing around from one side of an issue to the opposite notwithstanding the principled positions they ostensibly have staked depending on how it is framed. But we have argued that this impression that issue preferences are characteristically pliable is artifactual, a function of examining how citizens make choices when they are artificially sequestered and their attention restricted to only one side of a public issue. In the real world of politics, those who are competing for public support strive to frame issues to their advantage. And just so far as there is competition over how issues should be framed, ordinary citizens tend to be exposed to competing frames.

In the "government spending" experiment we saw that when citizens are simultaneously exposed to competing frames (rather than being artificially confined to only one), they are far more likely to make issue choices that are consistent with their underlying principles. This result, if reliable, impeaches the apparent implication of framing studies that the balance of opinion can be tipped in one or another direction depending on how an issue is framed. But how reliable is it? The "rally" experiment, which is focused on a different issue domain and employs altogether different measures, provides an independent opportunity to assess the robustness of this result.

Table 5.5 contrasts the choices that citizens make if the issue is framed in a way that is at odds with their basic political orientation—the counterframe condition—or if they simultaneously are exposed to competing ways of framing the issue—the dual frame condition. As before, in assessing the extent to which they draw on their basic values in making decisions about specific issues, we take account of both their general orientation toward the claims of order versus freedom and their level of political information.

Consider first the responses of those who, as a general matter, prefer freedom to order. They are markedly more likely to take the side of the issue consistent with their general political orientation when they hear both sides of the argument: the proportion choosing consistently goes from 53 percent in the counterframe condition to 75 percent in the dual frame condition. Nor is the gain from being able to hear opposing sides confined to, or even concentrated among, the most politically aware and sophisticated. On the contrary, in this instance political argument most facilitates the reasoning of the least well-informed.[30] Thus, only 30 percent of the least well-informed who profess to value freedom over order support the right of a group with extreme views to hold a public rally if they hear only the opposite side of the argument (the counterframe condition). By contrast, if they hear both sides (the dual frame condition), 84 percent support it.

TABLE 5.5
Support for Public Rally of an Extreme Group as a Function of Counter- and
Dual Framing, Political Information, and Commitment to Individual Freedom or
to Law and Order

	Individual Freedom Adherents				
	Political Information				
	Low	Medium	High	Total	
Counterframe	.30[a]	.51	.82[a]	.53	(n = 98)
Dual frame	.84[b]	.66	.76[b]	.75	(n = 78)
	Law and Order Adherents				
	Political Information				
	Low	Medium	High	Total	
Counterframe	.88[a]	.79	.76[a]	.81	(n = 162)
Dual frame	.42[b]	.44	.56[b]	.46	(n = 163)

[a] The difference between the low political information respondents and the high political information respondents is statistically significant (p < .05).

[b] The difference between the low political information respondents and the high political information respondents is statistically insignificant (p > .05).

Data from the Multi-Investigator II

The pattern, moreover, is the same for those who attach a greater importance to law and order. Among the least well-informed, when they have a chance to hear only the opposite side of the argument (the counterframe condition), the overwhelming majority—88 percent—supports the right of a group with extreme views to hold a public rally. By contrast, when they can hear both sides (the dual frame condition), a clear majority—58 percent—opposes it. The same pattern holds, as inspection of Table 5.5 shows, for all levels of political information.

The results of the "rally" experiment thus replicate those of the "government spending" experiment on the crucial point at issue. Both show that when citizens can hear the clash of political argument the positions they take on specific issues are markedly more likely to be grounded in their underlying principles. Moreover, the results of the "rally" experiment also replicate those of the "government spending" experiment on both of the other standards of comparison. As Table 5.6 shows, although respondents are more likely to make a consistent issue choice in the congruent frame condition, the choices that they make differ only modestly (and, indeed, in the case of those who favor law and order do not differ significantly) from those that they make in the dual frame condition. In a word, hearing the other side of an argument does extract a price, but it is a small one.

TABLE 5.6
Support for Public Rally of an Extreme Group as a Function of Alternative
Framing Forms and Commitment to Individual Freedom or to Law and Order

	Congruent Frame	Dual Frame	Default
Individual freedom adherents (n = 273)	.89[a]	.75	.83[b]
Law and order adherents (n = 482)	.37[b]	.46	.70[a]

[a] The difference from the Dual Frame is significant (p < .05).
[b] The difference from the Dual Frame is insignificant (p > .05).
Data from the Multi-Investigator II

There is a final comparison, one that focuses on the consistency of issue
choices when arguments are presented on opposing sides and when no arguments are expressly presented (the "default" condition). As Table 5.6
shows, there is a gain in consistency for those who favor freedom in the
default condition, although it is not statistically significant no doubt because of ceiling effects. By contrast, those who favor order are markedly
more likely to be consistent in the default condition. These results match
almost exactly those from the "government spending" experiment, and as
inspection of the means in the default condition will make plain, for the
same reason. The issue of freedom of speech, like that of helping the poor,
can be meaningful even in the absence of a "frame." To put the issue before citizens, formulated in terms of freedom of assembly, is to put an argument to them.

The results of the two experiments, then, are mutually supportive. But
in determining the broader conclusions that should be drawn from their
specific findings, and the measure of confidence that should be attached to
them, a number of factors deserve consideration.

QUALIFICATIONS

Five points of qualification deserve special emphasis.

First, the coverage of issues is limited. We have examined only a pair of
specific issues. The findings could well differ for other issues, especially if
they are so remote from people's ordinary focus of attention that they
have not worked through their connections with their deeper values and
political principles or, alternatively, if they are so immediate and emotion-
ally charged that people can call upon their own the range of arguments
both pro and con. On the other hand, the issues that we have examined—
government activism on behalf of the disadvantaged and freedom of expression—are two of the principal battlegrounds of contemporary politics
and between them illustrate different strands of political contention.

Second, the analysis and argument have proceeded in qualitative and exploratory terms. The findings show that citizens, if exposed to opposing sides of a political argument rather than being artificially sequestered and restricted to hearing only one, tend to make specific choices that are more in line with their underlying principles. But how large, even approximately, is this gain in consistency? Under what conditions is it maximized, under what conditions minimized? What, exactly, is the role of political awareness and sophistication? Are the gains in consistency of choice equivalent at any given level of political information or, as our own intuition suggests, larger the less attentive a person ordinarily is and the more well-stocked and well-organized his or her ideas about it are as a consequence? Are there differences in the matching of principles and issues choices, particularly among the politically aware, as a function of the specific structure of political choices, and, more specifically, is there something to recommend a distinction between issues like government spending, in which the opposing alternatives are equally legitimate, and in the politically most sophisticated stratum issues like permitting freedom of expression, in which one alternative dominates the other? To get a grip on these and a host of other questions, it will be necessary to move from an impressionistic and qualitative approach to a systematic and quantitative mode.

Third, our findings will apply just so far as there are incentives and opportunities for opposing points of view to obtain public expression. This limits their application, most obviously, to democratic polities that are genuinely competitive. Less obviously, but just as importantly, our results have only a limited applicability even within genuinely competitive political systems. Political parties and the candidates who campaign under their banner do not compete on all issues. The party holding an electorally unpopular position frequently will assimilate its position to that of its competitors, minimizing and blurring its distinctiveness, leaving voters not with a choice but an echo (Petrocik 1996). Indeed, as E. E. Schattschneider (1975) and William Riker (1986) recognized, one of the most important consequences of the logic of electoral competition is to ensure that some issues, so far from being contested, are taken off the public agenda.

Fourth, our argument rests on an implicit premise that needs to be excavated and made explicit. The standard studies of framing have erred, we have argued, by contrasting citizens' reactions only when they hear either one side of a political argument or the other. The vital contrast, we have contended, is when they hear both because in real politics that is precisely what competing candidates and parties are bent on doing—making sure that voters are exposed to their side of the issues. It is, however, important to emphasize the difference between the state of affairs in real politics, in which political contestants broadcast and otherwise disseminate messages summarizing their views, which is an integral element in political competition in properly democratic polities, and the state of affairs in our studies, in which experiments are carried out in a way to assure that respondents receive these messages. Exposure to a message is one thing; reception, another. This difference between exposure and reception applies with special force the less well-informed or attentive citizens are to politics. It follows that in the world as it really is (as opposed to the way it is represented in the experiments of our study), political debate may not have so corrective an effect on the political reasoning of ordinary citizens, particularly if they are politically disengaged or politically ill-informed. On the other side, on exactly the same reasoning, the politically least well-informed are the least likely to take in arguments at odds with their general political orientation, so far as they have formed them, and thus should be the least likely to be deflected by them.[31]

Fifth, our interest is in the conditions under which citizens can exercise political judgment. We have taken as our standard of political judgment the extent to which their specific choices conform to their avowed principles. This is, we think, a necessary condition of citizenship: if citizens are easily blown off course by the crosswinds of political debate, it is hard to understand the sense in which they can be said to be capable of exercising political judgment. On the other hand, even if being able to bring to bear one's principles is a necessary condition of being able to exercise political judgment, it is not a sufficient one. For it also is necessary that citizens be able to make their decisions in the light of distinctive features of specific alternatives they are asked to weigh. How well, if at all, ordinary citizens are capable of taking account of individuating characteristics of political choices—and in particular under what conditions, if any, they are capable of tempering their convictions in response to the (occasionally) unique features of ordinarily well-rubbed choices—is not a question that we have examined.

CONCLUSION

Our findings point to two broad lessons, one methodological, the other substantive.

We begin with the methodological moral. Framing theorists, as part of their very own argument, called attention to the competitive character of political argumentation. Indeed, the whole launching point for the framing argument, as we observed, is the express claim that politics characteristically involves "an environment that carries roughly evenly balanced communications on both sides of issues."[32] But as we have seen, their theoretical argument and their methodological design collide. All studies of framing carried out to this point have conformed to the so-called split-ballot design in which there are, by standard, only two experimental

conditions. It was natural, therefore, for framing experiments just to contrast reactions when respondents are presented with one side of an argument
with their reactions when presented with an opposing side. But overlooking the politically crucial circumstance when they are exposed to both
sides leads, as we have shown, to a hugely inflated impression of the plia-
bility of the ordinary citizen's judgment. The moral to draw is unequivocal. Methodological designs should follow from the theoretical question
being treated rather than the treatment of the theoretical question following from the methodological design.

The substantive issue goes deeper. According to the framing theory of
public opinion, citizens are not capable of political judgment: the very
same person will approve a course of government action or oppose it depending on how the issue happens to be framed at the moment of choice.[33]
Citizens, a limited number of suitable exceptions to one side, are not able
to judge the alternatives open for consideration in the light of relevant
principles. They are instead puppets, voting thumbs up or down depending
on how issues are framed, their strings being pulled by elites who frame issues to guarantee political outcomes. The result is to call democracy itself
into question. As Entman has noted, "[I]f by shaping frames elites can determine the major manifestations of 'true' public opinion that are available
to government (via polls or voting), what can true public opinion be? How
can even sincere democratic representatives respond correctly to public
opinion when empirical evidence of it appears to be so malleable, so vulnerable to framing effects."[34]

We want to emphasize that, using the same design as framing studies, our
findings are the same as theirs. If the issue of government spending for the
poor is framed in terms of increasing opportunities for the poor, a majority
favors it; if it is framed in terms of increasing taxes, a majority opposes it.
Identically, if the question of allowing a group with extreme views to hold
a public rally is cast in terms of freedom of expression, a majority favors it; if
it is cast in terms of the risk of violence, a majority opposes it. Not everyone
switches sides. But in both experiments citizens look like puppets forming
majorities on either side of the issues depending on how they are framed.

These results notwithstanding, this whole body of studies on framing
has gone terribly wrong by overlooking politics itself. In a properly democratic polity opposing camps campaign on behalf of competing ways of
understanding what is at issue. And our findings demonstrate that political debate, being exposed to opposing sides, tightens the linkages of mass
belief systems and increases the constraint between basic principles and
specific issue choices. The deeper lesson of our findings is thus that the
clash of political arguments, so far from overwhelming or perplexing or
blinding the political judgments of ordinary citizens, may be a condition
of the possibility of their exercising it.

NOTES

This study is a component of the second Multi-Investigator Survey funded by the National Science Foundation (SBR-9818742). The research was also supported through an NSF Achievement-Based Award (SES-0111715). The fieldwork has been carried out by the Survey Research Center at the University of California, Berkeley. We wish to acknowledge, and to honor, the person primarily responsible for developing the instrument and directing all aspects of the fieldwork and preparation of the data, Ms. Karen Garrett. We also wish to thank Paul Beck for a sympathetically stringent critique.

1. See Berelson, Lazarsfeld, and McPhee 1954.
2. See, for example, Gamson and Modigliani 1989.
3. Gamson and Modigliani (1989:3), emphasis in original.
4. The distinction that Gamson and Modigliani (1989) draw between "framing devices" and "reasoning devices," strictly defined, like so many of their fine-grained distinctions, have been lost in the more coarsely woven framing analysis that has subsequently appeared.
5. Kinder and Sanders 1990; Nelson and Kinder 1996; Zaller 1992.
6. Gamson and Modigliani 1987:143.
7. Zaller 1992:82.
8. Nelson and Kinder 1996:1057. See also Entman 1993.
9. Nelson and Kinder 1996:1057.
10. Gamson and Modigliani 1989:3.
11. Obviously, the class of framing effects of the second kind, involving alterations in the balance of opinion on an issue, must logically include that of framing effects of the first kind, involving alteration of the reasons for taking a position on an issue.
12. Gamson and Modigliani (1987) advanced the ambivalence argument; see also Zaller and Feldman 1992.
13. Zaller 1992:93.
14. Nelson and Kinder 1996:1058.
15. Zaller and Feldman 1992:585.
16. Zaller 1992:93.
17. Ibid., 55.
18. Ibid., 54.
19. Zaller 1992:95.
20. Nelson and Kinder 1996:1058. See also Hochschild 1981; Chong 1993.
21. Lane 1962.
22. Zaller 1992:59.
23. Nelson and Kinder 1996:1058.
24. Gamson and Modigliani (e.g., 1989) point to, among other things, the inherent contestability of frames and the foundational role, even for obtrusive issues, of meaning-generating experiences in people's everyday lives.
25. Since the response rate is 56 percent we have carried out a multipoint comparison between the sample characteristics and the Current Population Survey, examining the joint distributions of gender, age, education, and race. The fit for whites is extremely close (e.g., the proportion of less-than-high-school-educated

white males in the sample between the ages of 18 and 29 in our weighted sample is 7.2, as compared to 9.7 in the CPS.

26. We follow here an inventory of Rawls 1993.

27. Giving strength to this suspicion, Kinder and Sanders (1990) observe that the balance of opinion on affirmative action was not affected by the alternative ways they choose to frame the issue.

28. The Multi-Investigator political information parallels the standard National Election Studies measure, gauging awareness of elementary facts about political institutions.

29. We recognize that Converse, introducing the term *constraint,* deployed it only to index consistency across issue positions. We use the term more broadly to refer to the tightening of belief system linkages.

30. The rally experiment focuses on support for a societally approved norm, freedom of speech, and there not surprisingly is a ceiling effect constraining the difference to be observed between the counter- and dual-frame conditions among the best informed.

31. Nor is it irrelevant that in their immediate circle of acquaintances, they are likely to be predominantly surrounded by people whose outlook broadly matches their own. See Mutz 1998.

32. Zaller 1992:59.

33. It surely is true that the balance of opinion in public referenda can shift, from a majority in support to a majority in opposition, depending on how the issue is defined. Referenda on affirmative action are a case in point. If the question is defined in terms of prohibiting discrimination on the basis of race, as it was for example in elections in California and in Washington, then a majority backs it. If it is defined in relatively neutral terms, then a majority backs this. It is worth underlining that the ballot is a setting precisely where citizens are not simultaneously exposed to opposing formulations.

34. Entman 1993:57.

Appendix

Question Wording for Table 5.1:

> *"Higher Taxes" Frame:* Are you in favor of or opposed to a big increase in government spending to increase opportunities for poor people, *even if it means higher taxes?*

> *"Getting Ahead" Frame:* Are you in favor of or opposed to a big increase in government spending to increase opportunities for poor people *so they can have a better chance of getting ahead in life?*

> *Commitment to Equality or Economic Growth:* How about narrowing the gap between the rich and the poor OR increasing economic growth? If

you had to choose between these two, which would you say is more important?

Question Wording for Table 5.2:

"Higher Taxes" Frame: Are you in favor of or opposed to a big increase in government spending to increase opportunities for poor people, *even if it means higher taxes?* [This is the counterframe for the egalitarians.]

"Getting Ahead" Frame: Are you in favor of or opposed to a big increase in government spending to increase opportunities for poor people *so they can have a better chance of getting ahead in life?* [This is the counterframe for the economic growth proponents.]

Dual Frame: Taking into account both the fact that programs for the poor could mean higher taxes and the need for poor people to have a better chance of getting ahead in life, are you in favor of or opposed to a big increase in government spending to increase opportunities for poor people? [Half of the time the frames were reversed.]

Commitment to Equality or Economic Growth: How about narrowing the gap between the rich and the poor OR increasing economic growth? If you had to choose between these two, which would you say is more important?

Question Wording for Table 5.3:

"Higher Taxes" Frame: Are you in favor of or opposed to a big increase in government spending to increase opportunities for poor people, *even if it means higher taxes?* [This is the congruent frame for the economic growth proponents.]

"Getting Ahead" Frame: Are you in favor of or opposed to a big increase in government spending to increase opportunities for poor people *so they can have a better chance of getting ahead in life?* [This is the congruent frame for the egalitarians.]

Dual Frame: Taking into account both the fact that programs for the poor could mean higher taxes and the need for poor people to have a better chance of getting ahead in life, are you in favor of or opposed to a big increase in government spending to increase opportunities for poor people? [Half of the time, the frames were reversed.]

Default: Are you in favor of or opposed to a big increase in government spending to increase opportunities for poor people?

Commitment to Equality or Economic Growth: How about narrowing the gap between the rich and the poor OR increasing economic growth? If you had to choose between these two, which would you say is more important?

Question Wording for Table 5.4:

This next question is about a group that has very extreme political views. Suppose they wanted to hold a public rally to express their ideas.

"Violent Risk" Frame: Given the risk of violence, would you be in favor of or opposed to allowing this group to hold the rally?

"Free Speech" Frame: Given the importance of free speech, would you be in favor of or opposed to allowing this group to hold the rally?

Commitment to Law and Order: How about guaranteeing law and order in society OR guaranteeing individual freedom? If you had to choose between these two, which would you say is more important?

Question Wording for Table 5.5:

This next question is about a group that has very extreme political views. Suppose they wanted to hold a public rally to express their ideas.

"Violent Risk" Frame: Given the risk of violence, would you be in favor of or opposed to allowing this group to hold the rally? [This is the counterframe for the individual freedom adherents.]

"Free Speech" Frame: Given the importance of free speech, would you be in favor of or opposed to allowing this group to hold the rally? [This is the counterframe for the law and order adherents.]

Dual Frame: Taking into account both the importance of free speech and the risk of violence, would you be in favor of or opposed to allowing this group to hold the rally? [Half of the time the frames were reversed.]

Commitment to Law and Order or Individual Freedom: How about guaranteeing law and order in society OR guaranteeing individual freedom? If you had to choose between these two, which would you say is more important?

Question Wording for Table 5.6:

This next question is about a group that has very extreme political views. Suppose they wanted to hold a public rally to express their ideas.

"Violent Risk" Frame: Given the risk of violence, would you be in favor of or opposed to allowing this group to hold the rally? [This is the congruent frame for the law and order adherents.]

"Free Speech" Frame: Given the importance of free speech, would you be in favor of or opposed to allowing this group to hold the rally? [This is the congruent frame for the individual freedom adherents.]

Dual Frame: Taking into account both the importance of free speech and the risk of violence, would you be in favor of or opposed to allowing this group to hold the rally? [Half of the time the frames were reversed.]

Default: Would you be in favor of or opposed to allowing this group to hold the rally?

Commitment to Law and Order or Individual Freedom: How about guaranteeing law and order in society OR guaranteeing individual freedom? If you had to choose between these two, which would you say is more important?

REFERENCES

Berelson, Bernard R. 1964. *Human Behavior: An Inventory of Scientific Findings.* New York: Harcourt, Brace, and World.
Berelson, Bernard R., Paul R. Lazarsfeld, and William N. McPhee. 1954. *Voting: A Study of Opinion Formation in a Presidential Campaign.* Chicago: University of Chicago Press.
Chong, Dennis. 1993. "How People Think, Reason, and Feel about Rights and Liberties." *American Journal of Political Science* 37:867–99.
Entman, Robert M. 1993. "Framing: Toward Clarification of a Fractured Paradigm." *Journal of Communication* 43:51–58.
Gamson, William, and Andre Modigliani. 1987. "The Changing Culture of Affirmative Action." *Research in Political Sociology* 3:137–77.
———. 1989. "Media Discourse and Public Opinion: A Constructionist Approach." *American Journal of Sociology* 95:1–37.

Hochschild, Jennifer. 1981. *What's Fair? American Beliefs about Distributive Justice.* Cambridge, MA: Harvard University Press.

———. 1983. "Disjunction and Ambivalence in Citizens' Political Outlooks." In *Reconsidering the Democratic Public,* ed. George E. Marcus and Russell L. Hanson. University Park: Pennsylvania State University Press.

Jackman, Simon, and Paul M. Sniderman. 2002. "The Institutional Organization of Choice Spaces: A Political Conception of Political Psychology." In *Political Psychology,* ed. Kruten Renwick Monroe. Mahwah, NJ: Lawrence Erlbaum.

Kahneman, Daniel, and Amos Tversky. 1984. "Choices, Values, and Frames." *American Psychologist* 39:341–50.

Kinder, Donald R., and Lynn M. Sanders. 1990. "Mimicking Political Debate with Survey Questions: The Case of White Opinion on Affirmative Action for Blacks." *Social Cognition* 8:73–103.

Lane, Robert E. 1962. *Political Ideology: Why the American Common Man Believes What He Does.* New York: Free Press of Glencoe.

Lippmann, Walter. 1922. *Public Opinion.* New York: Harcourt Brace.

McClosky, Herbert, and Alida Brill. 1983. *Dimensions of Tolerance.* New York: Russell Sage.

Mutz, Diana C. 1998. *Impersonal Influence: How Perceptions of Mass Collectives Affect Political Attitudes.* New York: Cambridge University Press.

Nelson, Thomas E., and Donald R. Kinder. 1996. "Issue Frames and Group-Centrism in American Public Opinion." *Journal of Politics* 58:1055–78.

Petrocik, John E. 1996. "Issue Ownership in Presidential Elections." *American Journal of Political Science* 40:825–50.

Rawls, John. 1993. "The Domain of the Political and Overlapping Consensus." In *The Idea of Democracy,* ed. David Copp, Jean Hampton, and John E. Roemer. Cambridge: Cambridge University Press.

Riker, William H. 1986. *The Art of Political Manipulation.* New Haven: Yale University Press.

Schattschneider, E. E. 1975. *The Semisovereign People: A Realist's View of Democracy in America.* Fort Worth, TX: Harcourt Brace Jovanovich College Publishers.

Sniderman, Paul M. 2000. "Taking Sides: A Fixed Choice Theory of Political Reasoning." In *Elements of Reason: Cognition, Choice, and the Bounds of Rationality,* ed. Arthur Lupia, Mathew D. McCubbins, and Samuel L. Popkin. New York: Cambridge University Press.

Sniderman, Paul M., and Edward G. Carmines. 1997. *Reaching beyond Race.* Cambridge, MA: Harvard University Press.

Sniderman, Paul M., and Erica Gould. 1999. "Dynamics of Political Values: Education and Issues of Tolerance." In *Education and Racism: A Cross-National Inventory of the Positive Effects of Education on Ethnic Tolerance,* ed. Louk Hagendoorn and Shervin Nekuee. Aldershot: Ashgate.

Sniderman, Paul M., Getchen C. Crosby, and William G. Howell. 2000. "The Politics of Race." In *Racialized Politics: The Debate about Racism in America,* ed. David O. Sears, James Sidanius, and Lawrence Bobo. Chicago: University of Chicago Press.

Sniderman, Paul M., Joseph F. Fletcher, Peter H. Russell, and Philip E. Tetlock.

1996. *The Clash of Rights: Liberty, Equality and Legitimacy in Pluralist Democracies.* New Haven: Yale University Press.

Stouffer, Samuel. 1955. *Communism, Conformity, and Civil Liberties.* New York: Doubleday.

Zaller, John. R. 1992. *The Nature and Origins of Mass Opinion.* New York: Cambridge University Press.

Zaller, John, and Stanley Feldman. 1992. "A Simple Theory of the Survey Response: Answering Questions versus Revealing Preferences." *American Journal of Political Science* 36:579–616.

CHAPTER 6

Floating Voters in U.S. Presidential Elections, 1948–2000

John Zaller

POORLY INFORMED voters are more likely to shift back and forth during presidential campaigns. They are also less likely to cast votes that can be readily explained in terms of their political attitudes. These findings, along with side evidence of nonattitudes and "ideological innocence" among the less informed, feed the impression that they vote haphazardly. They tend to be, as early voting studies put it, "floaters" (Daudt 1961).

This chapter focuses on these low information voters in U.S. presidential elections from 1948 to 2000. Contrary to the general view, it finds that they are typically more responsive to the content of individual elections than their better informed counterparts. Low information voters are more apt to reward incumbents who preside over strong national economies and punish those who do not. Poorly informed voters are also more reactive to changes in the ideological location of the candidates. And finally, low information voters are at least as likely as other voters, and perhaps more so, to respond to presidential success or failure in foreign affairs.

These novel findings depend on a novel study design—one that infers the causes of voting from variation across elections rather than, as in most studies, correlations within elections. Thus, if one checks which voters change sides from one election to the next in response to bad economic times or the nomination of an extremist, low information voters appear most responsive to election content. But if one examines correlations within a single election, the better informed do a better overall job of matching their policy positions with the appropriate candidate.

This pattern of findings reflects well-known attitude differences within the two groups: less informed voters, who lack consistent policy-based ties to parties, are more responsive to election-specific forces, including the moderation of the candidates. High information voters, whose policy ties to parties are more consistent, vote on the basis of those ties, thereby resisting short-term forces. Emphasizing the kind of political responsiveness that predominates among high information voters, as past studies have done, sells low information voters short.

The paper has four sections. The first provides theoretical background. The second discusses measurement of key variables. The third presents empirical findings and tests their robustness. A conclusion explores the implications of the chapter's novel findings for theories of political behavior, for improvement of current methodology, and for the functioning of democracy.

THEORETICAL BACKGROUND

Political Information and Voting Behavior

From the Greek philosophers to the American Founders, theorists have worried that citizens lack the political sophistication necessary for self-government. Modern opinion research has reinforced this concern. Numerous studies have shown that voters often lack basic information about the political process and, further, that voters who are less informed, educated, or interested in politics are less able to connect their attitudes and interests to vote decisions.

One of the most important of these studies is that of Stimson (1975). Working with data from the 1972 election, he found that the party attachments and policy attitudes of voters having high "cognitive ability" explained 56 percent of the variance in their vote choices, compared to only 26 percent for voters having low cognitive ability. The choices of less sophisticated voters thus appeared notably less systematic and organized.

Researchers neither wanting nor expecting to find this pattern have nonetheless done so. Fiorina (1981) set out in *Retrospective Voting* to show that citizens who know little about issues and policy debates can at least look back over the previous four years and retrospectively judge whether the country did well or badly under the incumbent. But he ends up writing, "Previous studies have consistently found that high education, interest, and information accompany increased reliance on issues when people vote. I had expected that the lack of such civic virtues would predispose people toward a heavy reliance on retrospective evaluations. As shown, the data fall in between but with a noticeable lean toward the traditional findings" (54). In other words, less informed voters relied less on issues and yet also relied somewhat less on non-issue-based retrospective cues.

In 1990, John Ferejohn and James Kuklinski edited a volume called *Information and Democratic Processes*. Contributors accepted the existence of differences between the informed and uninformed, but mostly downplayed their importance. For example, Sniderman, Glaser, and Griffin found that better educated voters in the 1980 election based their decisions on a broad array of policy considerations and that less educated voters gave little weight to issues. However, they found that low education voters relied on their evaluations of the national economy and of the incumbent president. On the basis of these and other findings, Sniderman, Glaser, and Griffin asked: "Are [poorly informed voters] incapable of making a rational choice because of their lack of information? Not necessarily, if our analysis is correct. The poorly informed voters may lack the information to make the kind of choice the well-informed voter can, that is, a choice that turns on comparison of the candidates, for instance, with respect to policy commitments. All the same, the poorly informed voter . . . is in a position to judge if the incumbent's performance is satisfactory" (133).

In another study of presidential voting in that volume, Rahn et al. estimated a multistage model of the vote decision. The issue effects in the models of the less sophisticated voters generally matched those of the more sophisticated, from which the authors concluded: "We have found variations in political expertise to be of strikingly little importance."

Reviewing these and other studies in a 1993 essay, Sniderman observed that research had recently moved from documenting the limitations of less sophisticated citizens to showing how they "overcome informational shortfalls" and thereby "achieve a measure of coherence" (221). But Sniderman's evidence focused more on attitudes than voting behavior, and when Bartels (1996) investigated whether less informed presidential voters were able to overcome their lack of information, he found they were not: all else equal, voters who were poorly informed did not vote in presidential elections in the same way that their better informed counterparts did.

The most comprehensive study of information effects is probably *What Americans Know about Politics and Why It Matters* by Delli Carpini and Keeter (1996). As they write: "Poorly informed citizens are less likely to participate [in presidential elections], and when they do participate, they are less likely to tie their actions effectively to the issue stands and political orientations they profess to hold" (265). These authors found that low information voters did not even link their retrospective evaluations of the national economy to vote choice.

One methodological point: these studies use a variety of measures to capture voter information, some of which contain few or no actual tests of political information. The study that relies most exclusively on information—that of Delli Carpini and Keeter—finds the largest and most consequential effects of lack of information.[1] Research on topics other than voting also finds larger effects for political information than for such related measures as education and interest (Luskin 1987; Zaller 1990). It is therefore probable that some studies would have produced bigger information effects if measures of information had been used.

Taken as a whole, then, existing research indicates that less informed voters are less sensitive to the policy content of elections and perhaps less sensitive to economic factors as well. This chapter, which relies relatively heavily on information tests and examines a larger set of elections than any previous study of the subject, turns up findings that challenge this research.

Determinants of Presidential Voting

The first step in investigating the voting behavior of low information voters is to ask what factors generally affect the outcomes of presidential elections *and* can be reliably measured across elections from 1948 to 2000.

One obvious answer is the incumbent's management of the economy over the previous four years. Many studies have shown that economic voting occurs and measured it from government statistics that span our period. But what else? Of several possibilities, I focus on two for which the theoretical warrants are strong and measurement is, as I show below, feasible: the incumbent's handling of foreign policy and the ideological location of the candidates.

An incumbent administration's management of foreign policy is the natural complement of its management of the economy—the other major domain in which voters may wish to play the role of "rational god of vengeance and reward," as V. O. Key Jr. puts it. In this regard, Doug Hibbs (1987, 2000) has provided strong evidence that unsuccessful war affects presidential voting. There is also evidence that foreign policy actions short of war, such as President Jimmy Carter's handling of the Iran hostage crisis, can affect voting behavior (Iyengar and Kinder 1987; see more generally, Aldrich, Sullivan, and Borgida 1989).

Voters may not only look backward at how the incumbent administration has managed the country but forward at what the candidates promise to do if elected. In a cross-election study of this kind, these promises can be summarized in terms of a candidate's general ideological location. For at least five decades, theorists have known that, in a two-party system, the optimal location for candidates on political issues is at the center of the ideological spectrum (Downs 1957). But because party activists pressure candidates to take non-centrist positions (Aldrich 1995: chap. 6), candidates often stray from the middle of the road. When they do, they tend to be punished by voters (Rosenstone 1983; MacKuen et al. 2002; Canes-Wrone, Brady, and Cogan 2002; and Moon 2002).

I propose that this set of three variables captures a big fraction of what presidential elections are about—retrospective voting on the economy and on foreign policy, and responsiveness to the policy preferences of the median voter. But it clearly does not capture everything. It does not, in particular, capture the conservative, upper-class, and, more recently, fundamentalist orientation of the Republican Party, or the liberal, working-class, secular orientation of the Democratic Party. Voters who care most about these longstanding differences in the party agendas may be, for this reason, less responsive to the election-specific factors that are at the heart of this study.[2]

Measurement of Key Variables

This voting study requires measurement of a total of five variables, all of which present issues that require discussion.

Measuring the Vote: The Accuracy of CPS/NES Surveys

In this study, as in almost all other studies of the presidential vote over multiyear periods, I confine my analysis to vote shares for the two major parties, the Democrats and Republicans. Third-party votes, when they occur, are omitted on the grounds that the effects of information on third-party voting would require a major study in its own right.

Since the aim of this chapter is to examine the effect of information on voting, it must rely on survey measures of the vote rather than the official vote. The survey measures are from the presidential election studies that began in 1948 at the Center for Political Studies (CPS) at the University of Michigan and have continued there since 1980 as the National Election Studies (NES).

Like any data, the CPS/NES surveys are prey to both random and systematic error. The systematic error in the CPS/NES survey is an over-report for the winner that averages about 2 percent. This is not large as survey error goes, but given that the standard deviation (SD) of the incumbent vote is 5.8 percent, a 2 percent over-report is a large fraction of what the aggregate variables are trying to explain. This over-report could, moreover, lead to bias: suppose that economic performance causes the actual vote, and that actual vote causes over-report for the winner in surveys. Given this, an incumbent who won because the economy is strong will win by an even greater margin in the reported vote, thereby making the economy seem like it affects the vote more than it does.

To correct for over-report, I first calculate the fraction of individual voters who must have over-reported in order to produce the aggregate amount of over-report that exists. Then, working with the 0-1 individual-level data, I subtract that fraction from the value of each reported vote for the winner. Here is an example: suppose that in a sample of 100 voters, 60 percent report voting for the winner, but that the winner got only 50.01 percent of the actual vote. Given these numbers and ignoring sampling fluctuation, 10 of the 60 who claimed to have voted for the winner must have over-reported. I do not know which particular voters they are, so I assume that each of the winner's supporters has a one-sixth chance of having over-reported. I therefore count each of their votes for the winner as only 5/6 of a vote. Thus, instead of a vote variable with values of 0 and 1, I have a vote variable with values of 0 and .833. If I adjust each year's individual-level vote variable in this manner, the result is that the mean of the NES vote exactly matches the mean of the actual vote.

When I used the corrected vote variable in analyses of the effects of the economy and other aggregate determinants of the vote, I obtained coefficient estimates that were essentially identical to those obtained from using the actual vote. This was true whether I used the survey vote in the form of 14 aggregate means or individual-level regressions having some 16,000 cases.

Although producing a perfectly calibrated vote measure, this correction procedure has a shortcoming. It assumes that all kinds of voters—including voters who differ by political information—are equally likely to over-report. As we shall see, this assumption is empirically plausible. Still, in a study of information effects, I do not want the findings to be vulnerable to the suspicion that they may have been driven by differences in over-report.

I deal with this problem in two ways. First, I redo the over-report correction on the hypothesis that low information voters contribute disproportionately to over-report and show that the key findings of this chapter remain intact. Second, I undertake a parallel analysis of vote intention from pre-election surveys, showing that information effects are the same as for vote report.

A survey question about vote intention has been carried on the pre-election wave of all 14 of CPS/NES surveys and typically reads as follows:

Who do you think you will vote for in the election for president?

The concern with this question is that since CPS/NES samples are collected over a six- to eight-week period during the campaign, the question might fail to accurately capture vote intentions on Election Day. And, indeed, it does not. The vote intention variable overstates support for the winner by about the same amount as the reported vote.

One might suspect that over-report in the two measures derives from the same psychological impulse—to associate oneself with the winner. If this mechanism were at work, it would lead to more over-report as Election Day grew closer, since it would be increasingly clear who the winner would be. Yet what happens is the opposite: over-report for the eventual winner virtually disappears in the last fourteen days of the campaign. What, then, is the problem? It turns out that many presidential races tighten at the end. Thus, whatever the winning candidate's margin on Election Day, it was probably greater at an earlier point. Hence, vote intentions averaged over the entire campaign overstate the support that exists on Election Day. The overstatement is not a bias, but an accurate reflection of vote intentions at the time they were measured. But since overstatement remains a concern, I focus on vote intention at the end of the campaign.

Level of Political Information

I turn now to a brief discussion of the measurement of political information. The advantage of the CPS/NES election series, compared to other survey data, is that they typically carry items designed as tests of information. The main exception is the 1952 study, in which I had to build a scale that more nearly resembles a measure of involvement than information. But even the 1952 scale has some information items, and in other years the scales are mostly or entirely based on tests of political information.[3] In recoding the items and combining them into scales, I followed the general procedures described in Zaller 1992.[4] The SPSS code for constructing these scales in the various election studies and merging them is available on my Web page.[5]

Studies indicate that despite increases in education, Americans are about as politically informed today as in 1950 (Smith 1989; Delli Carpini and Keeter 1996). In light of this, I have constructed my information scales so as to produce a constant mean and variance across time.

Measuring Economic Performance

The difficulty in measuring economic performance is a true embarrassment of riches—more data and combinations of data than can be meaningfully evaluated on the basis of a mere fourteen elections. Among the primary data series made available by the U.S. government are inflation, unemployment, real disposable income (RDI) per capita, and gross domestic product (GDP). All of these measures, and more, have been tried, but RDI generally works best in the United States.

But even a decision to focus on RDI leaves an open question. RDI can be measured over varying time periods—the incumbent's whole term of office, the calendar year of the election, or just one or two quarters before the election (Lewis-Beck 1988). The question is one of time horizons—how far back do voters look when deciding whether the economy is good or bad?

The most elegant approach to the problem of time horizons is that of Hibbs (2000), who develops a model that uses economic data from each quarter of a president's term except the first. The Hibbs model explicitly estimates whether voters place an equal weight on all quarters, place more weight on more recent quarters, or perhaps place all weight on economic performance in the quarter of the election.

Hibbs's approach, although elegant, has no guaranteed empirical advantage. Hence I test it against two other approaches. The first is to measure economic performance in the 12 months prior to the election (quarters 12 to 15 of the presidential term); in this way, I assume that performance in of the four most recent quarters matters equally and that performance in other quarters matters not at all.[6] The other measure comes from the Michigan Survey on Consumer Attitudes and Behavior. As proposed by Nadeau and Lewis-Beck (2001), the measure is the percent who think "business conditions" have gotten better over the last year minus the percent who think they are worse. Nadeau and Lewis-Beck call this the National Business Index, or NBI. Its value, they argue, is that public perceptions of economic performance may matter more than the reality. They further argue that perceptions may embody the effects of many factors, as they seem relevant to the public at the time, rather than only RDI.

The NBI measure, however, has an endogeneity concern. People planning to vote for an incumbent may feel compelled to report that the economy is strong, unconsciously telling themselves, "If I'm voting for the incumbent, the economy must be good." As Duch, Palmer, and Anderson (2000) have shown, this kind of psychological process does operate in the context of NES surveys. Another problem with the NBI is that it is available only for elections from 1956 to 2000.[7] But both difficulties can be solved by building an instrument for economic perceptions and using it to estimate perceptions for the missing years, and I have done so.[8]

This yields a total of three measures of economic performance that are, as expected, strongly correlated. Yet the measures are by no means identical, as shown in Table 6.1.[9] The availability of these theoretically equivalent but empirically distinct indicators affords us leverage in assessing the stability of results in our small data set, as we shall see below.

Measuring Candidate Positions on Issues

The first scholar to use candidate ideology in an aggregate model of presidential elections is Rosenstone (1983). He obtained his measure by asking some forty scholars of presidential politics to rate each major party nominee from 1948 to 1980 on two ideological dimensions, New Deal social welfare liberalism and racial liberalism. As he explains, "[Raters] were instructed not to judge how the public perceived the candidates, or

TABLE 6.1
Correlations between Measures of Perceived Economic Performance

	Previous 12 Months RDI	*Hibbs weighted RDI*
NBI (instrument)	0.68	0.83
Hibbs weighted RDI per capita	0.85	

to recall the results of public opinion polls. Rather, I asked the scholars to score the candidates' actual positions on these dimensions 'the way an insightful political observer of the day would have evaluated the actions and positions of the candidate prior to the election'" (174). The ratings thus obtained are a strong predictor of the presidential vote.[10]

I collapse Rosenstone's two dimensions into one set of scores and use them to gauge candidate location from 1948 to 1968. For elections from 1972 to 2000, I use the CPS/NES election series, which asked its respondents to place presidential candidates on a seven-point scale running from extremely liberal to extremely conservative. Of course, many voters lack the knowledge to perform this rating task. Hence, in the analysis that follows, I use candidate location estimates only from NES voters who score one or more SDs above average on information and who rate the Democratic candidate at least one point to the left of the Republican candidate. This procedure uses roughly the top 15 percent of the electorate as if it were a panel of experts judging the ideological location of candidates.[11]

We have, then, two partially overlapping measures of candidate location. For my analysis, I recoded the 1 to 7 NES measure so that -3 was the most conservative position, $+3$ was the most liberal, and 0 was the midpoint. I then spliced the two measures into a single scale, using the three elections (hence six candidates) on which they overlap to scale the Rosenstone ratings to the NES metric. In the final measure, Rosenstone's ratings from the 1972 to 1980 elections were used only to put the two sets of ratings on a common metric.[12] Results are shown in Figure 6.1A.

The positions of the candidates matter only in relation to the position of the median voter. Where, we must therefore ask, is the median voter located on the ideology scale? After analysis, I concluded that the median voter should be placed at the 0-point on the scale. Voters do, of course, change locations, but when they do, candidates tend to adjust so as to keep voters in the middle (see Wlezien 2000; Erikson, MacKuen and Stimson 2002).[13]

Given the 0-point assumption, we can calculate which candidate is closer to the median voter by simply summing their scores, as shown in Figure 6.1B. Understanding how this works is essential to what follows, so the reader should attend carefully to the next few sentences. Look first at the locations of the two candidates in 1964. These are in Figure 6.1A. The Republican (Goldwater) is rated as -2.1 and the Democrat (Johnson) is $+1.5$. Hence the sum is $-.60$, meaning that Johnson is about .60 points closer to the 0-point than Goldwater. Accordingly, the number plotted in Figure 6.1B is $-.60$. Given the scoring in Figure 6.1B, negative numbers indicate that the Democrat is closer to the 0-point and positive numbers indicate that the Republican is closer to the 0-point. The theoretical

A. Scale positions of candidates

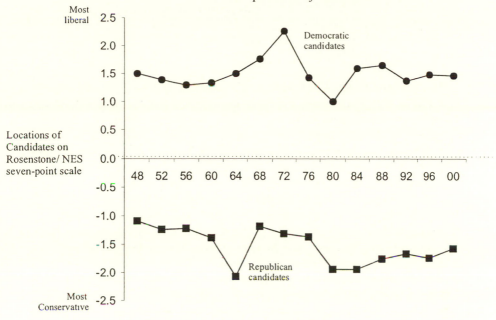

Most
liberal

Locations of
Candidates on
Rosenstone/ NES
seven-point scale

Most
Conservative

Democratic
candidates

Republican
candidates

B. Relative positions of parties and candidates

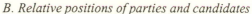

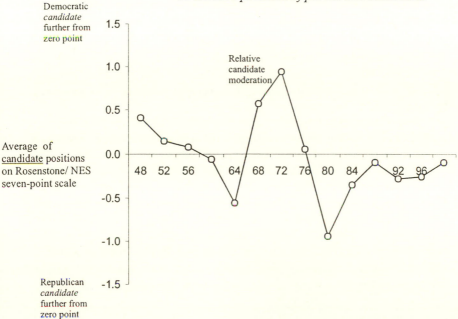

Democratic
candidate
further from
zero point

Average of
<u>candidate</u> positions
on Rosenstone/ NES
seven-point scale

Republican
candidate
further from
zero point

Relative
candidate
moderation

Figure 6.1 Spatial locations of candidates and parties, 1948–2000.

expectation is that the candidate who is closer to the midpoint of the electorate in a given election will have an advantage over an opponent who is further away.

Measuring Foreign Policy Performance

The leading model of U.S. presidential elections is what Doug Hibbs calls a "bread and peace" model. Peace—or, actually, war—is measured in this model as battlefield deaths. In practice, however, the only politically damaging wars in this period are Korea and Vietnam, and they produced nearly equivalent numbers of deaths by the time of the 1952 and 1968 elections. Hence, the war variable is essentially a variable with two cases scored 1 and the rest 0.

But are Vietnam and Korea the only foreign policy events that affected presidential elections? It seems unlikely. The notion that foreign policy affects public opinion is pervasive in the modern study of international relations (Aldrich, Sullivan, and Borgida 1989; Fearon 1994; Holsti 1996; Schultz 1998; Sobel 2001).

In an effort to measure a broader range of foreign policy influences, I asked a group of foreign policy scholars to rate the election-year success of presidents in advancing American interests in the international sphere. More specifically, I asked the scholars to:

> evaluate success or failure of the administration's conduct of foreign policy in defending or advancing American interests, as seen from the perspective of a person who follows events in the newspapers and judges them in light of mainstream values of his own day.

Raters were to make their evaluations on a 7-point scale, ranging from "highly unsuccessful" (-3) to "highly successful" (+3). The 0-point was not labeled. My instructions focused on the year of the election because research on economic performance indicates that voters give most weight to events close to the election.[14]

A total of nine sets of rankings were obtained[15] and are displayed in Figure 6.2. The solid line shows the mean ranking and the dotted lines show +/-2 standard errors from the mean at each point.

The key point in Figure 6.2 is that, in the view of foreign policy scholars, postwar presidential performance was notable for much more than the Korean and Vietnam wars. Jimmy Carter, who was unable to rescue the U.S. hostages seized by Iran, was rated almost as badly as Truman in 1952 and Johnson in 1968. But some presidents got good marks. Harry Truman was given uniformly high ratings for his handling of foreign policy in 1948, including the Marshall Plan and the Berlin airlift, which occurred in the midst of the fall campaign and might have contributed to his fabled

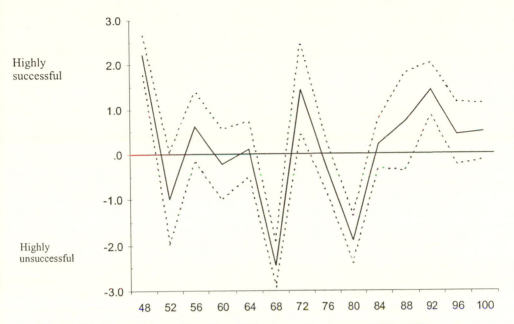

Figure 6.2 Expert ratings of presidential foreign policy success, 1948–2000.
  Note: Solid line shows mean rating of nine judges; dotted lines show ± two standard errors from mean.

rally. Similarly, Richard Nixon got high marks in 1972, the year of his famous trip to China. A high rating for George Bush in 1992 no doubt reflected the collapse of the Soviet Union and American success in the Gulf War, the aftermath of which was often in the headlines in 1992.

A scale based on a simple average of the nine sets of ratings has an alpha reliability of .92, which is quite high. But as with the expert rankings of ideological location, one must worry that experts know which presidents were popular and shade their ratings accordingly.

To avoid this problem, I make no direct use of these ratings in my analysis. Rather, I create a new foreign policy performance variable that awards one point of credit or blame for the six cases in which all coders agreed that it was due and nothing in other cases. Thus, following Figure 6.2, I have created a foreign policy performance scale that takes the value of -1 in 1952, 1968, and 1980, the value of +1 in 1948, 1972, and 1992, and the value of 0 in all other years.

The new variable is crude in that it rates the Vietnam War, in which 35,000 Americans died by the time of the 1968 election, as equal in gravity to several events that involved no deaths. But it is a good variable in

TABLE 6.2
Voter Instability from Pre- to Post-Election: All Voters

	Low Information		Middle Information		High Information
Percentage unstable from pre- to post-election	26.5%	20.6%	16.6%	14.5%	11.8%

that it has a strong basis in expert judgments about a variety of unquestionably major events and yet is essentially free of concern that it has been shaded in the direction of presidents who were electorally successful.[16]

MAIN FINDINGS: LOW INFORMATION VOTERS IN PRESIDENTIAL ELECTIONS

Are Low Information Voters Really Different?

Our first question is whether low information voters are in any obvious way different from other voters. The answer is that they are more volatile—much more. Table 6.2 updates the findings of Converse (1962) and Dryer (1971) on intra-campaign change from 1948 to 2000.

The measure of instability in these data is a straightforward one: respondents voting in the election report the same preference in both the pre- and post-election waves of the CPS/NES surveys. Movements from undecided to a vote decision, or from one candidate to the other, count equally as instances of instability. As it happens, most of this instability is due to movement from undecided to a vote choice. Table 6.3 demonstrates what happens if we limit the analysis to voters who state an initial preference and subsequently change.

Thus, two-thirds or more of the change that occurs over the course of the campaign consists of forming an initial preference, and about one-third consists of changing one's initial preference.

But these data do not address an arguably more important type of change, namely, party change *between* elections. It is consistent with these data, though perhaps unlikely, that *within* campaign change is due to voters

TABLE 6.3
Voter Instability from Pre- to Post-Election Voters with an Initial Preference

	Low Information		Middle Information		High Information
Percentage change from pre- to post-election	8.8%	6.5%	5.8%	3.6%	5.6%

returning home to the party they supported in the last election. Berelson, Lazarsfeld, and McPhee (1954) emphasized this sort of change in their study of the 1948 election.

Figure 6.3 offers two ways of assessing *between* election change. The graph on the left shows support for the Democratic candidate by political information, with a line for each election from 1948 to 2000. Thus, the line labeled 1964 shows that 90 percent of low information voters supported the Democrat in 1964, while the line labeled 1972 shows that only 37 percent of low information voters voted Democratic in that year—a huge swing. Meanwhile, high information voters were far more stable: 42 percent voted for the Democrat in 1964 and 39 voted for him in 1972. The numbers below the graph show the standard deviation of the inter-election vote swing at each level of political information. As can be seen both visually and by the statistical descriptions, there is far more inter-election variability among lower information voters.[17]

A difficulty with this approach, however, is that it fails to distinguish secular change from wild swings. If, for example, low information voters were migrating from one party to the other over a series of elections, we would be mistaken to describe the movement in terms of "instability" or "floating." Only if voters swing back and forth would we describe the change in such terms.

In light of this ambiguity, the graph at the bottom shows swings between pairs of adjacent elections, with each trend line formed by subtracting Democratic support in one election from Democratic support in the last. Again, the standard deviations of the inter-election swings are shown at the bottom of the graph. The SDs show, as previously, that low information voters are far more volatile than high information ones.

Aggregate data, as shown in Figure 6.3, can obscure individual-level patterns. Fortunately, however, the CPS/NES series includes three panels that permit individual-level tests of vote stability. Panels are from 1956 to 1960, from 1972 to 1976, and from 1992 to 1996. In each case, informed voters were substantially more stable than the uninformed. Change rates in the bottom quintile of information averaged 27 percent; in the top quintile, they averaged 11 percent.[18]

Analysis of Self-Reported Vote

We are now ready for the main findings of the paper. Without further ado, I introduce them in preliminary form in Figure 6.4, which shows scatterplots of presidential vote against economic performance for voters in the bottom third, middle third, and top third of the political information scale. Economic performance is measured by the Hibbs method and the effect of party of the incumbent has been partialed out.[19] As can be seen in the

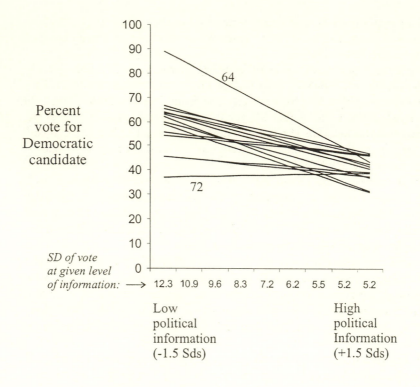

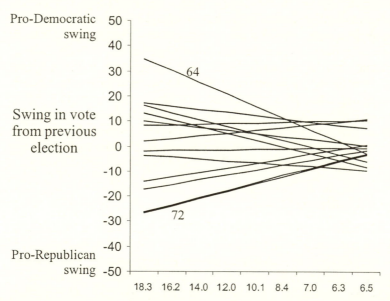

Figure 6.3 Swings in the presidential vote by political information, 1948–2000.

A. Low political information

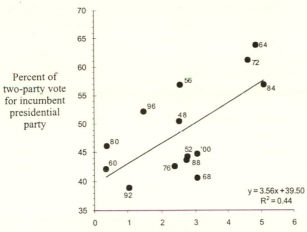

Percent of two-party vote for incumbent presidential party

Percent change in Real Disposable Income per capita, as weighted by Hibbs method, over the 15 quarters of president's term in office. See Hibbs (2000).

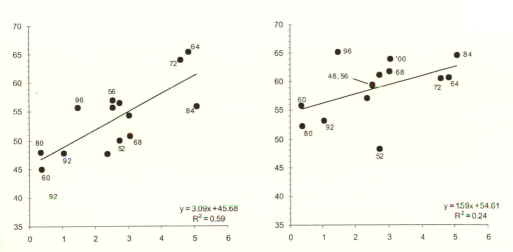

Figure 6.4 Impact of economic performance on presidential vote by level of political information.

figure, the effect of economic performance is about twice as large among low information voters as high information voters. One can also see that in years in which the incumbent has a large advantage on ideological moderation—1964, 1972, and 1980 (see Figure 6.1B)—the points fall above the trend line for low information respondents but not for high information ones. Note, finally, that the point for 1968—a year in which the incumbent has a disadvantage on war and moderation—falls further below the line for low information voters. Preliminary examination of the raw data thus suggests what multiple regression will soon confirm: low information voters are generally more sensitive to economic performance, moderation, and foreign policy performance.

Note that the data in Figure 6.4 are quite noisy. The average number of cases per cell is about 50 with an SD of 10. The point for high information voters in 1952 has only 32 voters, which no doubt explains why it is so far off trend.[20]

The next step is to test the patterns in Figure 6.4 in a multiple regression. I do so in Table 6.4 and Figure 6.5, which show multiple regression results within each of five information subgroups, based on 14 aggregate mean votes for the incumbent party from 1948 to 2000.

Table 6.6 (see below) estimates these same information interactions in an individual-level model involving some 16,000 individual observations rather than 14 aggregate means.

The aggregate and individual-level analyses are complementary rather than redundant: the aggregate analysis—because based on a separate regression within each subgroup—places no restriction on how information can interact with economic performance and other determinants of the vote. In particular, non-monotonicity is allowed. The downside is that purely chance variation is given wide scope to produce oddball results. The individual-level analysis, for its part, imposes a strong constraint on the data—any interactions with information must be strictly linear. But in so doing, it protects from chance variation, tests the statistical significance of any linear interactions that turn up, and accommodates control variables. Any patterns that show up in both the individual and aggregate models, and across all three measures of economic performance, thereby gain credibility.

I begin with Table 6.4, which uses the Hibbs model to estimate the effects of economic performance, foreign policy performance, and moderation on vote for the incumbent party. I use the Hibbs model because of its treatment of voter time horizons, as discussed above. Separate estimates are shown in column 1 for the actual vote in the electorate as a whole, and in columns 2 to 6 for the survey-measured vote within quintiles of political information.

TABLE 6.4
Determinants of the Presidential Vote, 1948–2000

	Actual Vote	Survey measure of vote				
		Low Information		Middle Information		High Information
Percent growth in RDI	2.97	3.01	3.64	3.84	3.34	1.45
se =	0.97	1.60	1.24	1.10	0.84	2.02
one-sided statistical significance	.01	0.05	.01	.00	.00	.25
Weight	0.85	0.77	0.78	0.87	0.91	0.92
se =	.13	0.26	0.16	0.11	0.09	0.49
foreign policy	3.41	5.26	0.74	4.47	4.26	2.19
se =	2.81	4.72	3.64	3.16	2.35	5.61
significance =	.13	.15	.42	.10	.05	.35
Moderation	2.72	7.57	6.37	0.03	1.20	−1.87
se =	2.56	4.03	3.10	2.95	2.32	5.66
significance =	.16	.05	.04	.50	.31	.37
Democratic Inc.	−0.57	7.98	3.33	−0.17	−5.49	−8.08
se =	1.18	2.17	1.63	1.32	1.00	2.42
significance =	.32	.00	.04	.45	.00	.01
Intercept	45.1	46.6	43.3	43.1	44.0	46.7
Adjusted R^2	.61	.68	.66	.62	.86	.53

Note: Dependent varible is percent of the two-party vote for the party of the incumbent in presidential elections from 1948 to 2000. One-tailed tests of statistical significance are shown in parentheses. The weight parameter is estimated in the model proposed by Hibbs (2000). Information is measured by items in CPS/NES surveys of the period. The survey data are used in aggregate form; that is, the dependent variable consists of group means by level of information in each of the 14 election studies. The overall *n* is 16,000; the average *n* of cases for each of the 5 × 15 group means is 213.

I begin with the strongest finding in Table 6.4: low information voters are far more sensitive to ideological moderation than high information voters. The pattern is as clear as it is unexpected from existing literature. The coefficient of 7.6 in column 2 means, for example, that Johnson's score of +.60 over Goldwater in 1964 (see Figure 6.1B) won him about

7.6 percentage points among voters in the bottom quintile of the information measure. Among high information voters, however, Johnson's relative moderation apparently gained him nothing.

The pattern of coefficients for foreign policy is more ragged, but suggests that low information voters are at least as responsive as other segments of the electorate, and probably more so. The coefficient of 5.3 in column 2 indicates that positive events, like Nixon's trip to China in 1972, gained an additional 5.3 percent of the vote for the incumbent among the less informed, and that negative events, like the Korean War, cost the incumbent a like amount. High information voters appear to be about half as responsive to foreign policy performance.

The impact of economic performance involves two coefficients, the weight and impact coefficients in the Hibbs model, each of which requires separate treatment. I begin with the weight parameter. Recall that the incumbent president has been in office for fifteen quarters at the time elections occur. The Hibbs model therefore asks: how much do voters weight quarters early in the term compared to recent quarters when judging economic performance? What, in other words, is their time horizon? The weight parameter answers this question by fixing the fraction of each quarter's performance that carries over into voters' assessments in the next quarter. A low weight (near 0) indicates that early quarters matter little and voters decide mostly on the basis of recent experience. A high weight (near 1) would indicate that past performance counts almost as much current performance, with each quarter in the past weighed almost as heavily as the current quarter. A weight of, say, .50 would indicate that half of a quarter's performance carries over from one quarter to the next; thus, economic performance three quarters previous to the current quarter would get a weight in the voter's mind of only $.5 \times .5 \times .5$, or .125, compared to a weight of one for the current quarter.

As can be seen in Table 6.4, the estimated weight is .77 for low information voters and .92 for high information voters. This difference, aggregated over 15 quarters, is actually quite large, with low information voters giving much more weight to recent performance compared to past performance. Specifically, a simple calculation shows that in evaluating whether the economy has performed well or badly over a president's term, low information voters put a 66 percent weight on the four quarters immediately prior to the election (and 34 percent on the previous 11). For high information voters, the weight on the most recent four quarters is 39 percent. Thus, low information voters have shorter time horizons than high information voters.

These weights are used in the Hibbs model to create separate measures of economic performance for each group, depending on the group's time horizon. Thus, the economic performance measures of low and high information groups have different means and variances, and correlate with one another at only $r = +.86$.

TABLE 6.5
Typical Vote Swing by Economic Performance and Voter Information

	Low	LM	Middle	MH	High
Typical vote swing due to change in economic performance	4.5%	5.4%	5.0%	4.2%	1.8%

The other coefficient in the Hibbs model is the impact coefficient, which gives the direct effect of a one-point change in weighted RDI over the president's term (as perceived by that group) on vote choice. This effect is higher for low information voters (3.0) than high information voters (1.4), but takes its peak value for middle information voters (3.8).

The best overall gauge of information effects is to multiply these impact coefficients by the SD of economic performance, as perceived by each group. These products give the size of the typical election-by-election swing in the vote attributable to economic performance, as follows in Table 6.5.

These data exhibit a non-monotonic trend with a skew toward greater sensitivity among the less informed. However, in view of the thinness of the data and the monotonic trends on other variables, a simpler conclusion seems warranted: low information voters are generally more sensitive to economic performance than high information voters.

Let us now turn to Figure 6.5, which visually displays the effects of economic performance, foreign policy performance, and moderation from the Hibbs model, along with comparable effects from models using the National Business Index (NBI) and RDI in the twelve months prior to the election. The results in Figure 6.5 are the same results we have been discussing, except that they are presented in graphical rather than tabular form.

As can be seen, the informational gradients are roughly comparable in all three models, with low information voters consistently more responsive to economic performance, moderation, and foreign policy performance. This consistency is important. The three models are based on empirically distinct measures of economic performance—especially the NBI measure—yet all three yield the same pattern. This stability adds to our confidence in the results.

Table 6.6 tests these same relationships at the level of some 16,000 individual survey respondents. Because the model is at the individual level, it can include a variety of controls: party identification, race, white southerner, and education.

The most important of the control variables is party identification, coded 1 for party of the incumbent, -1 for party of the challenger, and 0 otherwise. In light of Brody's (1991) finding that the direction of party

A. Economic effects

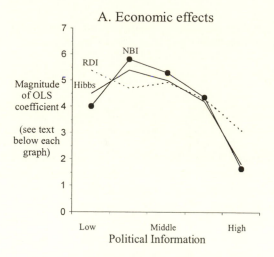

Graph presents mean election-by-election swing in presidential vote due to economic change, by level of information. Each point shows product of OLS coefficient X SD of a measure of economic performance.

B. Moderation effects

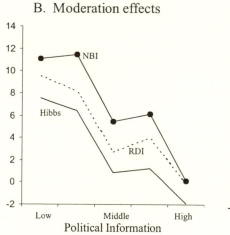

Graph presents OLS coefficients for impact of *Incumbent Party Moderation* on vote for president in models using three different measures of economic performance, by political information. Mean of Moderation = .0, SD = .47.

C. Foreign policy effects

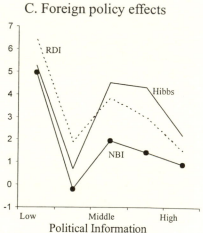

Graph presents OLS coefficients for impact of incumbent's *Foreign Policy* on vote for president in models using three different measures of economic performance, by political information. Foreign Policy takes values -1, 0, +1.

Figure 6.5 Coefficients showing impact on vote by level of political information.

TABLE 6.6
Interactive Effects of Information on Presidential Vote, 1948–2000

	Simple vote correction			Over-corrected vote		
	Hibbs (1)	NBI (2)	RDI (3)	Hibbs (4)	NBI (5)	RDI (6)
Economy X information	-0.81	-0.39	-0.67	-0.63	-0.08	-0.41
se =	0.20	0.21	0.20	0.20	0.21	0.20
Foreign policy X information	-0.61	-0.98	-0.52	-0.22	-0.52	-0.23
se =	0.65	0.64	0.66	0.65	0.64	0.66
Cand. moderation X information	-3.15	-3.57	-4.18	-1.96	-2.14	-2.62
se =	0.77	0.78	0.81	0.77	0.78	0.81
Incumbent Party ID (−1, 0, +1)	33.81	33.80	33.8	33.83	33.82	33.83
se =	0.4	0.4	0.41	0.4	0.41	0.4
Dem. incumbent X information	2.48	2.50	2.48	2.46	2.48	2.47
se =	0.41	0.41	0.41	0.41	0.41	0.41
Political information	1.21	0.12	0.99	0.81	-0.62	0.33
se =	0.65	0.66	0.69	0.65	0.66	0.69
(Average = .22; SD = .94)						
Adjusted R^2	.39	.39	.40	.39	.39	.39
SE of estimate	38.7	38.7	39	38.8	38.8	38.8
n =	16019	16019	16019	16019	16019	16019

Note: Dependent variable is "corrected" incumbent party vote; the scale before correction took values of 0 and 100. The party variable was on a scale of +1, −1, and 0 prior to the endogeneity correction. All regressions contain "fixed effect" dummy variables for each election year except one and other control variables, as explained in the text. The Hibbs, NBI, and RDI have been rescaled to have the same mean and SD as the RDI measure, thus facilitating comparison of effects. The weight parameter for the Hibbs measure has been set at .77, a value estimated from the actual vote, rather than estimated in this regression.

attachment is stable but that strength varies with political context, I expected this scoring to minimize endogeneity, but the variable nonetheless
responded to economic performance, candidate moderation, and even
foreign policy performance. Hence I ran a first-stage equation to purge
the party variable of this endogenous influence.[21] The 1948 study lacks a
party identification variable, so rather than omit either the variable or the
year, I gave all 1948 respondents a value of 0, which is the mean of the
purged party variable.[22] To capture the notion that party attachment may
be stronger among high information voters, I include an interaction for
party × information and party × information × incumbent.

To capture party realignment among white southerners, party for white
southerners is interacted with "post–Civil Rights Act." Each individual-
level variable is included as a main effect term and as an interacted term
that is multiplied by -1 when Republicans are the incumbent party.

In order to obtain correct standard errors in a pooled cross-section
analysis, one must add a 0–1 dummy variable for each election year except
one. These terms make it impossible to estimate the direct effects of aggregate variables, since the dummies explain all across-year variation. However, interactions between political information and each aggregate variable
can be included to explain within-year variation, and these interactions are
our principal interest.

The model thus specified has interactions between information and five
variables—economic success, foreign policy success, moderation, incumbent party, and party identification—plus a handful of controls. Given that
we have 16,000 individual-level cases, this may seem like a modest number of variables. But crucial variance still comes from only 14 aggregate
cases, so the instability and multicollinearity of previous regressions are by
no means absent from these.

The results, in the first three columns of Table 6.6, are easy to summarize because they vary little across specification. Political information has
highly statistically significant negative interactions with economic performance and candidate moderation. Information also interacts with foreign policy management, but more weakly. These effects are over and
above controls for party identification and party × information, but are
roughly the same without any controls at all.

Note that all these interactions are negative. This should be interpreted
as follows: economic performance, foreign policy performance, and candidate moderation all have direct *positive* effects on the vote. The *negative* interactions with information indicate that those positive effects diminish as
information increases, which leaves low information voters most responsive.

Although none of the foreign policy interactions approaches statistical
significance, their size implies nontrivial information effects: it can be calculated that a voter who scores -1.2 SD on information places about 65

percent more weight on foreign policy performance than a voter who scores $+1.2$ SDs on information.

Given all that has been written about effects of political information, these results, which mirror those of the aggregate analysis, are highly notable. However, the findings still face an important threat—the possibility that they stem from survey bias.

As discussed earlier, CPS/NES respondents tend to overstate their votes for the winning candidate by about two percentage points, an amount that tends to inflate the impact of aggregate variables on the vote. I corrected for the over-report, but I did so in a way that assumed all respondents were equally likely to over-report. But what if, as seems plausible, low information respondents are more likely to over-report than high information ones? This could, in principle, explain much if not all of the evidence of information interactions examined so far.

To assess this threat, I created a new vote variable on the assumption that low information voters are three times more likely to over-report than high information voters and two times more likely to do so than middle information voters. I assumed, in other words, that over-report occurs in proportions of 3-2-1 among low, middle, and high information voters. Results for this "over-corrected" variable are shown in columns 4 through 6 of Table 6.6.

As can be seen, the interactions with candidate moderation remain statistically significant on two-tailed tests. The results for economic performance remain statistically significant in two cases but become quite small (though still negatively signed) in the third. The weakest interaction effects—with foreign policy—fall by an average of about 40 percent and remain far from statistically significant, but they do remain consistent in terms of sign.

Even with the "over-corrected" vote measure, then, all signs on all interaction terms continue to point toward greater responsiveness on the part of low information voters. The most conservative reading of this evidence would conclude that low information voters are at least as responsive as high information voters and probably more so.

Analysis of Vote Intention

Before reaching a final conclusion, we must examine vote intention. If the pre-election measure of vote intention shows the same pattern as the post-election measure of reported vote, it would increase confidence in the results.

As noted earlier, vote intention in the last fourteen days of the campaign accurately reflects the final vote, but early in the campaign it exhibits over-support for the winner. Hence, in the analysis that follows, I use vote intentions in the last fourteen days.[23] This analysis is shown in Table 6.7, which reports regressions exactly parallel to those in Table 6.6, except that

TABLE 6.7
Interactive Effects of Information on Vote Intentions in Final Two Weeks of
Political Presidential Campaigns, 1948–2000

	Hibbs (1)	NBI (2)	RDI (3)
Economy × information	-1.20	-0.96	-0.96
se =	0.45	0.46	0.44
Foreign policy × information	-0.46	-1.15	-0.30
se =	1.10	1.09	1.13
Cand. moderation × information	-2.75	-3.70	-4.36
se =	1.50	1.50	1.56
Political information	1.47	0.96	1.04
se =	1.41	1.47	1.45
(Average = .22; SD = .94)			
Adjusted B^2	0.41	0.41	0.41
SE of estimate	35.7	35.7	35.7
n =	3188	3188	3188

Note: Dependent variable is pre-election intention to vote for the incumbent party candidate, which takes value of 0, 50, and 100. Regressions are identical in form to those in Table 6.6.

vote intention is now the dependent variable. As can be seen, magnitudes of the information interactions are, on average, close to what they are in columns 1 to 3 of Table 6.6—and notably bigger than those in columns 4 to 6. It thus appears that my "over-corrected vote" really is an over-correction. But the main point is that information interactions with vote intention at the end of the campaign match results obtained with self-reported vote, thereby increasing confidence in both sets of results.

Yet, the information interactions with vote intention *early* in the campaign do not match those obtained from vote self-report. To show this and to understand what it means, I return to aggregate data, regressing vote intention (or vote report) on the usual independent variables at three points in time: the first half of the campaign, the second half of the campaign, and Election Day itself. Regression coefficients from this analysis are shown graphically in Figure 6.6 for low, middle, and high information voters. All data in Figure 6.6 are based on respondents who were interviewed before the election and were reinterviewed afterward and reported that they had voted for a major-party candidate. This means there are no

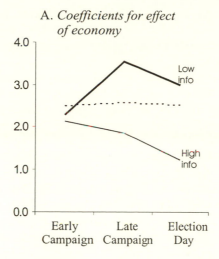

A. *Coefficients for effect of economy*

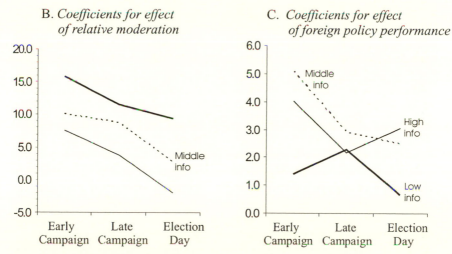

B. *Coefficients for effect of relative moderation*

C. *Coefficients for effect of foreign policy performance*

Figure 6.6 How causes of vote vary over the course of campaign.

Note: Figures show coefficients predicting vote for the incumbent party in aggregate regressions at three points in the campaign. The measure of economic performance is the Hibbs measure. Regressions contain a variable controlling for the party of the incumbent.

compositional differences between the campaign samples and the post-election sample, and that nonvoters are excluded from the campaign sample. The figure uses results from the Hibbs measure of economic performance, but results from the NBI and RDI measures show the same patterns.

The most notable pattern in Figure 6.6 is that high information voters become less responsive over the course of the campaign to all three causal forces—the economy, foreign policy, and moderation. The CPS/NES data were not intended to explore campaign dynamics in this way,[24] but a pattern as clear as this one should receive some attention. What should we make of it?

The existing literature provides two theoretical expectations for how campaigns influence vote choice. Berelson, Lazarsfeld, and McPhee (1954) found in the 1948 election that the campaign caused partisan mobilization—the return of errant partisans to their customary party. More recently, Gelman and King (1993) have proposed that campaigns educate voters about the real conditions of the country.

If these are the theoretical choices, the effect of the campaign on the highly informed must be one of partisan mobilization. For middle information voters, the effect of the campaign is much more partisan mobilization than education. The pattern of campaign effects for low information voters is unclear. These voters seem to become more responsive to economic and foreign policy performance during the campaign, but then less responsive on Election Day.[25] With respect to moderation, the pattern is one of declining responsiveness. Hence we get no overall sense how campaigns affect the less informed—perhaps because, on balance, it doesn't much affect them.

Fuzzy as this evidence is, it contributes at least a suggestion about why information has the effects it does. The suggestion is that campaigns are more about partisan mobilization than voter education. High information voters are more sensitive to the mobilizing effect of the campaign and hence end up, by Election Day, less responsive to election-specific influences. Because low information voters are less sensitive to partisan mobilization—perhaps because they are less partisan, or perhaps because they are less exposed to mobilizing communication—they end up more responsive to election-specific influences that are largely in place at the start of the campaign. I would like to press analysis further, but the data have been pushed to their limit.[26]

Before closing out the empirical analysis, I have three matters to wrap up:

- Figure 6.6 shows that low information voters are not more responsive to campaign content in the early stage of the campaign. But how about after the campaign? Had these same low information voters become more responsive to economic conditions than high information voters? The answer is yes. Low information voters interviewed early in the campaign were as responsive to campaign content on Election Day as were low information voters interviewed late in the campaign—and both groups were more responsive than were high information voters.
- Figure 6.5 also suggested the possibility of non-monotonic interactions with political information, such that voters near the bottom of the information scale,

rather than at the very bottom, might be most responsive to the aggregate determinants of the vote. To my eye, the suggestion is a weak one, since the data are noisy and non-monotonicity is not present for most indicators. Most likely, the responsiveness curve slopes gently downward from low to middle information and turns more steeply downward at that point. But the idea of non-monotonicity is plausible, so it is useful to formally evaluate it. I did so and found essentially no evidence of non-monotonicity across the three variables.[27]

- Finally, it is natural to wonder what happens when variables other than information are used to capture voters' engagement with the political process. I have briefly tried two in individual-level models: formal education and interest in the campaign. As would be expected from past research, both variables produce results that resemble those obtained from an information variable but are not as consistently strong. Formal education generates no interaction with economic performance but solid interactions with foreign policy performance and with candidate moderation. A simple three-point scale of "interest in the campaign" produces some statistically significant interactions with economic performance, moderation, and foreign policy performance. Even when strong, the results from the political interest variable are difficult to interpret, because political interest may wax and wane in ways highly endogenous to vote choice, whereas political information is an unusually stable individual-level characteristic (Delli Carpini and Keeter 1996). Campaign interest may capture little more than the partisan exuberance of voters supporting their customary party. Still, the result is worth reporting.

CONCLUSIONS

Implications for Theories of Political Behavior

My analysis so far has aimed to establish a novel factual conclusion: low information voters are at least as responsive to election-specific content as high information voters and most likely more so. I now turn to explanation. The question is: how shall we understand findings that few voting experts would confidently have predicted?

An initial answer may be found in Figure 6.7. It shows the self-described ideological positions of Democratic, Republican, and Independent voters, broken down by political information. As can be seen, low information partisans tend to be centrist in their self-described position on the left-right scale, whereas high information partisans are more polarized. High information Democrats tend to call themselves liberals and high information Republicans call themselves conservatives. Figure 6.7 also shows that the nominees of the two parties are polarized: Democratic nominees range from "slightly liberal" (on the NES scale) to "liberal," while Republicans range from "slightly conservative" to "conservative." The latter data are from Figure 6.1.

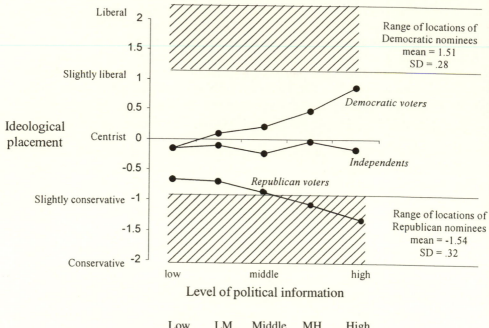

Figure 6.7 Ideological location of voters and presidential candidates, 1948–2000.
Note: Shaded areas give range of ideological locations of presidential candidates, 1948–2000 (from fig. 6.1). Data points show mean self-locations of voters on ideological rating scales in NES surveys, 1972–2000. Independent leaners are counted as members of party to which they lean. Number of cases, including numbers of voters unable to classify themselves on ideology, are shown below.

Given this configuration of voter and candidate locations, an explanation for the effect of information on vote choice follows readily: high information voters of both parties tend to be close to their own party nominee's location and far from that of the opposition. Hence, small election-specific changes do not impel them to change sides. However, low information voters fall between the two candidates. Thus cross-pressured, they may react to small differences in relative moderation or the incumbent party's record as manager of economic and foreign affairs.

Thus, high information voters tend to be more responsive to factors that are largely stable from one election to the next (party ideology) and low information voters tend to be more responsive to factors that often do change (relative centrism, record of the incumbent).

Ideological self-description is, however, a crude summary of political location, and it can be especially misleading when used in connection with low information voters, most of whom offer no ideological self-label. Figure 6.8 therefore examines the policy stances of voters. For each of five policies—defense spending, level of government services, government aid to blacks, job guarantees, and national health insurance—the figure shows the rough distribution (histogram) of attitudes by party and information, as in Figure 6.7. The pattern is striking: among well-informed voters, attitudes fall into distinct clusters that reinforce party attachment. Among low information voters, attitudes are less ideologically consistent and hence do less to tie voters to parties.[28]

Figure 6.8 also makes clear that low information voters are not really centrists. Their attitudes may average to a centrist position, but they are, from a left-right point of view, all over the map. Given this lack of ideological coherence, and given the ideological consistency of most party nominees, low information voters are likely to be less than completely happy with either candidate. To the extent they want to vote on the basis of issue proximity, they must trade off competing concerns. I speculate that a tradeoff between racial conservatism and economic liberalism may be especially common among low information voters, and that how they make this tradeoff varies across elections, depending on context and candidates.

High information voters surely care about issues as much as low information voters, but they have less need to balance competing concerns and hence less reason to switch parties. The closer candidate will normally be the candidate of one's own party. I therefore infer that issue voting for low information voters will often require change from one election to the next and that issue voting for high information voters will mainly involve stable party voting.

I note that the abortion issue, not shown in Figure 6.8, has a different pattern than the others. Fully 70 percent of high information Democrats take the most extreme liberal position, as do 36 percent of high information Republicans.[29] This suggests that if a Republican nominee were to urge a ban on abortions, the party would lose support among its high information partisans. So far, Republican nominees have avoided this problem, but the possibility reinforces my argument: high information voters do care about issues and are prepared to change parties over them, but they are rarely driven to do so because their attitudes usually line up with party ideology.

I acknowledge that although Figures 6.7 and 6.8 make this argument plausible, they do not prove it. Proof will require identifying the particular issues that are important to low information voters in particular elections

A. High information Democrats (solid line) and high information Republicans (dotted line)

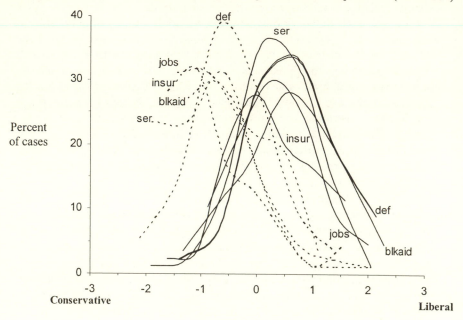

B. Low information Democrats (solid line) and low information Republicans (dotted line)

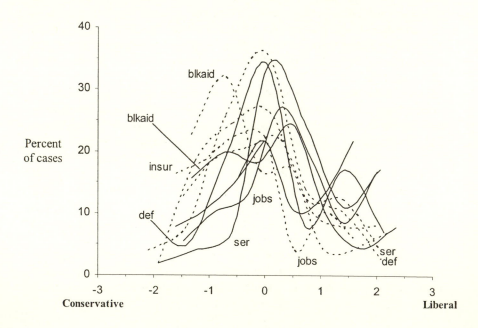

and showing their effect on vote choice. This remains a task for future research. Nonetheless, I suspect most scholars will accept that low information voters lack attitude consistency and are weakly attached to any party
for this reason. Many may also find it plausible that low information voters react strongly to the economy. What may surprise scholars is the claim
that these voters pay enough attention to notice and react systematically to
the relative moderation of presidential candidates. Let me therefore survey
the particular elections in which the candidate moderation variable took
high values, because these are the cases that produced the low information
voting behavior we are trying to explain:

- 1964. Goldwater, insisting that "extremism in the defense of liberty is no
  vice," opposed Social Security and racial integration. He hinted at using nuclear bombs in Vietnam and joked about lobbing a nuclear weapon "into the
  men's room at the Kremlin."
- 1968. Humphrey is remembered by liberals as the timid supporter of Johnson's Vietnam policy, but Rosenstone's coders saw him as a civil rights fire-
  brand in a year of racial disturbances and George Wallace's backlash third-party
  candidacy.
- 1972. McGovern favored a "reverse income tax" to redistribute wealth to the
  poor, an immediate pullout of U.S. troops from a war that seemed to be end-
  ing on U.S. terms, busing to end racial segregation of Northern public schools,
  and major cuts in defense.
- 1980. In this third run for the presidency, Reagan sought to present himself
  as a moderate. But as late as 1976, he had spoken against Social Security and
  even the Tennessee Valley Authority. He was also accused of being a "cow-
  boy" on foreign policy.

The "extreme" candidates against whom low information voters re-
acted, then, were candidates who rejected important elements of the postwar
status quo—a status quo that was presumably where it was because main-
stream opinion wanted it there. Voters need not know anything about ideology to recognize such challenges. They need only be able to recognize
challenges to a status quo that serves their interests or preferences.

Figure 6.8 Distribution of attitudes on five issues, by party and political information. *Note:* The lines show the distribution of attitudes on each of four 7-point
NES policy scales. Solid lines represent Democratic voters and dotted lines represent Republican voters. "Jobs" is the NES item on job guarantees; "def" is the item
on defense spending; "ser" is the item on level of government services; "blkaid" is
the item on government aid to blacks; "insu" is national health insurance. Results
have been converted to z-scores. The figure shows scores of the top and bottom
quintile of the information scale. *Source:* 1996 National Election Study.

How exactly low information voters become aware of such threats is unclear from my limited data. Perhaps they take cues from trusted reference groups, such as unions or church leaders, as Sniderman, Brody, and Tetlock (1991), Lupia (1994), and Lupia and McCubbins (1998) suggest. Or perhaps "gut-level rationality" enables them to spot and reject oddballs, as Popkin (1994) would argue. Or perhaps extremism evokes anxiety, which motivates a search for information, as Marcus, MacKuen, and Neuman (2001) argue. My preferred explanation is that, whatever their shortcomings, presidential campaigns do, in the end, a good job of communicating essential information. The news media maintain massive audiences and delight in unmasking political weakness through such contrivances as gaff watches, ridicule, invented controversy, and "gotcha" journalism. Campaign advertising, like news, thrives on calling unkind attention to political deviancy, and it can reach voters whether or not they care about politics (Jamieson 1996; West 2001; Geer 2003). Altogether, then, many nonideological mechanisms could enable low information voters to recognize ideological threats to a generally popular status quo.

This set of interpretations is consistent with much of the existing canon of political behavior. It accepts, in particular, the argument from chapter 10 of *The American Voter* (Campbell et al. 1960) that highly involved voters tend to be more partisan and ideological, and that low involvement voters tend to be oriented toward "nature of the times" and "candidate qualities."[30] It also accepts the important standard claim that left-right attitude consistency declines as a function of political information.

But the argument of this section departs from the canon in certain ways. Most obviously, it finds issue content in the behavior of the least sophisticated voters, a group whose mindset is characterized in the levels of conceptualization as having "no issue content." However, in discussing this characterization, Campbell et al. add that "some proportion of people classified [as no issue content] are placed there not because they are unable to comprehend [politics], but because the times do not focus their attention on the relevant political phenomena" (1960:256). What Campbell et al. may have underestimated, then, is the extent to which information from modern presidential campaigns can reach even voters who aren't well-informed.

But can poorly informed citizens respond in critical fashion to the political communication they receive? This brings us to another point at which existing theory may need revision. In his classic paper, "Information Flow and the Stability of Partisan Attitudes," Converse (1962) held that low information voters have little "inertial" basis for resisting the persuasive communication they encounter in campaigns. Hence, they tend to change their opinions in the direction of whatever message is sufficiently intense to reach them. What has not been clear in this argument is whether those less involved voters who are prone to change actually understand and react critically to the messages that move them. Are they, in other words, simply pushed about by whichever communication flow is more intense, as I have written (Zaller 1992:311), or do they choose in meaningful fashion among competing messages? The findings of this chapter show that at least in presidential elections, the latter position is correct. Although the two major parties generate roughly equal news and advertising, low information voters consistently favor the party that has the better record in managing national affairs and the better positioned candidate. The inference is hard to escape that they are responding critically to the mix of communication they receive.[31]

Methodological Implications

The question addressed in this section is why this chapter has generated different findings from past research. The answer, I believe, is that a set of three methodological artifacts has skewed past research toward finding greater policy voting among the highly informed. All three artifacts are, as it happens, ameliorated by the cross-election design of this study.

One artifact is the tendency of many voters—especially high information voters—to allow their vote decisions to (endogenously) influence their policy preferences (as well as vice versa). A number of studies have sought evidence of such influence, but they have not, to my knowledge, taken account of how political information affects this process.

A clear example of this problem arises in studies of economic performance and vote choice. As individual-level studies have shown, voters who perceive the economy to have improved in the last year tend to vote for the incumbent party, while voters who think conditions have worsened tend to vote against the incumbent. Indeed, it is standard to control for this relationship in voting studies. Past studies, however, fail to take into account that for many voters, ideological consistency extends to perceptions of economic performance. That is, many voters take a partisan view of economic performance, such that they say conditions are improving when their party is in power and worsening when the other party is in power (Wlezien, Franklin, and Twiggs 1997; Krause 1997). Table 6.8 shows how such partisan rationalization looks in two cases. When, in 1980, a Democratic incumbent was presiding over a weak economy, self-identified Republicans were quick to say that the economy was getting worse. But when, in 1992, a Republican president was in charge, Democrats were more likely to assert that the economy was worsening.

This form of biased perception appears in each NES since the new question on economic perceptions was added in 1980. Moreover, the size of the bias is, as past research on ideological consistency would suggest,

TABLE 6.8
Perceptions That the Economy Has Gotten "Much Worse" over Last Year by
Party Attachment, 1980 and 1992

	Strong Republican	Weak and Leaning Republican	Pure Independent	Weak and Leaning Democrat	Strong Democrat
1980	61.3	49.1	38.3	35.6	31.2
	(124)	(271)	(81)	(306)	(186)
1992	13.2	25.0	47.7	42.9	59.1
	(220)	(444)	(149)	(508)	(337)

Note: Cell entries are percent of voters who say economy has gotten "much worse" over last year. All respondents, including DK respondents, are included in the denominator from which cell entries are calculated.
Source: National Election Study surveys.

much larger among voters scoring high on political information. Evidence for this assertion is found in Table 6.9, which shows that the effect of partisanship on perceptions of economic performance more than doubles for high information voters compared to low information voters.

When biased perceptions of this sort are then used to predict vote choice in individual-level models, it makes it seem that high information partisans vote more on the basis of economic performance. Figure 6.9 offers a graphical illustration from the 1992 election: economic performance seems to have a huge effect on the vote choice of high information voters and a small one on the vote choice of low information voters.[32] As demonstrated in this chapter, however, low information voters are actually more sensitive to economic performance (see Duch, Palmer and Anderson 2000).[33]

Generalizing this argument, I suggest that a key reason this analysis reaches different findings about low information voters is that it avoids letting survey respondents (in effect) explain their own votes, using aggregate-level explanatory variables rather than individual-level ones. Thus, instead of asking respondents their perceptions of the economy, it uses actual economic performance. Instead of asking respondents how the president managed foreign affairs, it asks a panel of foreign policy scholars. Instead of asking respondents their perceptions of candidate proximity on issues, it uses aggregate estimates of ideological location. The analysis does use party attachment as a control variable in individual-level models, but shows that findings hold up in aggregate analysis in which partisanship is measured as a mere dummy variable for party of the incumbent (Table 6.4). The only independent variable always measured as an individual-level attitude variable is political information.

TABLE 6.9
The Effect of Party Bias on Perception of Economic Performance, 1980 to 2000

	Slope (b)	S.E.	Beta	t-ratio	Two-tailed p-value
Incumbent Pary ID (values: −1, 0, 1)	0.15	0.05	0.11	3.0	.000
Political information (range: 1–5)	.06	.018	0.05	5.6	.000
Information × Incumbent party ID	0.057	0.01	0.14	4.2	.000
Year 1984 (range 0–1)	1.6	0.04	0.54	40	.000
Year 1988	1.1	0.04	0.37	27	.000
Year 1992	.25	0.04	0.09	6	.000
Year 1996	1.60	0.04	0.50	38	.000
Year 2000	1.5	0.04	.49	36	

Adjusted R^2 = 0.37

N = 6829

Note: The dependent variable is an item asking whether the performance of the economy has gotten better or worse over the past year. It is scored from −2 (much worse) to +2 (much better).

Source: National Election Studies

A second artifact is measurement error. It is well-known both that measurement error in independent variables attenuates their impact and that the attitude statements of low information voters are more prone to measurement error (Feldman 1988; Zaller 1990). Use of aggregate measures of key variables, as in this study, will at least equalize measurement error across information groups and probably reduce its size as well.

The third artifact centers on how exactly policy voting works. The problem here is subtle and requires some exposition. Existing research shows that voters weight some issues more heavily than others in choosing between candidates. The weights vary across voters, so that one person may vote on the basis of race, another on the basis of taxes, and so forth (Krosnick 1988; Rivers 1988; Valentino, Hutchings, and White 2002). For a variety of reasons, this variability is difficult to model and political scientists mostly ignore it. But ignoring the problem can create distorted results—especially, as it happens, in estimating the incidence of policy voting among low and high information voters. To see how, imagine an election

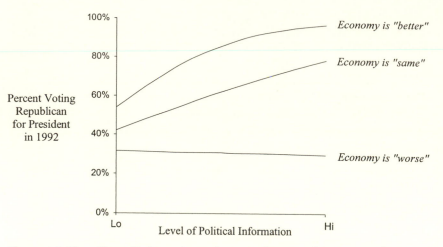

Figure 6.9 The effect of information and economic perceptions on vote for president in 1992. *Note:* Methodological information in note 32 of text. *Source:* 1992 National Election Study.

in which there are two issues, two candidates, and two kinds of voters, as follows:

- *Issues.* The two issues each have a liberal and conservative side.
- *Candidates.* The two candidates are ideologically consistent on the two issues.
- *Voters.* There are two kinds of voters, ideologues and nonideologues. The first kind takes ideologically consistent positions on the issues and the second does not. All voters vote strictly on the basis of issue proximity to the candidates, but they also weight the issues differently. For the sake of simplicity, I assume that each voter idiosyncratically bases her vote on one issue and entirely ignores the other.

A political scientist now arrives on the scene, conducts an NES–style survey, and runs standard multiple regressions to determine the causes of voting. For the sake of simplicity, I assume the political scientist runs separate regressions in the two groups of voters.

Given this setup, what does the political scientist find? Even without knowing how voters weight the issues, the political scientist finds that among ideologues, both attitudes (because correlated) predict vote choice, which inappropriately make the ideologues look like policy voters on both issues. But among the nonideologues, neither attitude correlates with vote choice. This is because, for each voter, one of the issues is positively correlated with vote choice and the other is negatively correlated, for an average correlation of zero across all voters. The political scientist could uncover the policy voting that exists among the nonideologues, but only if he knew which issue to weight for which voter, which he generally does not. Thus, the political scientist would find misleadingly abundant evidence of issue voting among the ideologues and chaos among the nonideologues.

What this example shows is that, given the kind of data and methods political scientists typically employ, it is, all else equal, easier to detect issue voting among attitudinally consistent voters (like high information voters) than among attitudinally inconsistent ones (like low information voters). I do not claim that all else is equal between the two groups, but I do claim that standard methods are biased against finding issue voting among the less informed.

One way around this potential problem is to measure issue importance at the individual level (though there might still be problems with endogeneity and measurement error). Another is to examine multiple elections, using differences in candidate emphasis on issues across elections to infer the motivation of the nonideologues. The latter, in effect, is the strategy of this chapter.

I doubt many readers would at this point challenge the value of cross-election data for understanding the determinants of the presidential vote. But the same problems—endogenous independent variables, higher levels of measurement error among the less informed, and heterogeneous decision models—arise in a great many contexts in which public opinion research is done, thereby creating the same problems and same need for care.[34]

Altogether, then, the results in this chapter challenge more than the notion that low information voters are less responsive to national political forces. They also raise doubt about the methods on which the standard view is based. More specifically, the results suggest that researchers should use more caution than they customarily do in deploying individual-level opinion statements as causal variables. The danger is that when survey respondents are allowed, in effect, to explain their own behavior, the highly informed may look more different from the poorly informed than they really are—a triumph of "survey behavior" over actual "political behavior."

Implications for Democratic Theory

Findings reported in this chapter ought to refurbish the reputation of low information voters, whose political acumen has been underestimated in past research. One might even be so bold as to argue that because low information voters are more responsive to election-specific conditions, they are more politically rational than anyone else. This, however, would be going too far. One could just as easily argue that it is rational for voters to ignore short-term factors and vote on the basis of party and ideology, as the highly informed tend to do. Thus, a recent paper by Achen and Bartels

(2002) shows that simple retrospective voting of the kind that predominates among low information voters is a crude decision rule and can lead to strange outcomes, as when incumbents lose support over failure to prevent floods, droughts, or coastal shark attacks.

One should also not conclude that the low information voters who perhaps sensibly preferred centrists in the period 1948 to 2000 would be so inclined in every context. Even in the absence of pertinent data, one would, for example, assume that in the Great Depression low information voters were more likely to embrace what would, in the terms of this chapter, be called the "extremist" policies of Franklin D. Roosevelt.[35] I therefore propose to summarize the propensities of the less informed as follows: *They are less strongly attached to, or socialized into, the dominant ideological and partisan structures of society and therefore more apt to abandon them when societal problems arise.* And they are not so uninformed about politics that they fail to recognize problems when they occur. Thus, low information voters are more apt to reject their party when it nominates an ideological oddball in normal times, and more apt to reject any sort of incumbent with a bad economic record, even if that means embracing an extremist, such as Roosevelt. The possibility that low information voters might have embraced an even more radical candidate in the 1930s, as many German voters did, is not, I think, contradicted by the findings reported in this chapter if these findings are understood as relative lack of attachment to existing ideas and organizations. If low information voters are often seen nowadays through the more normatively positive frame of "retrospective voters," it may be more because the nature of the times has changed since the perilous days of fascism, mass communism, and world depression than because the propensities of low information voters have changed.

In sum, findings that low information voters seem to be rationally retrospective and sensibly centrist in elections since World War II do not show that low information voting is no concern for democracy. It surely is a concern, even in contemporary elections. Because the least informed are most likely to swing election outcomes, the kinds of arguments that make sense to them are likely to dominate campaigns. If these arguments stress emotion more than reason, emotion will gain the upper hand in elections. If pivotal voters can't or won't attend to the details of policy debates, campaign discourse will ignore the details, even when "the devil is in the details." The whole electorate will be treated to sound bite democracy instead of real discussion. Perhaps most critically, the policies that presidents adopt in office may be policies they can defend to the least informed part of the electorate rather than policies they believe in. None of this—emotional appeals, overly simple arguments, pandering policies—can be good for democracy.

Consider, by way of illustration, presidential decision making on the Vietnam War, which is arguably America's worst policy blunder of the last century. Much evidence indicates that neither Kennedy nor Johnson thought it wise for the United States to become involved, but that each man feared electoral retribution for backing down. As Kennedy told a friend in 1963, "We don't have a prayer of staying in Vietnam. Those people hate us. They are going to throw our asses out of there at almost any point. But I can't give up a piece of territory like that to the Communists and then get the American people to re-elect me."[36] If, as this chapter suggests, "losing Vietnam" is the kind of foreign policy failure that an opposition party would try to exploit and low information voters would punish, then Kennedy and later Johnson were, in effect, catering to low information voters.

How often this sort of problem comes up is difficult to assess—and impossible to assess in a few sentences at the end of a long essay. But it is an important part of assessing the effects of political information. My findings that low information voters know enough to reject incumbents who preside over recessions and candidates who openly espouse extreme policies are far from demonstrating that these voters know enough to defend their own interests—or the nation's—from crafty manipulators.

NOTES

1. The study that finds negligible effects, that of Rahn et al. (1990), uses a scale composed of years of education, a three-point political interest item, and four information tests. The Stimson study (1975) uses a measure that gives equal weight to information and education.

2. Three other factors that I might have examined are the length of the incumbent party's tenure in the White House, the president's approval ratings, and "macro-partisanship," or mean level of partisan attachment in the electorate (Erikson, MacKuen, and Stimson 2002). The difficulty with the latter two variables is that they are endogenously affected by economic and foreign policy management, a complication that I cannot accommodate in this chapter.

The omission of "incumbent party fatigue," or long incumbency in the White House, is a tougher call, but I omit it for two reasons: first, omission does not affect the conclusions of the paper; second, due to multicollinearity, I cannot, in any case, get a clear fix on whether it interacts with information. See the Float Appendix on my Web page (www.sscnet.ucla.edu/polisci/faculty/zaller) for analysis of incumbent party fatigue.

3. The 1956 and 1960 surveys were also scarce on information items, but they were part of a panel study that, in its 1958 wave, carried good items. Hence I merged the 1958 information data with the 1956 and 1960 studies, building instruments for persons not in the 1958 survey.

4. In constructing the information scales, I tried to avoid missing data. If a person failed to answer a few items, I assigned an average based on items to which he did respond. If a person missed most items, I imputed scores from demographics and of political involvement. The weights in the imputation were determined by OLS. R-squares in the imputation models averaged .50. No attempt was made to adjust standard errors in the main analysis to reflect the uncertainty of data imputation. After imputation, missing data on the information scales averaged only about 0.2 percent of respondents who reported voting for one of the major party candidates.

5. The code runs on the 1948–1997 National Election Studies CD-ROM, plus the version of the 2000 study that was on the NES Web page in December 2001. This code is organized so that Tables 6.6 and 6.7 below, which are the heart of the paper, can be replicated with a single SPSS run. My Web page is www.sscnet.ucla.edu/polisci/faculty/zaller/.

6. In previous work, I have also used RDI in the 12 months of the calendar year of the election—that is, quarters 13 to 16 of the presidential term. However, that measure is correlated at .95 with RDI in the previous 12 months—that is, quarters 12 to 15, so I omit it.

7. I thank Richard Nadeau for making the 2000 value on his measure available to me.

8. As instruments, I use unemployment, inflation, real GDP, and RDI per capita in the year of the election. These variables yield a model with an R^2 of .88 and an adjusted R^2 of .81.

9. The Hibbs measure is based on a weight parameter of .77, the value obtained from estimating the Hibbs model on actual electoral data and no other independent variables.

10. The methods version of the paper on my Web page, called Float Appendix, examines empirically the possibility that the raters might have unconsciously rated the winning candidate nearer the center of the electorate.

11. I made an extensive effort to apply the Brady-Sniderman (1985) model of group location to data on candidate location. Although this model generates estimates of candidate location that are highly similar to those generated by the simple method described in the text, it did not work as theoretically expected in that information led to divergent rather than convergent estimates of location. In these circumstances, I decided to use the simpler method.

12. To accomplish the splicing, I collapsed left-right locations into extremity locations by folding the scales at their midpoint and taking absolute values. The two sets of ratings—but only six common points—were then regressed on one another. The resulting coefficients were used to scale the two series to a common metric, and, as the final step, the Republican scores were multiplied by -1 to restore the ratings to left-right space.

13. The mean of voters' self-identification on the NES ideology scale is right-of-center. However, many liberal-leaning groups, including blacks, women, and those having less education and income, fail to rate themselves on this scale, thereby biasing the mean. Interested readers may consult the Float Appendix on my Web page for further analysis of this issue.

I made an extensive analysis of the validity of these ratings, including comparisons to Poole's Common Space (1998) measures of candidate location and positions taken by the parties in their platforms, as measured by a group called the "Comparative Manifesto Project" and reported in Budge et al. 2001. See the Float Appendix on my Web page for this analysis.

14. Exact wording is available upon request.

15. Nine of the ten scholars I contacted provided ratings. I thank Richard Eichenberg of Tufts University, Ole Hosti of Duke University, Rick Sobel of Harvard University, and from UCLA: Matt Baum, Russ Burgos, Debbie Larsen, Marc Trachtenberg, Ken Schultz, and Art Stein.

16. The Float Appendix evaluates Hibbs's "War Only" variable as well as the newer variable.

17. The data in Figure 3 are corrected for this over-report.

18. Here as elsewhere, calculations omit third-party voters. If panel data were available for 1964, I suspect they would show many high information Republicans in the North defecting to Johnson and high information Democrats in the South defecting to Goldwater, thereby giving a misleading impression of partisan stability at the aggregate level. If such individual-level change occurred, however, it probably had the character of a realignment rather than a short-term shift. No other cases come to mind in which aggregate-level stability might be misleading in this way.

19. To partial out the effect of party, I ran a preliminary regression of incumbent vote on party of the incumbent and removed the effect of party before creating the scatterplots in Figure 6.4.

20. This could reflect sensitivity to war, but the high information point in 1968 suggests it is not.

21. The first-stage equation includes year dummies, interactions between information and each aggregate variable, and information. The interactions permit the party attachment of the less informed to be more responsive to aggregate forces.

22. One other compromise was necessary to retain the 1948 case: since 1948 did not carry a variable for state or region, I assigned the constant value of .15 to the South variable in this year, as estimated from the 1952 study. Race and a truncated education variable were included in the 1948 study, fortunately. Data imputation via a program like Amelia should have been used to assign party identification and South values in the 1948 sample, but I have not had time to do it.

23. No time of interview variable is available for 1948, but since all interviews were done in October, it is included in this analysis.

24. Interviews were conducted on different schedules in different years, and the separate halves of the sample are not intended to constitute a random sample.

25. The pattern is different if the 1948 point is included in the late campaign and Election Day readings, as it is in Tables 6.5 and 6.6. In particular, the importance of foreign policy among low information voters increases notably if the 1948 case is included.

26. I expected that a Time × Party Identification term in individual-level models would show that party becomes more important over the campaign, at least for the highly informed; this did not occur. However, my measure of party is quite attenuated, as described above.

27. Adding a series of interaction terms with the square of information would invite a multicollinear explosion. So I developed a constrained model on the following logic. Suppose we take the absolute value of an information variable that

runs from -2 to +2. The result would be a variable, folded on the 0-point, in which low scores on information are the same as high scores. If this variable had a larger effect than the original variable, it would be evidence of a non-monotonic effect, since high scores have the same effect as low ones. Now suppose we start with the same information scale, add +1 to it, take absolute value, and test its effect in a model. If the effect of this variable, folded at the value of -1, were thereby enhanced, it would be evidence of a non-monotonic effect with the inflection point at -1 rather than zero. This is the approach I followed, except that I created a parameter to estimate the inflection point. The results disclosed only minimal hints of non-monotonicity in the overall effect of the information variable. However, further exploration of the question is warranted.

28. Simple calculation reinforces this point. Suppose the Republican and Democratic candidates stake out positions at -1 and +1 on each issue in Figure 6.8. Also suppose that voters want to choose the candidate who is closer to them on these five issues. Given this, one can calculate the net policy distance of each voter from each candidate. For example, if a Democratic voter has a position of +.5 on an issue, his distance from the Republican candidate on that issue is $|-1-.5| = 1.5$ and his distance from the Democrat is $|1-.5| = .50$ Calculating over all issues, I find that when the average high information Democrat or Republican votes for the opposition party rather than his own, it results in a 120 percent increase in average policy distance. But when the average low information partisan opts for the opposition, it results in a mere 32 percent average increase in policy distance. If these calculations are made in terms of squared policy distance, the figures are 277 percent and 54 percent.

29. The abortion issue is also measured on a different scale than the other issues, which partly explains why so many voters are in the extreme liberal category.

30. As Converse, Clausen, and Miller (1965) remark, many candidate-centered comments—such as that Goldwater is "impulsive"—may be stand-ins for policy judgments.

31. Recall that much of this critical response occurs very early in the campaign, perhaps at the time of the national conventions (see Figure 6.6). But I do not see that this affects my argument.

32. Information in Figure 6.9 is measured additively by v5915 to v5921. The economic perceptions item is v3531. The information × perceptions interaction term is statistically significant at $p < .01$ in a logit analysis that also includes year dummies. If party identification is added to the model, the magnitude of the interaction drops by about 15 percent. Additional control variables further weaken the impact of the interaction term, but not my point, which is that high information respondents are more apt to rationalize votes in the politically conventional manner.

33. Past research has found little evidence of such endogeneity, but none, so far as I know, has taken account of the large information interactions that exist.

34. Experiments, quasi-experimental designs, measurement models, and out-of-sample data can help with the first two problems, but they do not help with heterogeneous decision models.

35. Class, a correlate of information, became a strong predictor of support for Roosevelt after 1934 (Sundquist 1983).

36. Cited in Zaller 2003.

REFERENCES

Achen, Chris, and Larry Bartels. 2002. "Blind Retrospection: Electoral Responses to Drought, Flu, and Shark Attacks." Paper given at annual meeting of American Political Science Association, Boston.

Aldrich, John H. 1995. *Why Parties?* Chicago: University of Chicago Press.

Aldrich, John H., John L. Sullivan, and Eugene Borgida. 1989. "Foreign Affairs and Issue Voting: Do Presidential Candidates 'Waltz before a Blind Audience?'" *American Political Science Review* 83:123–41.

Bartels, Larry M. 1996. "Uninformed Votes: Information Effects in Presidential Elections." *American Journal of Political Science* 40:194–230.

Bartels, Larry M., and John Zaller. 2001. "Presidential Vote Models: A Recount." *PS.* 34:9–20.

Berelson, Bernard, Paul F. Lazarsfeld, and William McPhee. 1954. *Voting: A Study of Opinion Formation in a Presidential Campaign.* Chicago: University of Chicago Press.

Brady, Henry E., and Paul S. Sniderman. 1985. "Attitude Attribution: A Group Basis for Political Reasoning." *American Political Science Review* 79:1061–78.

Brody, Richard A. 1991. "Stability and Change in Party Identification: Presidential to Off-Years. In *Reasoning and Choice,* ed. Paul M. Sniderman, Richard A. Brody, and Phillip E. Tetlock. New York: Cambridge University Press.

Budge, Ian, Hans-Dieter Klingeman, Andrea Volkins, and Judith Bara. 2001. *Mapping Policy Preferences—Estimates for Parties, Electors, and Governments, 1945–1998.* New York: Cambridge University Press.

Campbell, Angus, Philip Converse, Warren Miller, and Donald E. Stokes. 1960. *The American Voter.* New York: Wiley.

Canes-Wrone, Brandice, David W. Brady, and John F. Cogan. 2002. "Out of Step, Out of Office: Electoral Accountability and House Members' Voting." *American Political Science Review* 96:127–40.

Converse, Philip. 1962. "Information Flow and the Stability of Partisan Attitudes." *Public Opinion Quarterly* 26:578–89.

———. 1964. "Nature of Belief Systems in Mass Publics." In *Ideology and Discontent,* ed. David Apter. New York: Free Press.

Converse, Philip, Agae Clausen, and Warren Miller. 1965. "Electoral Myth and Reality: The 1964 Election." *American Political Science Review* 59:321–36.

Daudt, H. 1961. *Floating Voters and the Floating Vote: A Critical Analysis of American and English Election Studies.* Leiden, Holland: Kroese.

Delli Carpini, Michael X., and Scott Keeter. 1996. *What Americans Know about Politics and Why It Matters.* New Haven: Yale University Press.

Downs, Anthony. 1957. *An Economic Theory of Democracy.* New York: Harper and Row.

Dryer, Edward C. 1971. "Media Use and Electoral Choices: Some Political Consequences of Information Exposure." *Public Opinion Quarterly* 35:544–53.

Duch, Raymond M., Harvey D. Palmer, and Christopher J. Anderson. 2000. "Heterogeneity in Perceptions of National Economic Conditions." *American Journal of Political Science* 44:635–52.

Erikson, Robert S., and Christoper Wlezien. 1999. "Presidential Polls as a Time Series: The Case of 1996." *Public Opinion Quarterly* 63:163–77.

Erikson, Robert S., Michael B. MacKuen, and James A. Stimson. 2002. *The Macro Polity.* Cambridge: Cambridge University Press.

Fearon, James D. 1994. "Domestic Political Audiences and the Escalation of International Conflict." *American Political Science Review* 88:577–92.

Feldman, Stanley. 1988. "Structure and Consistency in Public Opinion: The Role of Core Beliefs and Values." *American Journal of Political Science* 32:416–40.

Ferejohn, John A., and James H. Kuklinski, eds. 1990. *Information and Democratic Processes.* Urbana: University of Illinois Press.

Fiorina, Morris 1981. *Retrospective Voting in American National Elections.* New Haven: Yale University Press.

Free, Lloyd S., and Hadley Cantril 1967. *The Political Beliefs of Americans.* New Brunswick: Rutgers University Press.

Geer, John 2003. "Campaigns, Attack Advertising, and Democracy." Center for the Study of Democratic Politics, Princeton University.

Gelman, Andrew, and Gary King. 1993. "Why Are American Presidential Election Campaign Polls So Variable When Elections Are So Predictable?" *British Journal of Political Science* 23:409–51.

Hibbs, Douglas A., Jr. 1987. *The American Political Economy: Macroeconomics and Electoral Politics.* Cambridge, MA: Harvard University Press.

———. 2000. "Bread and Peace Voting in U.S. Presidential Elections." *Public Choice* 104:149–80.

Holsti, Ole R. 1996. *Public Opinion and American Foreign Policy.* Ann Arbor: University of Michigan Press.

Iyengar, Shanto, and Donald R. Kinder. 1987. *News That Matters.* Chicago: University of Chicago Press.

Jamieson, Kathleen. 1996. *Packaging the Presidency.* New York: Oxford University Press.

Johnston Richard, Andre Blais, Henry Brady, and Jean Crete. 1993. *Letting the People Decide.* Palo Alto: Stanford University Press.

Key, V. O., Jr., with Milton C. Cummings. 1966. *The Responsible Electorate.* New York: Vintage.

Kramer, Gerald H. 1971 "Short-Term Fluctuations in Voting Behavior, 1896–1964." *American Political Science Review* 65:131–43.

Krause, George A. 1997. "Voters, Information Heterogeneity, and the Dynamics of Aggregate Economic Expectations." *American Journal of Political Science* 41:1170–1200.

Krosnick, Jon A. 1988. "The Role of Attitude Importance in Social Evaluation: A Study of Policy Preferences, Presidential Candidate Evaluations, and Voting Behavior." *Journal of Personality and Social Psychology* 55:196–210.

Lewis-Beck, Michael S. 1988. *Economics and Elections: The Major Western Democracies.* Ann Arbor: University of Michigan Press.

Lupia, Arthur. 1994. "Shortcuts vs. Encyclopedias: Voting Behavior in California Insurance Reform Elections." *American Political Science Review* 88:63–76.

Lupia, Arthur, and Mathew D. McCubbins. 1998. *The Democratic Dilemma.* New York: Cambridge University Press.

Luskin, Robert C. 1987. "Measuring Political Sophistication." *American Journal of Political Science* 31:856–99.

MacKuen, Michael B., Robert S. Erikson, and James A. Stimson. 2002. *The Macropolicy.* New York: Cambridge University Press.

Marcus, George, Michael MacKuen, and Russell Neuman. 2001. *Affective Intelligence and Political Judgment.* Chicago: University of Chicago Press.

Moon, Woojin. 2002. "Resource Constrained Electoral Competition: Theory, Tests, and Applications." PhD diss., UCLA.

Nadeau, Richard, and Michael S. Lewis-Beck. 2001. "National Economic Voting in U.S. Presidential Elections." *Journal of Politics* 63:159–81.

Popkin, Samuel L. 1994. *The Reasoning Voter.* Chicago: University of Chicago Press.

Rahn, Wendy, John Aldrich, Eugene Borgida, and John Sullivan. 1990. "A Social-Cognitive Model of Candidate Appraisal." In *Information and Democratic Processes,* ed. John A. Ferejohn and James H. Kuklinski, 136–59. Urbana: University of Illinois Press.

Rivers, Douglas. 1988. "Heterogeneity in Models of Electoral Choice." *American Journal of Political Science* 32:737–57.

Rosenstone, Steven J. 1983. *Forecasting Presidential Elections.* New Haven: Yale University Press.

Schultz, Kenneth. 1998. "Domestic Opposition and Signaling in International Crises." *American Political Science Review* 92:829–44.

Smith, Eric R.A.N. 1989. *The Unchanging American Voter.* Berkeley: University of California Press.

Sniderman, Paul M. 1993. "The New Look in Public Opinion Research." In *Political Science: The State of the Discipline,* ed. Ada W. Finifter. Washington DC: American Political Science Association.

Sniderman, Paul M., Richard A. Brody, and Philip E. Tetlock. 1991. *Reasoning and Choice: Explorations in Political Psychology.* Cambridge: Cambridge University Press.

Sniderman, Paul M., James M. Glaser, and Robert Griffin. 1990. "Information and Electoral Choice." In *Information and Democratic Processes,* ed. John A. Ferejohn and James H. Kuklinski, 117–35. Urbana: University of Illinois Press.

Sobel, Richard. 2001. *The Impact of Public Opinion on U.S. Foreign Policy since Vietnam: Constraining the Colossus.* Oxford: Oxford University Press.

Stimson, James. 1975. "Belief Systems: Constraint, Complexity, and the 1972 Election." In *Controversies in American Voting Behavior,* ed. Richard Niemi and Herbert Weisberg, 138–59. San Francisco: Freeman.

Sundquist, James. 1983. *Dynamics of the Party System.* Washington, DC: Brookings.

Valentino, Nicholas A., Vincent L. Hutchings, and Ismail K. White, 2002. "Cues That Matter: How Political Ads Prime Racial Attitudes during Campaigns." *American Political Science Review* 96:75–90.

West, Darrel. 2001. *Air Wars.* Washington, DC: CQ Press.

Wlezien, Christopher. 2000. "An Essay on 'Combined' Time Series Processes." *Electoral Studies* 19:77–93.

Wlezien, Christopher, Mark N. Franklin, and Daniel Twiggs. 1997. "Economic Perceptions and Vote Choice: Disentangling the Endogeneity." *Political Behavior* 19:7–17.

Zaller, John. 1990. "Political Awareness, Elite Opinion Leadership, and the Mass Survey Response." *Social Cognition* 8:125–53.

———. 1992. *The Nature and Origins of Mass Opinion.* Cambridge: Cambridge University Press.

———. 1996. "The Myth of Massive Media Impact Revived: New Support for a Discredited Idea." In *Political Persuasion and Attitude Change,* ed. Diana Mutz, Richard Brody, and Paul Sniderman, 17–79. Ann Arbor: University of Michigan Press.

———. 2003. "V. O. Key's Concept of Latent Opinion." In *Electoral Democracy,* ed. M. MacKuen and G. Rabinowitz. Ann Arbor: University of Michigan Press.

PART IV

Attitude Strength and Attitude Stability

Importance, Knowledge, and Accessibility: Exploring the Dimensionality of Strength-Related Attitude Properties

George Y. Bizer, Penny S. Visser, Matthew K. Berent, and Jon A. Krosnick

THE TERM *attitude strength* has been used often throughout the social sciences during the last century, but it has been used in many different ways and has rarely been formally defined in conceptual and operational terms. Recently, however, Krosnick and Petty (1995) proposed a definition pointing to four essential qualities of strong attitudes. In doing so, they drew an analogy between strong attitudes and people who are physically strong. Strong people are difficult to move and have a relatively easy time moving others. Likewise, strong attitudes can be thought of as those that resist change, which leads them to be especially stable over time. Strong attitudes are also influential, in that they powerfully direct information processing and have a substantial impact on behavior. Thus, the strength of an attitude is *defined* in terms of four dimensions—resistance to change, persistence over time, strength of impact on thinking, and strength of impact on behavior.

When defined in this way, it is immediately obvious that, like attitudes, many other constructs of broad interest to social scientists are likely to vary in strength. Behavioral intentions and a range of beliefs, including attributions, stereotypes, self-concepts, and much more, can all be conceived as varying in their imperviousness and in their consequentiality. Therefore, understanding the nature, origins, and consequences of attitude strength can in principle help us understand the workings of these other psychological phenomena as well.

Many other attributes of attitudes have been shown to be positively correlated with the four defining features of attitude strength (see e.g., Krosnick and Abelson 1992). We refer to these other properties as "strength-related attitude attributes." They include attitude importance, knowledge, elaboration, certainty, ambivalence, accessibility, intensity, extremity, structural consistency, and others. As Krosnick and Petty (1995) outlined, some of these attributes are features of the attitude itself (e.g., extremity), others are aspects of attitude structure (e.g., accessibility, knowledge, structural consistency), others are subjective beliefs about attitudes or attitude objects (e.g., importance and certainty), and others refer to processes through which attitudes are formed, changed, and maintained (e.g., elaboration).

Because these attributes are positively correlated with one another and with the four defining features of strength (Krosnick and Abelson 1992; Krosnick et al. 1993), the temptation of parsimony has led some investigators to presume that multiple attributes reflect a single underlying construct. That is, the origins and consequences of multiple attributes have been presumed to be identical, an assumption that has many convenient implications. Most important, theory building can be accomplished efficiently. Rather than trying to understand the unique causes and effects of twelve or more attributes, we need only account for a small handful of latent constructs. Furthermore, on a practical level, averaging together measures of multiple attributes would presumably yield a reliable measure of the construct they reflect, thus facilitating the assessment process.

Because parsimony is appealing in principle, it makes little sense to develop theories of attitude strength that are unnecessarily complex or differentiated. However, we will argue here that complexity and differentiation are the reality of the psychology of attitudes and must therefore be represented in our theories of their functioning. In particular, we will advocate a view of attitude attributes that requires individual theory building for each, paying careful attention to each attribute's inherent nature and identifying antecedents and consequences in ways faithful to that nature.

We begin by reviewing the bulk of work to date on the structure of strength-related attitude features, which has employed factor analytic methods. We show that the results of such work has been conflicting and ultimately uninformative on the matter of latent structure. We then describe new studies taking a different approach to identifying structure, examining whether two strength-related attitude properties have the same causes and the same effects. The focus of the studies described here has been on the relations of attitude importance to the volume of attitude-relevant knowledge and to attitude accessibility.

FACTOR ANALYTIC STUDIES

The largest segment of the literature suggesting commonalties among strength-related attributes reported factor analyses. In some studies, exploratory factor analyses or principal components analyses were implemented to identify underlying dimensions based on covariances among attributes (e.g., Abelson 1988; Bassili 1996a). For example, Pomerantz, Chaiken, and Tordesillas (1995) reported factor analyses suggesting the one set of strength-related attributes (including extremity and certainty) reflects an individual's commitment to an attitude, and a second set of attributes (including knowledge volume and attitude importance) reflects the degree to which the attitude is embedded within a large, interconnected cognitive structure.

However, the results of such exploratory factor analyses have varied considerably across studies and sometimes even within studies. Some investigations have yielded support for the notion that many strength-related features reflect a single underlying construct (Verplanken 1989, 1991), whereas other studies suggest that there are two (e.g., Bassili 1996a) or three (Abelson 1988) underlying factors. And different studies have reached different conclusions about which attributes reflect the same underlying construct and which reflect different constructs.

In an effort to get past the ambiguities inherent in exploratory factor analysis, Krosnick et al. (1993) explicitly tested the plausibility of a number of different latent factor models, beginning with one proposing that a single underlying factor could account for covariation among some or all of thirteen attributes. Specifically, these investigators tested the goodness-of-fit of various structural equation models positing pairs, trios, or larger sets of attributes loading on a single underlying factor, each possibility derived from existing theories and research. Across three studies, Krosnick et al. (1993) found almost no consistent evidence suggesting that a group of attributes reflected a common underlying strength factor. And all three studies yielded evidence rejecting the claim that a single latent factor could account for all the covariation among all dimensions. Lavine et al. (1998) also conducted similar confirmatory factor analyses, which supported the same conclusion.

This factor analysis approach employs just one of many possible ways to diagnose latent structure. In essence, a factor analysis will support the conclusion that two measures reflect a single underlying construct if correlations of the two measures with other measures in the model show similar patterns. But in past studies, the only "criterion" dimensions used to gauge similarity have been other strength-related attitude attributes thought to possibly reflect the same underlying constructs. In the research described in this chapter, we took a different, complementary approach, expanding the scope of criterion variables, and focused on the causes and consequences of attributes. If two attributes are in fact simply surface manifestations of a single underlying construct, then they should have the same origins, and they should have the same effects. So if two attributes turn out to be distinct in terms of causes and consequences, this would suggest that they are not surface manifestations of a single latent factor.

We have been employing this approach to gauge the relations between various pairs of strength-related attitude attributes. In this chapter, we describe two lines of work done thus far, the first examining the relation of attitude importance to the volume of attitude-relevant knowledge, and the second exploring the relation of importance to accessibility.

ATTITUDE IMPORTANCE AND KNOWLEDGE

One Construct?

The amount of importance that people attach to an attitude and the volume of knowledge they have stored in memory about it are two of the most widely studied strength-related attitude attributes. Past exploratory factor analyses have generally found these two attributes to load on a single factor. And in the literature on importance and knowledge, no evidence shows that a cause of importance is not a cause of knowledge, that a cause of knowledge is not a cause of importance, that an effect of importance is not an effect of knowledge, or that an effect of knowledge is not an effect of importance. All this is therefore consistent with the claim that these two attributes are manifestations of one single underlying construct.

Three causes of attitude importance documented thus far are (1) acknowledgment that the attitude object impinges on one's material self-interest, (2) identification with reference groups or individuals who attach importance to the attitude object or whose material interests are linked to the object, and (3) recognition of a link between the attitude and one's core values (Boninger, Krosnick, and Berent 1995). In addition, Roese and Olson (1994) suggested that attitude accessibility may be a cause of attitude importance, and Haddock, Rothman, and Schwarz (1996) and Haddock et al. (1999) suggested that people's perceptions of the accessibility of attitude-supportive and attitude-challenging information in memory may cause importance. Finally, Pelham's evidence (1991) indicates that attitude importance may be adjusted in order to promote a person's self-esteem. No evidence to date has tested whether any of these factors cause knowledge, so it is conceivable that these are all causes of knowledge as well (as the single latent factor perspective would suggest).

The primary origins of knowledge documented thus far are (1) direct experiences with an attitude object (Fazio and Zanna 1981) and (2) exposure and attention to information about the object provided by other people, through conversations or mass media (McGuire 1986; Roberts and Maccoby 1985). Knowledge about social and political issues is especially likely to be acquired through the latter route: exposure and attention to information about the attitude object conveyed by the news media (Clarke and

Fredin 1978; Perse 1990). To date, no studies have tested whether importance is enhanced by direct experience or exposure to information from informants; it is conceivable that these causal processes do indeed occur (again as the single latent factor perspective assumes).

Quantity of attitude-relevant knowledge has been shown to be associated with stronger consistency between attitudes and behavior, greater ability to encode new information about an object, reduced reliance on peripheral cues in evaluating persuasive messages, more extensive thinking about attitude-relevant information, greater sensitivity to the quality of arguments in evaluating a persuasive message, and greater resistance to attitude change (Biek, Wood, and Chaiken 1996; Davidson 1995; Wilson et al. 1989; Wood 1982; Wood and Kallgren 1988; Wood, Rhodes, and Biek 1995). In line with three of these findings, attitude importance has also been shown to be associated with greater attitude-behavior consistency (e.g., Budd 1986; Parker, Perry, and Gillespie 1974; Rokeach and Kliejunas 1972), more extensive thinking about attitude-relevant information (Berent and Krosnick 1993; Celsi and Olson 1988; Howard-Pitney, Borgida, and Omoto 1986), and greater resistance to attitude change (Fine 1957; Gorn 1975; Zuwerink and Devine 1996). However, the other documented correlates of knowledge have not yet been investigated with regard to importance, so it is conceivable that importance has these consequences as well. In addition, various documented effects of importance (e.g., the motivation to acquire information about the attitude object [Berent and Krosnick 1993]; consistency between attitudes and core values [Jackman 1977; Judd and Krosnick 1989]) have not yet been investigated with regard to knowledge, so it is conceivable that they follow from high knowledge as well.

Distinct Effects?

However, when considered less mechanically and more conceptually, it seems likely that the causes and effects of importance and knowledge will be different. Attitude importance is a subjective judgment—a person's sense of the concern, caring, and significance he or she attaches to an attitude. To attach great importance to an attitude is to care tremendously about it and to be deeply concerned about it. There is nothing subtle about attitude importance, particularly at its highest levels: people know very well when they are deeply concerned about an attitude, and they know just as well when they have no special concern about one.

In our view, attitude importance is consequential precisely because of its status as a belief: perceiving an attitude to be personally important leads people to use it in processing information, making decisions, and taking action. Consistent with this reasoning, attitude importance has been shown to motivate people to seek attitude-relevant information (Berent and Krosnick 1993; Zaichkowsky 1985) and to think carefully about that information (Berent 1990). Importance also motivates people to use an attitude: more important attitudes have more impact on judgments of liking for other people (Byrne, London, and Griffitt 1968; Clore and Baldridge 1968; Granberg and Holmberg 1986; Krosnick 1988; McGraw, Lodge, and Stroh 1990), on voting behavior in elections (Krosnick 1988; Schuman and Presser 1981), and on trait inferences (Judd and Johnson 1981). Thus, importance appears primarily to be a motivator.

In contrast, knowledge is not in and of itself motivational—it is simply a store of information in memory. As such, its effects seem most likely to be ability based in character. Knowledge has been shown to enhance recall (e.g., Cooke et al. 1993; Fiske, Lau, and Smith 1990; McGraw and Pinney 1990; Schneider et al. 1993), improve comprehension (Eckhardt, Wood, and Jacobvitz 1991; Engle, Nations, and Cantor 1990), increase the speed of judgments (e.g., Fiske, Lau and Smith 1990; Paull and Glencross 1997), improve cue utilization in decision tasks (Paull and Glencross 1997), enable appropriate inferences (Pearson, Hansen, and Gordon 1979), facilitate the learning of new topic-relevant information (Hansen 1984; Kyllonen, Tirre, and Christal 1991; Willoughby et al. 1993), and enable the generation of effective counterarguments to a persuasive appeal (Wood 1982; Wood, Rhodes, and Biek 1995). Thus, although knowledge seems to enable people to perform various relevant cognitive tasks more effectively, there is no reason why it should, in and of itself, *motivate* people to engage in any behavior.

These characterizations suggest that importance and knowledge are likely to have distinct effects on thought and behavior. For example, importance, but not knowledge, may induce selective affiliation: people who care passionately about an issue may be motivated to associate with others who share their views on the issue. In contrast, people who simply happen to know a great deal about the issue may not be especially likely to use the issue as a criterion for deciding with whom to affiliate. On the other hand, knowledge, but not importance, may lead to better memory for relevant information: possessing a large network of information about a topic may enhance one's ability to integrate and store new attitude-congruent information, thereby facilitating retrieval later.

In addition, importance and knowledge may interact with one another. For example, having both the motivation to behave in accordance with one's attitude and the ability to identify and carry out the appropriate behavior may lead to greater attitude-behavior correspondence than either motivation or ability alone.

Distinct Causes?

In addition to being distinct in terms of their consequences, importance and knowledge seem likely to be distinct in terms of their origins as well. As we outlined previously, knowledge seems to accumulate simply as the result of exposure to information about an object, either through direct behavioral experience with it or through indirect learning from other people. But simply being exposed to information is only likely to lead a person to attach importance to an attitude if that information makes a compelling case of a linkage between the object and a person's self-interest, reference groups or individuals, or values. Thus, knowledge acquisition is unlikely to have a uniform direct effect on importance.

Information acquisition sometimes occurs intentionally, because a person seeks out new knowledge. And people who attach great personal importance to an object are likely to be motivated to gather information about it. Thus, importance seems likely to be a cause of knowledge accumulation.

TESTING THESE HYPOTHESES

Having laid out these hypotheses regarding distinctions between importance and knowledge in terms of their causes and effects, we turn now to reviewing the recent work of Visser, Krosnick, and Simmons (2002) to test them. These investigators began by replicating previous exploratory factor analyses. Using data collected from 159 undergraduate respondents, Visser, Krosnick, and Simmons factor analyzed strength-related attitude attributes for two separate attitudes (toward capital punishment and legalized abortion). Both sets of data revealed a similar latent factor structure to the one that has emerged in previous research: importance and knowledge loaded on a common factor, along with elaboration; certainty, extremity, and affective-cognitive consistency loaded together on a second factor. But then Visser, Krosnick, and Simmons proceeded to demonstrate that the causes and effects of these two constructs are anything but identical.

ORIGINS OF IMPORTANCE AND KNOWLEDGE

To gauge the origins of attitude importance and knowledge regarding the issue of legalized abortion, ordinary least squares regressions were conducted predicting importance and knowledge with four potential antecedents: self-interest; the importance of the issue to reference groups and individuals; value-relevance; and news media use. Consistent with previous research (Boninger, Krosnick, and Berent 1995), self-interest, the importance of the issue to reference groups and individuals, and value-relevance were all significant predictors of attitude importance. Media use, on the other hand, was unrelated to importance. Media use was a significant predictor of knowledge, however, as were self-interest and value-relevance. The importance of the issue to reference groups and individuals was not a significant predictor of knowledge.

These associations may reflect direct effects of each of the antecedents. That is, self-interest, perceptions of the links between an issue and reference groups or individuals, and value-relevance may have led directly to increases in attitude importance. Similarly, media use, self-interest, and value-relevance may have led directly to the accumulation of knowledge about legalized abortion. Alternatively, some of these associations may have been mediated by others.

For example, the impact of self-interest on knowledge may have been mediated by its impact on importance: recognizing that one's material interests are at stake in an issue may lead people to attach importance to an attitude, which in turn may motivate them to seek out relevant information about it (Berent and Krosnick 1993). If this is so, the relation between self-interest and knowledge may have been mediated by importance.

However, another causal account is possible as well. Perhaps recognizing that an attitude object impinges on a person's material interests directly inspires him or her to gather information about the attitude object. Having accumulated a great deal of such information, people may then come to decide that the attitude is important to them. Such a process could occur if people were motivated to rationalize why they invested the effort in information gathering, or if people infer importance based on how much knowledge they have about objects (e.g., "if I know this much about an object, then it must be personally important to me"). If this account is correct, the association between self-interest and importance would be mediated by knowledge.

When Visser, Krosnick, and Simmons tested these mediational hypotheses, clear evidence emerged: controlling for importance eliminated both the associations between self-interest and knowledge and between value-relevance and knowledge. This suggests that self-interest and value-relevance each increased the importance people attached to their attitudes, which in turn led them to accumulate attitude-relevant information.

However, controlling for knowledge did not alter the associations between self-interest and importance, between the views of significant others and importance, or between value-relevance and importance. This suggests that knowledge did not mediate any of these relations. Instead, increases in each led directly to increases in attitude importance.

Taken together, these results suggest the causal model presented in Figure 7.1, which Visser, Krosnick, and Simmons estimated using covariance

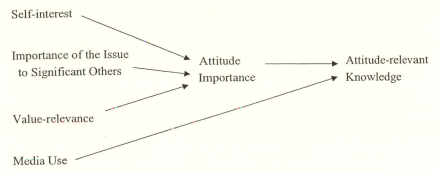

Figure 7.1 The causes of attitude importance and knowledge.

structure modeling techniques and found it fit the data quite well. Self-interest, the importance of the issue to significant others, and value-relevance each led to increased attitude importance, and increases in attitude importance led to increased knowledge about the issue. Knowledge increased as a function of media use, but media use had no impact on attitude importance. These results suggest that importance and knowledge spring from largely distinct sources.

CONSEQUENCES OF IMPORTANCE AND KNOWLEDGE

To the extent that importance and knowledge are manifestations of a single underlying construct, they should regulate the impact of attitudes on thought and behavior in the same ways. To test this possibility, Visser, Krosnick, and Simmons conducted a series of studies examining the effects of importance and knowledge on (1) selective information gathering, (2) attitude-expressive behavior, and (3) perceived social support for one's views.

Information Gathering

As we suggested earlier, people seem likely to be motivated to acquire information relevant to attitudes to which they attach importance, as Berent and Krosnick (1993) found. If we perceive an attitude to be important, we are indeed likely to selectively expose ourselves to information regarding that attitude object. On the other hand, knowledge, when characterized simply as a store of information in memory, seems unlikely to motivate such information gathering.

To test these hypotheses, undergraduate respondents were told that they would receive information about twelve different political candidates, each of whom they would be asked to evaluate. Respondents were told that for each candidate, they could choose three out of six possible issues and would learn the candidate's positions on those issues. As expected, people who attached more importance to an issue requested candidates' positions on the issue significantly more often. However, for both issues, possessing more knowledge had no impact on respondents' information selection, nor was the interaction between importance and knowledge significant in either case. Attaching importance to an issue apparently motivated respondents to seek information that enabled them to use their attitudes when evaluating candidates, but possessing knowledge did not.

Attitude-Expressive Behavior

In a similar manner, the independence of importance and knowledge can be tested by analyzing whether they both regulate attitude-behavior consistency to the same degree. Performing an attitude-expressive behavior requires sufficient motivation to do so, but it also requires sufficient knowledge to plan appropriate behavioral strategies and to execute them effectively. If importance and knowledge provide such motivation and ability, respectively, we might expect them both to regulate the impact of attitudes on behavior. This hypothesis was tested in two studies.

In a study of abortion activism, undergraduates reported whether they had ever performed seven specific behaviors expressing their attitudes toward legalized abortion (e.g., contacting a public official to express their views on the issue, giving money to an organization concerned with the issue). Similar measures were included in a telephone survey of a representative national sample of American adults, focusing on the issue of global warming.

As predicted, importance and knowledge were associated with increases in attitude-expressive behavior in both studies. Respondents who attached more importance to their attitudes performed more behaviors. Likewise, respondents who possessed more attitude-relevant knowledge performed more behaviors. Furthermore, a significant interaction between importance and knowledge showed that the combination of high importance and high knowledge was associated with a particularly pronounced surge in attitude-expressive behavior. This is consistent with the notion that importance conferred the motivation to behave in attitude-expressive ways and that knowledge conferred the ability to do so, both of which were necessary for maximal attitude-congruent behavior.

Social Support

The false consensus effect offers another opportunity to explore differential effects of importance and knowledge. People are often influenced by their own attitudes toward an object when estimating others' attitudes toward the object, leading to exaggeration of the degree of social support for one's views. A number of explanations for this "false consensus" effect have been posited, some of which have implications for the moderating roles that importance and knowledge might play.

One explanation holds that the false consensus effect is the result of the relative salience of one's own attitude when estimating the views of others (e.g., Marks and Miller 1985). People may use their own attitudes as a starting point from which to adjust their final estimates of others' attitudes. But because such adjustments are rarely sufficient (Tversky and Kahneman 1974), final estimates may be unduly influenced by a person's own attitude. Because important attitudes are brought to mind frequently, they are more accessible and more salient in memory than unimportant attitudes (e.g., Krosnick 1989). As a result, important attitudes may be especially likely to serve as powerful anchors when estimating others' views on a topic, producing a positive association between attitude importance and the magnitude of the false consensus effect.

If this account of the false consensus effect is correct, possessing much knowledge about an attitude object seems unlikely to exacerbate the phenomenon. In fact, the more knowledge one has about an object, perhaps the less salient one's attitude toward it becomes, because activation of the attitude in consciousness may be accompanied by activation of this other relevant information as well. Therefore, knowledge may be unrelated to the magnitude of the false consensus effect and may even be negatively related to it.

Other theoretical accounts of the false consensus effect have also been proposed, including motivations such as self-esteem maintenance, need for social support, and social interaction goals (Marks and Miller 1987). For example, perceiving that one's attitudes are widely shared by other people is likely to enhance a person's sense that his or her views are correct, which may contribute to positive self-esteem. Thus, to the extent that people are especially concerned about the correctness of attitudes that are personally important, they may be more strongly motivated to perceive widespread support for their more important attitudes. In contrast, possessing a great deal of knowledge about an attitude may itself contribute to an increased sense of the correctness of one's views, perhaps reducing the motivational drive to look to social support for the attitude as evidence of its correctness. This perspective, too, suggests that importance may be positively associated with the magnitude of the false consensus effect, whereas knowledge may be unrelated or negatively related.

Finally, the motivation to affiliate with others with whom one agrees, particularly with regard to important attitudes, may further contribute to a positive association between importance and perceived social support. In general, people prefer to affiliate with others with whom they agree in terms of their attitudes; this preference leads people to be surrounded by like-minded others (Byrne, London, and Griffitt 1968). And doing so is especially likely in terms of important attitudes. In contrast, the abilities associated with holding a large store of knowledge seem irrelevant to attitude-based friend selection, so more knowledge may not be associated with having more like-minded friends. If people generalize from the biased sample of people with whom they interact when estimating the proportion of others who share their views (Marks and Miller 1987), importance (but not knowledge) may regulate the magnitude of the false consensus effect.

To explore these hypotheses, undergraduate respondents were asked to estimate the proportion of others who shared their views on the issue of capital punishment. They also rated the degree to which they perceived themselves to be in the minority in their views on this issue. On both measures, significant effects of attitude importance were evident: people who attached more importance to their attitudes generated higher estimates of social support for their views, and they perceived themselves to be in the minority on this issue significantly less often. Knowledge, on the other hand, had no impact on either measure, nor did knowledge and importance interact.

This investigation of the causes of the false consensus effect therefore bolsters the notion that importance and knowledge should not be conceptualized as manifestations of a single construct. The fact that importance moderated the false consensus effect while knowledge did not suggests that the two strength-related attributes are—at least to some degree—independent of each other. If the single-construct conceptualization were correct, either, both, or neither of the two attributes would have moderated the effect.

CHANGES IN IMPORTANCE AND KNOWLEDGE OVER TIME

If importance and knowledge are surface manifestations of a single underlying construct, they must rise and fall in parallel over time in the course of daily life, as the underlying construct they reflect rises and falls. If people come to attach more importance to an attitude object over the course of weeks or months, they must also manifest comparable increases in the amount of knowledge they possess about it. If importance and knowledge are discrete constructs, on the other hand, they may rise and fall independently. People may come to attach more importance to an attitude but not gain any new knowledge about it. They may also gain information about an object but not perceive the attitude to be any more important to them. Importance and knowledge may even change in opposite directions: as people learn more about an attitude object, for example, they may come to attach less importance to it.

To explore this possibility, Visser, Krosnick, and Simmons took advantage of a unique real-world opportunity provided by the White House Conference on Global Climate Change, held on October 6, 1997, drawing national attention and sparking a vigorous national debate about global warming. During the subsequent months, hundreds of stories on this issue appeared on television, in newspapers, on the radio, and in news magazines. Advertisements paid for by industry organizations and other advocacy groups further expanded the national discussion.

The impact of this flood of information was explored by conducting telephone interviews with two nationally representative samples of American adults. The first sample was interviewed just before media attention to global warming surged, and the second sample was interviewed several months later, after the media had turned their attention elsewhere.

The deluge of media attention led to a marginally significant increase in the personal importance the American public attached to this issue. Mediational analyses indicated that the public debate increased Americans' perceptions of links between global warming and their core values, leading them to attach greater importance to the issue. Interestingly, the public debate did not alter the amount of knowledge American citizens said they possessed about global warming. Thus, importance and knowledge exhibited different trajectories over time, suggesting that they reflect not one but two underlying constructs that rise and fall independently.

CONCLUSIONS

The effects of importance and knowledge documented in this research are summarized in Figure 7.2. Importance and knowledge were both related to the degree of attitude impact, but these relations were not identical. Importance was a cause of selective exposure to attitude-relevant information and of the false consensus effect, whereas knowledge volume influenced neither of these outcomes. And importance and knowledge interacted to inspire attitude-expressive behavior. These findings therefore resonate with the evidence summarized in Figure 7.1 that importance and knowledge have different causes.

The portrait that emerges from this research stands in contrast to the image of these two strength-related attitude features suggested by exploratory factor analyses. These two constructs are clearly positively associated. But rather than being manifestations of a single underlying construct, importance and knowledge seem better described as discrete constructs possessing

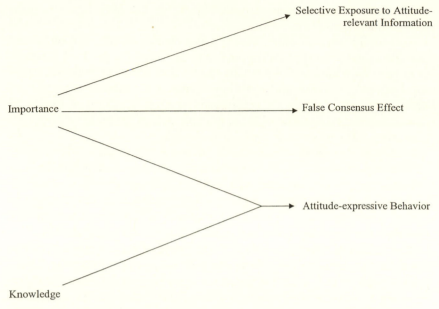

Figure 7.2 The effects of importance and knowledge.

distinct psychological properties, arising from different origins, producing disparate outcomes, and operating via separate causal processes. The findings reported here are consistent with our suspicion that attitude importance motivates people to protect and use their attitudes, whereas knowledge amounts to a stock of information that confers the ability to use an attitude successfully.

ATTITUDE IMPORTANCE AND ACCESSIBILITY

Theory

The next set of evidence we review focuses on the relation of attitude importance to attitude accessibility. Past research has shown that importance and accessibility are positively correlated (e.g., Krosnick 1989). One possible reason for this relation is causal impact of one on another, a notion consistent with some existing research. For example, thinking about an attitude object has been shown to increase attitude extremity (Millar and Tesser 1986; Sadler and Tesser 1973; Tesser and Conlee 1973; Tesser and Cowan 1975), and attaching importance to an object inspires thinking about relevant information (Berent and Krosnick 1993). Roese and Olson (1994) and Bizer and Krosnick (2001) explored the possibility of mutual impact with regard to importance and accessibility, and we review their findings here.

The approach taken in their research presumes that if two strength-related attributes do indeed reflect a single underlying construct, then this can be documented by studying changes in them induced by experimental manipulation or real-world events. After observing or causing a change in one attribute, researchers can explore whether other strength-related attributes changed in parallel. According to the single-construct view, if an increase in one attribute is observed, *all other* manifestations of the construct should also increase. But if these attributes are independent, they may not necessarily change in parallel. And even if parallel changes do occur, they may be due to an effect of one variable on the other, which would also challenge the single-construct view.

With regard to importance and accessibility, two contradictory causal hypotheses have been advanced about their reciprocal impact. Krosnick (1989) suggested that attitude importance is likely to be a cause of attitude accessibility. Once a person decides to attach personal significance to an attitude, he or she is likely to seek out information relevant to it and to think deeply about that information. As a result, the attitude is likely to become more accessible over time. Thus, the effect of importance on accessibility would be mediated by selective exposure and selective elaboration.

As we mentioned earlier, Roese and Olson (1994) asserted the opposite. These investigators suggested that people's internal cues regarding the personal importance of their attitudes may often be weak and ambiguous, forcing people to make inferences through self-perception. These investigators suggested one useful cue in such situations may be the speed with which one's attitude comes to mind. If an attitude comes to mind quickly, people may infer that it must be important to them, whereas if an attitude comes to mind slowly, people may infer that it must not be very important to them.

To test these latter hypotheses, Roese and Olson (1994) manipulated the accessibility of attitudes and then measured the importance of those attitudes. Specifically, these investigators induced some people to express some attitudes repeatedly while not expressing other attitudes at all. Consistent with previous research (e.g., Fazio et al. 1982), this manipulation increased the accessibility of the repeatedly expressed attitudes. Roese and Olson also found that the manipulation increased the degree of personal importance people said they attached to those attitudes. The fact that importance and accessibility both increased as a result of repeated expression is consistent with the notion that both attributes are simple derivatives of one single latent construct.

Roese and Olson attempted to test more directly the notion that attitude accessibility caused attitude importance reports. They reasoned that if attitude importance judgments are in fact derived from attitude accessibility, then accessibility should have mediated the impact of their repeated expression manipulation on importance reports. That is, repeated expression should have caused increased accessibility, which in turn caused increased importance ratings.

However, the partial correlations that Roese and Olson estimated to conduct their critical mediational analyses were accidentally not computed properly (Roese, personal communication, 1995). The experimental design entailed computing repeated-measures within-subjects associations of the manipulation with importance and accessibility across attitude objects, so the partial correlation analysis needed to be computed using within-subjects repeated-measures as well. But accidentally, only between-subject differences were controlled for (Roese, personal communication, 1995). Consequently, the reported mediational analyses do not shed light on the causal effects accessibility and importance may have on one another. All we can infer from this study is that repeated expression can cause increases in both accessibility and importance.

Bizer and Krosnick (2001) replicated Roese and Olson's (1994) study twice in order to compute the proper partial correlations. Bizer and Krosnick's (2001) third study manipulated importance in an effort to assess whether it might cause accessibility. Finally, their fourth investigation examined naturally occurring changes in importance and accessibility via a panel survey to see whether one variable could predict subsequent changes in the other.

In the first three of these studies, Bizer and Krosnick observed the impact of a change in one attribute on the other. If both of these attributes reflect a single underlying construct, then any manipulation that influences one should influence the other. But if the two attributes represent distinct constructs, then a cause of one will not necessarily influence the other. Finally, if both are influenced simultaneously by a manipulation, then the impact of the manipulation on one attribute may be mediated by the other. Consequently, these studies offered opportunities to explore the latent structure of these attributes in a novel way.

Experimental Manipulation of Accessibility

In Studies 1 and 2, accessibility was manipulated by inducing repeated attitude expression. The effect of the manipulation on accessibility and importance could then be assessed, as could mediation. Respondents first reported their attitudes on four target issues on written questionnaires. For each respondent, two attitudes were expressed five times each, while the other two attitudes were expressed only once. Respondents then reported their attitudes on each issue and the personal importance of each attitude on a computer. To measure attitude accessibility, the computer recorded the time it took respondents to report that they supported or opposed a policy on a dichotomous measure (Study 1) or on a five-point rating scale (Study 2). Attitude importance was measured on a nine-point scale with only the endpoints verbally labeled in the first study; importance was measured more reliably (on a five-point scale with all points verbally labeled) in the second study.

The results of these two studies were consistent. First, repeatedly expressed attitudes were reported significantly more quickly than were attitudes not repeatedly expressed in both studies. However, repeated expression did not increase importance ratings in either experiment. Because importance did not increase, there was no need to examine whether importance mediated the effect of the manipulation on accessibility in either study. The fact that accessibility increased without a parallel increase in importance suggests that both attributes are not simply surface manifestations of the same underlying construct, challenging the singular-construct models of attitude strength.

Experimental Manipulation of Importance

Bizer and Krosnick (2001) next conducted a study looking for an effect of importance on accessibility. To do so, they drew on the findings of Boninger, Krosnick, and Berent (1995), which showed that attitude importance is caused by self-interest. Bizer and Krosnick therefore thought that manipulating respondents' self-interest in an issue would alter the importance they attached to it, so they could see whether accessibility changes as a result as well.

During this study, respondents read news articles from a "computerized bulletin board service." Two articles discussed policies that were to be instituted at their own university (e.g., "Ohio State to give all students free lunches"), whereas the other two had been rejected at a faraway university (e.g., "University of Southern Wales will not give all students free lunches"). This was the manipulation of self-interest, with respondents presumably having more interest in the former issues than in the latter.

Because the impact of importance on accessibility would presumably be mediated by selective exposure or selective elaboration, respondents were given the opportunity to be selective in either their exposure to or their thinking about the articles. Respondents were shown the headlines of the articles and were able to choose which of the corresponding articles they wished to read. Bizer and Krosnick expected that people would choose to read or think about the articles relevant to their self-interest more than to the articles irrelevant to their self-interest.

Respondents then reported their attitudes on the four target issues; the computer measured response latencies of these reports. Finally, respondents completed a paper-and-pencil questionnaire that assessed their perceptions

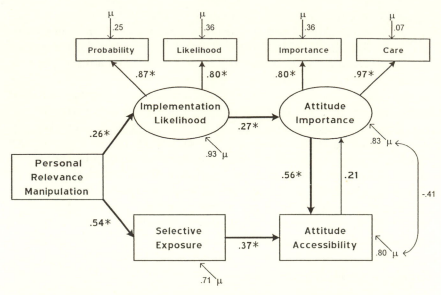

Figure 7.3 Documenting the impact of a manipulation of personal relevance on perceived likelihood of policy implementation, attitude importance, and accessibility. *p < .05.

of the likelihood that each of the four policies would be enacted at their university and the personal importance of each issue to them.

As expected, policies that were said to be personally relevant to respondents were indeed perceived to be more likely to be implemented at the respondents' own university than the remaining policies. Furthermore, attitudes on personally relevant issues were more personally important and reported more quickly than were attitudes on nonrelevant issues.

To assess the impact of importance and accessibility on each other, Bizer and Krosnick specified the causal model shown in Figure 7.3. This model allowed for the possibility that the manipulation of personal relevance may have enhanced the perceived likelihood of implementation and inspired selective exposure (by leading people to be more interested in reading articles on topics that might affect them). In turn, perceived likelihood of implementation was allowed to affect attitude importance (on the assumption that greater perceived likelihood of implementation would enhance perceptions of self-interest, which would in turn increase importance), while selective exposure was allowed to affect attitude accessibility (on the assumption that simply reading an article on a topic makes relevant knowledge in memory more accessible).

This model fit the data excellently. Enhancing the personal relevance of a policy did have the expected, positive direct effect on selective exposure

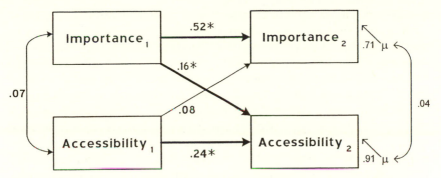

Figure 7.4 Documenting the impact of attitude importance and accessibility on one another. *p < .05.

and on perceptions of implementation likelihood. Perceived likelihood had a significant and positive effect on importance, and selective exposure had a significant and positive effect on accessibility. In contrast, the effect of accessibility on importance was not significant. Thus, there was no hint that people inferred the importance of their attitudes from the speed with which they came to mind.

TRACKING THE CAUSES OF NATURALLY OCCURRING CHANGES

In a final study, Bizer and Krosnick (2001) analyzed the data from the telephone survey study of public attitudes on global warming we described earlier. During each interview, respondents were asked to report how important the issue of global warming was to them personally and to report their attitudes toward global warming. Using a technique developed by Bassili (1996b), interviewers marked the length of time between the completion of asking the attitude question and the beginning of respondents' answers, which was treated as a measure of attitude accessibility.

The national debate about global warming that occurred between the two interviews offered Americans the opportunity to talk, think, and learn about the issue. During this time, people could have been selective in their exposure to and processing of this information based on their preexisting levels of the personal importance of the issue to them. Therefore, high initial levels of importance may have instigated increases in the accessibility of relevant attitudes.

To test this idea, Bizer and Krosnick estimated the parameters of the causal model in Figure 7.4, which fit the data perfectly, because the model is just-identified. Attitude importance manifested a moderately high level of stability over time, and accessibility manifested a somewhat lower but nonetheless reliable amount of stability over time. Furthermore, initial attitude importance predicted subsequent changes in accessibility in the expected direction. That is, increased initial levels of personal importance were associated with increases in accessibility over time. This result is consistent with the notion that importance is a cause of accessibility. Initial levels of attitude accessibility did not predict subsequent changes in importance.

Taken together, Bizer and Krosnick's first three studies challenge the claim that people simply infer attitude importance from attitude accessibility, presuming that an object must be important to them if their attitude toward it came to mind quickly. In Study 1, a manipulation caused increases in attitude accessibility, but no changes in importance were observed. In Study 2, a manipulation caused increases in attitude accessibility and yielded a marginally significant *decrease* in importance. And in Study 3, increased accessibility did not cause increases in importance. All this suggests that attitude accessibility does not subsume attitude importance.

These findings have clear implications regarding the structure of strength-related attitude attributes, complementing the existing literature that is dominated by factor analytic studies. If importance and accessibility were both simply surface manifestations of a single underlying factor, they would always change in parallel with one another. But in Studies 1 and 2, Bizer and Krosnick found that manipulations that increased one strength-related dimension did not always increase the other dimension, challenging the single latent construct hypothesis. Furthermore, Study 3 suggested that one variable (i.e., importance) mediated a manipulation's effect on another (i.e., accessibility). And in Study 4, importance guided subsequent changes in accessibility, but not vice versa. All this is inconsistent with the notion that both variables are manifestations of the same construct, inconsistent with the claim that accessibility subsumes importance.

CONCLUSION

Throughout much of this century, psychologists conceptualized intelligence as one general dimension of ability along which people vary, as instantiated, for example, by Spearman's "g-factor" (1904, 1927). Not only is this notion intuitively plausible and appealing because of its simplicity, but various sorts of empirical evidence supported it as well. Most notably, factor analyses of ability measures pointed to a great deal of shared variance among these indicators, presumably attributable to a single underlying construct. Evidence consistent with this view dates back as early as Spearman's (1904, 1927) demonstrations that aptitudes as diverse as French, math, and music all loaded on g (see Jensen 1998).

Over the years following Spearman's argument for a *g* factor, a range of evidence has been uncovered challenging this relatively simple claim, leading other researchers to argue for the existence of a few general intelligence factors. For example, Cattell (1971) asserted that fluid ability (g_f) and crystallized ability (g_c) should be distinguished from one another. Likewise, Willis and Schaie (1986) argued for the existence of four principal factors: fluid reasoning, crystallized knowledge, memory span, and perceptual speed.

In recent years, however, it has become clear that even these intermediate-range theories of the structure of intelligence oversimplify matters (e.g., Gardner 1983; Sternberg 1984; Schank 1986; Snow 1986). This research, in various ways, shows that the conceptualizations of intelligence as one single factor or a few general factors is flawed: intelligence is too complex to be thought of in such simplistic terms. A wide range of techniques have been developed to assess a wide array of abilities, and nearly all of these many abilities demonstrate some empirical independence from the others. For example, one of the most widely used intelligence assessment tests, the Wechsler Adult Intelligence Scale, yields a four-factor intelligence score, providing intelligence scores on the dimensions of verbal comprehension, perceptual organization, freedom from distractibility, and processing speed (cf. Kaufman 1994).

As we have seen, the notion of attitude strength has had a similar history in the social sciences. As with intelligence, it is attractive to consider attitude strength as a global construct. Such a conceptualization is parsimonious, easy to understand, and even somewhat intuitive. However, the research we have reviewed here suggests that such a conceptualization compromises validity, a price that is not worth paying.

In their chapter in the *Handbook of Social Psychology* titled "Attitude Structure and Function," Eagly and Chaiken (1998) reviewed the existing literature on the latent structure of strength-related attitude properties and noted that factor analytic studies had suggested a distinction between cognitive and affective dimensions of attitude strength. But these authors noted as well that "although several findings have . . . suggested the utility of distinguishing cognitive from affective aspects of attitude strength, subsequent work may well yield other useful distinctions beyond, or within, these two broad dimensions" (291). Eagly and Chaiken called upon researchers to "go beyond the question of strength's dimensionality to the question of whether such distinctions matter. If all aspects of attitude strength produced the very same effects, the theoretical importance of distinguishing types of strength would be hollow" (291).

The research reviewed in this chapter was done in the spirit of Eagly and Chaiken's recommendation, confirming their expectations. We have indeed uncovered further distinctions among strength-related dimensions than just the cognitive-affective one, and we have seen that different attributes have different origins and different effects. Although a common factors model would certainly be more parsimonious, the truth appears to be that strength-related properties are interrelated but distinct.

In the simplest evidence, correlations among the attributes, although typically significantly different from zero, are not so strong as to suggest that all are surface manifestations of the same latent construct (Krosnick and Abelson 1992). Confirmatory factor analyses suggest uniformly that pairs of these attributes do not reflect a single underlying factor. Manipulations that increased one attribute did not necessarily lead to increases in other attributes. And extensive research comparing importance with attitude-relevant knowledge and accessibility showed that treating these two constructs as isomorphic is ill-advised. Thus, though it is certainly more parsimonious to lump strength-related attitude attributes into one or several higher-order strength factors, it seems best to consider these attributes as related, yet not simple outgrowths of hypothetical higher-order factors.

The work we have described helps to fill in gaps in the portraits of various strength-related attributes. For example, attitude importance appears to be, at its core, a motivation to protect and use one's attitude, whereas knowledge constitutes a reservoir of ability, facilitating behavioral strategizing. We have also seen some illustrations of what a construct is *not*. For example, knowledge seems not to attenuate such cognitive biases as the false consensus effect. Lastly, we have seen evidence regarding the mechanisms by which effects occur. For example, self-interest and value-relevance affect knowledge only by inspiring increased importance. We hope that cataloging these sorts of findings along with others will eventually lead to a full and rich account of the origins and consequences of attitude strength.

Future research on this topic might borrow two of the approaches employed here and apply them anew. One design is that used by Bizer and Krosnick (2001): implement an experimental manipulation narrowly designed to alter just one strength-related attitude (e.g., importance), and observe the consequences that follow. Analogous manipulations can presumably be implemented to alter knowledge, certainty, and other features and obscure their consequences. Other studies might employ the technique used by Visser, Krosnick, and Simmons, whereby multiple dimensions are measured, and multivariate analysis is used to isolate their independent effects and interactions. When many studies employing these and other approaches document the full range of causes and effects of various attributes, we will be in a strong position to build a general, integrative theory.

NOTES

The authors wish to thank Richard Petty, Marilynn Brewer, Gifford Weary, Bill von Hippel, Timothy Brock, and Philip Tetlock for their very helpful suggestions regarding this research. The authors also wish to thank Jamie Franco for her help in preparation of the manuscript.

REFERENCES

Abelson, R. P. 1988. "Conviction." *American Psychologist* 43:267–75.

Bassili, J. N. 1996a. "Meta-Judgmental versus Operative Indexes of Psychological Attributes: The Case of Measures of Attitude Strength." *Journal of Personality and Social Psychology* 71:637–53.

———. 1996b. "The How and Why of Response Latency Measurement in Telephone Surveys." In *Answering Questions: Methodology for Determining Cognitive and Communicative Processes in Survey Research,* ed. N. Schwarz and S. Sudman, 319–46. San Francisco: Jossey-Bass.

Berent, M. K. 1990. "Attitude Importance and the Recall of Attitude-Relevant Information." Master's thesis, Ohio State University.

Berent, M. K., and J. A. Krosnick. 1993. "Attitude Importance and Selective Exposure to Attitude-Relevant Information." Paper presented at the Midwestern Psychological Association Annual Meeting, Chicago.

Biek, M., W. Wood, and S. Chaiken. 1996. "Working Knowledge, Cognitive Processing, and Attitudes: On the Determinants of Bias." *Personality and Social Psychology Bulletin* 22:547–56.

Bizer, G. Y., and J. A. Krosnick. 2001. "Exploring the Structure of Strength-Related Attitude Features: The Relation between Attitude Importance and Attitude Accessibility." *Journal of Personality and Social Psychology* 81:566–86.

Boninger, D. S., J. A. Krosnick, and M. K. Berent. 1995. "Origins of Attitude Importance: Self-Interest, Social Identification, and Value Relevance." *Journal of Personality and Social Psychology* 68:61–80.

Boninger, D. S., J. A. Krosnick, M. K. Berent, and L. R. Fabrigar. 1995. "The Causes and Consequences of Attitude Importance." In *Attitude Strength: Antecedents and Consequences,* ed. R. E. Petty, and J. A. Krosnick, 159–90. Mahwah, NJ: Lawrence Erlbaum.

Budd, R. J. 1986. "Predicting Cigarette Use: The Need to Incorporate Measures of Salience in the Theory of Reasoned Action." *Journal of Applied Social Psychology* 16:633–85.

Byrne, D. E., O. London, and W. Griffitt. 1968. "The Effect of Topic Importance and Attitude Similarity-Dissimilarity on Attraction in an Intrastranger Design." *Psychonomic Science* 11:303–04.

Cattell, R. B. 1971. *Abilities: Their Structure, Growth, and Action.* Boston: Houghton Mifflin.

Celsi, R. L., and J. C. Olson. 1988. "The Role of Involvement in Attention and Comprehension Processes." *Journal of Consumer Research* 15:210–24.

Clarke, P., and E. Fredin. 1978. "Newspapers, Television, and Political Reasoning." *Public Opinion Quarterly* 42:143–60.

Clore, G. L., and B. Baldridge. 1968. "Interpersonal Attraction: The Role of Agreement and Topic Interest." *Journal of Personality and Social Psychology* 9:340–46.

Cooke, N. J., R. S. Atlas, D. M. Lane, and R. C. Berger. 1993. "Role of High-Level Knowledge in Memory for Chess Positions." *American Journal of Psychology* 106:321–51.

Davidson, A. R. 1995. "From Attitudes to Actions to Attitude Change: The Effects of Amount and Accuracy of Information." *Attitude Strength: Antecedents and Consequences,* ed. R. E. Petty and J. A. Krosnick, 315–36. Mahwah, NJ: Lawrence Erlbaum.

Eagly, A. H., and S. Chaiken. 1998. "Attitude Structure and Function." In *The Handbook of Social Psychology,* ed. D. T. Gilbert, S. T. Fiske, and G. Lindzey, 269–322. New York: McGraw Hill.

Eckhardt, B. B., M. R. Wood, and R. S. Jacobvitz. 1991. "Verbal Ability and Prior Knowledge: Contributions to Adults' Comprehension of Television." *Communication Research* 18:636–49.

Engle, R. W., J. K. Nations, and J. Cantor. 1990. "Is 'Working Memory Capacity' Just Another Name for Word Knowledge?" *Journal of Educational Psychology* 82:799–804.

Fazio, R. H., and M. P. Zanna. 1981. "Direct Experience and Attitude-Behavior Consistency." In *Advances in Experimental Social Psychology,* ed. L. Berkowitz, 14:161–202. San Diego: Academic Press.

Fazio, R. H., J. Chen, E. C. McDonel, and S. J. Sherman. 1982. "Attitude Accessibility, Attitude-Behavior Consistency, and the Strength of the Object-Evaluation Association." *Journal of Experimental Social Psychology* 18:339–57.

Fine, B. J. 1957. "Conclusion-Drawing, Communicator Credibility, and Anxiety as Factors in Opinion Change." *Journal of Abnormal and Social Psychology* 5:369–74.

Fiske, S. T., R. R. Lau, and R. A. Smith. 1990. "On the Varieties and Utilities of Political Expertise." *Social Cognition* 8:31–48.

Gardner, H. 1983. *Frames of Mind: The Theory of Multiple Intelligences.* New York: Basic Books.

Gorn, G. J. 1975. "The Effects of Personal Involvement, Communication Discrepancy, and Source Prestige on Reactions to Communications on Separatism." *Canadian Journal of Behavioural Science* 7:369–86.

Granberg, D., and S. Holmberg. 1986. "Political Perception among Voters in Sweden and the U.S.: Analyses of Issues with Specific Alternatives." *Western Political Quarterly* 39:7–28.

Haddock, G., A. J. Rothman, and N. Schwarz. 1996. "Are (Some) Reports of Attitude Strength Context Dependent?" *Canadian Journal of Behavioural Science* 28:313–16.

Haddock, G., A. J. Rothman, R. Reber, and N. Schwarz. 1999. "Forming Judgments of Attitude Certainty, Intensity, and Importance: The Role of Subjective Experiences." *Personality and Social Psychology Bulletin* 25:771–82.

Hansen, J. 1984. "The Role of Prior Knowledge in Content Area Learning." *Topics in Learning and Learning Disabilities* 3:66–72.

Howard-Pitney, B., E. Borgida, and A. M. Omoto. 1986. "Personal Involvement: An Examination of Processing Differences." *Social Cognition* 4:39–57.

Jackman, M. R. 1977. "Prejudice, Tolerance, and Attitudes toward Ethnic Groups." *Social Science Research* 6:145–69.

Jensen, A. R. 1998. *The G Factor: The Science of Mental Ability.* Westport, CT: Praeger.

Judd, C. M., and J. T. Johnson. 1981. "Attitudes, Polarization, and Diagnosticity: Exploring the Effect of Affect." *Journal of Personality and Social Psychology* 41:26–36.

Judd, C. M., and J. A. Krosnick. 1989. "Attitude Centrality, Organization, and Measurement." *Journal of Personality and Social Psychology* 42:436–47.

Kaufman, A. S. 1994. *Intelligent Testing with the WISC-III.* New York: Wiley.

Krosnick, J. A. 1988. "The Role of Attitude Importance in Social Evaluations: A Study of Policy Preferences, Presidential Candidate Evaluations, and Voting Behavior." *Journal of Personality and Social Psychology* 55:196–210.

———. 1989. "Attitude Importance and Attitude Accessibility." *Personality and Social Psychology Bulletin* 15:297–308.

Krosnick, J. A., and R. P. Abelson. 1992. "The Case for Measuring Attitude Strength in Surveys." In *Questions about Survey Questions,* ed. J. Tanur, 177–203. New York: Russell Sage.

Krosnick, J. A., and R. E. Petty. 1995. "Attitude Strength: An Overview." In *Attitude Strength: Antecedents and Consequences,* ed. R. E. Petty and J. A. Krosnick, 1–24. Mahwah, NJ: Lawrence Erlbaum.

Krosnick, J. A., D. S. Boninger, Y. C. Chuang, M. K. Berent, and C. G. Carnot. 1993. "Attitude Strength: One Construct or Many Related Constructs?" *Journal of Personality and Social Psychology* 66:1132–51.

Kyllonen, P. C., W. C. Tirre, and R. E. Christal. 1991. "Knowledge and Processing Speed as Determinants of Associative Learning." *Journal of Experimental Psychology: General* 120:57–79.

Lavine, H., J. W. Huff, S. H. Wagner, and D. Sweeney. 1998. "The Moderating Influence of Attitude Strength on the Susceptibility to Context Effects in Attitude Surveys." *Journal of Personality and Social Psychology* 75:359–73.

Marks, G., and N. Miller. 1985. "The Effect of Certainty on Consensus Judgments." *Personality and Social Psychology Bulletin* 11:165–77.

———. 1987. "Ten Years of Research on the False-Consensus Effect: An Empirical and Theoretical Review." *Psychological Bulletin* 102:72–90.

McGraw, K. M., and N. Pinney. 1990. "The Effects of General and Domain-Specific Expertise on Political Memory and Judgment." *Social Cognition* 8:9–30.

McGraw, K. M., M. Lodge, and P. K. Stroh. 1990. "On-Line Processing in Candidate Evaluation: The Effects of Issue Order, Issue Salience, and Sophistication." *Political Behavior* 12:41–58.

McGuire, W. J. 1986. "The Myth of Massive Media Impact: Savagings and Salvagings." In *Public Communication and Behavior,* ed. G. Comstock, 1:173–257. San Diego: Academic Press.

Millar, M., and A. Tesser. 1986. "Thought-Induced Attitude Change: The Effects of Schema Structure and Commitment." *Journal of Personality and Social Psychology* 51:259–69.

Parker, H. A., R. W. Perry, and D. F. Gillespie. 1974. "Prolegomenon to a Theory of Attitude-Behavior Relationships." *Pakistan Journal of Psychology* 7:21–39.

Paull, G., and D. Glencross. 1997. "Expert Perception and Decision Making in Baseball." *International Journal of Sport Psychology* 28:35–56.

Pearson, P. D., J. Hansen, and C. Gordon. 1979. "The Effect of Background Knowledge on Young Children's Comprehension of Explicit and Implicit Information." *Journal of Reading Behavior* 11:201–09.

Pelham, B. W. 1991. "On Confidence and Consequence: The Certainty and Importance of Self-Knowledge." *Journal of Personality and Social Psychology* 60:518–30.

Perse, E. M. 1990. "Media Involvement and Local News Effects." *Journal of Broadcasting and Electronic Media* 34:17–36.

Pomerantz, E. M., S. Chaiken, and R. S. Tordesillas. 1995. "Attitude Strength and Resistance Processes." *Journal of Personality and Social Psychology* 69:408–19.

Roberts, D. F., and N. Maccoby. 1985. "Effects of Mass Communication." In *Handbook of Social Psychology,* ed. G. Lindzey and E. Aronson, 3rd ed., 2:539–98. New York: Random House.

Roese, N. J., and J. M. Olson. 1994. "Attitude Importance as a Function of Repeated Attitude Expression." *Journal of Experimental Social Psychology* 30:39–51.

Rokeach, M., and P. Kliejunas. 1972. "Behavior as a Function of Attitude-Toward-Object and Attitude-Toward-Situation." *Journal of Personality and Social Psychology* 22:194–201.

Sadler, O., and A. Tesser. 1973. "Some Effects of Salience and Time upon Interpersonal Hostility and Attraction during Social Isolation." *Sociometry* 36:99–112.

Schank, R. C. 1986. "Explaining Intelligence." In *What Is Intelligence?,* ed. R. J. Sternberg and D. K. Detterman, 121–31. Norwood, NJ: Ablex.

Schneider, W., H. Gruber, A. Gold, and K. Opwis. 1993. "Chess Expertise and Memory for Chess Positions in Children and Adults." *Journal of Experimental Child Psychology* 56:328–49.

Schuman, H., and S. Presser. 1981. *Questions and Answers in Attitude Surveys: Experiments on Question Form, Wording, and Context.* New York: Academic Press.

Snow, R. E. 1986. "On Intelligence." In *What Is Intelligence?,* ed. R. J. Sternberg and D. K. Detterman, 133–39. Norwood, NJ: Ablex.

Spearman, C. 1904. "'General Intelligence,' Objectively Determined and Measured." *American Journal of Psychology* 15:201–93.

———. 1927. *The Abilities of Man: Their Nature and Measurement.* New York: MacMillan.

Sternberg, R. J. 1984. "Toward a Triarchic Theory of Human Intelligence." *Behavioral and Brain Sciences* 7:269–316.

Tesser, A., and M. C. Conlee. 1973. "Recipient Emotionality as a Determinant of the Transmission of Bad News." *Proceedings of the Annual Convention of the American Psychological Association,* 247–48.

Tesser, A., and C. L. Cowan. 1975. "Some Effects of Time and Thought on Attitude Polarization." *Journal of Personality and Social Psychology* 31:262–70.

Thompson, M. T., M. P. Zanna, and D.W. Griffin. 1995. "Let's Not Be Indifferent about (Attitudinal) Ambivalence." In *Attitude Strength: Antecedents and*

Consequences, ed. R. E. Petty and J. A. Krosnick, 361–86. Mahwah, NJ: Lawrence Erlbaum.

Thurstone, L. L. 1938. *Primary Mental Abilities.* Chicago: University of Chicago Press.

Tversky, A., and D. Kahneman. 1974. "Judgment under Uncertainty: Heuristics and Biases." *Science* 185:1124–31.

Verplanken, B. 1989. "Involvement and Need for Cognition as Moderators of Beliefs-Attitude-Intention Consistency." *British Journal of Social Psychology* 28:115–22.

———. 1991. "Persuasive Communication of Risk Information: A Test of Cue versus Message Processing Effects in a Field Experiment." *Personality and Social Psychology Bulletin* 17:188–93.

Visser, P. S., J. A. Krosnick, and J. P. Simmons. 2002. "Understanding the Relations among Strength-Related Attitude Features: Lumping versus Splitting." Paper presented at the annual convention of the Midwestern Psychological Association, Chicago.

Wänke, M., H. Bless, and B. Biller. 1996. "Subjective Experience versus Content of Information in the Construction of Attitude Judgments." *Personality and Social Psychology Bulletin* 22:1105–13.

Willis, S. L., and K. W. Schaie. 1986. "Practical Intelligence in Later Adulthood." In *Practical Intelligence,* ed. R. J. Sternberg and R. K. Wagner, 236–68. New York: Cambridge University Press.

Willoughby, T., T. G. Waller, E. Wood, and G. E. MacKinnon. 1993. "The Effect of Prior Knowledge on an Immediate and Delayed Associative Learning Task Following Elaborative Interrogation." *Contemporary Educational Psychology* 18:36–46.

Wilson, T. D., D. S. Dunn, D. Kraft, and D. J. Lisle. 1989. "Introspection, Attitude Change, and Attitude-Behavior Consistency: The Disruptive Effects of Explaining Why We Feel the Way We Do." In *Advances in Experimental Social Psychology,* ed. L. Berkowitz, 22:287–343. New York: Academic Press.

Wood, W. 1982. "Retrieval of Attitude-Relevant Information from Memory: Effects on Susceptibility to Persuasion and on Intrinsic Motivation." *Journal of Personality and Social Psychology* 42:798–810.

Wood, W., and C. A. Kallgren. 1988. "Communicator Attributes and Persuasion: Recipients' Access to Attitude-Relevant Information in Memory." *Personality and Social Psychology Bulletin* 4:172–82.

Wood, W., N. Rhodes, and M. Biek. 1995. "Working Knowledge and Attitude Strength: An Information-Processing Analysis." In *Attitude Strength: Antecedents and Consequences,* ed. R. E. Petty and J. A. Krosnick, 283–313. Mahwah, NJ: Lawrence Erlbaum.

Zaichkowsky, J. L. 1985. "Measuring the Involvement Construct." *Journal of Consumer Research* 12:341–52.

Zuwerink, J. R., and P. G. Devine. 1996. "Attitude Importance and Resistance to Persuasion: It's Not Just the Thought That Counts." *Journal of Personality and Social Psychology* 70:931–44.

CHAPTER 8

Stability and Change of Opinion: The Case of Swiss Policy against Pollution Caused by Cars

Hanspeter Kriesi

THE QUESTION of the stability of opinion about government policies has been a hotly debated issue among social scientists for many decades. Panel surveys have typically found a lot of instability with respect to individual opinions between successive interviews. In the American debate, this instability has usually not been attributed to genuine change of opinion but interpreted as some kind of chance variation. The debate has focused on the type of chance variation and the reasons why there is so much of it. There are two approaches. On the one hand, Converse's approach maintains that this instability is indicative of widespread non attitudes. In his seminal essay, "The Nature of Belief Systems in Mass Publics," Converse (1964) claims that "large portions of an electorate do not have meaningful beliefs, even on issues that have formed the basis of intense political controversy among elites for substantial periods of time" (245). Accordingly, large parts of the citizenry may be susceptible to political manipulations of all kinds and their political choices may be singularly ill-considered. Converse's point of view has been strongly challenged by the measurement error approach (e.g., Achen 1975; Judd and Milburn 1980), which attributes the chance variations in individuals' responses to the inherent difficulty of survey questions to measure individual opinions correctly. Compared to the unsettling consequences of Converse's interpretation, the implications of this approach are quite attractive. According to the measurement error approach, we can put our trust in the citizens. They have real, stable opinions; it is our measurement instruments that are unreliable, the deficiencies of which are easily remedied by standard psychometric techniques.

The two approaches employ different methodologies to arrive at their respective conclusions, and one might suspect that the discrepancy between them is an artifact of the differences in the methodology employed. Commenting on the discrepancy between these two approaches, Sniderman, Brody, and Tetlock (1991) go one step further and suggest that behind the choice of a method for data analysis lie different ontological assumptions: "[T]he propriety of techniques for estimating the facts depends on prior assumptions about the facts of the matter" (17). To the extent that it accepts the idea that differences in methodology necessarily lead to different results, this comment is misleading. It is, however, revealing in so far as it points to the importance of the theoretical models about the "facts of the matter," which guide the analysis of the data. Within the framework of one and the same methodological approach, we can, indeed, arrive at quite different conclusions, depending on the kind of theoretical models we apply. This has been graphically illustrated by the exchange between Jagodzinski and his collaborators (Jagodzinski and Kühnel 1987; Jagodzinski, Kühnel, and Schmidt 1987, 1990) on the one hand, and Saris and van den Putte (1987) on the other.

In this essay I would like to build on the methodology employed by the measurement error approach without, however, sharing all its traditional assumptions about the "facts of the matter." I start from three sets of assumptions concerning citizens' attitudes and opinions. First, I assume that citizens hold some *general political attitudes*. In line with the measurement error approach, I expect these attitudes to guide, to some extent, the specific opinions they hold on given public policy issues. But, closer to Converse's original idea that mass belief systems suffer from a triple lack of crystallization—horizontally, between opinions on issues; vertically, between general concepts and specific preferences on concrete issues; and temporally, between positions taken at different moments in time on a given issue—I assume that these attitudes are *not very reliable guides* for an individual's policy-related opinions at a given point in time. The general attitudes may be rather vague in the first place. Moreover, citizens may fail to connect the specific policy issues to their underlying general attitude. Citizens may not have the cues allowing them to make the necessary connections. In addition, the issue-related considerations that come up in the individual's mind at the time of the interview may vary from one occasion to the other (Zaller 1992). Individuals may bring different considerations to the evaluation of the same question for reasons that directly depend on the interview situation: most questions are open to multiple interpretation and their order and framing may have an influence on the type of considerations that will be most salient in the mind of the respondents when asked to give their opinions. But the considerations that are immediately salient in a given interview situation may also be influenced by the political context of the moment: the intensity of the public debate on the issue in question and the saliency of certain arguments in this debate may vary over time. The respondents may have heard a pertinent argument just the other day in the news or in a discussion with a friend, and this argument may become the decisive consideration when she is expressing her opinion in the interview.

Second, I assume that *not all individuals are alike*. Some people are more politically *aware* (Zaller 1992) or *sophisticated* (Luskin 1987; Sniderman, Brody, and Tetlock 1991) than others, and this has important consequences for the crystallization of their opinions on political issues. Moreover, some policies are more relevant for some people than for others. Those who are directly *concerned* about a given policy are more likely than the average citizen to monitor the policy process in question, and, as a consequence, they are more likely to have crystallized opinions about it. Take, for example, a group of retired persons: they are rather likely to follow the ups and downs of the policy cycle in the area of old-age pensions and to have stable opinions about it. In addition, and most important, some individuals feel more strongly about a given issue than others. *Opinion strength* or the lack of it may have multiple origins. The largely unconscious presence of opposing considerations in an individual's mind—what Zaller (1992:59) calls ambivalence—may be at the origin of weak opinions. Opinions may be weakened by an underlying inner conflict that cannot be resolved in the interview situation—what Alvarez and Brehm (1995:1056; 1997) call ambivalence. Weak opinions may also result from uncertainty due to a lack of information about the issue in question, or from a combination of these factors (Steenbergen, Brewer, and Vercellotti 1997). While I am agnostic about the origins of a possible lack of opinion strength, I would like to suggest that opinion strength is a crucial factor with respect to the stability of individual opinions. Converse (1964) has already pointed out that strong opinions are more resistant to change. Eagly and Chaiken (1993:580ff.) and Krosnick and Fabrigar (1995:51–52) review a formidable array of evidence in support of this proposition: strong opinions are more persistent over time.

Third, I assume that the stability of individual opinions is a function of the *issue* in question. Policies most likely to give rise to crystallized opinions are those that are *familiar* to the respondents. These are issues that have been extensively debated, have given rise to a policy consensus among the elites. In turn, these elites have seen that consensus implemented by specific measures whose effects are well-known to the respondents from personal experience. As Converse (1970) has observed, "[T]here is a very real sense in which attitudes take practice" (177). In addition, *constraining* issues are likely to give rise to crystallized opinions. The constraints can be of a moral or of a more material kind. On the basis of the principles or costs involved, people are likely to feel more strongly about a constraining issue. Finally, the *complexity* of the issues may also play a role. The more complex an issue, the more likely it is that people will lack knowledge and will have a weak opinion about it.

SOURCES AND DATA

This analysis is based on a panel study consisting of four waves of interviews with a representative sample of Swiss citizens. In this study, the respondents were asked about their opinions concerning various policy measures against air pollution caused by cars. The first wave took place in December 1993, the second and third occurred in May and June 1994, and the last one was held in October 1995. The panel study was designed around three different "natural experiments." Between the first two waves, a public debate took place about transportation issues, in particular about the introduction of a tax on CO_2, one of the measures involved in the study. Between the next two waves, a Choice Questionnaire (see Bütschi 1997) was administered to the respondents. During the fifteen months between the last two interviews, half of the sample received additional information about the increase of the concentration of CO_2 in the atmosphere and possible measures to prevent it, while the other half of the sample did not receive anything. The original representative sample included some 2,000 Swiss residents who were at least eighteen years old and who had the right to vote. For the second wave, the original sample size was reduced to one half (n = 1,062), due to budgetary reasons. In the following waves, additional respondents were lost. All in all, for six issues, between 668 and 674 respondents answered the complete set of questions during the four waves, which corresponds to roughly two-thirds of the original sample of the second wave.

The six issues are all concerned with measures against air pollution caused by cars, but they differ with regard to the three aspects I highlighted above: their familiarity, complexity, and the degree to which they are constraining. Arranged according to the degree to which they impose individual constraints, these are their characteristics:

- *Electrical vehicles:* promoting electrical vehicles; a familiar, but complex measure, originally supported by 72.4 percent of the sample.
- *Car-free zones:* closing down town centers to car traffic; a highly familiar, straightforward measure, originally supported by 81.5 percent of the sample.
- *Parking restrictions:* raising parking fees in town centers and extending zones with restricted parking throughout entire areas of the cities; a familiar, straightforward measure, originally receiving 65.4 percent support.
- *Tax on CO_2:* introducing a tax on CO_2, which would raise the price of gas by 10 cts/l (presently at about 1.20 Sfr.). The tax receipts would be redistributed to the taxpayers and, thus, contribute to their future revenues; an unfamiliar, complex, and rather constraining measure, originally supported by 52.5 percent of the sample.

- *Speed limits:* introducing speed limits of 100 km/h (presently 120 km/h) on highways; a highly familiar, straightforward, and very constraining measure, as far as Swiss drivers are concerned, originally supported by 45.6 percent of the sample.
- *Price of gas to Sfr 2/l:* raising the price of gas beyond the 10 cts proposed by the tax on CO_2, step by step up to Sfr 2/l until 2000; a very unfamiliar, complex (link to the tax on CO_2), and highly constraining measure, originally supported by 40.1 percent of the respondents.

In the first wave, the respondents were asked about their opinions in a two-step procedure. First, they were provided with a brief sketch of the measure and asked whether they had already heard about it before. Then they were asked to give their opinion about the measure.[1] Five response categories were offered: "strongly disagree," "disagree," "agree," "strongly agree," and a "no opinion" option. Note that there was no middle alternative: the respondents were forced to take a stance—except for the "no opinion" option, which provided them with a possible escape from the forced choice. This commonly used approach measures direction and strength of an opinion. *Strength* is measured as an opinion's extremity or intensity.[2]

"Awareness," or more precisely "ecological awareness," was operationalized following procedures proposed by Zaller (1992) or Luskin (1987); that is, by a measure of information holding that counts the number of factual items the respondent has correctly answered.[3] More specifically, this measure of ecological awareness is composed of five subscales, each measuring a specific subset of a respondent's ecological awareness. The subscales concern issues related to radioactivity (3 items), air pollution caused by CO_2 (4 items), air pollution more generally measured (4 items), more practical environmental questions such as the price of electricity or the disposal of batteries (4 items), and the number of ecological organizations spontaneously mentioned in response to an open question. The resulting scale corresponds to the sum of these subscales and ranges from 0 to a maximum of 20 possible correct answers. The mean for the Swiss sample on this summary scale is situated just below 11 (10.83), with a standard deviation of 3.34. On the basis of this result, we may conclude that the Swiss are generally quite aware of environmental problems.

If it is generally difficult to capture the policy-relevant constraints of an individual's situation, the issue of private transportation offers the advantage of a relatively simple "objective" indicator of situational constraints. People who do not have a car of their own and who do not use a private car of some other member in their household can be considered to be unconstrained by any of the proposed measures. Our indicator of *objective constraints* distinguishes, therefore, between those who do not drive a private car and those who own a private car or regularly use the car of another member in their household.

THE UNDERLYING ATTITUDE

For the analysis of the first set of assumptions concerning the impact of a general, underlying attitude with respect to environmental protection, I propose to construct a so-called latent state-trait model, a type of model introduced by Steyer and Schmitt (1990). This model offers a conceptual framework for the simultaneous consideration of two fundamental aspects of the variation of individual opinions: the variable association of the different opinions with the underlying attitude and the intertemporal variation of the underlying attitude. One can conceive of this particular type of model as a two-tiered factor model. On the first level, the six opinions at time t_i constitute six different indicators of the "state" of the attitude at this moment in time. On the second level, the four time-specific "states" of the attitude are treated as indicators of its stable underlying "trait." Figure 8.1 presents this model. The latent states are indicated by the four factors η_j. Each observed measurement y_i depends on the effect of the respective latent state (λ_{ij}) and its associated error term ε_i. Each latent state, in turn, depends on the effect (γ_{j1}) of the latent trait ξ_1 and the situation-specific error (ζ_j). On the first level, the variances of the error terms ($\Theta\varepsilon_{ii}$) give an idea of the extent to which a given opinion is determined by the underlying attitude at time t_j. On the second level, the variances (ψ_{jj}) of the situation-specific error (ζ_j) indicate the extent to which the attitude at a given moment in time deviates from the "true" underlying attitude.

Table 8.1 shows how the six opinions are correlated with each other at each point in time. An inspection of this table reveals that one issue—the promotion of electrical vehicles—lies on a plane that is quite different from that of the other issues. The other five issues are only moderately correlated among themselves. To estimate the model, I assume equal error terms for the four measurements of one and the same opinion.[4] In addition, I allow for autocorrelated errors between corresponding measurements of the same issues at different points in time.[5] Finally, I also allow for correlated errors between different but related opinions at each point in time— the opinions about the two fiscal incentives, on the one hand, and about the two urban issues, on the other. A test of this model clearly suggests that it should be rejected ($\chi^2 = 812.91$, 242 df). The model can be considerably improved by allowing for variable error terms for the issue of electrical vehicles ($\chi^2 = 549.35$, 238 df), and by adding correlated errors

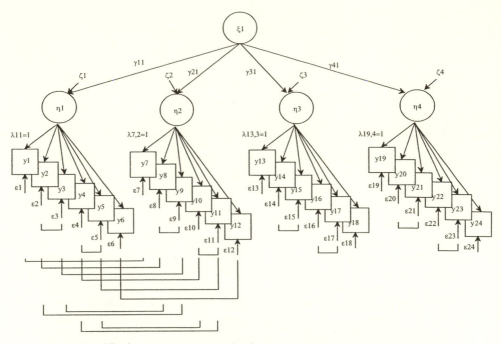

Figure 8.1 The latent state-trait model for the six issues and the four waves of interviews.

between the opinions on the two urban issues and the two fiscal incentives across points in time ($\chi^2 = 325.30$, 214 df).[6]

The results of this model are presented in Table 8.2. The first part of the table corresponds to the first tier of the model. It confirms that, indeed, the opinion on electrical vehicles has virtually nothing to do with the underlying attitude about environmental protection. Among the remaining issues, the more constraining ones tend to be more closely associated with the underlying factor. But even in the best of all cases, the opinion about speed limits (the only issue that is at the same time constraining and familiar), more than half (55.8 percent) of the variance in the individual opinions cannot be accounted for by the underlying attitude. This is only in part due to measurement error. In part, this also stems from a lack of validity: to a variable degree, the individual opinions on policy issues are determined by factors other than the supposed underlying attitude.

The second part of the table concerns the stability of the underlying trait. It shows this trait to be quite stable. The state-specific error variances range from 2.7 percent to 13.9 percent. Interestingly enough, at the second interview, the state-specific factor scores correspond most closely to the underlying attitude (the "trait"). This is in line with the idea of a

TABLE 8.1
Correlations between Six Opinions at Four Different Points in Time: Pearson
Correlation Coefficients

Issues	1	2	3	4	5
Time 1					
1 electrical vehicles	–				
2 car-free zones	.163	–			
3 parking restrictions	.076	.474	–		
4 tax on CO_2	.158	.302	.430	–	
5 gas at Sfr 2/l	.189	.330	.435	.750	–
6 speed limits	.157	.323	.370	.430	.427
Time 2					
1 electrical vehicles	–				
2 car-free zones	.133	–			
3 parking restrictions	.095	.394	–		
4 tax on CO_2	.113	.259	.400	–	
5 gas at Sfr 2/l	.117	.247	.453	.768	–
6 speed limits	.072	.294	.352	.377	.438
Time 3					
1 electrical vehicles	–				
2 car-free zones	.004	–			
3 parking restrictions	-.032	.467	–		
4 tax on CO_2	-.069	.217	.415	–	
5 gas at Sfr 2/l	-.092	.258	.462	.717	–
6 speed limits	-.035	.236	.373	.488	.505
Time 4					
1 electrical vehicles	–				
2 car-free zones	.081	–			
3 parking restrictions	.094	.375	–		
4 tax on CO_2	.149	.321	.425	–	
5 gas at Sfr 2/l	.137	.362	.396	.759	–
6 speed limits	.143	.317	.386	.491	.518

TABLE 8.2
Results of the Latent State-Trait Model for Six Measures: Standardized Effects

A. First Tier of the Model

Effect	Electric Vehicles	Car-free Zones	Parking Restrict.	Tax on CO_2	Speed Limits	Gas at Sfr 2/l
λ_{ik}	.241(t_1)	.568	.602	.620	.665	.630
	.180(t_2)					
	-.060(t_3)					
	.161(t_4)					
$\Theta\varepsilon_{ii}$	.942(t_1)	.677	.635	.615	.558	.602
	.968(t_2)					
	.996(t_3)					
	.974(t_4)					

B. Second Tier of the Model

Effect	t_1	t_2	t_3	t_4
γ_{jk}	.928	.986	.953	.955
ψ_{jj}	.139	.027	.092	.108

"Socratic effect" typically noted in panel studies (McGuire 1960; Saris and van den Putte 1987). Respondents are clarifying their ideas in the course of a panel survey and, as they reflect and learn more about the subject matter, get closer to their "true attitude."

As a result of this first step of the analysis, we may conclude that there is, indeed, an underlying attitude about environmental protection, which turns out to be rather stable over time, but which, as expected, does not help us a great deal to understand the opinions about specific ecological policy measures in the area of transport policy. The variability (around 60 percent) in these opinions apparently depends on many factors other than the underlying attitude.

VARIATIONS BETWEEN ISSUES

Given that the underlying attitude is unable to elucidate much of the variation in our opinions, we take a closer look at the stability of each one of the six opinions. The corresponding correlations are given in Table 8.3. Inspecting his panel data from the American elections in the late 1950s, Converse

TABLE 8.3
Correlations between the Four Measures for Six Opinions: Pearson Correlation
Coefficients

Time	t_1	t_2	t_3
Electrical vehicles n = 674			
t_1	–		
t_2	.387	–	
t_3	.364	.488	–
t_4	.501	.443	.434
Car-free zones n = 669			
t_1	–		
t_2	.503	–	
t_3	.467	.599	–
t_4	.517	.505	.540
Parking restrictions n = 668			
t_1	–		
t_2	.487	–	
t_3	.428	.575	–
t_4	.477	.448	.439
CO_2-tax n = 672			
t_1	–		
t_2	.536	–	
t_3	.523	.660	–
t_4	.583	.601	.575
Speed limits n = 674			
t_1	–		
t_2	.652	–	
t_3	.666	.752	–
t_4	.637	.659	.703
Gas at Sfr 2/l n = 670			
t_1	–		
t_2	.582	–	
t_3	.576	.716	–
t_4	.556	.607	.610

(1964:242) noted to his surprise that the correlations between the opinions given at the initial interview in 1956 and the terminal interview in 1960 were of the same order of magnitude as the correlations between opinions given at each one of these moments and opinions measured at the interview in 1958. In other words, one could just as easily predict 1960 opinions on most of the issues on the basis of individual opinions in 1956 alone as one could with a knowledge of the more proximal 1958 responses. As it turns out, we find the same surprising phenomenon in our panel data: with one exception, the correlations between the four measurements are approximately stable over time. The exception concerns the transition between t_2 and t_3, for which the stability turns out to be most sizable for all the opinions in our study. This is actually not so exceptional, given that the two measurements at t_2 and t_3 were typically only a few days, but at most three to four weeks apart. It was this surprising stability of correlations that led Converse to propose his famous black-and-white model, and it was this phenomenon that was interpreted by Achen (1975) to be a result of measurement error. Achen argued that correlations will be equal across time periods when respondents are stable in their views, and all observed variability is measurement error.

For the analysis of the stability of the individual opinions, it is no longer possible to rely on the latent state-trait model. Since I have only one measurement for a given opinion at each point in time, this model is not identified. A possible solution might have been to use estimates for the measurement quality of the opinions, which have been made available by systematic evaluations of measurement instruments in public opinion research (see Scherpenzeel 1995; Scherpenzeel and Saris 1993; Költringer 1993). Such estimates would, however, have been identical for all our opinions, since we measured them by the same instruments and for all time points, since we always used the same questions. This turned out to be unfeasible, given that the assumption of equal measurement errors led to incoherent results in the case of some issues.[7] A possible alternative, true score models in the tradition of Wiley and Wiley (1970), did not fit our data in most cases. This is why I finally turned to a straightforward factor model as presented in Figure 8.2. The four measurements are all taken as indicators of an underlying "true" issue-specific opinion. The error terms of the second and third measurements are allowed to be correlated, given their proximity in time.

As in Figure 8.1, the error term in this model does not only cover measurement error. It also indicates a lack of validity of the interview response. More specifically, the response to the interview question does not necessarily measure what it is supposed to measure, because it aims at a moving target. Thus, ambivalence in Zaller's terms will contribute to an increase in the error term. According to Zaller (1992:38), depending on the immediate context of the interview, a variable set of considerations will be

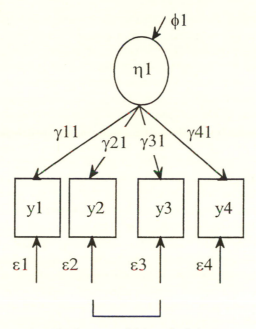

Figure 8.2 The factor model for a single issue.

salient and accessible for an individual. This means that respondents do not have "just one opinion" toward one and the same political issue but "multiple potential opinions." As Zaller points out, "[F]or most people, most of the time, there is no need to reconcile or even to recognize their contradictory reactions to events and issues" (93). Ambivalence in the sense of a deep value conflict is also likely to contribute to the error term: it may imply that the individual will resolve her conflict differently from one interview to the other. Finally, uncertainty resulting from a lack of information may also contribute to the error term: individuals may just base their response on whatever short-term information they can grasp. Notice that in each case, their response is not entirely random. Even if their opinion changes, people may express real feelings and react to short-term changes in the context. In Zaller's words: "Although the perceptions of the issue may change over time, the responses they generate are not, for that reason, lacking in authenticity" (1992:94).

The factor model has the advantage of being very flexible. I have tested four versions of the model, a version that

- allows all four error terms to vary independently (1)
- provides for a change in error terms between t_1 and t_2, but not thereafter (2)
- imposes equal error terms for t_1 and t_4, and for t_2 and t_3 (3)
- imposes equal error terms for all time points (4).

The first model allows for variable, short-term effects at each moment in time. The second model takes into account a stable effect at t_2, but apart from that does not allow for any other particular period effect. This effect corresponds to the pervasive panel-effect, which is, however, confounded in our case with the effect of our first "natural experiment," i.e., the effect of the public debate on the tax on CO_2. The third model presupposes that this panel-cum-public debate effect is of a short-term nature and fades away toward the end of the study, implying a return to the original variation in the error term. The final model constitutes the baseline, given that it postulates no discernible variation in the error terms at all.

For each issue, I estimated the models with LISREL 7, on the basis of the correlation matrices from Table 8.3. Table 8.4 presents the results. The upper part of the table contains the χ^2-statistics and P-values of the four types of models for each issue. The lower part of the table presents the standardized effects (λ_{ij}) of the underlying opinions on the observed scores and the error variances ($\Theta\varepsilon_{ii}$) and covariances ($\Theta\varepsilon_{23}$). The results depend on the type of issue. While the first model fits all the issues, it turns out to be the best model only for electrical vehicles and the tax on CO_2. For both of these issues, the error variance is far lower at the end of our study than it is at the beginning. For electrical vehicles, our study seems to have had a destabilizing effect at first, before it contributed to a stabilization of the individual opinions indicated by a sizable reduction in the error variance at t_4. For the tax on CO_2, by contrast, the opinions were stabilizing in step-wise fashion. In the case of the urban policies—car-free zones and parking restrictions—the baseline model applies, and for the most constraining issues—speed limits and an increase of the price of gas up to Sfr 2/l—there is only an indication of an effect at t_2. A return to the original situation as assumed by model 3 does not seem to hold in any case.

The original and final sizes of the variances of the error terms also vary from one issue to the next. Originally, these variances tended to be lower among the more constraining issues, except for the two fiscal incentives, which had particularly large error variances: these unfamiliar and complex issues met with great uncertainty on the part of the respondents. It is interesting to note, however, that for both of the fiscal incentives, and most notably for the tax on CO_2, the size of the error variances decreased considerably in the course of our study. The case of the tax on CO_2 is especially revealing, since it was this issue that was most intensely debated in the public during the period between our first two interviews; this issue also constituted the object of our experiment between the last two interviews. We can conclude from this result that the experiments in the course of our study have contributed to the clarification and stabilization of some individual opinions, at least in this most intensely debated case. Finally, as expected, the error terms at t_2 and t_3 are always positively and significantly correlated.

TABLE 8.4
Results of the Factor Model for Each Single Issue: χ^2-statistics, P-values, and Standardized Effects

Effect	Electric Vehicles	Car-free Zones	Parking Restrict.	Tax on CO_2	Speed Limits	Gas at Sfr 2/l
1. All ϵ free	.39	1.15	2.06	.64	1.27	.96
χ^2, 1 df; P	.534	.284	.151	.422	.260	.327
2. $\epsilon 22 = \epsilon 33 = \epsilon 44$	19.20	4.30	4.79	7.84	3.36	2.60
χ^2, 5 df; P	.002	.507	.443	.166	.645	.761
3. $\epsilon 11 = \epsilon 44$; $\epsilon 22 = \epsilon 33$	9.31	6.76	5.40	22.23	7.57	14.45
χ^2, 5 df; P	.097	.239	.369	.000	.181	.013
4. $\epsilon 11 = \epsilon 22 = \epsilon 33 = \epsilon 44$	20.0	6.80	5.48	22.34	9.24	17.46
χ^2, 7 df; P	.006	.450	.602	.002	.236	.015
λ_{11}	.579	.633	.665	.602	.756	.617
λ_{21}	.528			.687	.809	.743
λ_{31}	.471			.654		
λ_{41}	.744			.790		
$\Theta\epsilon_{11}$	.665	.599	.558	.637	.429	.619
$\Theta\epsilon_{22}$	.721			.528	.345	.449
$\Theta\epsilon_{33}$	.778			.572		
$\Theta\epsilon_{44}$	.446			.376		
$\Theta\epsilon_{23}$	.081*	.106***	.096***	.119***	.054**	.087***

* $p < .05$; ** $p < .01$; *** $p < .001$

INTRODUCING GROUP HETEROGENEITY

The measurement error approach has been criticized for its assumption that the given population is more or less homogenous with respect to the question of stability of opinion. Thus, Luskin (2002) maintains that the exclusive use of correlation matrices by the measurement error approach implies that despite requiring individual-level data, it gives only aggregate results. On the basis of this approach, he seems to suggest, one can only say something about the stability of opinions of the public at large. By contrast, Converse's approach takes issue with the assumption of population homogeneity.

His basic idea is that the population is not homogenous as far as the individual capacity to develop stable opinions with respect to public policies is concerned. In his famous black-and-white model, he postulates that there are in fact *two groups in the population:* one with perfectly stable opinions, and one that gives perfectly random responses over time and which, therefore, is characterized by what he called nonattitudes.

However, contrary to what Luskin seems to suggest, the measurement model approach does not preclude the possibility of taking into account group heterogeneity. We may apply our preferred models to different subgroups as well. Following the approach of Converse, we may in fact divide the sample into different subgroups that are expected to differ systematically from each other with regard to the stability of their opinion. Converse distinguished between just two groups—the entirely stable and the entirely random group. On the basis of the three individual characteristics (which I discussed at the outset, each dichotomized into two categories), I propose to form eight distinct groups of individuals. For *ecological awareness,* I dichotomize the sample at the median into persons who are "unaware" and persons who are "aware." For *situational constraints,* I distinguish between individuals who do not have a car—the unconstrained group—and those who either have a car or drive someone else's. For *opinion strength,* the two groups to be distinguished include individuals with weak or no opinions, on the one hand, and individuals with strong opinions, on the other. Table 8.5 presents the distributions of the sample over the resulting eight combinations for each one of the six issues. The number of cases per combination varies from one issue to the other, because the extent of opinion strength is issue dependent. The reader may also note that several of these groups are rather small. This is a consequence of the unequal distribution of the Swiss population on one of the independent variables: only about one-fourth of the Swiss do not drive a car and are, therefore, unconstrained according to our definition.

The different groups vary enormously with respect to the stability of their opinions. This can be seen from Table 8.6, which compares the correlation matrices of four subgroups for the examples of speed limits—the issue with the most stable opinions on the average—and electrical vehicles—the issue with the least stable average opinions (see Table 8.3). Moreover, an inspection of the various correlation matrices shows no consistent patterns. In particular, we no longer find the pattern that has given rise to Converse's black-and-white model. Given that there is no discernible common pattern among the correlations, I shall use the most flexible version of the four-factor model I introduced above, i.e., model 1 (Table 8.1). Since there are six issues and eight subgroups per issue, ideally we obtain four estimates of error variances ($\Theta\varepsilon_{ii}$) for 48 group-specific models. I have again estimated each model with LISREL 7. In five cases, the estimation

TABLE 8.5
Distribution of the Sample on the Eight Groups Defined by the Combination of Individual Characteristics, by Issue: Absolute Numbers

Groups[a]	Electric Vehicles	Car-free Zones	Parking Restrict.	Tax on CO_2	Speed Limits	Gas at Sfr 2/l
1 = 1-0-1	87	153	123	122	142	135
2 = 0-0-1	66	108	90	84	107	91
3 = 1-1-1	196	127	157	160	141	145
4 = 0-1-1	156	111	130	136	114	130
5 = 1-0-0	30	63	49	42	39	39
6 = 0-0-0	34	44	33	28	39	30
7 = 1-1-0	59	27	40	48	51	51
8 = 0-1-0	41	31	41	47	36	44
Total	669	664	663	667	669	665

[a]The first index refers to awareness, the second to ambivalence, and the third to constraints:

    awareness: 0 = unaware; 1 = aware
    ambivalence: 0 = not ambivalent; 1 = ambivalent
    constraint: 0 = unconstrained; 1 = constrained

procedure did not provide reliable estimates.[8] In four out of the 43 remaining cases, all concerning urban issues, the model did not fit very well. (See Table 8.A1 in the appendix. Table 8.A2 in the appendix gives the 172 estimated error variances [$\Theta\varepsilon$'s] for the 43 models for which the estimation procedure converged.)

EXPLAINING THE DIFFERENCES

I then tried to explain these estimates on the basis of the characteristics of the different groups, issues, and states by applying multiple regression procedures. The results of the regression analyses are reported in Table 8.7. To the extent that it is possible to identify systematic variation in the error variances as a function of the indicated characteristics, we shall be able to exclude measurement error as a source of error variance.

Table 8.7 reports the impact of the different types of characteristics taken both separately and combined. Let us first look at the *issue* characteristics. As expected, the error variances diminish significantly for the more constraining issues, indicating that opinion stability is greater among the

TABLE 8.6
Correlation Matrices for Four Subgroups, the Cases of Speed Limits and
Electrical Vehicles

A. Speed Limits

Group 1: aware-strong-constrained
	1	2	3	4
1	–			
2	.857	–		
3	.839	.931	–	
4	.765	.836	.844	–

Group 4: unaware-weak-constrained
	1	2	3	4
1	–			
2	.428	–		
3	.471	.725	–	
4	.346	.495	.697	–

Group 5: aware-strong-unconstrained
	1	2	3	4
1	–			
2	.731	–		
3	.755	.836	–	
4	.764	.645	.584	–

Group 8: unaware-weak-unconstrained
	1	2	3	4
1	–			
2	.354	–		
3	.382	.474	–	
4	.183	.362	.457	–

B. Electrical Vehicles

Group 1: aware-strong-constrained
	1	2	3	4
1	–			
2	.581	–		
3	.408	.531	–	
4	.702	.619	.522	–

Group 4: unaware-weak-constrained
	1	2	3	4
1	–			
2	.417	–		
3	.382	.498	–	
4	.438	.428	.327	–

Group 5: aware-strong-unconstrained
	1	2	3	4
1	–			
2	.676	–		
3	.681	.575	–	
4	.577	.490	.563	–

Group 8: unaware-weak-unconstrained
	1	2	3	4
1	–			
2	.556	–		
3	.461	.204	–	
4	.280	.422	.285	–

---

issues imposing stronger constraints. Familiarity, as expected, also decreases error variances, but the effect becomes significant only if we control for group and state characteristics as well. Complexity has no effect at all, which is why I shall drop it from the subsequent analyses. Next, let us turn to group characteristics. Contrary to expectations, neither a high level of awareness with respect to environmental problems nor having or driving a car contributes in any way to greater stability of individual opinions. But *opinion strength* turns out to have the expected effect: the weaker the opinion, the greater the error variance. For the following analyses, I shall only retain opinion strength. Combining issue and group characteristics, it is

TABLE 8.7
Determinants of Error Variances ($\Theta\epsilon$): Standardized Regression Coefficients (BETA) and Adjusted R^2 (n = 172)

Predictor Variables	1	2	3	4	5	6
Issue Characteristics						
Familiarity	-.18	.	-.18*	-.18*	-.18*	.03
Constraining	-.30**	.	-.30***	-.30***	-.30***	-.02
Complexity	.01	.	.	.	.	.
Group Characteristics						
Weak Opinions	.	.36***	.36***	.36***	.79***	.79***
Awareness	.	-.07	.	.	.	.
Constraint	.	.00	.	.	.	.
States						
t_2	.	.	.	-.11	.16	-.02
t_3	.	.	.	-.10	.22*	.14
t_4	.	.	.	-.22**	-.04	-.04
Interactions						
t_2—weak opinions	.	.	.	.	-.41***	-.38***
t_3—weak opinions	.	.	.	.	-.49***	-.46***
t_4—weak opinions	.	.	.	.	-.27*	-.27*
t_3—speed limits	.	.	.	.	.	-.24**
t_2, t_3—parking restrict.	.	.	.	.	.	.23**
t_2, t_3—electrical vehicles	.	.	.	.	.	.19**
t_2, t_3—tax on CO_2	.	.	.	.	.	.17*
R^2 adj. (all groups)	.03	.12	.16	.18	.25	.35
R^2 adj. (constrained groups only)	.09	.31	.39	.43	.45	.54

* $p < .05$; ** $p < .01$; *** $p < .001$

possible to explain roughly one-sixth of the variance in the error terms (refer to the line with the adjusted R^2 for all groups).

In the next step, we add dummy variables for time points t_2, t_3, and t_4. The corresponding effects indicate to what extent the error variances at these time points differ from those at t_1. As we know from the previous analysis (Table 8.4), the opinions on a given issue tend to get closer to the respective "true" opinion in the course of our study. Accordingly, we expect the error variances to decrease with respect to t_1. They, indeed, do so, as is shown in column 4 of Table 8.7, but, contrary to the impact of issue and group characteristics, the reduction turns out to be significant only at the end of our study (t_4).

Next, consider the possibility that the panel effect, the impact of the public debate, the impact of the Choice Questionnaire, and the impact of our last experiment are not the same for all groups of individuals. In particular, I would like to suggest that these various elements above all contributed to clarification in the minds of persons who originally had weak opinions. The additional information and the occasion to think about the issues in question provided by the different phases of the study should have been especially useful for the groups with weak opinions. To check for this possibility, I create three interaction terms, i.e., dummy indicators, which take the value of 1 for groups with weak opinions at t_2, t_3, and t_4 respectively, and 0 otherwise. These three interaction terms all turn out to be highly significant and negative, confirming the idea that above all, it is the people with weak opinions who clarify their opinions in the course of the study. The interaction terms for time points t_2 and t_3 are more substantial than for t_4, which suggests that the public debate plus panel effect on the one hand, and the Choice Questionnaire effect on the other, were particularly important. Introducing the three interaction terms has some repercussions on the original effects of the variables involved: the direct effect of weak opinions is strongly reinforced, while the direct state effects become insignificant (t_4) or even change their signs (t_2 and t_3). This leads to two conclusions. First, taking into account the fact that weak opinions in particular have been considerably clarified in the course of our study only reinforces the notion that originally weak opinions are especially unstable. Second, only the groups of people with weak opinions were able to clarify their opinions in the course of our study. In the groups with originally strong opinions, the various events in the course of our study had a rather destabilizing effect, if they had any effect at all. The Choice Questionnaire in particular seems to have had a significant destabilizing effect on people who had strong opinions at the outset. Introducing these interaction terms raises the share of explained variance in the error terms to 25 percent.

Finally, it is possible that the events in the course of our study have had a stabilizing or destabilizing effect only with respect to certain issues. Thus, it is conceivable that the arguments presented in the Choice Questionnaire with respect to a given issue were more convincing than others and allowed a significant part of the respondents to clarify their issue-specific opinions. By contrast, it is also conceivable that the public debate, the Choice Questionnaire, and the press experiment introduced arguments that were new to some respondents who had held previously strong opinions, and made them uncertain with respect to the issues at stake. It is difficult to make a general argument about which issues should have been particularly susceptible to these kinds of effects. An inspection of the data in Table 8.A2 and previous results not reported here in detail suggest the introduction of four interaction effects accounting for an issue-specific impact at t_2 and/or t_3. On the one hand, the Choice Questionnaire is expected to have had a clarifying effect in the case of speed limits; on the other hand, both the public debate and the Choice Questionnaire are expected to have made some respondents more uncertain with respect to the tax on CO_2, parking restrictions, and electrical vehicles. Indeed, these effects all turn out to be significant in the expected direction. Introducing these effects renders the direct effects of state t_3 and of the issue characteristics (familiarity and constraints) insignificant, while the other effects remain largely unchanged. This suggests that except for the effect of opinion strength, the four issue-specific interaction effects, which I have just introduced in a more or less ad hoc fashion, account for all of the differences between states and issues, which we have found above.

Note that the introduction of these effects raises the share of the explained variance to about one-third. In other words, we can trace at least one-third of the variance in the error terms to some systematic variation due to issue, group, or state characteristics. In fact, it is quite plausible to assume this share of systematic variation in the error terms to be even more substantial. Remember that some of the groups involved were rather small (see Table 8.5), which implies that the parameter estimates obtained for these groups are bound to lack precision. Indeed, if we redo the regressions retaining only the subset of groups that are constrained (i.e., the groups that are larger in size and, therefore, provide us with more precise estimates of the model parameters), we arrive at R^2 estimates that are considerably larger in size: about one half of the variance in the error terms now appears to have a systematic origin.

Conclusion

This analysis has shown that the measurement error approach allows one to uncover systematic sources of opinion change. By breaking down the sample into more homogenous subgroups, I was able to show that there are systematic elements of change associated with each moment of measurement, which is equivalent to observing that our natural experiments had systematic effects on individual opinions—effects which, unfortunately, are confounded with the pervasive panel effect. Next, it was possible to show the crucial importance of opinion strength for the determination of the stability of individual opinions: people with weak opinions are much more likely to change them than people with strong opinions. In addition, issue characteristics such as the degree to which issues are familiar and constraining also have an effect on the stability of individual opinions.

These systematic effects determine the size of the variances in the error terms in the models of the measurement error approach. This has important consequences for the interpretation of these models. While we dispute the claim of the adherents of the measurement error approach that stable underlying attitudes allow for the explanation of the enormous instability we typically find on the level of individual issue-specific opinions, we should refrain from interpreting this instability only as so much random noise. The error variances, which indicate the extent of the instability in the measurement error models, do not only contain measurement error. They also indicate meaningful short-term reactions of respondents to new information, which they obtain in the course of public debates on the issues in question. While the changes in the individual opinions are "authentic," i.e., in a meaningful way responsive to information that reduces or increases individual uncertainty about the issues at stake, such changes are not necessarily permanent.

As far as democracy is concerned, this result is somewhat reassuring. "Politics, at its core, is about arguments—about the justification advanced for a policy, about the criticism leveled against it" (Sniderman and Carmines 1997:154). And democratic politics is about the full and open exchange of arguments in a process of deliberation among the principal groups, bodies, and representatives of a polity. Not all citizens participate actively in this debate, and not all of those who participate vicariously by following the spectacle of the debate in the public space already have a definite opinion about the issues at stake. Deliberation is an opinion-forming process: "[T]he participants should not have fully or definitively formed opinions at the outset; they are expected to engage in meaningful discussion, which means that they should be ready to modify initially held opinions in the light of arguments of other participants and also as a result of new information which becomes available in the course of the debate" (Hirschman 1991:169). Stability of individual opinions, then, is not necessarily an ideal of democratic politics. The truly democratic citizen should have an open mind, ready to change on the basis of the arguments exchanged in the public debate.

Moreover, deliberation implies not only the possibility of rational opinion change. It also implies the possibility of opinion formation among those who did not hold any opinion before. In many individual cases, this process may not go very far at any given moment in time, and its outcome may be reversible under changing circumstances. However, its outcome at any given moment in time is not entirely random, but to some extent reflects the contents of the arguments exchanged: as Sniderman and Carmines also point out, "[A]ll arguments are not equal" (1997:154). Some arguments are more easily received than others, and some resonate better with the political predispositions of some groups of people. Although the present analysis has not entered into the details of opinion change, its results are quite compatible with the notion that citizens respond to the arguments exchanged in public space in a meaningful way.

NOTES

I would like to thank Willem Saris for his help with the statistical models and for his crucial comments on an earlier draft of this paper. Without his continuing support, this paper could not have been written.

1. For the project of a tax on CO_2, the questions read as follows: "The government is currently discussing the introduction of a tax on CO_2, which is designed to be levied on all types of fuel. This measure is proposed to restrict the energy consumption of every individual. For gasoline, the tax discussed would amount to 10 cents/liter. The revenue raised by this tax would be returned to the population: that is, every taxpayer would get about 60 francs a year. Have you already heard of this measure? What is your opinion about the introduction of such a tax on CO_2?" For well-known or less complex measures, the introduction was more concise.

2. Converse and Presser (1986:37f.) have criticized this approach because it confounds extremity and intensity. I do not think this point is important, since both extremity and intensity are aspects of the multidimensional concept of strength (see Krosnick and Fabrigar 1995).

3. According to Luskin (1987:890), the best measures of "political sophistication," i.e., political awareness in our terminology, are combinations of measures operationalizing consistency, level of abstraction, and information holding. However, simple counts of information come in a close second. For example, simple counts work better than "active use" measures such as the measures for the "level of conceptualization" used by Campbell et al. (1960).

4. As noted by Saris and van den Putte (1987:129), for the analysis of correlation matrices this assumption is plausible if the same instruments are used at different points in time and the error distribution remains approximately the same through time. Throughout our study, we have used the same format for the questions about the individual opinions. However, the interview method varied from one wave to another. The first and the last interviews were done by telephone, while the second interviews were face-to-face and the third measurement was based on a written questionnaire. I nevertheless maintain this assumption.

5. Table 8.1 does not show them all. It just indicates the kind of correlations for the two time periods t_1 and t_2.

6. Again, Table 8.1 does not show all of these additional correlations between error terms, but just indicates them for the two time periods t_1 and t_2.

7. Most notably, this assumption led to negative estimates of state-specific error variances for the time points closest to the true scores in the case of the most constraining issues.

8. In four cases, the estimation procedure did not converge, and in one case it did not even start, given that one of the variables was a constant (due to small group size).

APPENDIX

TABLE 8.A1
χ^2- and P-values for 48 Estimated Models, 2 df

	1	2	3	4	5	6	7	8
Electrical vehicles								
χ^2	1.30	1.50	.20	.66	.23	2.20	.86	.11
P	.253	.221	.654	.416	.633	.138	.354	.739
Car-free zones								
χ^2	11.33	2.87	7.43	.23	[a]	[b]	1.99	.05
P	.000	.090	.006	.632			.158	.830
Parking restrictions								
χ^2	2.57	5.55	.23	1.05	2.55	.57	[b]	[b]
P	.109	.018	.635	.305	.110	.451		
Tax on CO_2								
χ^2	.47	.02	.26	.00	.59	.16	.08	1.02
P	.492	.891	.608	.980	.442	.690	.776	.312
Speed limits								
χ^2	1.44	.47	.03	2.12	1.83	.35	.43	.07
P	.230	.494	.854	.145	.176	.554	.512	.787
Gas at Sfr 2/l								
χ^2	.27	.28	.25	.06	[b]	.00	.90	.96
P	.604	.597	.615	.806		.954	.343	.327

[a] No variation at t_1: only people in favor of the measure
[b] No convergence after 27 iterations

TABLE 8.A2
Estimated Coefficients for the 48 Subgroups: $\Theta\epsilon$ Coefficients

	1	2	3	4	5	6	7	8
Electrical vehicles								
$\Theta\epsilon_{11}$	.372	.617	.765	.547	.260	.334	.829	.604
$\Theta\epsilon_{22}$	.496	.851	.780	.593	.402	.585	.507	.187
$\Theta\epsilon_{33}$	.680	.510	.768	.712	.357	.742	.606	.500

TABLE 8.A2 *cont.*

	1	2	3	4	5	6	7	8
$\Theta\epsilon_{44}$	.215	.114	.468	.577	.550	.843	.425	.802
$\Theta\epsilon_{23}$	(.129)	.233	.261	.156	(-.046)	(-.153)	(-.051)	(-.433)
Car-free zones								
$\Theta\epsilon_{11}$	.460	.530	.692	.652	a	b	.655	.284
$\Theta\epsilon_{22}$	.397	.400	.712	.547			.073	.607
$\Theta\epsilon_{33}$	.282	.677	.573	.576			.998	.355
$\Theta\epsilon_{44}$	.268	.566	.449	.467			.437	.542
$\Theta\epsilon_{23}$	(.031)	(.162)	.299	(.028)			(.308)	(.288)
Parking restrictions								
$\Theta\epsilon_{11}$	.373	.330	.677	.927	.092	.214	b	b
$\Theta\epsilon_{22}$	.286	.336	.653	.887	.820	.641		
$\Theta\epsilon_{33}$	.393	.673	.642	.910	.721	.733		
$\Theta\epsilon_{44}$	.379	.608	.647	.252	.402	.701		
$\Theta\epsilon_{23}$	(.064)	(.031)	(.159)	.371	.353	(.346)		
Tax on CO_2								
$\Theta\epsilon_{11}$	.199	.528	.740	.723	.705	.453	.919	.833
$\Theta\epsilon_{22}$	.334	.478	.514	.357	.604	.550	.893	.510
$\Theta\epsilon_{33}$	.370	.507	.584	.607	.685	.580	.783	.430
$\Theta\epsilon_{44}$	.157	.294	.487	.748	-.030	.292	-.164	.520
$\Theta\epsilon_{23}$	.133	(.101)	(.162)	(.071)	(-.176)	(.199)	(.208)	(-.006)
Speed limits								
$\Theta\epsilon_{11}$	.223	.303	.735	.763	.070	.232	.811	.839
$\Theta\epsilon_{22}$	.063	.307	.368	.453	.416	.661	.520	.307
$\Theta\epsilon_{33}$	.075	.364	.485	.043	.395	.165	.023	.036
$\Theta\epsilon_{44}$	.243	.209	.557	.496	.371	.599	.688	.739
$\Theta\epsilon_{23}$	(.000)	.113	(.054)	(.002)	.242	(-.114)	(-.180)	(-.343)
Gas at Sfr 2/l								
$\Theta\epsilon_{11}$	.257	.484	.787	.867	b	.281	.633	.617
$\Theta\epsilon_{22}$	.185	.279	.597	.381		.111	.696	.480

TABLE 8.A2 *cont.*

	1	2	3	4	5	6	7	8
$\Theta\epsilon_{33}$	.252	.399	.382	.390		.399	.378	.423
$\Theta\epsilon_{44}$	.228	.570	.463	.726		.525	.683	.447
$\Theta\epsilon_{23}$	(.025)	(.015)	(.141)	(.033)		(-.031)	(.139)	.091

[a] Estimation impossible because one variable was a constant due to small group size.
[b] Estimation procedure did not converge.

REFERENCES

Achen, Christopher H. 1975. "Mass Political Attitudes and the Survey Response." *American Political Science Review* 69:1218–31.

Alvarez, R. Michael, and John Brehm. 1995. "American Ambivalence towards Abortion Policy: Development of a Heteroskedastic Probit Model of Competing Values." *American Journal of Political Science* 39(4):1055–82.

———. 1997. "Are Americans Ambivalent towards Racial Policies?" *American Journal of Political Science* 41(2):345–74.

Bütschi, Danielle. 1997. *Information et opinions: Promesses et limites du questionnaire de choix.* PhD diss., Department of Political Science, University of Geneva.

Campbell, Angus, Philip E. Converse, Warren E. Miller, and Donald E. Stokes. 1960. *The American Voter.* New York: Wiley.

Converse, Philip E. 1964. "The Nature of Belief Systems in Mass Publics." In *Ideology and Discontent,* ed. David Apter, 206–61. New York: Free Press.

———. 1970. "Attitudes and Non-Attitudes: Continuation of a Dialogue." In *The Quantitative Analysis of Social Problems,* ed. Edward R. Tufte, 168–89. Reading, MA: Addison-Wesley.

———. 1980. "Comment: Rejoinder to Judd and Milburn." *American Political Science Review* 45:644–46.

Converse, Jean M., and Stanley Presser. 1986. *Survey Questions: Handicrafting the Standardized Questionnaire.* London: Sage.

Diekmann, Andreas, and Peter Preisendoerfer. 1992. "Persoenliches Umweltverhalten. Diskrepanz zwischen Anspruch und Wirklichkeit." *Koelner Zeitschrift fuer Soziologie und Sozialpsychologie* 44(2):226–51.

Eagly, Alice H., and Shelly Chaiken. 1993. *The Psychology of Attitudes.* New York: Harcourt, Brace, Jovanovich.

Hirschman, Albert O. 1991. *The Rhetoric of Reaction.* Cambridge, MA: Belknap Press of Harvard University Press.

Jagodzinski, Wolfang, and Steffen M. Kühnel. 1987. "Estimation of Reliability and Stability in Single-Indicator Multiple-Wave Models." *Sociological Methods and Research* 15(3):219–58.

Jagodzinski, Wolfgang, Steffen M. Kühnel, and Peter Schmidt. 1987. "Is There a 'Socratic Effect' in Nonexperimental Panel Studies? Consistency of an Attitude toward Guestworkers." *Sociological Methods and Research* 15(3):259–302.

———. 1990. "Searching for Parsimony: Are True-Score Models or Factor Models More Appropriate?" *Quality and Quantity* 24:447–70.

Judd, Charles M., and Michael A. Milburn. 1980. "The Structure of Attitude Systems in the General Public: Comparisons of a Structural Equation Model." *American Sociological Review* 45 (August):627–43.

Költringer, R. 1993. "Messqualität in der Sozialwissenschaftlichen Umfrageforschung." Endbericht Projet P8690-SOZ des Fonds zur Förderung der Wissenschaftlichen Forschung (FWF) Wien.

Luskin, Robert C. 1987. "Measuring Political Sophistication." *American Journal of Political Science* 31:856–99.

———. 2002. "Political Psychology, Political Behavior, and Politics: Questions of Aggregation, Causal Distance, and Taste." In *Thinking about Political Psychology,* ed. James H. Kuklinski. New York: Cambridge University Press.

McGuire, William J. 1960. "A Syllogistic Analysis of Cognitive Relationships." In *Attitude Organization and Change,* ed. M. J. Rosenberg, C. I. Hovland, W. J. McGuire, R. P. Abelson, and J. W. Brehm, 65–111. Westport, CT: Greenwood Press.

Peffley, Mark, and Jon Hurwitz. 1993. "Models of Attitude Constraint in Foreign Affairs." *Political Behavior* 15:61–90.

Saris, Willem E., and Bas van den Putte. 1987. "True Score or Factor Models: A Secondary Analysis of the ALLBUS-Test-Retest Data." *Sociological Methods and Research* 17(2):123–57.

Scherpenzeel, Annette. 1995. *A Question of Quality: Evaluating Survey Questions by Multitrait-Multimethod Studies.* Ph.D. diss., University of Amsterdam.

Scherpenzeel, Annette, and Willem E. Saris. 1993. "The Evaluation of Measurement Instruments by Meta-Analysis of Multitrait-Multimethod Studies." *Bulletin de Methodologie Sociologique* 39:3–19.

Schumann, Howard, and Stanley Presser. 1981. *Questions and Answers in Attitude Surveys: Experiments on Question Form, Wording and Context.* New York: Academic Press.

Sniderman, Paul M., and Edward G. Carmines. 1997. *Reaching beyond Race.* Cambridge, MA: Harvard University Press.

Sniderman, Paul M., Richard A. Brody, and Philip E. Tetlock. 1991. *Reasoning and Choice: Explorations in Political Psychology.* New York: Cambridge University Press.

Steenbergen, Marco R., Paul Brewer, and Timothy Vercellotti. 1997. "Generalized Value Conflict and Uncertainty in Public Opinion." Paper prepared for the conference "No Opinion, Instability and Change in Public Opinion Research." October 6–8, Amsterdam.

Steyer, R., and M. Schmitt. 1990. "The Effects of Aggregation across and within Occasions on Consistency, Specificity, and Reliability." *Methodika* 4:58–94.

Wiley, David E., and James A. Wiley. 1970. "The Estimation of Measurement Error in Panel Data." *American Sociological Review* 35:112–17.

Zaller, John R. 1992. *The Nature and Origins of Mass Opinion.* New York: Cambridge University Press.

CHAPTER 9

Attitude Strength and Response Stability of a Quasi-Balanced Political Alienation Scale in a Panel Study

Jaak Billiet, Marc Swyngedouw, and Hans Waege

THE STABILITY of attitude measures is not what it should be. A recent study of the reliability of survey measurement estimated the test-retest reliability of 41 attitude items from the U.S. National Elections Study panels (1950–1970) to be 55 percent on average. This means that only somewhat more than half of the response variance is true (Alwin and Scott 1996:81). This figure is not very high. This conclusion, reached previously by Philip Converse (1964) after his analysis of the Survey Research Center's National Election Panels, was confirmed in one of our own surveys in 1997. In that particular survey, in which 85 percent of the respondents (N = 556) filled out a short, self-administered questionnaire within two weeks after they were interviewed, change of the underlying attitude was very unlikely. The average test-retest correlation of eight 5-point Likert items belonging to a balanced ethnocentrism scale was 0.54 (range 0.42–0.60). The average test-retest correlation for ten more abstract 7-point Likert items measuring cultural conformism and cultural dissent was even worse: 0.49 (range .32–.63). This is problematic, even when we take into account differences in method (interview versus self-administered), which led to some underestimation of the test-retest reliabilities. To be sure, the stability of composite measures is higher (Achen 1975; Lord and Novick 1968; Groves 1989:492). It is 0.77 for our composite ethnocentrism scale, 0.65 for the "cultural dissent" scale, and 0.73 for the "cultural conformism" scale. Still, this is problematic, taking into account that no substantial attitude change could have occurred and that the effect of memory is not completely excluded.

A second observation that needs our attention is the difference in stability between individuals with lower and higher levels of education. That education is positively related to response stability was first proposed by Converse (1964) but later largely withdrawn by him (Converse 1975). More recently, differences in test-retest stability between more and less educated respondents are found when *balanced* scales are used to measure left-right and liberal-authoritarian attitudes (Evans and Heath 1995; Curtice 1996:139). The test-retest correlation was lower among the less educated in the case of balanced scales, but the difference with the more educated disappeared when *unbalanced* scales were used. It was concluded that acquiescence had helped to exaggerate the consistency of the unbalanced scales among the less educated respondents (Curtice 1996:139). The same observations are made in our own panels. For example, the average correlations between pairs of identical items rose from 0.45 among the less educated to 0.58 among the more educated in the Flemish General Elections panel surveys (N = 1,736) held in 1991 and 1995. Observers may conclude that the attitudes of the less educated are less stable than the attitudes of the more educated, but that conclusion is risky since instability may refer to real attitude change, to unreliability of the measurements (random measurement error), as well as to inconsistency of the responses to opinion items. Why are the test-retest correlations among the more educated more stable than among the less educated? Is it because they are better informed and have more crystallized attitudes in the sense of prior existence and persistence (Schuman and Presser 1981:251)? Is it because they hold stronger attitudes in the sense that they are more personally involved in the issues with which opinion questions are dealing (Krosnick and Abelson 1992:185)? Or is it because they are less likely to be influenced by the media because they hold more prior knowledge about the issues (Krosnick and Abelson 1992:181)?

In *The Nature and Origins of Mass Opinion*, Zaller (1992) points to the consequences of asking uninformed people to express their opinions on topics to which they have given little if any previous thought. The consequences are quite predictable: the opinion statements of uninformed people will be rough and superficial, and they vacillate randomly across repeated interviews of the same respondents (Zaller 1992:28). Several interpretations are provided for these shifts.

One interpretation is that many respondents undergo substantial opinion change between interviews that are repeated after several months. However, when the same respondents are asked the same questions on three different occasions, one can typically predict their opinion on the third interview as easily from the first interview as from the second. This would not be possible if changes between the first and second interviews represented systematic opinion change (Converse 1964; Zaller 1992:30).

Another interpretation deals with attitude crystallization. According to Converse (1964), opinion instability in samples must be assigned mainly to individuals who lack strong feelings on the issues but nevertheless provide answers by choosing randomly from the response options offered by the interviewers. Converse suggested that many respondents "simply do not have meaningful beliefs even on issues that have formed the basis for intense political controversy among the political elite for substantial periods of time" (1964:245). In line with this reasoning, the instability of responses to opinion statements is due to the respondents with weak attitudes or even nonattitudes (Smith 1988). The respondents with strong and firmly crystallized attitudes should show more stable responses to opinion statements (Krosnick 1988; Schuman and Presser 1981:253–64). This argument is consistent with the observation about the discrepancy between the less and more educated respondents.

Converse's evaluation of the panel data and his conclusions about the prevalence of nonattitudes have been challenged by investigators who argue that although the responses to opinion statements fluctuate, respondents have underlying "true" attitudes that are stable (Zaller 1992:31; see Smith 1988 for an overview). They contend that instrument unreliability, rather than nonattitudes, is the cause of low correlations. In this interpretation, the fluctuations in the responses on the observed variables are attributed to measurement error inherent in the response scales that are offered, e.g., the number of response categories (Alwin 1992). One of the consequences of this interpretation of response instability is that the correlations which are attenuated by random measurement error can be increased by applying correction coefficients that are, for example, derived from Multitrait-Multimethod studies (see Andrews 1984; Saris and Münnich 1995; Scherpenzeel 1995).

Zaller does not hold the conventional view that citizens possess "true attitudes" on every issue about which they are interviewed, but he also abandons the idea of nonattitudes. He proposed a model that specifies how individuals construct opinion reports in response to particular stimuli presented to them. The model is based on the ideas about information accessibility in cognitive psychology. Individuals do not possess just one opinion toward issues but multiple potential opinions. People are continuously exposed to a stream of political information that can push their opinion in one direction or another. Mostly unconsciously, they fill their minds with inconsistent information. When asked a survey question, they call to mind as many of those ideas as are immediately accessible and use them to make choices among the options offered to them. The basic claim of Zaller's model is that "survey responses are a function of immediately accessible 'considerations.'" In his view, it is the flow of information in elite discourse that determines which considerations are salient (Zaller 1992:35–36).

Both Converse's interpretation (attitude crystallization) and Zaller's model (multiple opinions) argue that attitude measurements are expected to be more stable among those who are informed and who are strongly involved in the issue. These respondents are less likely to choose response categories randomly (Converse) or to be influenced by changing considerations (Zaller). In this study, we will explore the differences in stability of responses to a balanced set of items measuring "political alienation" in a two-wave panel according to attitude strength measured by the level of knowledge (information) about politics.

ATTITUDE STRENGTH AND RESPONSE STABILITY

At first glance, the concept of "attitude crystallization" seems fruitful as an explanation of attitude stability over time. However, it is not very useful for empirical analysis since the explained variable (response stability measured by test-retest correlations) is a part of the definition of crystallization itself, namely persistence. The non-tautological aspect of crystallization is the more difficult part to operationalize (Schuman and Presser 1981:251–52). Nevertheless, attitude strength, which is theoretically not equivalent to "crystallization" but closely related to it, is useful for explaining response stability.

Attitude strength, as distinguished from the direction of attitudes (pro or con), refers to the salience of the issue, the centrality of the issue, or to personal involvement with the issue (Schuman and Presser 1981:231–32). Krosnick and Abelson (1992:179–81) proposed five dimensions of attitude strength: (1) extremity in the sense of departure from the neutral midpoint;[1] (2) intensity defined as the strength of one's feelings about an attitude object; (3) certainty or the degree to which an individual is certain that his or her attitude toward an object is correct; (4) importance, or the degree to which an individual considers an attitude to be important personally for him or her; and (5) knowledge that refers to the amount of information about the attitude object. Several measurements are proposed to measure these dimensions: the position on the response scale (extremity); questions about how intense feelings toward the object are (intensity); asking how difficult the respondent found it to answer the question (certainty); asking how important the attitude object is (importance); asking how important the attitude is in view of certain decisions (centrality); asking for a list of everything respondents know about an attitude object (knowledge); and committed actions (see Krosnick and Abelson 1992:179–81; Schuman and Presser 1981:233–48).

In our own research we have used open why-questions, comparative judgments, knowledge questions, the number of "no-opinion" responses, and open or closed questions about what is the most important for the respondents in combination with sorting tasks (Billiet, Carton, and Huys 1990:225–33; Billiet 1993). These are all attitude-specific measurements for attitude strength. General measurements are also proposed: for example, interest in the news, arguing about public issues, or asking how strongly attitudes are held in general (Schuman and Presser 1981:256). In general, specific measures perform better than general ones.

It was expected that the introduction of attitude strength could lead to better predictions of behavior from attitudes, or that respondents who are most susceptible to response effects could be separated from others (Krosnick and Abelson 1992:185–93). Krosnick and Schuman (1988), who explored the impact of attitude importance, intensity, and certainty on the susceptibility to response effects found little evidence of such an impact. However, in particular cases, some impact of attitude strength on response effects was detected (Bishop 1990; Waterplas, Billiet, and Loosveldt 1988). It remains unclear what role attitude strength plays in regulating the occurrence of response effects, but it is very plausible to expect that it exerts an influence on the stability of test-retest correlations.

One of the problems in measuring specific attitude strength is that this aspect should be measured completely independently of attitude direction. There is evidence that the various aspects of attitude strength do not all reflect a single dimension (Krosnick and Abelson 1992:183), and because of that, valid measurement of the dimensions of attitude strength will require a good deal of additional investigation. It is recommended, but it is not always possible in practice, to measure the strength of several attitudes at the same time. In this study, we will evaluate the impact of both a rather simple subjective and an extremely extensive and objective measurement of attitude strength on the stability between item correlation in a panel design.

DATA AND METHODS

The data of this study come from a two-wave panel survey held in 1995 and 1996 in Flanders concerning Flemish knowledge about many issues concerning the new federal structures in Belgium.[2] The sample was constructed using the equal probability method and was representative of the Flemish population of 18–75 years of age.[3] The 1995 sample contained 710 randomly selected respondents, of whom 532 were reinterviewed after twelve months, in principle by identically trained interviewers of the Institute of Social and Political Research (ISPO). Because of the simulated pre-test/post-test design of the study, in the period of the second wave, 455 randomly selected new respondents were also interviewed (Cambré, Billiet, and Swyngedouw 1996).

CONCEPTS AND MEASUREMENTS

This study focused on the stability of the following eight items that are intended to measure *political alienation* (Gamson 1968; Dierickx, Gijselinckx, and Thijssen 1996:643):

I1. There's no sense in voting; the political parties do what they want to do anyway.

I2. Most of our politicians are competent people who know what they are doing.

I3. In the elections, one party promises more than the other, but in the end, nothing much happens.

I4. The political parties are interested only in my vote, not in my opinions.

I5. If people like me let the politicians know what we think, then they will take our opinions into account.

I6. So many people vote in elections that my vote doesn't make any difference.

I7. People like me do have an influence on what political authorities do.

I8. Politicians have never learned to listen to people like me.

The items were (quasi) balanced (i.e., positively and negatively worded), in order to control for acquiescence (Martin 1964; Cloud and Vaughan 1979; Ray 1979). We will elaborate on this in the section in which the measurement models are tested.

Attitude strength is measured by two constructs: the knowledge about and interest in politics. Both fall between specific and general measures of attitude strength for the attitude toward politicians and the political system. They do not measure directly the strength of political alienation, but they are far more specific than the general strength measures mentioned by Schuman and Presser (1981:256) because they deal with the semantic field of "politics" and not only with the interest in public issues in general.

The *knowledge* about politics measures the knowledge dimension of attitude strength (Krosnick and Abelson 1992:181) more extensively than in other studies since this was the focus of the survey. Knowledge is operationalized as the number of correct answers given to exam-style questions that required more cognitive sophistication than is usual in political knowledge measures (Luskin 1987; Maddens and Dewachter 1993; Delli Carpini and Keeter 1993). The knowledge[4] was about the federal structures, about the basic principles and policies of the federal state and Flemish government. These subjects were relevant because Belgian state reform had arrived at a crucial stage in 1995. For the first time, the direct election of representatives for the separate regional legislative chambers was planned for the 1995 national elections. In order to make adequate and conscious use of their basic democratic voting rights, the citizens were supposed to be able to distinguish among the three legislative bodies (chamber, senate, and council), among the federal and regional policies and programs, and among politicians functioning on different levels. The knowledge about federal structures consists of three sets of knowledge questions: (1) nine "true/false/do not know" questions about the basic principles of the federal logic (*structu*), including questions about the number of regions, the authority of the federal and regional prime ministers, the composition of the Flemish council, the authority of the Flemish council, and the structure of the Flemish public administration; (2) a set of nine "true/false/do not know" questions about the typical Flemish policy (*policy*) on the domains of information, scientific research, education, environment protection, ethics, and the state budget; and (3) a question in which the respondents must classify sixteen policy domains in the correct category of responsible authorities (*authority*) (Flemish authority, federal authority, mixed, none, do not know). For each set, the correct answers were counted resulting in a score from zero to the maximum number of correct answers. The mean scores are 2.7 (SD = 2.17) for the 9 structure questions, 5.2 (SD = 2.1) for the 9 policy questions, and 8.1 (SD = 3.7) for the 16 authority questions. The three (observed) political knowledge scales are clearly indicators of a common latent construct "political knowledge" (factor loadings are 0.70, 0.66, and 0.77).

Political interest (Van Deth 1990) is conceived as a proxy variable for the importance dimension of attitude strength since it is reasonable to assume that citizens with strong attitudes toward politics are more concerned about it. Several objective questions were used concerning the frequency of reading domestic and international news about political, social, and economic affairs in daily newspapers, the frequency of listening to or watching political programs, the frequency of reviewing political information during elections, and the frequency of discussion about politics with family members, friends, or colleagues. These five indicators could not be explained by one underlying factor. The underlying structure consists of two different dimensions that are strongly related (r = .70). The first construct, the one we will use in this study, strictly speaking, measures interest in discussions and debates about politics. These three indicators represent what has been labelled the "positive saliency" of politics (Nie and Andersen 1974:572; Van Deth 1990:285–86).

Finally, we also included the level of *education* in our analysis since we can expect that the more educated are more informed about political issues. Education is a four-level ordinal variable ranging from less to more education. The correlation between education and political knowledge is strong (r = 0.54), but we will investigate the differences in their impact on attitude stability. The correlation between knowledge and interest is also substantial (r = 0.35), but the correlation between interest and education is rather weak (r = 0.10). Each of these three variables (knowledge, interest, and education) is recoded into two extreme categories and one middle category (30 percent respondents with lowest scores and 30 percent with highest scores, and about 40 percent in the middle). The analysis is focused on the contrasts between the two extreme groups defined by each variable.

RESPONSE INSTABILITY: REAL CHANGE, UNRELIABILITY, OR RESPONSE INCONSISTENCY?

A final remark about methods deals with the ambiguity in meaning of "response stability." In this study, we are not so much interested in instability in the sense of random measurement error (unreliability), or in real (systematic) attitude change, as in differences in test-retest stability as an indication of differences in attitude strength. Respondents with a weak or even nonexistent attitude are expected to be more likely to give inconsistent answers over time to the same questions. Are our panel data useful for this aim? Is it possible to differentiate among those three aspects of instability: random measurement error (unreliability), response inconsistency, or real change? It is often suggested that reliability can be operationalized by measuring an attitude at two or more points in time, provided that both memory of the previous response and "true value" change can be ruled out as factors affecting response consistency (Schuman and Presser 1981:252; Groves 1989). This must be completed by a third assumption about the stability of the method effects (Saris 1995:14–15). These assumptions are very strong and it is hard to provide evidence that are true. The use of three repeated measurements would have been better since one can formulate propositions about the correlations among the three measurements in order to distinguish random fluctuations and change (Heise 1969; Wiley and Wiley 1970; Alwin and Scott 1996:94). In such a case, one does not have to assume that the true scores did not change, but it is still necessary to assume no memory effects and stable method effects. Even with three repeated measurements, it is still not possible to distinguish between random measurement error and response inconsistency because of a weak or even nonexistent attitude, unless one can rely on information about random measurement error of the instrument derived from other studies.

We are not in the situation of having a three-wave panel, and the study was not designed as a reliability study. Being interested now mainly in the stability of the political alienation items and scale, we must provide arguments to support the stability of the true values and the method effects. We should not worry about memory effects since the distance in time between the repeated measurements is long. The stability of the method effect is easy to accept. The research team, the layout of the questions and response cards, the wording and the context of the questions, the number of response categories, and even most of the interviewers are unchanged. The stability of the true value is harder to demonstrate. Here we must fall back on the inspection of the marginal distributions, means, and standard deviations (Schuman and Presser 1981:252, 262), and on arguments about the political context.

The idea that true value change can be observed in the marginal distributions or in the means and standard deviations is based on the assumption that systematic change in the true values would be manifested in shifts in the marginals in the time 1 by time 2 turnover tables, and in the mean values and standard deviations. Certainly, real change on the individual level can cancel out on the aggregate level, but this is unlikely unless several subgroups had changed in different directions. If any real change had occurred in that particular case, then we would expect more political alienation in the first wave because the interviews were held in a period (February–April 1995) in which the so-called Agusta affair broke out, with daily discussions in the media about corruption among top politicians. General elections were announced and organized for May 24 (Platel 1996). Media messages about all kinds of affairs were still present in the period of the reinterviews (April–June 1996), but they were not as common as in the first half of 1995. Unfortunately, the potential temporary media effect that we can expect cannot be separated from "true value" change, and it is precisely this kind of inconsistency in which we are interested.

Let us evaluate some of the measures for the composite political alienation scale. The internal consistency of the scale, measured by Cronbach's alpha, is 0.74 in the first and 0.78 in the second wave. For the panel respondents, the mean on the political alienation scale is 3.365 (SD = 0.719) in the first interview and 3.339 (SD = 0.721) in the reinterview. This mean score is slightly higher in the first wave as was expected, but the difference is very small. Is the difference significantly different from zero? We cannot test this hypothesis with a classical t-test since the observations are dependent, but we can perform a paired difference t-test, or a nonparametric analogue (Schlotzhauer and Littell 1987:200–205). We can conclude that the average difference between the pairs of observations is not significantly different from zero (mean = -0.027; T: mean = 0 = 0.955, p = 0.34).[5] On the basis of that, we can conclude that no systematic shift in one direction had occurred.

Table 9.1 shows that the respondents with little political knowledge scored significantly higher on political alienation in both the first and second waves, but there is nearly no difference in mean scores between the waves in the two groups (more educated, 0.014; less educated, 0.009). The standard errors are equal in both the two waves and the two knowledge groups.

TABLE 9.1
Test of Equality of Means and Variances of the Composite Measurement of Political Alienation (Additive Likert scale) for Respondents with Low and High Political Knowledge in 1995 and 1996

	1995				1996			
	Mean	SE	t-value	Prob.	Mean	SE	t-value	Prob.
Political knowledge								
Low	3.586	0.050	6.904	< .0001	3.600	0.053	6.881	< .0001
High	3.072	0.055			3.063	0.057		
Ho: var. equal	F = 1.25; prob. > F = 0.152				F = 1.17; prob. > F = 0.325			

We can also compare the mean of the political alienation scale in the complete 1995 sample (N = 710) with that of the fresh sample from 1996 (N = 455). The means are 3.324 and 3.059 and the null hypothesis (difference) must be rejected (t = 6.39; p < 0.001), indicating that the respondents scored somewhat higher on the political alienation scale in 1995. This was expected because of the media effect in 1995.

Most important for further analysis is that the difference in mean scores between the waves largely disappeared among the panel respondents who remained in this study. This is due to the dropout of the politically least-interested respondents in the second wave. This conclusion is based on an analysis of panel attrition. The attrition was 25 percent among those with low political interest and only 10 percent among the most politically interested (Cambré, Billiet, and Swyngedouw 1996:15). It seems plausible to assume that no real true value change occurred among the panel respondents and that the instability of the test-retest correlations is due to unreliability (random error) and inconsistency because of the weakness of the attitude. We can obtain an impression of this source of instability if we can separate it from random error. This strategy is possible by adjusting the test-retest correlations for random measurement error or by observing the stability of the latent variable behind the set of indicators.

RESULTS

The observed test-retest correlations of the 1995–1996 political alienation items are in the range 0.30–0.48 (average 0.37). This is low if we assume that significant real change was very unlikely. It is, for example, consistently lower than the test-retest correlations in a set of eight negatively

TABLE 9.2
Observed Test-Retest Correlations (Pearson) of the Political Alienation Items in 1995 and 1996, According to Level of Education, Level of Political Knowledge, and Political Interest

Items	Education			Political Knowledge			Political Interest		
	Low	High	H−L	Low	High	H−L	Low	High	H−L
I1	.423	.447	.024	.347	.492	.145	.393	.421	.028
I2	.353	.361	.008	.333	.496	.169	.454	.440	-.014
I3	.269	.412	.143	.173	.270	.097	.289	.282	-.007
I4	.255	.381	.126	.195	.363	.168	.244	.347	.103
I5	.397	.423	.026	.339	.459	.120	.352	.438	.086
I6	.397	.484	.087	.270	.422	.152	.352	.379	.027
I7	.391	.458	.067	.297	.532	.235	.270	.294	.024
I8	.239	.400	.161	.230	.356	.126	.275	.407	.132
Mean diff.			.080			.151			.047

worded Likert items expressing feelings of threat toward immigrants, as shown in Table 9.2.[6]

Among the less educated respondents, the test-retest correlations are in the range 0.24–0.42. This is systematically lower than among the higher educated (range 0.36–0.48). Let us compare this again with the "feeling threatened by the immigrant" items where an analogous difference in stability between the less-educated (range 0.39–0.53) and the higher-educated respondents (range 0.55–0.67) was found. On average, the differences between the higher and the less educated are of the same order as the differences in response stability between the low and high political interest groups. The knowledge variable performed best in discriminating groups with weaker and stronger response consistency. The differences in correlations between those groups are in the range 0.10–0.24 (mean = 0.15).

The third item in the set ("In the elections, one party promises more than the other, but in the end, nothing much happens") shows very weak correlations for the whole sample (0.30) as well as within the two extreme knowledge groups. Surprisingly, this correlation is the highest in group with medium knowledge (0.39). We do not know the reason for this extremely low correlation or for these differences. Is it because the subject of the statement was the elections that were held between the first and second waves? Let us see in Table 9.3. The percentages of respondents agreeing with the statement are about the same in 1995 and 1996 (about 72

TABLE 9.3
Responses to the Item "In the elections, one party promises more than the other, but in the end, nothing much happens" According to Moment of Interview (Absolute Numbers and Marginal)

		1996					
		Compl. agree	*Agree*	*Neither . . . nor*	*Disagree*	*Compl. disagree*	*Total (%)*
1995	Compl. agree	93	78	15	8	4	198 (37.8)
	Agree	32	96	31	16	3	178 (34.0)
	Neither . . . nor	11	29	28	15	2	85 (16.3)
	Disagree	4	21	9	10	1	45 (8.6)
	Compl. disagree	6	4	3	3	1	17 (3.3)
	Total	146	228	86	52	11	523
	(%)	(27.9)	(43.6)	(16.4)	(9.9)	(2.1)	(100.0)

percent) but the responses are more extreme in 1995, partly during the pre-electoral campaign. Fifty-six percent of the respondents who disagreed or strongly disagreed with the statement in 1995 (strongly) agreed with it in 1996. And vice versa, 49 percent of those who rejected the statement in 1996 had supported it in 1995. The skewness of the distributions, the changes in extremity, and shifts in pro, con, and neutral positions are responsible for the low correlation.

Differences in the Corrected Test-Retest Correlations between the Items

Are the differences in response stability, evaluated by the test-retest correlations of the particular items (see Table 9.2), larger than one might expect by pure chance? In order to answer that question, we shall perform a two-group comparison with LISREL (Jöreskog and Sörbom 1993). However, before starting the test, the observed correlations must be corrected for measurement error because these measures contain both random error and correlated error due to similar methods employed (i.e., 5-point Likert-type items) (Scherpenzeel and Saris 1997:372). Correction is not possible unless estimates of the reliability and the validity of the measures are available.

According to Saris and Scherpenzeel (1996), the validity and reliability estimates can be obtained by Multitrait-Multimethod (MTMM) studies in which one can evaluate the quality of measurement instruments. Researchers who do not have direct MTMM-based information about the validity and reliability of their particular measurements are advised to use a set of correction coefficients, which are based on a meta-analysis of a large number of MTMM studies (Scherpenzeel 1995:117–50; Scherpenzeel and Saris 1997; Saris, Van Wijk, and Scherpenzeel 1998). According to these scholars, the average reliability and validity of a measurement should be adjusted depending on the effects of characteristics of the measurement instrument that is actually used (i.e., the subject or domain of the study, the response scale, the data collection, the position in the questionnaire, the country, etc.). Since we were involved in the MTMM experiments, we have specific information about the necessary adjustments for nearly all of the characteristics of our instruments. We used exactly the same methodology in the present study as in our previous MTMM study (the same interviewers, the same instructions for interviewers, the same kind of questionnaire and response cards, etc.). In the domain of life satisfaction that was used in our MTMM experiment, the validity coefficient of the 5-point scale is 0.895 and its reliability is 0.835. These coefficients must be adjusted for the subject of the study, i.e., politics. This means that according to the meta-analysis of Scherpenzeel and Saris (1997:362), rather large adjustments are necessary, namely -0.07 for the validity coefficients and -0.10 for the reliability coefficient. This results in a validity coefficient (b_{ij}) of 0.825 and a reliability coefficient (h_{ij}) of 0.735. The estimation of the method effect (or invalidity coefficient g_{ij}) is then 0.565 (this is $(1 - b^2_{ij})^{1/2}$).

It should be mentioned that these estimations of the validity and the reliability coefficients of the 5-point scale are not independent of the two other methods used in the MTMM models in which they are estimated (De Wit and Billiet 1995:53–56). In a context in which other methods are combined, these estimates for the 5-point scale might be somewhat different.[7] Moreover, the rather large adjustments of the validity and reliability estimates because of the domain to which these items belong (politics) may somewhat inflate the differences in the corrected test-retest correlations. However, we do not have better estimations for the domain of politics. In any case, using coefficients that are not adjusted for the political domain do not lead to substantially different conclusions about the differences in stability between the groups of respondents.

The correction for measurement error of the observed test-retest correlations $r(y_{i1}y_{i2})$ of the items is obtained by the following equation proposed by Saris and Scherpenzeel (1996:61) and which is based on the true-score model[8] (see figure 9.1).

$$\rho(F_{i1}F_{i2}) = [r(y_{i1}y_{i2}) - (h_{i1} \times g_{i1} \times h_{i2} \times g_{i2})]/$$

$$(h_{i1} \times b_{i1} \times h_{i2} \times b_{i2}) \qquad (Eq.\ 9.1)$$

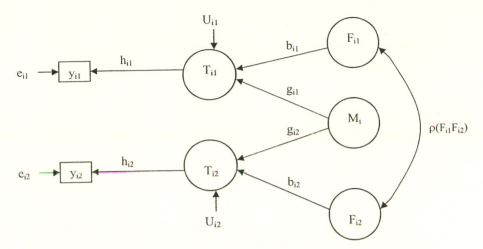

Figure 9.1 The true-score model for the test-retest correlation of a variable incorporating method-effects, unique components and random error. *Source*: Saris and Scherpenzeel 1996.

Legend:

y_{i1} and y_{i2}: observed indicator i at time 1 and time 2;
T_{i1} and T_{i2}: true score at time 1 and time 2;
M_i: method effect for item i;
F_{i1} and F_{i2}: state of the latent indicator at time 1 and time 2;
e_{i1} and e_{i2}: random measurement error for item i at time 1 and time 2;
h_{i1} and h_{i2}: the reliability coefficients for item i at time 1 and time 2;
b_{i1} and b_{i2}: the validity coefficients for item i at time 1 and time 2;
g_{i1} and g_{i2}: the method effect on the true score at time 1 and time 2;
u_{i1} and u_{i2}: the residual variance of the true score at time 1 and time 2;
$\rho(F_{i1}F_{i2})$: the correlation between the two latent indicators.
Assumptions in the test-retest situation: $h_{i1} = h_{i2}$; $b_{i1} = b_{i2}$; $g_{i1} = g_{i2}$.

In this equation, $\rho(F_{i1}F_{i2})$ refers to the correlation between an unobserved variable i measured at two points in time by an identical indicator i. We may assume that the method effect of the 5-point scale is stable over the whole set. For that reason, the true-score validity coefficients (b_{ij}), the reliability coefficients (h_{ij}), and the method effects (g_{ij}) do not need subscripts for items i and time j since both are constant for this set of indicators. Therefore equation 9.1 can be simplified as follows:

$$\rho(F_{i1}F_{i2}) = [r(y_{i1}y_{i2}) - (h \times g)^2]/(h \times b)^2 \qquad \text{(Eq. 9.2)}$$

The corrected test-retest correlations $\rho(F_{i1}F_{i2})$ and their corresponding t-values are shown in the last two columns of each second row in Table 9.4. As already discussed, the stability of the third item is extremely low.

TABLE 9.4
Test of the Equality of the Adjusted Test-Retest Correlations between Items in
the Samples of the Respondents with Low and High Political Knowledge
(Goodness of Fit Indices, Correlations, and t-values)

Item	Model	χ^2	df	p.	RMSEA	p-value of close fit	ϕ^1_{12} (t)	ϕ^2_{12} (t)
I1	$\phi^1_{12} = \phi^2_{12}$	74.72	3	.000	.269	.000	.68 (10.239)	
	$\phi^1_{12} \neq \phi^2_{12}$	.00	2	1.0	–	–	.49 (6.495)	.87 (12.941)
I2	$\phi^1_{12} = \phi^2_{12}$	91.56	3	.000	.299	.000	.67 (10.070)	
	$\phi^1_{12} \neq \phi^2_{12}$	.00	2	1.0	–	–	.44 (5.884)	.88 (13.202)
I3	$\phi^1_{12} = \phi^2_{12}$	7.702	3	.053	.069	.238	.14 (2.514)	
	$\phi^1_{12} \neq \phi^2_{12}$	.00	2	1.0	–	–	.00 (.018)	.28 (3.714)
I4	$\phi^1_{12} = \phi^2_{12}$	22.999	3	.000	.142	.002	.30 (5.166)	
	$\phi^1_{12} \neq \phi^2_{12}$	.00	2	1.0	–	–	.07 (.854)	.52 (7.507)
I5	$\phi^1_{12} = \phi^2_{12}$	35.257	3	.000	.180	.000	.62 (9.546)	
	$\phi^1_{12} \neq \phi^2_{12}$	.00	2	1.0	–	–	.45 (6.008)	.78 (11.628)
I6	$\phi^1_{12} = \phi^2_{12}$	33.03	3	.000	.174	.000	.47 (7.699)	
	$\phi^1_{12} \neq \phi^2_{12}$	.00	2	1.0	–	–	.25 (3.118)	.68 (10.249)
I7	$\phi^1_{12} = \phi^2_{12}$	345.551	3	.000	.587	.000	.67 (10.087)	
	$\phi^1_{12} \neq \phi^2_{12}$	.00	2	1.0	–	–	.35 (3.226)	.98 (14.859)
I8	$\phi^1_{12} = \phi^2_{12}$	15.096	3	.002	.110	.028	.39 (6.616)	
	$\phi^1_{12} \neq \phi^2_{12}$	.00	2	1.0	–	–	.22 (2.881)	.55 (8.065)

Now we are ready to test the between group equality of the stability over time of each latent indicator, which is represented by the corresponding observed indicator.[9] We start with a model in which the adjusted test-retest correlation in the two groups is constrained to be equal. In the second step, the equality constraint is freed and the drop in χ^2 value for the loss of one degree of freedom is evaluated.

The null hypothesis stating that there is no difference in correlations between the two groups is rejected for all the items. In each case, there is a substantial improvement of the model fit when the equality constraint between the correlations is dropped The difference in stability of item 7 about the influence on political authorities is extremely large. In the high knowledge group, the adjusted correlations between the repeated measurements of the items are considerably higher than in the low knowledge group.

DIFFERENCES IN THE STABILITY OF THE LATENT VARIABLE BEHIND THE SET OF ITEMS

In substantive research, one is often not so much interested in single attitude items as in the stability of the measurement of the latent variable behind the set of items. In order to evaluate the stability of the latent variable at two points in time, a measurement model is presented within each of the political knowledge groups. The focus is on the equality of the correlation between the two measurements of the latent variable "political alienation" in the two knowledge groups. A number of decisions must be made about the structure of the model for the different groups and time periods. The model used is confirmed as usual in equation 9.3:

$$\Sigma^i_t = \Lambda^i_t \Phi^i_1 \Lambda^i_t + \Theta^i_t \text{ where } t = 1995 \text{ or } 1996 \text{ and } i \text{ group } 1 \text{ or } 2 \quad (Eq.\ 9.3)$$

1. We specify three latent variables behind the eight indicators, which are measured twice: political alienation in 1995 (POLAL95), political alienation in 1996 (POLAL96), and a style factor (STYLE) that measures acquiescence. This is a typical method effect for agree-disagree items. For an extensive discussion of this, we refer to Billiet and McClendon (2000), who identified a style factor that correlates 0.93 with a score for agreeing (number of times the respondents agreed from 14 items).

2. The *structures* of the factor loadings (λ) and the residual (co-)variances (θ) for political alienation are the same:

$$\Lambda^1_t \cong \Lambda^2_t; \Theta^1_t \cong \Theta^2_t.$$

3. Within each political-knowledge group, the factor loadings are identical across the waves:

$$\Lambda^1_1 = \Lambda^1_2; \Lambda^2_1 = \Lambda^2_2.$$

4. As is observed, and to some extent tested in Table 9.1, within each political-knowledge group, and across the waves, the variances of political knowledge are equal (see Table 9.3):

$$\Phi^1_1 = \Phi^2_1 = \Phi^1_2 = \Phi^2_2.$$

5. The style factor had identical loadings on all the items (in time 1 and time 2) within each political knowledge group, but they vary across these groups:

For all i: λ^1_i = constant; λ^2_i = constant

$$\Lambda^1 \neq \Lambda^2.$$

6. We expect that the loadings on style are larger for the low knowledge group since we may assume that those who have more information and who have a stronger attitude are less subject to acquiescence (Evans and Heath 1995):

For all i: $\lambda^1_i > \lambda^2_i$.

7. The variances of the style factor are not identical for the two knowledge groups:

$$\Phi^1_s \neq \Phi^2_s.$$

We expect that the variance of the style factor in the low knowledge group is higher than this variance in the high knowledge group, but this is not tested.

8. We may assume that the style factor is not correlated with the substantive factor, thus the covariance between the substantive variable in the two waves and the style factor is zero in the two groups:

$$\Phi^1_{13} = \Phi^1_{23} = \Phi^2_{13} = \Phi^2_{23} = 0.$$

In the first model in Table 9.5, the covariance of political alienation (Φ_{12}) in the two waves is fixed to be equal across the two groups. In the second model, this equality constraint is lost and the hypothesis states that the covariances are not equal.

The difference in χ^2 between Model 2 and Model 1 is -6.13 for a loss of one degree of freedom; thus we can accept the second model.[10] So there is reason to reject the model with equal correlations and accept the model with unequal correlations. The standardized and unstandardized parameters as estimated under Model 2 are reported in Table 9.6. The equality constraints of the parameters are exactly as they were specified. The variance of the style factor is larger in the group with little political knowledge, and the factor loadings are also smaller. However, a model in which the variance of the style factor is constrained to be equal in the two knowledge groups is likewise acceptable since there is only a small increase in χ^2 units (+2.02) for one additional degree of freedom.

TABLE 9.5
Test of Equality of the Test-Retest Correlation of the Construct "Political Alienation" across High and Low Political Knowledge Groups (Goodness of Fit Indices, Correlations, and t-values)

Model	χ^2	df	p.	RMSEA	p-value of close fit	ϕ^1_{12} (t)	ϕ^2_{12} (t)
(1) $\phi^1_{12} = \phi^2_{12}$	287.36	210	.0003	.033	.999	.66 (5.008)	
(2) $\phi^1_{12} \neq \phi^2_{12}$	281.23	209	.001	.032	.999	.52 (3.880)	.76 (5.131)

Table 9.6
Parameters of Model 2. Difference in Test-Retest Correlation of "Political Alienation" in the High and Low Political Knowledge groups.

Group 1. Low Political Knowledge (N = 164)

Items	Political Alienation 1995			Political Alienation 1996			Style (Acquiescence)		
	Unstand.	(t-value)	Stand.	Unstand.	(t-value)	Stand.	Unstand.	(t-value)	Stand.
I95_1	1	(fixed)	.703	0			1	(fixed)	.234
I95_2	-.567	(-4.676)	-.398	0			1	–	.234
I95_3	.868	(7.645)	.610	0			1	–	.234
I95_4	.957	(8.080)	.672	0			1	–	.234
I95_5	-.797	(-6.772)	-.560	0			1	–	.234
I95_6	.606	(4.905)	.426	0			1	–	.234
I95_7	-.577	(-4.688)	-.405	0			1	–	.234
I95_8	.897	(7.462)	.630	0			1	–	.234
I96_1	0			1	(fixed)	.703	1	–	.234
I96_2	0			-.567	(-4.676)	-.398	1	–	.234
I96_3	0			.868	(7.645)	.610	1	–	.234
I96_4	0			.957	(8.080)	.672	1	–	.234
I96_5	0			-.797	(-6.772)	-.560	1	–	.234
I96_6	0			.606	(4.905)	.426	1	–	.234
I96_7	0			-.577	(-4.688)	-.405	1	–	.234
I96_8	0			.897	(7.462)	.630	1	–	.234

	ϕ^1_1			ϕ^1_2			ϕ^1_3		
	Unstand.	(t-value)	Stand.	Unstand.	(t-value)	Stand.	Unstand.	(t-value)	Stand.
ϕ^1_1	.494	(5.703)	1						
ϕ^1_2	.255	(3.880)	.516	.494	(5.703)	1			
ϕ^1_3	.0			.0			.055	(3.606)	1

Group 2. High Political Knowledge (N = 169)

Items	Political Alienation 1995			Political Alienation 1996			Style (Acquiescence)		
	Unstand.	(t-value)	Stand.	Unstand.	(t-value)	Stand.	Unstand.	(t-value)	Stand.
I95_1	1	(fixed)	.703	0			1	(fixed)	.172
I95_2	-.621	(-5.610)	-.436	0			1	–	.172

TABLE 9.6 *cont.*

Items	Political Alienation 1995			Political Alienation 1996			Style (Acquiescence)		
	Unstand.	(t-value)	Stand.	Unstand.	(t-value)	Stand.	Unstand.	(t-value)	Stand.
I95_3	.812	(7.771)	.571	0			1	–	.172
I95_4	1.177	(9.581)	.827	0			1	–	.172
I95_5	-1.020	(-9.186)	-.717	0			1	–	.172
I95_6	.699	(6.752)	.491	0			1	–	.172
I95_7	-1.061	(-8.217)	-.745	0			1	–	.172
I95_8	.849	(7.885)	.596	0			1	–	.172
I96_1	0			1	(fixed)	.703	1	–	.172
I96_2	0			.621	(-5.610)	-.436	1	–	.172
I96_3	0			.812	(7.771)	.571	1	–	.172
I96_4	0			1.177	(9.581)	.827	1	–	.172
I96_5	0			-1.020	(-9.186)	-.717	1	–	.172
I96_6	0			.699	(6.752)	.491	1	–	.172
I96_7	0			-1.061	(-8.217)	-.745	1	–	.172
I96_8	0			.849	(7.885)	.596	1	–	.172

	ϕ^2_1			ϕ^2_2			ϕ^2_3		
	Unstand.	(t-value)	Stand.	Unstand.	(t-value)	Stand.	Unstand.	(t-value)	Stand.
ϕ^2_1	.494	(5.703)	1						
ϕ^2_2	.374	(5.131)	.757	.494	(5.703)	1			
ϕ^2_3	.0			.0			.030	(3.070)	1

More important, the correlation between the repeated measurements of the latent variable is considerably higher among the respondents who are much better informed about politics than among the respondents with little political knowledge. Since the latent variables are purified from random error (unreliability), the difference in instability between the two knowledge groups must be ascribed to a difference in real change or to a difference of response consistency.

CONCLUSION AND DISCUSSION

The purpose of this study was to estimate the effect of attitude strength on the stability of a quasi-balanced political alienation scale. The basic two-wave model was modified in two important ways. First, we corrected the observed test-retest correlations for measurement error. This was done based on the results of meta-analysis. These adjustments are not optimal but they are the best we can currently obtain. Large numbers of MTMM studies with combinations of different methods for estimating the expected values of the coefficients of a particular method can lead to more stable estimates in the future. The corrections led to considerable changes in the correlation matrix. Second, we introduced a style factor to control for another aspect of invalidity: acquiescence bias. The acquiescence factor was stable over time and significant in the two groups of respondents, those with weak and those with strong attitudes. After correction for these two aspects of invalidity, we found that respondents with weak attitudes, in the sense that they have little information about politics, are more likely to give inconsistent responses over time.

Because we have only a two-wave study, it is not completely obvious whether the instability must be conceived as real change or as a response inconsistency among respondents with weak attitudes. On the basis of the marginal distributions in the observed variables and the means of the composite variable "political alienation" in the sample of the panel respondents, we assumed that no substantial real change occurred in the two knowledge groups. If this assumption is correct, then we may conclude that a difference in the response consistency between ill- and well-informed respondents was responsible for the difference in response stability. Since political knowledge was conceived as an indicator of attitude strength, we may assume a low degree of commitment to the issue (politics) is responsible for the instability over time.

These conclusions can be drawn for both individual items and the latent variable alienation. In both cases, a correction is made for unreliability and aspects of invalidity of the measurement instrument. This suggests that Converse was right in arguing that there are different types of people: those with an opinion and those without an opinion or a weak opinion. By making the distinction between different groups on the basis of knowledge, one can get a better impression of the strength or weakness of the opinions of the respondents. This is important for public opinion research because it gives an impression of how easily public opinion can be changed.

Together with other theoretical and empirical impressions, the result of this study justifies further attention to the empirical study of the relation between response instability and attitude strength in public opinion research.

The model presented in this study can be elaborated in several respects. A three-wave panel study would enable us to differentiate between change and random fluctuations. Concerning the measurement of attitude strength, we presented a well-developed measure of the information dimensions. Other dimensions like importance, certainty, and intensity were less elaborated and could be incorporated. Subsequently, the relative importance of these aspects of attitude strength could be distinguished.

This contribution seems to bolster Converse's argument that the main issue is the problem of attitude crystallization. But Zaller's main hypothesis, the multiple accessible opinions and their different "activation," is not really tested in this study nor is Converse's hypothesis sufficiently tested since we are without three-wave panel data. It would be interesting to research two distinct aspects of Zaller's hypothesis: first, the differences between relevant subgroups on the logical integration of multiple opinions in one general opinion or attitude; second, the differences between relevant groups concerning the variability of opinions on both levels of abstraction. This calls for a more ambitious research agenda and the inclusion of methods other than general surveys.

NOTES

The research project on the reliability and validity of scales is supported by the National Research Fund-Flanders (G.0209.95) and by a research grant of the Research Fund Katholieke Universiteit Leuven (OT/94/3).

1. Extremity is considered a refinement of attitude direction (pro-con) by Schuman and Presser (1981:231) and not an aspect of attitude strength.

2. The survey was sponsored by the Flemish government in order to study the impact of its information campaigns to the public. The knowledge of the Flemish citizens about the authorities, institutions, and policies of the Flemish federal state within the context of the Belgian federation was the main subject of the study. The survey was conducted by the Institute of Social and Political Research (ISPO), which is located at the Department of Sociology, Katholieke Universiteit Leuven. The fieldwork was organized and supervised by Bart Cambré. Billiet and Cambré 1999.

3. A two-stage sample with equal probabilities was used. In the first stage, the municipalities were selected at random. Seventy-seven clusters of sample units were selected at random with a probability proportional to the number of inhabitants in each municipality; 64 Flemish municipalities out of 316 were included in the sample. In the second stage, for each cluster a random sample of respondents was selected from the national population registers. In the first wave, the non-response rate was 38 percent (refusals and non-contacts included). Face-to-face interviews (N = 710) were conducted by trained interviewers of ISPO. The response rate for panel respondents in the second wave was 79.2 percent (computed on the

basis of 672 respondents who had not at the end of the first interview explicitly refused to participate in a subsequent interview).

4. Political knowledge was measured in 1995 and in 1996. Some items were different because of the changed political situation (new governments and new policy). The correlation between both measures was high (.82). We are using the measurement from 1995.

5. The Wilcoxon Signed Rank test (a nonparametric analogue) leads to the same conclusion:

$$\text{Sgn Rank} = -21; \text{p} = 0.062.$$

6. The test-retest correlations of the threat items in the sample of 1,736 panel respondents in the General Elections study were in the range .50–.61, although the time gap was four times larger. The data were collected by the same research institute (ISPO) in the context of the 1991 and 1995 General Election surveys. The same sampling procedures, training program, interviewers, and type of questionnaires were used.

7. In our MTMM experiments, the 5-point scale was evaluated in the context of a 10-point and a 100-point scale. Large numbers of MTMM studies with combinations of different methods for estimating the expected values of the coefficients of a particular method can lead to more stable estimates.

8. We refer to Saris and Scherpenzeel (1997) for more details and for an excellent explanation of the true score model for measurement error.

9. For the analysis of ordinal variables, polychoric correlation and WLS estimation is preferable (Jöreskog 1990); however, the two subsamples are too small to estimate the asymptotic covariance matrix adequately. Coenders (1996) has shown that product-moment correlations and ML are mostly acceptable. We used that method with the covariances as input. ULS estimation was also performed. This does not affect the parameters, but the differences in χ^2 for equal degrees of freedom are larger, which means that the null hypothesis is more easily rejected.

10. The fit of the model can be improved by accepting more error correlations, but this does not substantially change the conclusion. Models that specify differences in over-time correlations are always more acceptable. For example, Model (1): $\chi^2 = 258.7$; df = 206; p = .007 versus Model (2): $\chi^2 = 253.6$; df = 205; p = .012.

REFERENCES

Achen, Christopher H. 1975. "Mass Political Attitudes and the Survey Response." *American Political Science Review* 69:1218–51.
Alwin, Duane F. 1993. "Information Transmission in the Survey Interview: Number of Response Categories and the Reliability of Attitude Measurement." In *Sociological Methodology*, ed. Peter V. Marsden, 83–118. Oxford: Blackwell.
Alwin, Duane F., and Jacqueline Scott. 1996. "Attitude Change: Its Measurement and Interpretation Using Longitudinal Surveys." In *Understanding Change in*

Social Attitudes, ed. Bridget Taylor and Katarina Thomson, 75–106. Aldershot: Dartmouth.

Andrews, F. M. 1984. "Construct Validity and Error Components of Survey Measures: A Structural Modelling Approach." *Public Opinion Quarterly* 48: 409–22.

Billiet, J. 1993. "Stabiliteit en verandering in de attitude tegenover vreemdelingen." In *Kiezen is Verliezen. Onderzoek naar de politieke opvattingen van de Vlamingen,* ed. M. Swyngedouw, J. Billiet, A. Carton, and R. Beerten, 147–62. Leuven: Acco.

Billiet, J., and B. Cambré. 1999. "Social Capital, Active Membership in Voluntary Associations and Some Aspects of Political Participation: An Empirical Case Study." In *Social Capital and European Democracy,* ed. Jan Van Deth, Marco Maraffi, Kenneth Newton, and Paul Whiteley. London: Routledge.

Billiet, J., and McKee J. McClendon. 2000. "Modeling Aquiescence in Measurement Models for Two Balanced Sets of Items." *Structural Equation Modeling: A Multidisciplinary Journal* 7:608–29.

Billiet, J., G. Loosveldt, and Lina Waterplas. 1986. *Het survey-interview onderzocht. Effecten van het ontwerp en gebruik van vragenlijsten op de kwaliteit van de antwoorden.* Leuven: SOI.

Billiet, J., B. Cambré, and M. Swyngedouw. 1997. "De kennis van de federale logica en van de bevoegdheden en het beleid van de Vlaamse overheid: Een Verklaringsmodel." *Res Publica* 39:609–27.

Billiet, J., A. Carton, and R. Huys. 1990. *Onbekend of onbemind? Een sociologisch onderzoek naar de houding van de Belgen tegenover migranten.* Leuven: SOI.

Bishop, G. F. 1990. "Issue Involvement and Response Effects in Public Opinion Surveys." *Public Opinion Quarterly* 54:209–18.

Cambré, B., J. Billiet, and M. Swyngedouw. 1996. *De kennis van de vlamingen en hun houding tegenover de vlaamse overheid. Resultaten van een effectpeiling.* Leuven: ISPO.

Cloud, J., and G. M. Vaughan. 1979. "Using Balanced Scales to Control Acquiescence." *Sociometry* 33:193–206.

Coenders, G. 1996. *Structural Equation Modelling with Ordinally Measured Survey Data.* Ph.D. diss., Universitat Ramon Llull, Barcelona.

Converse, Philip E. 1964. "The Nature of Belief Systems in Mass Publics." In *Ideology and Discontent,* ed. David Apter, 206–61. New York: Free Press.

———. 1975. "Public Opinion and Voting Behavior." In *Handbook of Political Science,* ed. F. I. Greenstein and N. W. Polsby, 4:75–169. Reading, MA: Addison-Wesley.

Curtice, John. 1996. "Why Methodology Matters." In *Understanding Change in Social Attitudes,* ed. Bridget Taylor and Katarina Thomson, 131–49. Aldershot: Dartmouth.

Delli Carpini, Michael X., and Scott Keeter. 1993. "Measuring Political Knowledge." *American Journal of Political Science* 37:1179–1206.

De Wit, H., and J. Billiet. 1995. "The MTMM Design: Back to the Founding Fathers." In *The Multitrait-Multimethod Approach to Evaluate Measurement Instruments,* ed. W. Saris and A. Munnich, 39–60. Budapest: Eötvös University Press.

Dierickx, G., and P. Thijssen. 1993. "Politieke effciëntie in Vlaanderen: Een verkennende analyse." In *Kiezen is Verliezen. Onderzoek naar de politieke opvattingen van Vlamingen,* ed. M. Swyngedouw, J. Billiet, A. Carton, and R. Beerten, 185–98. Leuven: Acco.

Dierickx, G., C. Gijselinckx, and Peter Thijssen. 1996. "Cultural Deprivation and Political Alienation: An Interim Report." *Res Publica,* 631–56.

Evans, G., and A. Heath. 1995. "The Measurement of Left-Right and Libertarian-Authoritarian Values: A Comparison of Balanced and Unbalanced Scales." *Quality and Quantity* 29:191–206.

Gamson, W. 1968. *Power and Discontent.* Homewood: Dorsey Press.

Groves, Robert, M. 1989. *Survey Errors and Survey Costs.* New York: Wiley.

Heise, D. R. 1969. "Separating Reliability and Stability in Test-Retest Correlation." *American Sociological Review* 34:93–101.

Jöreskog, K. 1990. "New Developments in LISREL: Analysis of Ordinal Variables Using Polychoric Correlations and Weighted Least Squares." *Quality and Quantity* 24:387–404.

Jöreskog, Karl G., and Dag Sörbom. 1993. *LISREL® 8 User's Reference Guide.* Chicago: Scientific Software International.

Krosnick, Jon A. 1988. "Attitude Importance and Attitude Change." *Journal of Experimental Social Psychology* 24:205–55.

Krosnick, Jon A., and Robert P. Abelson. 1992. "The Case for Measuring Attitude Strength in Surveys." In *Questions about Questions: Inquiries into the Cognitive Bases of Surveys,* ed. Judith M. Tanur, 177–203. New York: Russell Sage Foundation.

Krosnick, J. A., and H. Schuman. 1988. "Attitude Intensity, Importance, and Certainty and Susceptibility to Response Effects." *Journal of Personality and Social Psychology* 54:940–52.

Loosveldt, Geert. 1995. "The Profile of the Difficult-to-Interview Respondent." *Bulletin de méthodologie sociologique* 48:68–81.

Lord, F., and M. R. Novick. 1968. *Statistical Theories of Mental Test Scores.* Reading, MA: Addison-Wesley.

Luskin, Robert C. 1987. "Measuring Political Sophistication." *American Journal of Political Science* 31:356–99.

Maddens B., and W. Dewachter. 1993. "Politieke kennis." In *Kiezen is Verliezen. Onderzoek naar de politieke opvattingen van de Vlamingen,* ed. M. Swyngedouw, J. Billiet, A. Carton, and R. Beerten, 131–46. Leuven: Acco.

Martin, John. 1964. "Acquiescence: Measurement and Theory." *British Journal of Social and Clinical Psychology* 3:216–225.

Nie, N. H., and K. Andersen. 1974. "Mass Belief Systems Revisited: Political and Attitude Structure." *Journal of Politics* 36:540–91.

Platel, Marc. 1996. "Het Belgische politieke gebeuren in 1995." *Res Publica* 38:501–26.

Ray, John J. 1979. "Is the Acquiescent Response Style Problem Not So Mythical After All: Some Results from a Successful Balanced F-Scale." *Journal of Personality Assessment* 43:638–43.

Saris, W. E. 1995. "Designs and Models for Quality Assessment of Survey Measures." In *The Multitrait-Multimethod Approach to Evaluate Measurement In-*

struments, ed. W. E. Saris and A. Munnich, 9–37. Budapest: Eötvös University Press.

———. 1996. *Designs and Models for Evaluating the Quality of Survey Procedures.* Paper presented at the Fourth International Social Science Methodology Conference, Essex, July 1–5.

Saris, W. E., and A. Münnich. eds. 1995. *The Multitrait-Multimethod Approach to Evaluate Measurement Instruments.* Budapest: Eötvös University Press.

Saris, W. E., and A. Scherpenzeel. 1996. "Methodological Procedures for Comparative Research." In *A Comparative Study of Satisfaction with Life in Europe,* ed. W. E. Saris, R. Veenhoven, A. C. Scherpenzeel, and B. Bunting, 49–76. Budapest: Eötvös University Press.

Saris, W. E., T. Van Wijk, and A. Scherpenzeel. 1998. "Validity and Reliability of Subjective Social Indicators." *Social Indicators Research* 45:173–99.

Scherpenzeel, A. 1995. *A Question of Quality: Evaluating Survey Questions by Multitrait-Multimethod Studies.* Den Haag: Royal PTT Nederland.

Scherpenzeel, A., and W. Saris. 1997. "The Validity and Reliability of Survey Questions." *Sociological Methods and Research* 25(3):341–83.

Schlotzhauer, Sandra D., and Ramon C. Littell. 1987. *SAS© System for Elementary Statistical Analysis.* Cary, NC: Sas Institute.

Schuman, H., and S. Presser. 1981. *Questions and Answers in Attitude Surveys: Experiments on Question Form, Wording, and Context.* New York: Academic Press.

Smith, Tom W. 1988. "Nonattitudes: A Review and Evaluation." In *Surveying Subjective Phenomena,* ed. Charles F. Turner and Elizabeth Martin, 2:215–55. New York: Russell Sage Foundation.

Van Deth, J. W. 1990. "Interest in Politics." In *Continuities in Political Action: A Longitudinal Study of Political Orientation in Three Western Democracies,* ed. M. Kent Jennings and J. W. van Deth. New York: Walter de Gruyter.

Waterplas, L., J. Billiet, and G. Loosveldt. 1988. "De verbieden versus niet toelaten assysmetrie. Een stabiel formuleringseffect in survey-onderzoek?" *Mens en Maatschappij* 63:399–418.

Wiley, David E., and James A. Wiley. 1970. "The Estimation of Measurement Error in Panel Data." *American Sociological Review* 35:112–17.

Zaller, John, R. 1992. *The Nature and Origins of Mass Opinion.* Cambridge: Cambridge University Press.

PART V

An Alternative to the Standard Opinion Poll

CHAPTER 10

Coping with the Nonattitudes Phenomenon: A Survey Research Approach

Peter Neijens

PREVIOUS CHAPTERS in this volume give ample evidence that not all groups in society have (strong) attitudes on all public issues. This phenomenon is not only important from a methodological point of view. It is also important because it is related to the debate regarding whether "ordinary" citizens have "meaningful" opinions and whether they are able to participate meaningfully in decision-making processes, such as referenda. Bartels (2003), for example, states: "I shall argue that citizens have 'meaningful beliefs' but that those beliefs are not sufficiently complete and coherent to serve as a satisfactory starting point for democratic theory, at least as it is conventionally understood."

Many researchers have tried to account for the finding that respondents lack information and/or have not much about the issue at hand. They have attempted to gather measures of opinion that are of higher quality (i.e., better informed or more deliberative) than that recorded in typical mass opinion surveys (Price and Neijens 1998). Their techniques include information questionnaires (Saris, Neijens, and de Ridder 1984; Neijens et al. 1996), educational surveys (e.g., Kay et al. 1994a, 1994b), citizen planning cells (Dienel 1978; 1989), and deliberative polls (Fishkin 1995). (For an overview, see Price and Neijens 1997, 1998.)

In this chapter, we will discuss the Choice Questionnaire developed by Saris, Neijens, and de Ridder (1984). This questionnaire provides respondents with written information before asking them for their opinions. The instrument aims to fulfill two objectives: the measurement of *informed* opinions, and the measurement of these opinions that are *representative* of a population. In the developmental process, two questions had to be answered: which information should be presented and how should this be done so as to make adequate processing of the information possible? A third important question is whether the instrument is successful. Below we answer the design questions, and we will summarize the empirical evidence with respect to the success of the Choice Questionnaire. For this overview, we make use of the research shown in Table 10.1.

TABLE 10.1
Applications of the Choice Questionnaire Approach

Research Topic	Reference
Design and evaluation of the Choice Questionnaire	Saris, Neijens, and de Ridder 1984; Neijens, 1987
Car-free zones in the inner city	Neijens et al. 1996
Parking policy	Saris and van der Put 1996
Child care	Boomsma, Neijens and Slot 1996
Energy	Van Knippenberg and Daamen 1996; Van der Salm, Van Knippenberg, and Daamen 1997
Euthanasia	Van der Put 1995; Alcser, Neijens, and Bachman 1996
Ecological transport policy	Bütschi 1997a, 1997b, this volume
New housing estate IJburg	Molenaar, Neijens, and Saris 1997a
Metro system	Molenaar, Neijens, and Saris 1997b

DESIGN OF THE CHOICE QUESTIONNAIRE

The Type of Information

What type of information should be presented in the Choice Questionnaire? In answering that question we used criteria derived from (empirical) decision analysis because survey questions asked are, in general choice, questions for which this theory applies (see Keeney and Raiffa 1976; Edwards 1977). According to this theory, information about the consequences of each option and the probability of their occurrence are fundamental for making a responsible choice. Each consequence of an option can be broken down into attributes (or aspects), e.g., costs, environmental aspects, etc. This implies that if uncertainty is involved, each option is characterized by probability distributions over possible values (or states or outcomes) of the attributes.

Therefore, we decided that the information on an option should consist of statements whereby each statement describes a "consequence" of an option. That is to say, each statement mentions one aspect (attribute) and indicates the possible outcomes thereof as well as the extent to which they are likely to occur. Here is an example of a consequence of an option:

> Normally we can expect no victims. An accident with 50,000 victims, however, is possible. The probability of such an accident is very low.

Note that this example describes a distribution with a very good chance that outcome 0 will occur and that deviations from 0 are very unlikely, but possible. Thus, even an outcome of 50,000 is possible.

A different kind of distribution is the one in which a certain outcome is a very strong possibility and where (large) deviations from this outcome are very unlikely. This kind of "curve" could be described by the mean of the distribution and the statement that (large) deviations from this mean are not expected. It can also be said that outcome x is almost certain or very likely.

Obviously, precise information is not always available and in such cases only inexact information can be provided. The following example illustrates this point:

> The Netherlands is dependent on foreign supplies for its oil. This places the Netherlands in a very vulnerable position: the oil-producing countries can raise prices or halt supplies. It is also possible that they could make the supply dependent on political conditions. The use of option x means that Holland's supply of electricity is made more dependent on foreign suppliers.

In this example, the possibility of an outcome is described. The chance that this will happen is not indicated very specifically. Neither is the extent of the negative outcomes indicated (i.e., which political conditions? how high will the prices be?). If the available information is not more exact, we can do no more than to give this inexact information.

In an ideal situation, the information is not disputed. In reality, the experts often disagree about the facts, and it is impossible to decide who is right and who is wrong. In such cases we have to state the different opinions about the outcomes and probabilities. One could question whether the arguments that the conflicting parties advance for their positions also need to be given. We decided not to do so. By adding arguments, the disagreement only "shifts": behind the disagreement is another disagreement. Evaluation of the disagreement becomes even more difficult because of the technical aspects. Thus, on the one hand, the arguments do not help very much and, on the other, furnishing arguments can lead to providing an excess of information that is often overly technical.

To summarize, the information that should be included in the Choice Questionnaire for each option concerns information about the possible outcomes of each attribute (aspect) as well as the extent to which they are likely to occur. One has to look for simple descriptions of the "curve" of an attribute. Two examples have been given of types of curves that occur frequently. Where there is serious disagreement over the outcomes, the different expert opinions should be included in the information. When precise information is lacking, only the inexact information can be provided.

FRAMING

The studies by Tversky and Kahneman (1981) and Slovic, Fischhoff, and Lichtenstein (1982) established the effects of the framing of information about a decision-making problem. For example, it matters a great deal whether the (same) information about a decision problem has been formulated as, for example, "lives saved" or "lives lost" (framing of outcomes). Furthermore, a difference can be noted depending on whether a certain type of action is said to lead to a lower probability of a negative consequence or on whether the (same) information is presented by saying that the action causes one aspect of the consequence to disappear while the other aspect is left unaffected. This is known as the "framing of contingencies." And yet another framing effect (concerning the framing of acts) must be considered: "[D]ecision-makers appear to use only the information that is explicitly displayed in the formulation of the problem. Information that has to be inferred from the display or created by some mental transformation tends to be ignored." (Slovic, Fischhoff, and Lichtenstein 1982:24). That is, out of sight is out of mind. More recent framing studies are described in Neuman, Just, and Crigler (1992), Price, Tewksbury, and Powers (1997), and Valkenburg, Semetko, and de Vreese (1999).

Framing effects are related to Zaller's idea of considerations. His idea is that a respondent has "only" a couple of (*inconsistent*) *considerations* related to an issue (Zaller 1992). In other words, the respondent does have opinions on an issue, but does not have one, consistent, overall attitude. According to Zaller, respondents in survey research choose an answer category depending on which of the considerations with respect to an issue are "triggered" (for example, by the order or framing of the questions). Their answers express real feelings because people respond to the issue as they see it at the time of response (Zaller 1992:94).

This dependency of the measurement of (public) opinion on "context" is problematic for questionnaire designers, as Bartels (1998:22) notes: "What should a democratic theorist make of this context dependence? How might either context—or either outcome—be more appropriate than the other?" And according to Kinder and Sanders (1990:99): "[T]hose of us who design surveys find ourselves in roughly the same position as do those who hold and wield real power: public officials, editors and journalists, newsmakers of all sorts. Both choose how public issues are to be framed, and in both instances, the decisions seem to be consequential."

Bartels wants a normative account of what makes one frame more appropriate than another as a basis for democratic choice. But his problem is: "Neither Zaller (1992) nor any other analyst of political attitudes has actually proposed a concrete model specifying what a universe of potentially relevant considerations is supposed to consist of, or how it is supposed to be sampled from" (1998:36).

As specified above, our norm is derived from (empirical) decision analysis. We specify all outcomes and describe them shortly, according to specified rules. So we are able to give all contexts, many more than can be given in a standard survey research question. That makes the answers less dependent on an arbitrary chosen context.

Of course, some decisions regarding the providing of information are still difficult. The information has to be formulated in a certain way and there is not always an exclusively "correct" way of doing so. The problem plays a role even when individuals attempt to formulate a problem for themselves (Fischhoff, Slovic, and Lichtenstein 1980). How should these decisions regarding the information be taken? Slovic, Fischhoff, and Lichtenstein (1982:35) answer this question as follows:

> Making that decision takes one out of psychology and into the domains of law, ethics, and politics. . . . [E]xtreme care must be taken to select knowledgeable and trustworthy designers and program coordinators. We cannot propose a general solution here, as a competent and credible program staff would have to be put together in consultation with representatives of the people who were to be informed.

In the Choice Questionnaire approach, the most fruitful method is to select "blue ribbon" committees that are politically (and scientifically) balanced next to the application of explicit norms derived from decision analysis. The ultimate question is one of political legitimacy.

PRESENTATION OF THE INFORMATION

Three aspects of information presentation can be distinguished: format, structure, and order (Van Raaij 1977). One *format* aspect of the information in the Choice Questionnaire concerns whether the information should be stated in absolute terms (i.e., "to what extent will the status quo be changed by implementing this policy?") or in relative terms (i.e., options described in relation to each other). The information in the Choice Questionnaire is stated in absolute terms. Research has shown that information in an absolute format, compared to information in a relative format, is more difficult to process, resulting in extended processing and longer retention (Van Raaij 1977; Chestnut 1976).

Variation in the *structure* of the information presentation is possible. First, the information can be presented per option or per attribute, or the whole information matrix (option by attributes) can be shown at one time. Bettman and Kakkar (1977) showed that when information was given in an alternative or an attribute-centered way, subjects adapted the information processing to the way of presentation. Because a pilot study did not show a positive effect from an attribute-wise presentation, and because it is not possible to provide the whole information matrix at one time, it was decided to adopt a presentation per option. This choice also simplifies the design of the evaluation procedure, which will be presented in the next section.

Another question to consider is whether information about consequences *that will not occur* should also be given (i.e., the coal option does not have the consequence of a possible nuclear catastrophe, a consequence specified for nuclear power, one of the other options). We do not think so, since comparison of the options (when making a choice) brings the "missing" information to light. Consequences that are *the same* for all options are also left out, because there are many and they are not important for the choice among the options.

With respect to the *order* of the information presentation, research has shown that people possibly give more weight to the first mentioned aspect (primacy effect) or the last mentioned aspect (recency effect). Therefore, a choice could be made to vary the order of the presentation between respondents.

AIDING INFORMATION PROCESSING

The provision of information can easily create an "information overload" situation (Slovic and Lichtenstein 1971; Jacoby, Speller, and Berning 1974a; Jacoby, Speller, and Kohn 1974b). Research has shown that increasing the amount of information results in less attention being paid to each aspect (Svenson 1979). Therefore, as an aid to decision making, providing respondents with information only would not be satisfactory. "[I]nformation must be not only *available* to consumers, but also *processable*" (Russo, Krieser, and Miyashita 1975).

Bronner and de Hoog stated in this respect: "We think that many so-called 'information systems' fail because too much attention is paid to providing information, instead of trying to elicit the underlying decision process in which the information must fit in order to be meaningful for decision-makers. . . . Decision aiding facilities are not only important for aiding and structuring the decision process, but also for giving people a meaningful context for acquiring, storing, and handling information" (1984:126).

We tried to facilitate information processing in the Choice Questionnaire by an evaluation procedure. Respondents were asked to evaluate the attractiveness of each consequence. The rationale behind this procedure was our expectation that the respondents would absorb the information more thoroughly as a result of the various judgments they would have to make; they would be actively involved with the information. It was also assumed that an evaluation of the consequences in the same units would facilitate the respondents' comparison of the consequences (Slovic and Lichtenstein 1968; Slovic and MacPhillamy 1974; Svenson 1979).

Respondents were asked to make one evaluation of each consequence, thereby taking into account the outcomes of the aspect considered and the probabilities of their occurrence. This is shown in Figure 10.1. Respondents were first asked whether they considered the consequence to be important or unimportant. If they believed the consequence to be important, they were asked to indicate whether they considered it as advantageous or disadvantageous, and to give the magnitude of the advantage or disadvantage. A magnitude estimation scaling procedure was used (the following standard was employed: a (dis)advantage which is neither great nor small; modulus: 400).

Separate evaluations of "probabilities" and "outcomes" were not requested in order to restrict the number of evaluations the respondents have to give, and because the separate evaluations would provide no insight into the evaluations of the combination of "probabilities" and "outcomes." For example, some people cannot live with the idea of a small chance of a "disastrous" outcome, but others can. Also, research has shown that respondents take this into consideration in their evaluation of advantages and disadvantages (Bronner and de Hoog 1978; Schaefer, Swaton, and Niehaus 1981).

It was also believed that the respondents' task would be simplified if they summarized their evaluations of each option since this bookkeeping system would not require them to recall all the information when asked to make their choice. They were, therefore, asked to total the advantageous and disadvantageous evaluations, respectively, for each option.

After making these evaluations, the respondents were presented with a number of options, each written on a card. Each card contained the consequences of an option, the respondents' evaluations of these consequences, and the two overall evaluations. Respondents were asked to rank the various options according to preference. They were then asked to choose one option. No prescription or decision rule was given for the choice.

FIELD PROCEDURE

The field procedure for the Choice Questionnaire was as follows. Before the interviewer presented the Choice Questionnaire to the respondent, some questions were asked to elicit background information. The instructions for filling in the Choice Questionnaire were also given during this

15 EXTRA UNITS OF NATURAL GAS

Some experts suggest that 15 extra units of natural gas should be used. Others consider this excessive because of the disadvantages connected with it.

Below are listed the most important advantages and disadvantages of the use of approximately 15 extra units of natural gas.

- The price of natural gas is controlled by the Dutch government and is maintained at the same level as the price of oil. In the near future this price could vary enormously. In the long term this fuel will, however, almost inevitably become more expensive. The use of 15 extra units of natural gas will slightly raise the price of electricity. That will slightly raise the cost of living and will raise costs to industry.

- The money earned from the sale of natural gas for the generation of electricity goes largely directly to the Dutch treasury, which means that it is used for the general good of Dutch society. The use of 15 extra units of natural gas will provide the government with a considerable amount of extra money.

- The quantity of natural gas available in The Netherlands and elsewhere in the world is limited. The total world supply is sufficient for the coming 40 or 50 years. Here we should consider the fact that natural gas is eminently suitable for industrial use and for domestic heating and cooking. The use of 15 extra units of natural gas for generating electricity means that less is available for these applications.

- The burning of fossil fuels can affect the climate of the world in the long term. Like oil, natural gas is less of a problem than coal, but it can still contribute slightly to the risk. The consequence of this can be that the temperature worldwide will gradually rise (greenhouse effect) which leads to drastic changes in the climate: areas that at present are favourable for agriculture can gradually acquire a desert climate. In other regions, agricultural land can deteriorate because of an increase in rainfall. In addition, a higher worldwide temperature can cause a gradual melting of the polar ice-caps which will cause the sea-level to rise. It is not at all certain whether these consequences would, in fact, occur. But if they do, there is nothing that can be done to correct them. The use of approximately 15 extra units of natural gas would make a slight contribution to this risk.

- Atmospheric pollution resulting from the use of fossil fuels produces harmful effects. Natural gas is less of a problem than oil or coal, but it can still contribute in a very slight way, to these consequences. These consequences are harmful to the human breathing mechanism which means that people suffering from lung disease can face more problems. In addition, there are damaging consequences for plants and animals, for instance, crops and horticultural products. The use of approximately 15 extra units of natural gas contributes in a very slight way to these effects.

- The burning of fossil fuels can give rise to 'acid rain'. Natural gas is less of a problem than oil or coal, but it can still contribute in a very slight way, to this phenomenon. It seems very likely that acid rain has a harmful effect on life in the ground, on plants and trees and on life in the water. The use of 15 extra units of natural gas contributes to these effects in a very slight way.

PLACE A CROSS IN THIS COLUMN IF YOU THINK THAT THE CONSEQUENCE MENTIONED IS NOT IMPORTANT	Advantage AN ADVANTAGE THAT IS NEITHER GREAT NOR SMALL = 400	Disadvantage A DISADVANTAGE THAT IS NEITHER GREAT NOR SMALL = 400
		....
......	....	....
......	....	....
......	....	....
......	....	....
......	....	....
......	....	....
TOTAL	....	....

Figure 10.1 Example of an information card.

face-to-face interview. The respondent filled in an example under the guidance of the interviewer. In this way, the various steps in the Choice Questionnaire were clarified.

At the end of the interview, the interviewer handed the respondent a booklet containing the Choice Questionnaire and requested that it be filled in at home within a week.

When collecting the completed questionnaires, the interviewer asked some additional questions, which were intended to provide insight into the opinions of the respondent regarding the filling-in of the questionnaire.

Variations in the field procedure are possible. One could, for example, approach respondents via the telephone instead and mail the Choice Questionnaire to them, asking them to return it after completion (see below).

EVALUATION OF THE QUALITY OF THE CHOICE QUESTIONNAIRE

In this section we summarize the findings of the research with the Choice Questionnaire. If not stated otherwise, the findings stem from the "original" Choice Questionnaire: the Choice Questionnaire for the General Social Debate (Saris and Neijens 1983; Saris, Neijens, and de Ridder 1984; Neijens 1987; Neijens et al. 1992).

The General Social Debate (GSD) focused on alternative national programs for electricity production. Initiated by the Dutch government because of the substantial extra-parliamentary opposition to the use of nuclear power, the GSD sought to involve the Dutch population in determining a national energy policy. A steering committee, consisting of persons recruited from parties with different standpoints on the issue and respected by a broad spectrum of people, was given the task of organizing the debate. In the first phase, the information phase, the steering committee prepared an interim report containing the information pertinent to the choice-making problem. In this phase, the steering committee consulted with interested organizations and action groups, organized public hearings to discuss controversial aspects, and so on.

In the second phase, the committee collected the opinions of members from all strata of society. The Choice Questionnaire, which contained information based on the interim report, was used. The steering committee was responsible for the final formulation of the information in the questionnaire.

The interim report summed up (1) the various energy supply options for electricity production; (2) which attributes were considered relevant by the population; and (3) how the options scored on these attributes. As a result, the Choice Questionnaire for the GSD provided financial, social, health, and environmental consequences for a number of options. This information about the consequences of each option was presented on information cards in the Choice Questionnaire. The various consequences were given in the form of statements.

In the GSD Choice Questionnaire, six options were proposed: the use of specified amounts of energy resources (natural gas, oil, coal, nuclear power, and wind energy) plus a conservation strategy. Respondents were asked to choose three options. The options were constructed such that each combination of three would provide sufficient energy. Twenty combinations were, thus, possible. The number of information statements pertinent to each option varied between six and nine.

FINDINGS WITH RESPECT TO PARTICIPATION

In the GSD Choice Questionnaire, respondents participating in a face-to-face interview (a random sample of the Dutch population; N = 1,574) were asked to fill out a booklet with the Choice Questionnaire. They were given one week to do this. Nearly 7 percent of the respondents did not participate at all in the Choice Questionnaire; when the interviewer returned after a week, the booklet was completely blank. Not all of the other respondents filled out the Choice Questionnaire completely. For each task (evaluation of the consequences, determination of overall evaluations, and answering of questions regarding choices), there were approximately 3 percent of the respondents who failed to complete it. All the tasks were completed by 80.7 percent of the respondents (1,243 persons).

Although the extent of the nonparticipation is not unimportant, the nature of the nonparticipation is particularly important with respect to the usefulness of the Choice Questionnaire. If the nonparticipation is "random," the representativeness of the participants is not jeopardized. When studying the relationship between a number of background variables and the participation, we found that participation was not biased with respect to sex, residence, and the composition of the respondent's household. However, participation was biased with respect to education and age. The participants were somewhat underrepresented in the lower education categories and somewhat over-represented in the higher education categories. With respect to age, they were somewhat overrepresented in the younger age groups and somewhat underrepresented in the older age groups. The differences were small (explained variance in participation by these two variables was 5 percent).

The profile of the participants in the Choice Questionnaire thus differed only to a limited extent from the profile of the Dutch population as a whole. We thereby concluded that opinions measured with the Choice Questionnaire are (nearly) representative of those of the population.

MAIL

In the research of Molenaar, Neijens, and Saris (1997a, 1997b), a mail procedure was used. Respondents were selected from a random sample (of the Amsterdam population) participating in a public opinion survey (N = 1,690). They were asked for their participation in the mailed Choice Questionnaire. Of these, 1,054 respondents (62 percent) agreed and received a questionnaire; 372 (35 percent) filled it out and mailed it back. The profile of the respondents deviated slightly from the profile of the Amsterdam electorate. They had, for example, a higher political interest. In this case, the time for the respondents to mail back their questionnaire was only one week. Later we amended the procedure. Interviewers called the respondents after one week to ask whether "assistance was necessary." This improved the response rate.

The time needed for the telephone-mail Choice Questionnaire procedure (formulation of the information, telephone research for selection of respondents, mail Choice Questionnaire, analysis, and report) is only four weeks for not-too-difficult policy problems. This time can even be reduced when, instead of a mailed Choice Questionnaire, a telephone procedure is used. We do not know, however, what the effects of such a procedure would be.

FINDINGS WITH RESPECT TO THE QUALITY OF THE OPINIONS GIVEN

Two aspects of the findings are important: the quality of the evaluations (unimportant/advantages/disadvantages—see Figure 10.1), and the quality of the choices (selection of the options).

Quality of the Evaluations

Respondents are, of course, free to express their own values and personal concerns when evaluating the consequences of the options, but a number of checks are possible.

When halo effects are found, it is questionable whether the evaluations of the consequences are based on the information provided. A halo effect occurs when "[i]ndividuals who favor an alternative tend to rate it high on all desirable attributes, while individuals who dislike the alternative tend to rate it low on all attributes" (Beckwith and Lehmann 1975:265). Halo effects indicate that respondents evaluate the consequences in light of their existing preferences: the evaluations are then merely a proxy measure of the choice itself.

Halo effects result in high associations between the evaluations of the consequences of an option: supporters of the option give high (less negative) scores on all consequences, and opponents of the option give low (less high) scores on all consequences. An analysis of the evaluations shows that the correlations between the various consequences (per option) were very low, (as shown in Table 10.2). Three options (gas, oil, and coal) do show higher correlations (see the right-hand column). The reason for this is that these three options all have consequences of a similar sort: global climatic effects, atmospheric pollution, and acid rain. These high correlations are, of course, not suspect. Since the correlations are of a very low order, the hypothesis of halo effects can be rejected.

A number of other checks were carried out to see whether the evaluations of the respondents were unusual in light of the information provided. We investigated, for example, whether respondents evaluated consequences that only had negative outcomes as advantageous, or vice versa. Space does not permit a detailed discussion of these analyses here, but we concluded that in general the judgments were of good quality and were made in accordance with the information provided (see Neijens 1987; Neijens, de Ridder, and Saris 1988 for further details).

Quality of the Choices

To investigate whether the choice made by a respondent was based on the information provided, we checked whether his choice was *consistent* with his evaluations of the consequences of the options mentioned in the information provided.

A consistent choice is defined as choosing the most attractive option(s), where the attractiveness of an option is determined by a combination of

TABLE 10.2
Associations between Judgments Made of the Consequences (Per Option)

Option	Average	Minimum	Maximum
Gas	0.24	−0.13	0.73
Oil	0.24	0.10	0.68
Conservation	0.08	−0.26	0.32
Coal	0.25	−0.12	0.72
Nuclear power	0.25	0.08	0.49
Wind energy	0.12	−0.13	0.49
Average	0.20		

Table shows Pearson's correlation coefficients. Data from GSD Choice Questionnaire survey (N = 1,243). In the calculation of the correlation coefficients, the evaluations rated as disadvantageous have a minus sign. Consequences marked "unimportant" are given a zero value.

the evaluations of the consequences of that option. We found that 68 percent of the respondents who filled out the GSD Choice Questionnaire made completely consistent choices and that they did so by trading off the positive and negative consequences of an option in a compensatory way (the "addition of utilities decision rule," which assumes an addition of the evaluations of the consequences, whereby the disadvantageous evaluations are given a negative value).

We conclude that opinions measured with the Choice Questionnaire are informed opinions: the choices made are in accordance with respondents' evaluation of all aspects of the problem mentioned in the information.

WHICH ASPECTS OF THE PROCEDURE ARE IMPORTANT?

What are the contributions of the different aspects of the Choice Questionnaire to informed choices? Three aspects can be distinguished: provision of information, the evaluation of consequences task, and the bookkeeping system whereby the evaluations are totaled per option. We expected that the provision of information only might be inadequate and that the facilities to process this information (evaluation of the consequences and the bookkeeping system) are necessary to produce its effect.

To investigate this point we studied in the context of the GSD Choice Questionnaire the consistency of the choices under four conditions: (1) "no information" condition; (2) "information only" condition; (3) "information with a request to evaluate the consequences" condition; and (4) "information with a request to evaluate the consequences and to provide overall evaluations of the options" condition.

In each condition, a random sample of the Dutch population filled out a specific version of the questionnaire. The data in condition 4 were obtained from the GSD Choice Questionnaire discussed above. The data in the "information only" condition were obtained from a questionnaire in which the information was presented in story form in a booklet, but was otherwise the same as that in the Choice Questionnaire. The booklet was left with the respondents, who were asked to read through it. They were not asked to evaluate the individual consequences or make overall evaluations of the options but to make a choice after they had read the booklet. They were then requested to evaluate the consequences of the options, as in the Choice Questionnaire. This allowed subsequent investigation of the consistency between their choices and their evaluations of the consequences. Data for the other conditions were obtained in a similar way.

Table 10.3 shows that when no information was provided on the energy options, 37 percent of the respondents made a consistent choice (condition 1). A majority of the respondents, thus, made a choice that did not

TABLE 10.3
Percentage of Consistent Decisions under Four Conditions

Condition	% Offering Consistent Decision[a]	N[b]
1. No information[c]	37	300
2. Information only[c]	48	299
3. Information + evaluations of the consequences	57	300
4. Information + evaluations of the consequences + overall evaluations	68	1243

Data are drawn from Neijens (1987:184–187).

[a] A decision to select a particular option was deemed consistent if it agreed with a respondent's summed positive and negative evaluations of consequences across options. By chance alone, only 5 percent of respondents would have offered such a consistent decision.

[b] N includes only respondents who carried out the tasks given in the various conditions completely.

[c] In the "no information" and "information only" conditions, respondents completed their evaluations of consequences *after* selecting their favored option.

agree with their own judgment of the consequences of the options. Comparing conditions 1 ("no information") and 2 ("information only"), we see that the provision of information has an effect: the percentage of consistent decisions is eleven percentage points higher in condition 2. The task of evaluating the consequences also has an effect: the percentage of consistent decisions in condition 3 ("information + evaluations") is nine points higher than in condition 2. The determination of overall evaluations also has an effect on the percentage of consistent decisions: in condition 4 it is eleven points higher than in condition 3.

From these data, we conclude that all three aspects of the Choice Questionnaire contribute to its effect on the use of information. The contribution of each aspect is nearly the same (about ten percentage points). We also see that the provision of information alone is not enough. Although the percentage of consistent decisions rose by eleven percentage points in condition 2, the majority of the respondents still failed to make a consistent decision. The figure for the "no information" situation can be improved a further twenty percentage points by giving the respondents two extra tasks: evaluation of the consequences and determination of overall evaluations. We can conclude that the informed choices produced by the Choice Questionnaire stem from the information presented as well as from the evaluation procedures used in the processing of this information.

Table 10.3 also shows that the results are very systematically related to the various questionnaire types. This supports the interpretation that the results obtained with the Choice Questionnaire can be *attributed* to the information provided and the information processing aid offered, instead of being merely a result of the research situation itself.

Van der Salm, van Knippenberg, and Daamen (1997) also investigated whether the opinions measured with the Choice Questionnaire can be attributed to the information provided in the questionnaire. They state "As long as the provided information is not the only manipulated variable in evaluation research, other explanations for an effect on choice are possible (Cook and Campbell 1979; Neale and Liebert 1986)" (195). In their research, respondents were randomly assigned to one of two conditions. They were presented with identical Choice Questionnaire procedures but with slightly different information about the consequences of two of the options. The research demonstrated "that Choice Questionnaire respondents do base their preferences on the information provided: different information resulted in significantly different choices" (193).

FACTORS INFLUENCING THE EFFECTS OF THE CHOICE QUESTIONNAIRE

The influence of *questionnaire characteristics* is shown above. Further research has shown the role of *option characteristics* (Bütschi, chapter 11 in this volume; Alcser, Neijens, and Bachman 1996): the Choice Questionnaire especially effects choice related to complex, polarized, unknown topics and topics that do not touch basic values (such as euthanasia).

There are also effects due to *respondent characteristics*. "Cognitive ability" and "involvement with the issue" (variables taken from the elaboration likelihood model [ELM] [Petty and Cacioppo 1981]) were associated positively with the consistency of the choice. These variables, however, explain no more than 7 percent of the variation in consistency. Van Knippenberg and Daamen (1996) studied the role of these variables in detail. They found that more motivated and more able respondents tend to engage in more elaborate processing of the information presented. They also found that these respondents were more stable in their preferences, as shown by a second measurement of the preferences two months after the Choice Questionnaire research. "Again, results are in line with the prediction (based on the elaboration likelihood model) that more motivated and more able persons are more likely to engage in extensive information processing" (78). With respect to prior opinion, Bütschi investigated factors such as strength, instability, and inconsistency (see Bütschi, chapter 11 in this volume).

CONCLUSIONS AND DISCUSSION

This evaluation of the research shows that the Choice Questionnaire copes with the nonattitudes phenomenon in a satisfactory way: the questionnaire measures *informed* opinions, *representative* of the population as a whole.

Furthermore, it is a relatively simple instrument that can be applied in large-scale survey research. The Choice Questionnaire is, therefore, useful in decision-making processes where meaningful public input is sought.

The Choice Questionnaire is also a very useful instrument for research into effects of information providing on opinion formation processes at the individual and collective level. At the individual level, the Choice Questionnaire allows us to investigate in a real-life context the role of source (credibility, trustworthiness, expertise), persuasive context (argumentative or nonargumentative), prior opinion, and the order, format, and structure of the information provided. At the collective level, it is possible to study the role that this kind of "decision aid" plays in increasing citizen competence in participation processes. This research will contribute to information processing theories, the improvement of survey research techniques, and our democratic ways.

REFERENCES

Alcser, K. H., P. C. Neijens, and J. G. Bachman. 1996. *Using an Informed Survey Approach to Assess Public Opinion on Euthanasia and Physician-Assisted Suicide: A Cross-National Comparison between Michigan (USA) and the Netherlands.* Ann Arbor, MI: ISR.

Bartels, L. M. 2003. "Democracy with Attitudes." In *Electoral Democracy,* ed. Michael B. MacKuen and George Rabinowitz. Ann Arbor: University of Michigan Press.

Beckwith, N. E., and D. R. Lehmann. 1975. "The Importance of Halo Effects in Multi-Attribute Attitude Models." *Journal of Marketing Research* 12:265–75.

Bettman, J. R., and P. Kakkar. 1977. "Effects of Information Presentation Format on Consumer Information Acquisition Strategies." *Journal of Consumer Research* 3:233–40.

Bishop, Y.M.M., S. E. Fienberg, and P. W. Holland. 1975. *Discrete Multivariate Analysis: Theory and Practice.* Cambridge, MA: MIT Press.

Boomsma, P.J.S.M., P. C. Neijens, and J.J.M. Slot. 1996. *Brede Maatschappelijke Discussies. Bestuurlijke Vernieuwing Avant la Lettre* [General social debates. Administrative innovation avant la lettre.] *Bestuurskunde* [Management Science] 5(8):369–77.

Bronner, A. E., and R. de Hoog. 1978. *Politieke Voorkeur: Oordelen en Beslissen.* PhD diss., University of Amsterdam.

———. 1984. "The Intertwining of Information Search and Decision Aiding." *Acta Psychologica* 56:125–39.

Bütschi, D. 1997a. "How to Shape Public Opinion, If Possible At All? The Example of the 'Choice Questionnaire.'" Paper prepared for the conference, "No Opinion, Instability, and Change in Public Opinion Research." October 6–8, University of Amsterdam.

———. 1997b. *Information et opinions: Promesses et limites de questionnaire de choix*. Master's thesis, Department of Political Science, University of Geneva.

Chestnut, R. W. 1976. "The Impact of Energy-Efficiency Ratings: Selective vs. Elaborative Encoding." *Purdue Papers in Consumer Psychology* no. 160. West Lafayette, IN: Purdue University.

Converse, P. E. 1964. "The Nature of Belief Systems in Mass Publics." In *Ideology and Discontent,* ed. D. Apter. New York: Free Press.

Converse, J. M., and S. Presser. 1986. *Survey Questions: Handcrafting the Standardized Questionnaire*. Sage University Paper no. 63. Beverly Hills: Sage.

Cook, T. D., and D. T. Campbell. 1979. *Quasi-Experimentation: Design and Analysis Issues for Field Settings*. Boston: Houghton Mifflin.

Dienel, P. C. 1978. *Die Planungszelle: Ein Alternative zur Establishment-Demokratie*. Der Bürger Plant Seine Umwelt. Opladen: Westdeutscher Verlag.

———. 1989. "Contributing to Social Decision Methodology: Citizen Reports on Technological Projects." In *Social Decision Methodology for Technological Projects,* ed. Charles Vlek and George Cvetkovich. Dordrecht, Holland: Kluwer Academic Publishers.

Edwards, W. 1977. "Use of Multiattribute Utility Measurement for Social Decision Making." In *Conflicting Objectives in Decisions,* ed. D. E. Bell, R. L. Keeney, and H. Raiffa. New York: Wiley.

Fischhoff, B. 1984. "Informed Consent for Transient Nuclear Workers." In *Equity Issues in Nuclear Waste Disposal,* ed. R. Kasperson and R. W. Kates. Cambridge, MA: Oelgeschlager, Gunn, and Hain.

Fischhoff, B., P. Slovic, and S. Lichtenstein. 1980. "Labile Values: A Challenge for Risk Assessment." In *Society, Technology, and Risk Assessment,* ed. J. Conrad. London: Academic Press.

Fishkin, J. S. 1995. *The Voice of the People: Public Opinion and Democracy*. New Haven: Yale University Press.

Hagenaars, J.A.P. 1985. *Loglineaire Analyse van Herhaalde Surveys. Panel-, Trend-, en Cohortonderzoek*. PhD diss., University of Brabant.

Jacoby, J., D. E. Speller, and C. K. Berning. 1974. "Brand Choice Behavior as a Function of Information Load: Replication and Extension." *Journal of Consumer Research* 1(1):33–42.

Jacoby, J., D. E. Speller, and C. A. Kohn. 1974. "Brand Choice Behavior as a Function of Information Load." *Journal of Marketing Research* 11(1):63–69.

Kahneman, D., P. Slovic, and A. Tversky, eds. 1982. *Judgment under Uncertainty: Heuristics and Biases*. London: Cambridge University Press.

Kay, A. F., H. Henderson, F. Steeper, and C. Lake. 1994. *Interviews with the Public Guide U.S.: On the Road to Consensus*. St. Augustine, FL: Americans Talk Issues Foundation.

Kay, A. F., H. Henderson, F. Steeper, C. Lake, S.B. Greenberg, and C. Blunt. 1994. *Steps for Democracy: The Many versus the Few*. St. Augustine, FL: Americans Talk Issues Foundation.

Keeney, R. L., and H. Raiffa. 1976. *Decisions with Multiple Objectives: Preferences and Value Tradeoffs*. New York: Wiley.

Kinder, D. R., and L. M. Sanders. 1990. "Mimicking Political Debate with Survey Questions: The Case of White Opinion on Affirmative Action for Blacks." *Social Cognition* 8:73–103.

Molenaar, N. J. 1982. "Response Effects of 'Formal' Characteristics of Questions." In *Response Behaviour in the Survey Interview,* ed. W. Dijkstra and J. van der Zouwen. London: Academic Press.

Molenaar, F., P. C. Neijens, and W. E. Saris. 1997a. *IJburg-Keuze-Enquête.* Verslag van een Onderzoek naar Verschillende Presentatie- en Argumentatiestrategieën voor de Gemeentelijke Referendumcampagne [IJburg Choice Questionnaire. Report for Schoep and van der Toorn].

———. 1997b. *Keuze-Enquête Noord Zuid Metrolijn.* Onderzoek naar het Eeffect van Argumenten in Twee Strategieën van Communicatie in de Campagne voor het Amsterdamse Referendum. [North South Metro Choice Questionnaire. Rapport voor Communications Assets.]

Neale, J. M., and R. M. Liebert. 1986. *Science and Behavior: An Introduction to Methods of Research.* Upper Saddle River, NJ: Prentice-Hall.

Neijens, P. 1987. *The Choice Questionnaire. Design and Evaluation of an Instrument for Collecting Informed Opinions of a Population.* Amsterdam: Free University Press.

Neijens, P., J. A. de Ridder, and W. E. Saris. 1988. "Variation in Response Functions and Prescription for Information Integration." In *Variation in Response Behavior: A Source of Measurement Error in Attitude Research,* ed. W. E. Saris. Amsterdam: Sociometric Research Foundation.

Neijens, P. C., M. Minkman, J. A. de Ridder, W. E. Saris, and J.J.M. Slot. 1996. "A Decision Aid in a Referendum." *International Journal of Public Opinion Research* 8(1):83–90.

Neuman, W. R., M. R. Just, and A. N. Crigler. 1992. *Common Knowledge. News and the Construction of Political Meaning.* Chicago: University of Chicago Press.

Petty, R. E., and J. T. Cacioppo. 1981. *Attitudes and Persuasion: Classic and Contemporary Approaches.* Dubuque, IA: W. C. Brown.

Petty, R. E., G. A. Rennier, and J. T. Cacioppo. 1987. "Assertion versus Interrogation Format in Opinion Surveys: Questions Enhance Thoughtful Responding." *Public Opinion Quarterly* 51:481–94.

Price, V. E., and P. C. Neijens. 1997. "Opinion Quality in Public Opinion Research." *International Journal of Public Opinion Research* 9:336–60.

———. 1998. "Deliberative Polls: Toward Improved Measures of 'Informed' Public Opinion?" *International Journal of Public Opinion Research* 10:145–76.

Price, V. E., D. Tewksbury, and E. Powers. 1997. "Switching Trains of Thought: The Impact of News Frames on Readers' Cognitive Responses." *Communication Research* 24:481–506.

Pröpper, I.M.A.M., and H.J.M. ter Braak. 1996. "Interactief Bestuur." *Bestuurskunde* 5(8):356–68.

Russo, J. E., G. Krieser, and S. Miyashita. 1975. "An Effective Display of Unit Price Information." *Journal of Marketing* 39:11–19.

Saris, W. E., and P. Neijens. 1983. "De Gestructureerde Keuze-Enquête als Middel ter Afsluiting van de Brede Maatschappelijke Discussie." [The Choice Questionnaire as an aid in a public debate.] *Civis Mundi* 22:5–9.

Saris, W. E., and C. van der Put. 1996. *De KeuzeEenquête als Instrument voor Beleid*. Amsterdam: NIMMO.

Saris, W. E., P. C. Neijens, and J. A. de Ridder. 1984. *Kernenergie: Ja of Nee?* [Nuclear power: Yes or no?] Amsterdam: SSO.

Schaefer, R. E., E. Swaton, and F. Niehaus. 1981. *Measuring Attitudes towards the Use of Nuclear Power: An Analysis of a Measurement Instrument*. IIASA WP-81-24. Laxenburg, Austria: International Institute for Applied Systems Analysis.

Schuman, H., and S. Presser. 1981. *Questions and Answers in Attitude Surveys: Experiments on Question Form, Wording, and Context*. New York: Academic Press.

Slovic, P., and S. Lichtenstein. 1968. "The Relative Importance of Probabilities and Payoffs in Risktaking." *Journal of Experimental Psychology* (Monograph Supplement) 78:1–17.

———. 1971. "Comparison of Bayesian and Regression Approaches to the Study of Information Processing in Judgment." *Organizational Behavior and Human Performance* 6:649–744.

Slovic, P., and D. MacPhillamy. 1974. "Dimensional Commensurability and Cue Utilization in Comparative Judgment." *Organizational Behavior and Human Performance* 23:86–112.

Slovic, P., B. Fischhoff, and S. Lichtenstein. 1980a. "Informing People about Risk." In *Product Labeling and Health Risks*, ed. L. M. Mazis Morris and I. Barofsky. Banbury Report 6. Cold Spring Harbor, NY: Cold Spring Laboratory.

———. 1981. "Informing the Public about the Risks of Ionizing Radiation." *Health Physics* 41:589–98.

———. 1982. "Response Mode, Framing, and Information-Processing Effects in Risk Assessment." In *New Directions for Methodology of Social and Behavioral Science*, ed. R.M. Hogarth, 21–36. San Francisco: Jossey-Bass.

Svenson, O. 1979. "Process Descriptions of Decision Making." *Organizational Behavior and Human Performance* 11:172–94.

Tversky, Amos, and Daniel Kahneman. 1981. "The Framing of Decisions and the Rationality of Choice." *Science* 211:453–58.

Valkenburg, P. M., H. A. Semetko, and C. H. de Vreese. 1999. "The Effects of News Frames on Readers' Thoughts and Recall." *Communication Research* 26:550–68.

van Knippenberg, D., and D. Daamen. 1996. "Providing Information in Public Opinion Surveys: Motivation and Ability Effects in the Information-and-Choice Questionnaire." *International Journal of Public Opinion Research* 8:70–82.

van der Put, C. E. 1995. "De Euthanasie-KeuzeEenquête." PhD diss., University of Amsterdam.

van Raaij, W. F. 1977. "Consumer Choice Behavior: An Information-Processing Approach." PhD diss., University of Brabant.

van der Salm, C. A., D. van Knippenberg, and D.D.L. Daamen. 1997. "A Critical T-Test of the Choice Questionnaire for Collecting Informed Public Opinions." *Quality and Quantity* 31:193–97.

Zaller, J. R. 1992. *The Nature and Origins of Mass Opinion*. Cambridge: Cambridge University Press.

CHAPTER 11

The Influence of Information on Considered Opinions: The Example of the Choice Questionnaire

Danielle Bütschi

THIS CHAPTER considers how structured information offered in the form of a Choice Questionnaire encourages people to engage in a learning process and, eventually, how it affects their opinions. More precisely, it investigates whether structured information presenting arguments for and against different policy alternatives helps citizens develop informed opinions, and thus whether it increases their ability to fully participate in the democratic process. The following pages describe and discuss the results of an experiment held in Switzerland with a Choice Questionnaire addressing the question of pollution caused by privately owned cars.

The Choice Questionnaire used in this experiment was designed following the model developed by Saris and Neijens (Saris, Neijens, and de Ridder 1983; Neijens 1987; Neijens, chapter 10 in this volume). It was part of a bigger research project carried out in Switzerland with the aim of investigating fluctuation in opinions when confronted by different kinds of information (see Kriesi, chapter 8 in this volume). In this research program, a representative sample of Swiss citizens was interviewed in a four-wave panel study concerning policy measures directed toward car drivers and intended to achieve the objectives set by the Swiss government in the domains of energy consumption and air pollution. These policy measures, chosen in collaboration with experts in Swiss transport policy, propose promoting electrical cars, setting up car-free zones in inner cities, establishing parking restrictions and speed limits on highways, and, finally, creating a tax on CO_2 of 10 cts/l and a much more radical tax that would lead, in a span of about five years, to an increase in the price of gas up to two Swiss franks per liter (Sfr 2/l). An initial questionnaire was administered at the beginning of the project; in addition to questions related to these six measures, it included questions concerning environmental protection in general. About six months later, a face-to-face interview using the same opinion questions about these six measures and questions more closely related to transport policy was conducted with half of the original sample (i.e., 1,062 persons). At the end of this second interview, respondents received the Choice Questionnaire and instructions on how to fill it out. In this Choice Questionnaire, respondents had to assess the six policy measures at the core of the whole research project according to a set of pro- and counterarguments, then choose a package of three preferred measures, and, finally, give for a third time their opinion about them. It is mainly by comparing opinions given during the face-to-face interview and at the outset of the Choice Questionnaire that I shall assess the impact of information on individuals' opinions. Finally, eighteen months later, respondents were interviewed a last time about general questions related to the CO_2 issue and about the same six policy measures. This last questionnaire should produce some elements that allow an examination of the effects of a new set of information in the long run.

INFORMATION AND OPINIONS

Authors studying the impact of information on opinions generally concentrate their interest on media as possible agents of change. As a matter of fact, media are often considered the vehicle par excellence for transmitting political elite messages to the public and in this respect are feared for their potential power over mass opinion. Research, however, does not give credit to this widespread—and somewhat misleading—conception. In their seminal work on the impact of political campaigns on individuals' votes, Lazarsfeld and his colleagues (1948), for example, could not conclude that media create opinion. At best, media reinforce and activate existing opinion, and if media are to have an effect, it is indeed in a "two-step flow" through community leaders. Subsequent studies confirm this minimal effect (see Zukin 1981). Following this vein of research, we should not expect too strong or direct an effect of the Choice Questionnaire on opinions. But this does not mean that the Choice Questionnaire—or any kind of information—is not worth looking at. The Choice Questionnaire certainly affects processes of opinion formation and transformation and examining these processes should give some stimulating insights on how new information is used by people and under which conditions it might influence their opinions.

The Theory of Reasoned Action (TRA) of Fishbein and Ajzen (1975) might offer a first hint in understanding the way the Choice Questionnaire might affect opinions. These authors explain behavior by using a causal chain, where beliefs (about possible consequences of the action and about the judgment of others about the action) affect attitudes and subjective norms, which in turn affect intention and, at the end of the chain, behavior. This theory has been largely criticized,[1] but it nevertheless highlights the decisive impact of information as a means to influence behavior and opinion through beliefs. More specifically, when respondents assess the different consequences related to each alternative presented in the Choice Questionnaire, they actually define their beliefs, and, following the TRA, it should eventually affect their opinions.

This is, of course, a simplification of reality, and we have to consider other elements affecting the formation and transformation of opinions. Apart from sociological factors that determine opinions and attitudes, we have to consider that individuals may use different strategies—or heuristics—when assessing information. According to cognitive psychologists, individuals focus on the subset of information that enables them to use a simple decision rule to make a judgment or a decision (see Tversky and Kahneman 1974). Voters, for example, take various shortcuts to get an opinion, so that the logic prevailing can be described as a "low-information rationality" (Popkin 1992). In short, to understand the role of the Choice Questionnaire on opinions, we must acknowledge, along with Simon (1976), that individuals might be bounded in their rationality by their values and goals, as well as by other intellectual and psychological characteristics. And these limitations might vary from one individual to another, so that information offered by the Choice Questionnaire might not have the same impact on all respondents.

In this respect, Zaller's model on the nature and origins of mass opinions (1992) brings a stimulating insight into understanding how the Choice Questionnaire can affect opinions. According to his model, new information comes in addition to existing considerations. It is then in affecting this existing mix of consideration that new information might create or modify opinions. I recognize here the model of Fishbein and Ajzen (1975), but for new information to affect this mix of consideration and, eventually, to affect opinions, it must first be accepted (Zaller speaks here of "partisan resistance"). Second, the mix of existing considerations can be more or less "crystallized" so that well-informed people (i.e., people with a lot of existing considerations about an issue) might be more difficult to influence because of "inertial resistance." Finally, people are not safe from other messages that lead to the formation of countervalent considerations counteracting newly formed considerations. These observations prove how complex information processes are. I shall concentrate only on inertial resistance processes that occurred when respondents assessed the information contained in the Choice Questionnaire.[2] I shall examine, thus, whether information given to respondents will have differentiated effects depending on how much individuals have "crystallized" or, in other words, inconsistent considerations. The special design of the study allows one to consider crystallization from the point of view of previous (in)stability of opinions, the idea being that the more an individual's opinion on a given issue has been stable in the past, the more she should be impermeable to the kind of information provided by the Choice Questionnaire.

The interest of Zaller's model does not, however, only rely on the possibility of accounting for individual characteristics; it also recognizes variations according to the characteristics of the types of issues and communications. There are different patterns of opinion change according to the level of polarization of the issue, to its familarity, and to the intensity of the messages related to the issue. Similarly, when looking at the impact of the Choice Questionnaire, attention should also be paid to the nature of the different policy measures proposed to reduce air pollution caused by private traffic. As Kriesi has already pointed out in describing the research design in which the Choice Questionnaire is integrated (chapter 8 in this volume), the six policy measures considered here differ with regard to their constraining character, their familiarity, and their complexity. The two proposed taxes (the CO_2 tax and the increase to Sfr 2/l) and the speed limits are the most constraining measures. Thus, as they imply a worsening of the respondents' situation, people who are already against them should be more difficult to influence with regard to these measures. Moreover, the speed limits were well-known to the Swiss public at the time of the experiment, which increased the chances of inertial resistance. As Zaller (1992) states in his model of attitude formation and change, in such a situation inertia due to existing beliefs is too important for a new message to have any impact. Car-free zones in inner cities and electrical vehicles were also much discussed at this time, but they were also relatively complex measures. Complexity refers to a situation in which no clear judgment can be reached, and a measure will be considered complex if it can be viewed as positive in some respects and negative in other respects. New arguments might thus influence opinions about car-free zones and electrical vehicles, and I shall examine later on which one of these characteristics (familiarity or complexity) is better suited to understand opinion (in)stability about these two measures.

(IN)STABILITY OF OPINIONS IN TIME

This section looks in more detail at opinion changes induced by the Choice Questionnaire. The analysis will concentrate on a comparison between opinions recorded during the face-to-face interviews and those reported at the end of the Choice Questionnaire.

Table 11.1 considers the six measures proposed in the Choice Questionnaire and presents the proportion of respondents who changed their mind between the face-to-face interview, during which the questionnaire was handed out to respondents, and the completion of the questionnaire. First, I observe that most respondents kept the same opinion throughout. This result is, however, far from surprising, as only a short period of time separated the two questionnaires (respondents had two weeks to answer

TABLE 11.1
Respondents with Stable or Unstable Opinions (Percentages)

	Stable Opinion	Change: for → against	Change: against → for	Total (n)
Car-free zones in inner cities	84.0	7.4	8.6	100% (n = 907)
Electrical cars	77.3	11.4	10.3	100% (n = 910)
Parking restrictions	72.3	11.0	16.6	100% (n = 907)
Tax on CO_2 emissions	76.6	9.9	13.5	100% (n = 910)
Speed limit of 100 km/h on highways	83.0	6.9	10.1	100% (n = 913)
Price of gas at Sfr 2/l	79.7	8.4	11.9	100% (n = 906)

it). But other reasons might also be mentioned. It is clear, for example, that respondents already had more or less structured beliefs about the policy alternatives when filling out the Choice Questionnaire and thus did not change their mind so easily. Moreover, they had specific predispositions and constraints, which they did not easily forget. It should also be noted that information flows do not convey a single message but contradictory arguments. The media, for example, carry and transmit the messages of opposing groups, and therefore it does not come as a surprise that scholars could find only minimal effects of the media on opinions (Zaller 1996). Knowing this, we can easily understand that the presence of contradictory arguments in the Choice Questionnaire impairs the persuasive strength of this instrument. Finally, the extent of opinion changes may be limited if the information conveyed does not contradict prior opinions. In this case, the effect of a new message is to reinforce preexisting opinions rather than to change them (see Lazarsfeld, Berelson, and Gaudet 1948:48ff).

Nevertheless, some significant changes can be observed and the proportion of changes differs from one measure to another. On the whole, respondents are notably more unstable regarding electrical vehicles, parking restrictions, and the CO_2 tax. It is, however, difficult to understand what distinguishes these measures from the others. They all demand heterogeneous solutions. Electrical vehicles is, for example, a voluntary measure, whereas parking restrictions and the CO_2 tax are much more constraining for drivers. The promotion of electrical cars is a well-known measure, whereas parking restrictions and the CO_2 tax were not discussed as much at the time of the experiment. At this stage of the analysis, it is difficult to clearly state for what kind of issue a tool like the Choice Questionnaire is most suited.

It is also interesting to note that most changes occurred in a pro-ecological direction, except for measures advocating electrical cars. Moreover, the most constraining measures, for which it might be more difficult for a respondent to shift from a negative to a positive opinion because of sacrifices such a measure implies, get more positive opinion changes than negative ones. This result is particularly stimulating, knowing that changes observed between the first telephone interview and the face-to-face interview (i.e., six months) were directed toward anti-ecological positions (Bütschi and Kriesi 1994). In other words, despite a "natural" evolution toward anti-ecological positions, the Choice Questionnaire managed to reverse this trend for most measures, not because it only provided positive considerations (the questionnaire is a neutral tool and was in this case elaborated with experts of all positions), but because it made clear to respondents that constraining measures have other objectives apart from only annoying drivers.

At this stage of the analysis it is, however, difficult to state whether the Choice Questionnaire indeed affected opinions. Table 11.1 does not give any information about the reasons for the observed changes. The next section will consider in more detail whether these changes can be attributed—at least partly—to information processing.

THE REASONS FOR OPINION CHANGE

Since the discovery by Converse (1964) of an extremely volatile electorate, whose opinions fluctuate from one interview to another, the diagnosis of the reasons for opinion changes is far from consensual and remains actual. Supported by panel data, Converse identified a clear division in the American public and then formulated his now famous black-and-white model. According to this model, there are primarily two groups of citizens: individuals with perfectly stable opinions and individuals with purely random opinions. Whereas the first group fits quite well with the ideal of democracy and its participative institutions, the second group—which is also the largest—challenges such a vision. According to Converse, many citizens are not sufficiently informed about political issues to hold true attitudes when electing their representatives or reporting opinions in the course of a survey. Their choice is only the expression of nonattitudes. Such conclusions have, of course, strong normative implications for democracy and hence arouse strong refutations. Achen (1975), and then Erikson (1979), Judd and Milburn (1980), and Inglehart (1985), advocated the existence of true attitudes. They do not deny the existence of rather important opinion changes over time, but they consider those changes as being mainly due to measurement errors inherent in surveys. They maintain that behind the type of opinion changes that Converse could observe, individuals possess stable underlying (latent) attitudes.

These two interpretations of opinion changes differ drastically regarding their implication: the first casts doubts on citizens' ability to participate in democratic processes; the second questions the reliability of surveys. However, both consider opinion changes as a problem. Neither Converse nor Achen acknowledges that opinion changes can be reasoned and expected after new information has been transmitted to individuals. Converse was certainly right in insisting that opinion change was the fact of a specific group of people, but contrary to his conclusions, I expect this particular group not to change its mind randomly but to follow specific patterns suggested by the information received via the Choice Questionnaire.

First, let us look at the relationship between prior instability and opinion change that occurred after the Choice Questionnaire. People who changed their mind between the first telephone interview (t_1) and the face-to-face interview (t_2) are subject to "prior instability." Table 11.2 shows to what extent people who changed their mind between these first two interviews modified their opinion once more after having filled out the Choice Questionnaire(t_3). At this stage, I considered opinion change only as a change of sides, but as we shall see later on, similar results are also obtained when considering more subtle positional changes. The first column displays the proportion of people who changed from the pro to the opposite side during the interviews preceding the Choice Questionnaire and then either kept the same opinion after having filled out the questionnaire or changed their opinion once again. The second and third columns show the corresponding proportions of persons who kept the same opinion between the first two interviews, and those who shifted from an opposing to a favorable one during the first period. Normally, persons who changed their mind twice (once after the face-to-face interview and once again after the Choice Questionnaire) should have returned to their initial position: from a supportive position they move, for example, to an oppositional one, and then back again to their originally favorable assessment of the issue. One has to note that it is also possible for a person to change twice in one and the same direction, and thus not return to her initial position: somebody who changed her mind from the "in favor" to the "no opinion" position made a first negative change, and if she moved from there to a position "against" the measure in question, she made a second negative change.

The strong and positive association coefficients reported in Table 11.2 clearly show that persons who have already changed their mind between the first and the second interview are more likely to modify their opinion once again after having filled out the Choice Questionnaire. Thus, the proportion of respondents who had stable opinions between the first two interviews and then kept the same opinion after the questionnaire ranges from 80 percent to 90 percent, whereas the corresponding proportion for those who have already changed their mind between the first two interviews amounts to at most 70 percent and in some cases drops to as little as 40 percent. These results suggest that the questionnaire is not likely to

TABLE 11.2
Opinion Change and Prior (In)stability: Crosstabs Tables and Association Coefficients

	Electrical cars				Change t_1–t_2							
					Car-free zones in inner cities				Parking Restrictions			
	Change against (%)	Stable opinion (%)	Change in favor (%)	V-Cramer	Change against (%)	Stable opinion (%)	Change in favor (%)	V-Cramer	Change against (%)	Stable opinion (%)	Change in favor (%)	V-Cramer
Change t_2–t_3												
Change in favor → against	–	10.3	28.7		1.0	6.3	29.9		0.6	10.4	27.2	
Stable opinion	39.6	84.7	68.8		47.1	90.5	70.1		44.1	79.9	70.4	
Change against → in favor	60.4	4.9	2.5		52.0	3.2	–		55.3	9.6	2.4	
(n)	(96)	(649)	(157)	0.43	(102)	(730)	(67)	0.43	(161)	(613)	(125)	0.37

	Tax on CO$_2$ emissions				Change t_1–t_2							
					Speed limitation on highways				Gas increase up to Sfr 2/l			
	Change against (%)	Stable opinion (%)	Change in favor (%)	V-Cramer	Change against (%)	Stable opinion (%)	Change in favor (%)	V-Cramer	Change against (%)	Stable opinion (%)	Change in favor (%)	V-Cramer
Change t_2–t_3												
Change in favor → against	1.2	7.6	36.0		1.5	4.3	40.8		2.3	4.9	39.6	
Stable opinion	60.0	84.3	59.6		61.4	89.8	57.9		64.6	88.1	54.5	
Change against → in favor	38.8	8.1	4.4		37.1	5.9	1.3		33.1	7.1	5.9	
(n)	(170)	(618)	(114)	0.37	(132)	(697)	(76)	0.38	(175)	(622)	(101)	0.36

modify the opinion of those who have already clarified their point of view on a given issue in the past, but rather that it serves as an instrument helping *ambivalent* persons make up their mind. But, for the time being, this conclusion remains purely speculative, as we cannot exclude, at this stage of the analysis, that these results can also reflect problems of nonattitudes highlighted by Converse (1964, 1970). The details of the results of Table 11.2 allow us, however, to favor the hypothesis of reasoned changes, especially among ambivalent people. As a matter of fact, in the case of electrical cars, car-free zones in inner cities, and parking restrictions, the Choice Questionnaire clearly had a different impact on respondents who had previously changed their mind in favor of the policy measure and those who had previously turned against it. While less than 30 percent of those who were previously won over to support these measures changed their mind again, a majority of the previous defectors came back to their positive previous position. This means that, on balance, the Choice Questionnaire succeeded in gaining some support for these easy-to-accept measures among the previously unstable persons. For the remaining measures—which are also the most constraining ones—the patterns of change among the people who previously changed their mind in either a pro or counter direction are less differentiated. In every case, however, changes involve significantly less than 50 percent of the groups concerned, which suggests that the moves that did take place were not the exclusive result of chance behavior. Such interpretation must, of course, be investigated cautiously and there should be further examination in more detail as to whether opinion changes are related to the information provided by the Choice Questionnaire.

Information as such is not expected to have an impact on opinion change. In order to have an effect, it has to be understood, interpreted, and evaluated. In the case of the Choice Questionnaire, it is the way respondents evaluate the different arguments that is likely to be decisive for a possible opinion change. More specifically, as is suggested by Festinger's (1957) cognitive dissonance theory, evaluations that contradict prior opinions and place respondents in a dissonant situation are likely to induce them to change their mind. Accordingly, an indicator for the *subjectively felt "tension"* has been constructed, which measures the dissonance between the opinion someone held during the face-to-face interview in wave 2, and the overall evaluation the person gave to the corresponding measure presented in the Choice Questionnaire. For each measure, the Choice Questionnaire presents a set of relevant consequences, and the sum of evaluations (positive or negative, on a magnitude estimation scaling) given to these consequences is then the overall evaluation of the measure used for the construction of an indicator of subjectively felt tension. More precisely, this indicator of tension has been obtained by subtracting overall evaluation of a measure from opinion related to this same measure given at t_2.[3] This means that a positive value of the resulting difference is indicative of pressure toward a more favorable opinion about the given measure, while a negative value implies pressure toward a more unfavorable opinion.

Figure 11.1 presents the relationship between this indicator of tension and the opinion (in)stability for each of the selected policy alternatives between the face-to-face interview and the Choice Questionnaire. More precisely, for each level of tension, the proportion of people who changed their mind from the pro to the counter position, or the reverse, is reproduced. For reasons of presentation, the individual scores on this tension indicator have been rounded to the unit. Moreover, people with a tension greater or equal to 3 (or smaller or equal to -3) were brought together in the same category in order to get a sufficient number of cases.

On the basis of the results displayed in this figure, we can clearly see that a relationship exists between tension and opinion change. Respondents without any tension have more stable opinions than those who are in a cognitively dissonant situation after having filled out the Choice Questionnaire. In one case, however, people with a high tension (+3) follow unexpected patterns, as they seem more likely to have stable opinions. But this case must be considered cautiously, as it concerns only a limited number of respondents.

The extent to which an opinion change results from a subjectively felt tension between an overall evaluation and the corresponding prior opinion can be considered as an indicator of reasonable, motivated change. Previous results suggest, however, that opinion changes are also related to the ambivalence of individuals. We also have to account for a possible impact of prior instability on opinion change by some individuals, whatever is the tension between opinions expressed during the face-to-face interview and overall evaluations given in the course of the Choice Questionnaire. If such a relationship stands out from our analysis, we must then accept that some respondents comply with Converse's black-and-white model and hold so-called nonattitudes. But prior instability can also interact with the tension produced by the evaluation procedure: as a result of inertial resistance, it is possible that people with a previously stable opinion are resistant to change, even if they experience some subjectively felt tension. Conversely, the subjectively felt tension may have a particularly strong effect on individuals with previously unstable opinions, i.e., the Choice Questionnaire may be particularly effective in clarifying their opinions.

Table 11.3 provides a test of the impact on opinion change exerted, on the one hand, by subjectively felt tensions resulting from additional information (change motivated by information processing) and, on the other hand, by prior opinion change (nonattitudes). It presents the results of a regression analysis for the six policy measures, for which we have complete

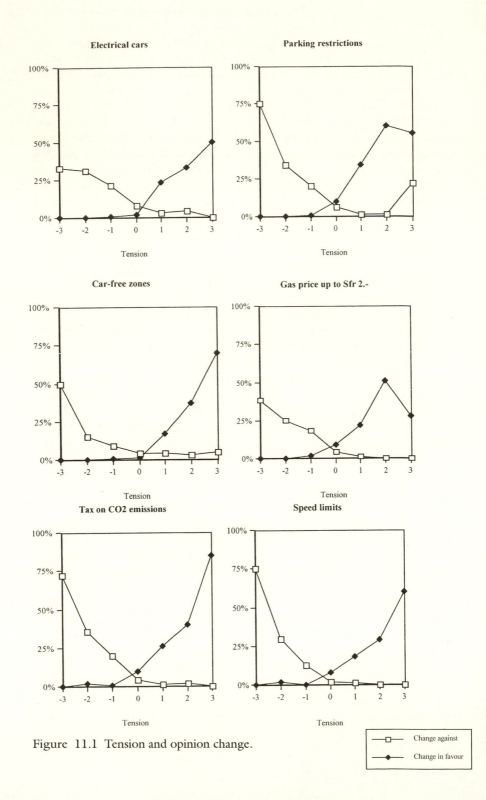

Figure 11.1 Tension and opinion change.

TABLE 11.3
The Reasons for Change: Standardized Regression Coefficients and Adjusted R^2s

	Electrical Vehicles	Car-Free Zones	Parking Restrictions	Tax on CO_2	Speed Limits	Gas at Sfr 2/l
Prior opinion change t_{12}	-.16***	-.22***	-.22***	-.22***	-.22***	-.13***
Tension	.40***	.28***	.46***	.39***	.30***	.30***
Tension * prior change t_{12}	.13***	.19***	.03	.14***	.19***	.23***
R^2 adjusted	.35	.33	.38	.39	.36	.32

* $p < .05$; ** $p < .01$; *** $p < .001$

information. In this regression, the indicators measuring opinion change—either between the first two interviews or after the experiment with the Choice Questionnaire—are now not only taking into account changes in sides as in the previous bivariate analysis, but they also account for minor changes between categories on the same side. That is, they are constructed as the differences between the original and subsequent opinions, each measured on a 5-point scale. Accordingly, these variables range from −4 (maximum negative change) to +4 (maximum positive change), with 0 indicating stability. An interaction term also has to be integrated in the analysis, so as to identify on whom the Choice Questionnaire might have the strongest effect. This interaction term is the product between the subjectively felt tension and a dummy indicator measuring whether one has changed sides (1) or not (0) between the interviews preceding the Choice Questionnaire, i.e., whether one's opinion has remained relatively stable or not.

The results displayed in Table 11.3 confirm the impact of the Choice Questionnaire on motivated, reasonable, and conscientious opinion change: the tension existing between prior opinions and overall evaluations generally has the biggest influence on opinion change for all six policy measures. Prior instability, independently of the subjectively felt tension, however, also has a significant, although clearly more limited, effect. The sign of this effect is negative, indicating that there is a general tendency for a previous move in a given direction to be turned back after having completed the Choice Questionnaire. There is, in other words, arbitrary moving back and forth between opposing camps, too. Finally, with the exception of parking restrictions, the interaction effects are also highly significant. That is to say, there is some inertial resistance on the part of the previously stable individuals: the Choice Questionnaire does not easily change opinions that rest on a large set of coherent considerations, even in cases where it creates a tension between these previous opinions and evaluations based on the information it has provided. But conversely, the questionnaire can affect the opinions of unstable and ambivalent people, at least if the newly acquired information puts them in a dissonant situation with regard to their previously held opinions. In this respect, we should consider the Choice Questionnaire more as a tool that aids in the decision-making process than a persuasive instrument.

LONG-TERM EFFECTS

So far I have only looked at the immediate effects of the Choice Questionnaire on individual opinions. Even though the questionnaire has been developed to help individuals reach an opinion at a certain point in time and not to form long-lasting attitudes, it might be worth studying how far the observed effects persist over time. The following section will consider the long-term effects of the Choice Questionnaire on the basis of the answers given in the last interview, which was administered one and a half years later.

If we refer to social-psychological literature, it appears that opinions formed on the basis of a rational examination of information are more stable than opinions based on heuristics or shortcuts (Chaiken 1980, 1987; Chaiken, Liberman, and Eagly 1989; Eagly and Chaiken 1993; Petty and Cacioppo 1986). As the Choice Questionnaire intends to induce such "rational" (or at least reasoned) evaluation of information, it should, thus, also be effective in the long term. However, social psychologists such as Underwood (1957) and Postman, Stark, and Fraser (1968) showed that interference processes may hinder the formation of new opinions and thus cancel the effects of a message conveyed either through the media or through instruments such as the Choice Questionnaire. Two kinds of interference may jeopardize the effects of additional information on opinions. First, processes of "proactive interferences" are present when previous beliefs (in our case, beliefs held at the time of the face-to-face interview) override newly acquired beliefs. Second, "retroactive interferences" occur when an individual is exposed to new messages after the experimental manipulations and acquires new beliefs that then cancel the observed opinion changes.[4] As individuals are continuously exposed to information flows, it is very likely that new messages interfered with beliefs acquired by way of the Choice Questionnaire during the eighteen months following the experiment. For example, the debate about a tax on CO_2 emissions was still underway after the experiment of the Choice Questionnaire, since the consultation procedure ended only six months later. And even then the debate was not over, as the Federal Council (the executive power) still had to work out a CO_2 bill. Other national or international events marked the political and environmental debate and may have eventually influenced opinions in the long term.[5] Even though these events were not directly related to private car use, which was at the core of the Choice Questionnaire, they might still have spilled over to this problematic and may thus have influenced the respondents' opinions in one way or another.[6]

Analogous to the previous analysis of the immediate effects of the Choice Questionnaire, the following pages will explore the persistence of its effects as a consequence of ambivalence and of the tension felt between overall evaluations given in the course of the experiment and prior opinions expressed at t_2. Several hypotheses will guide the analysis. First, individuals who had already changed their mind either during the first two interviews (t_{12}) *or* after having filled in the Choice Questionnaire (t_{23}) are, independently of the tensions they experienced after having filled in the questionnaire, more likely to change their mind once again between the period separating the Choice Questionnaire and the final interview. If this is the case, it would mean that there are individuals who do not have any attitudes at all and whose response behavior follows the random pattern suggested by Converse in his black-and-white model. Second, in the way of a refinement of this nonattitude hypothesis, individuals who changed their mind between the first two interviews *and* after having filled out the Choice Questionnaire will be considered separately. This group should be particularly volatile and have significantly greater probability of change during the last interview.

The possibility of delayed opinion changes due to the Choice Questionnaire will also be considered. A study realized in social psychology showed indeed that some types of messages only have effects in the long run. Under the telling name of "sleeper effect," Hovland, Lumsdaine, and Sheffield (1949) describe situations where changes measured immediately after a message are more limited than changes measured at some later point in time, as if the message "slept" for some time in the minds of the individuals. The idea that information might have a deferred impact on opinions is rather unconventional, but researchers explain such phenomena by the fact that, with time, negative elements of a message are put aside, and if the content of the message is strong enough, it may have an impact in the long run. Applied to the Choice Questionnaire's case, such sleeper effect would imply that some people who experienced a tension between the overall evaluations given in the course of the questionnaire and their prior opinions are only affected by this discrepancy in the long run and thus changed their mind during the one and a half years separating the questionnaire and the last interview.

As a final hypothesis, the possibility that the Choice Questionnaire might have durably converted respondents must be accounted for. As a matter of fact, it is possible that individuals who experienced a tension between their overall evaluations and their prior opinions, and consequently

TABLE 11.4
Long-Term Stability and Choice Questionnaire: Standardized Regression Coefficients and Adjusted R^2s

	Electrical Vehicles	Car-Free Zones	Parking Restrictions	Tax on CO_2	Speed Limits	Gas at Sfr 2/l
Minimum instability	.21***	.23***	.20***	.17***	.13***	.18***
Maximum instability	.04	-.01	.06	.07	.01	-.07
Tension	-.09	.02	.04	-.11*	-.05	.01
Tension * prior change t_{23}	.10	-.01	.10	.32***	.44***	.14*
Tension * ch. t_{12} * ch. t_{23}	-.04	.04	-.10*	-.11**	-.31***	.07
R^2 adjusted	.06	.05	.06	.12	.07	.07

* p < .05; ** p < .01; *** p < .001

changed their mind after completing the Choice Questionnaire, kept the same new opinion one and a half years later. In this respect, and following the idea that the questionnaire functions as a decision aid for ambivalent people, previously ambivalent individuals may be durably influenced by the process of information assessment they went through when filling out the Choice Questionnaire.

Table 11.4 presents a regression analysis testing the effects of these different hypotheses on the changes in opinions that occurred between the Choice Questionnaire and the last interview. Contrary to the short-term analysis reported in the previous section, this analysis only considers the distance of a move without taking into account its direction. Thus, the resulting indicators of issue-specific opinion change range from 0 to 4 (0 referring to stable opinion and 4 to the most unstable). Disregarding the change of direction facilitates the test of the hypotheses, because taking direction into account would imply nonlinear relationships. Given that the four hypotheses do not refer to the direction of change at all, this procedure does not result in any restriction of the generality of the results.

Four variables operationalize the hypotheses. Two of them account for the first couple of hypotheses referring to nonattitudes. *Minimal instability* describes persons who changed their mind once during the whole process (between t_1 and t_2 *or* between t_2 and t_3). Here also, for reasons of linearity, direction of change is ignored. A positive effect on opinion change during the final period is expected for minimal instability. *Maximal instability* refers to persons who changed twice, i.e., in periods t_{12} *and* t_{23}. Again, a positive effect is expected. Next, the sleeper effect hypothesis is operationalized by the same *subjectively felt tension* variable that was introduced in the last section, which indicates the dissonance between overall evaluations attributed to given issues in the course of the Choice Questionnaire and prior opinions. But here, too, only absolute values are considered. The higher the value of this variable, the more likely one is expected to change one's mind. This variable measures long-term changes net of any previous changes induced by the Choice Questionnaire. The last two variables are interactions that account for the persistence of changes provoked by the Choice Questionnaire. They refer to persons who changed their mind after having filled out the questionnaire as a result of the tension induced by the evaluation of the presented arguments. These variables operationalize permanent conversion, and, therefore, the expected relationships are negative. The first one of the two is a simple interaction between opinion change occurring as a result of the questionnaire and the subjectively felt tension, whereas the second one is a three-way interaction, where opinion change resulting from the questionnaire is a conditional effect of both tension and prior instability. Underlying this last variable is the idea that the chances of somebody changing durably as a result of the experiment of the Choice Questionnaire are particularly great if this change is a result of both tension induced by the questionnaire and ambivalence (i.e., prior instability).

Compared to short-term analysis, the variances explained by these regression models are quite low, and long-term opinion changes are certainly due to much more complex processes than the ones suggested here. But looking at the impact of the different indicators, minimal instability appears to be the most pervasive factor contributing to changes that occurred between the Choice Questionnaire and the last interview. The fact that some people changed their mind once in the whole process explains, for all policy alternatives under consideration, subsequent changes. This means that it is likely that some persons do not have true attitudes or, in other words, that some are easily influenced by proactive or retroactive interferences. Maximal instability, on the other hand, does not have a significant impact, which is to say that having changed one's opinion more than once does not further increase its volatility later on.

Tension—the indicator for the sleeper-effect—has no effect at all. In other words, the sleeper effect hypothesis must then be rejected. Moreover, the interactions between the tension and previous change are not systematically significant either. For half of the policy measures under consideration, no significant relationship exists between long-term opinion changes and the interaction terms accounting for the conditional effect of tension. And where a significant relationship exists, it does not go in the expected direction: in the case of the tax on CO_2 emissions, speed limits, and increases in the price of gas up to Sfr 2/l, the respective effects are positive. This suggests that the motivated opinion change induced by the

Choice Questionnaire is not particularly stable over time: in the case of rather constraining measures, such as the CO_2 tax, the increase of petrol up to Sfr 2/l, and speed limits, individuals who were induced to change their mind by the Choice Questionnaire tended, in fact, to go back to their initial position.

At least for parking restrictions, the tax on CO_2 emissions, and speed limits, the Choice Questionnaire nevertheless seems to have had a long-term effect for the particular group of ambivalent persons who had already changed their mind between t_1 and t_2 and then changed their mind a second time as a result of the tension created by the Choice Questionnaire. For these three measures and for this specific group of persons, the questionnaire seems to have a long-term effect, even though it is not clear why such a relationship exists in these particular cases but not for others (and especially not for the measure advocating an increase in the price of gas up to Sfr 2/l, which is similar to the CO_2 tax and even more constraining). Whatever causes this result, it supplies further evidence of the Choice Questionnaire's capacity to function as a tool that helps ambivalent people form an opinion. In this function, it can have a long-term effect.

CONCLUSION

The Choice Questionnaire has an effect on individual opinions in many ways. First, contrary to Converse's black-and-white model, it appears that the opinion change it induced is only marginally due to chance. Overall evaluations play a crucial role in determining observed change. Processes of opinion change rely, indeed, on the integration of new messages, here conveyed by the Choice Questionnaire, even though we are not in a position to state that individuals processed the information in a fully objective way. Second, analysis showed that the questionnaire should not be considered as an instrument of persuasion but rather as a decision-making tool for ambivalent respondents. As a matter of fact, information provided by the Choice Questionnaire primarily influenced respondents who did not have structured beliefs about the policy alternatives in question. Nevertheless, analysis also showed that the questionnaire has only a limited effect in the long run. In this respect, the questionnaire helps people with not much information to formulate well-considered opinions, and no more. Such an instrument cannot be expected to produce a long-term opinion change. It is an instrument to be used at a specific moment and in a specific context.

In sum, the Choice Questionnaire can be considered as an instrument that helps some people form considered opinions. It contributes to some extent to the citizens' "enlightened understanding" of the policy process.

It is an instrument that could prove useful at different levels of the political process, especially in the direct democracy institutions of Switzerland and the United States. There are at least three levels on which the political system might benefit from considered opinions. First, citizens are generally excluded from the elaboration phase of legislation. At this stage of the political process, policymakers are the main actors, and citizens remain in the background. Even in Switzerland, where opposition groups capable of launching a referendum against an act of legislation adopted by Parliament are typically integrated into the pre-parliamentary legislative process (Neidhart 1970), individual citizens are excluded from this step of the decision-making process. In direct democratic procedures, they only intervene at the end of the legislative process, once a bill that has been passed by Parliament is attacked by a referendum. The Choice Questionnaire could act as a sophisticated tool of public participation at this stage of policy elaboration. Traditional opinion surveys could, of course, also be used to assess the needs and attitudes of the general public at this stage of the policy process. This stage is, however, generally characterized by low levels of publicity about the issue under consideration, and it is thus very likely that citizens interviewed do not possess all the necessary facts to consider the issue in its entirety. By contrast, the Choice Questionnaire allows citizens to thoughtfully consider the proposed project and then form a reasoned opinion.

Second, in asking respondents to separately assess each consequence of a given issue, the Choice Questionnaire offers precious information for decision makers. This function is, of course, rather traditional as it means that the questionnaire gives policymakers important insights into the attitudes about a specific project, but it also allows for a more sophisticated analysis of the various arguments that are relevant for the public at large.

Third, the Choice Questionnaire can be of interest within direct democratic systems at the time referenda or popular initiatives are submitted to a vote (Neijens et al. 1996). In such democratic voting procedures, citizens deal with more or less complex issues, and the less politically sophisticated typically have some difficulty in fully participating in such procedures.[7] The Choice Questionnaire may generally help citizens to better understand voting issues and to express opinions that coincide with their own interests and values. On this point, it is interesting to take note of the results of an experiment carried out in Amsterdam just before a vote aimed at reducing traffic problems in the city (Neijens and de Ridder 1992; Neijens et al. 1996). A Choice Questionnaire was distributed to a representative sample of the population of Amsterdam, and it was shown that the respondents knew more about the issue at stake after having filled out the questionnaire than they did before. In addition, most of them took into consideration the information they received through the questionnaire at the time of making their final decision. It is clear that so long as the Choice

Questionnaire is distributed to a representative sample, only a minority of citizens will be in a position to benefit from its information and support. If the Choice Questionnaire is to be used in consulting the public, it should be distributed to all citizens in the form of an information booklet, for example. The Swiss federal government (as well as cantonal and local governments) already sends an information brochure to all citizens, which presents the issue to be voted on and its own recommendations for the vote, as well as the arguments of the opposition (generally, groups who demanded the referendum or launched the initiative). This information brochure could be completed (or replaced) by a Choice Questionnaire, allowing citizens to arrive at a structured evaluation of the different issues at stake.

NOTES

1. For a review of these critics, see Eagly and Chaiken 1993:177ff.
2. For a more detailed analysis of the Choice Questionnaire along the lines of Zaller's model, see Bütschi 1999.
3. Before subtracting overall evaluations from opinions, responses were first brought on a comparable scale.
4. For a review on proactive and retroactive interference, see Gordon 1989.
5. During this one-and-a-half-year period, the Alpine Railroad Tunnels were intensively discussed in the Swiss media. Moreover, it was also during this period that Greenpeace action against the Shell Platform Brent Spar took place, as well as the Berlin Conference on climate change and the resumption of nuclear tests in the Pacific by France.
6. For a discussion of the role of information during this one-and-a-half-year period, see Kriesi 1998.
7. Held (1987) describes such a situation as being a result of democratic inequalities, whereas Gaxie (1978) speaks of a "hidden census."

REFERENCES

Achen, Christopher H. 1975. "Mass Political Attitudes and the Survey Response." *American Political Science Review* 69:1218–31.
Bütschi, Danielle. 1999. *Le Questionnaire de choix. Raisonnement dans les processus démocratiques.* Paris: L'Harmattan.
Bütschi, Danielle, and Hanspeter Kriesi. 1994. *Dispositions des Suisses à l'égard d'une politique des transports respectueuse de l'environnement.* Congress of the Swiss Political Science Association. November 11–12, Balstahl.
Chaiken, Shelly. 1980. "Heuristic versus Systematic Information Processing and the Use of Source versus Message Cues in Persuasion." *Journal of Personality and Social Psychology* 39:752–66.

———. 1987. "The Heuristic Model of Persuasion." In *Social Influence: The Ontario Symposium,* ed. M. P. Zanna, J. M. Olson, and C. P. Herman, 3–39. Hillsdale, NJ: Lawrence Erlbaum.

Chaiken, Shelly, A. Liberman, and Alice H. Eagly. 1989. "Heuristic and Systematic Processing within and beyond the Persuasion Context." In *Unintended Thoughts,* ed. James S. Uleman and John A. Bargh, 212–52. New York: Guilford Press.

Converse, Philip. 1964. "The Nature of Belief System in Mass Publics." In *Ideology and Discontent,* ed. David Apter, 206–61. New York: Free Press.

———. 1970. "Attitudes and Non-Attitudes: Continuation of a Dialogue." In *The Quantitative Analysis of Social Problems,* ed. Edward R. Tufte, 168–89. Reading, MA: Addison-Wesley.

Eagly, Alice H., and Shelly Chaiken. 1993. *The Psychology of Attitudes.* New York: Harcourt Brace Jovanovich.

Erikson, Robert S. 1979. "The SRC Panel Data and Mass Political Attitudes." *British Journal of Political Science* 9:89–114.

Festinger, Leon. 1957. *A Theory of Cognitive Dissonance.* Stanford: Stanford University Press.

Fishbein, Martin, and Icek Ajzen. 1975. *Belief, Attitude, Intention and Behavior. An Introduction to Theory and Research.* Reading, MA: Addison-Wesley.

Gaxie, Daniel. 1978. *Le cens caché: Inégalités culturelles et ségrégation politique.* Paris: Seuil.

Gordon, William C. 1989. *Learning and Memory.* Pacific Grove: Brooks/Cole.

Held, David. 1987. *Models of Democracy.* Cambridge: Polity Press.

Hovland, C. I., A. A. Lumsdaine, and F. D. Sheffield. 1949. *Experiments in Mass Communication.* Princeton: Princeton University Press.

Inglehart, Ronald. 1985. "Aggregate Stability and Individual-Level Flux in Mass Belief Systems: The Level of Analysis Paradox." *American Political Science Review* 79(1):97–116.

Judd, Charles M., and Michael A. Milburn. 1980. "The Structure of Attitude Systems in the General Public: Comparisons of a Structural Equation Model." *American Sociological Review* 45(August):627–43.

Kriesi, Hanspeter. 1998. "Opinion Formation and Change: The Case of the Swiss Policy against Air Pollution Caused by Cars." Department of Political Science, University of Geneva.

Lazarsfeld, Paul H., Bernard Berelson, and Hazel Gaudet. 1948. *The People's Choice: How the Voter Makes up His Mind in a Presidential Campaign.* New York: Duell, Sloan, and Pearce.

Neidhart, Leonhard. 1970. *Plebiszit und pluralitäre Demokratie: Eine Analyse der Funktionen des Schweizerischen Gesetzreferendums.* Bern: Francke.

Neijens, Peter. 1987. *The Choice Questionnaire. Design and Evaluation of an Instrument for Collecting Informed Opinions of a Population.* Amsterdam: Free University Press.

Neijens, Peter, and Jan de Ridder. 1992. "De Keuze-Enquête Over de Auto in de Binnenstand." *In Het eerste Amsterdam ereferendum in perspectief,* ed. Willem E. Saris, Peter Neijens, and Jeroen Slot. Amsterdam: Cramwinckel.

Neijens, Peter, Mark Minkman, Jan de Ridder, Willem Saris, and Jeroen Slot. 1996. "A Decision Aid in a Referendum." *International Journal of Public Opinion Research* 8(1):83–90.

Petty, Richard E., and John T. Cacioppo. 1986. *Communication and Persuasion: Central and Peripherial Routes to Attitude Change*. New York: Springer Verlag.

Popkin, Samuel. 1992. *The Reasoning Voter*. Chicago: University of Chicago Press.

Postman, Leo, Karen Stark, and Janet Fraser. 1968. "Temporal Changes in Interference." *Journal of Verbal Learning and Verbal Behavior* 7:672–94.

Saris, Willem, Peter Neijens, and J. A. de Ridder. 1983. *Kernenergie: Ja of nee?* Amsterdam: SSO.

Simon, Herbert A. 1976. *Administrative Behavior*. New York: Free Press.

Tversky, Amos, and Daniel Kahneman. 1974. "Judgment under Uncertainty: Heuristics and Biases." *Science* 185:1124–31.

Underwood, Benton J. 1957. "Interference and Forgetting." *Psychological Review* 64(1):49–60.

Zaller, John R. 1992. *The Nature and Origins of Mass Opinion*. Cambridge: Cambridge University Press.

———. 1996. "The Myth of Massive Media Impact Revived: New Support for a Discredited Idea." In *Political Persuasion and Attitude Change,* ed. Diana C. Mutz, Paul M. Sniderman, and Richard A. Brody, 17–78. Ann Arbor: University of Michigan Press.

Zukin, Cliff. 1981. "Mass Communication and Public Opinion." In *Handbook of Political Communication,* ed. Dan D. Nimmo and Keith R. Sanders, 359–90. Beverly Hills: Sage.

PART VI

Looking Forward

CHAPTER 12

A Consistency Theory of Public Opinion
and Political Choice: The Hypothesis
of Menu Dependence

Paul M. Sniderman and John Bullock

IN THE END WE study the attitudes of citizens to understand the choices they make as citizens—the candidates they choose to vote for, the public policies they choose to support. Here we want to draw together some arguments that have run through this book, together with some that have been carried on outside it, to outline a general account of political choice.

The spine of this account is the concept of consistency. As with many social science terms, the concept of consistency is inconsistently used. In the context of research on public opinion and political choice, a trio of meanings can be distinguished. Consistency can be a synonym for constraint. Construed as constraint, consistency indexes the predictability of citizens' position on one issue given their positions on another.[1] Then again, consistency can be a synonym for stability. Construed as stability, consistency indexes the predictability of citizens' positions on an issue at one point in time given their positions on the same issue at an earlier point in time. Finally, consistency can be a synonym for congruence. Construed as congruence, consistency indexes the predictability of positions citizens take on specific issues given their general political orientations.[2]

Empirically, this trio—constraint, stability, congruence—is broadly related. The more tightly constrained citizens' positions across issues, the more stable their positions are likely to be over time; and the more stable and tightly constrained their positions, the more likely they are to be congruent with underlying basic orientations. The premise of the theory we present is thus that the first two senses of consistency are causally parasitic on the third. Positions tend to be constrained across issues or stable over time to the extent they are congruent with basic political orientations. And just so far as citizens possess basic political orientations together with the competence to call them into play, a consistency theory of public opinion has a causal leg to stand on.

But a consistency theory of public opinion that has just one leg has long appeared too wobbly to stand, special circumstances aside.[3] The dominant themes of two generations of research have been that citizens tend to be muddle-headed (the lack of constraint theme), empty-headed (the non-attitudes theme), or both. True, a strong qualifying note also has been sounded. Citizens can pull their ideas together conditional on political sophistication: the more of the latter, the more of the former.[4] But there has seemed no way to get consistency of choice, defined as congruence, out of the largest part of the public: they pay too little attention to politics, know too little about it, and invest too little in organizing their ideas about it.

We therefore want to point to a new conceptual path. It is necessary, we will suggest, first to take account of the characteristics of choices that citizens face, and then to attend to their characteristics as choosers. In politics, citizens characteristically are presented with an organized set, or menu, of choices.[5] The choices they make are dependent on the organization of this menu. Specifically, citizens are in a position to make coherent choices just so far as this menu is coherent. The distinctive feature of the consistency theory that we present is thus that it stands on two causal legs. It posits that consistency, understood as congruence, is *jointly* conditional on the characteristics of citizens as choosers and the menu of options they face as citizens.

Admittedly, in proposing any version of a consistency theory, we are making an uphill argument. A principal theme of half a century of public opinion research has been precisely the comparative absence of consistency in public opinion. Indeed, under the headings of nonattitudes and ambivalence, the lability of choices is a surface motif of many of the chapters of this book. And yet, so far as the studies in this book seek to give a causal analysis of the public's beliefs and choices that goes beyond a nonattitudes story, they are committed to a consistency account of some variety. So, by way of concluding commentary, it seems worthwhile to consider what the premises of such an account most plausibly are.

The most vital premise is this: in representative democracies citizens do not directly choose the alternatives. They only get to choose from among the alternatives on the menu of choices presented to them. That menu is simplified, coordinated, and advocated above all through electoral competition between political parties. Accordingly, we claim that citizens in representative democracies can coordinate their responses to political choices insofar as the choices themselves are coordinated by political parties.

To put our cards on the table at the start, the evidence backing our claim is patchy at best. This is partly because the claim has not yet been the object of systematic study and partly because this kind of claim is inherently difficult to study systematically.[6] Our consideration of previous research is therefore frankly opportunistic. Still, if future work shows that we were on the right track, we may be forgiven for giving our argument a speculative shove here and there.

We assume that people are motivated to be consistent in their beliefs and sentiments about politics, just as they are in their beliefs and sentiments about other areas of their lives.[7] The question is: how do they manage to achieve consistency in politics, to the extent they actually achieve it? By what means, given a set of alternatives, do they select one congruent with their general political orientations? How, for that matter, do they form general political orientations given the limited attention they pay to politics and public affairs?

We proceed in three steps. Our first step is to review critically the principal consistency-generating mechanisms so far proposed. They are part of an answer—but only as part of a broader perspective. Our second step is to outline this broader perspective. A substantial part of the public is able to achieve consistency in their political choices, we will suggest, just because their choices are menu dependent. Finally, given the speculative character of our account, our third step is to elaborate on some especially obvious qualifications.

ESTABLISHED MECHANISMS

How, so far as citizens are consistent in their political choices, do they manage to achieve consistency? There is no shortage of answers. By our count, four are commonly given: on-line tallies, group affect, basic values and political orientations, and judgmental heuristics.[8] Four mechanisms may seem three too many. But each can do solid work. The difficulty, we will suggest, is that even when taken together, they cannot do the necessary explanatory job.

Taking the quartet of explanatory mechanisms in order of explanatory reach, we start with the so-called Stony Brook account of motivated reasoning and on-line impression formation.[9] Lodge and his Stony Brook colleagues have proceeded from a simple intuition. Voters form initial impressions of candidates, stored in memory in the form of feelings (or affect). Exposed to subsequent information, the affective tally of past impressions comes to mind at the same time voters become aware of the affective "tag" attached to the new information. In the process voters update their running tally. Evaluations are thus constructed anew with each addition of new information. But the impact of each new piece of information is predicated on the tally of previous evaluations. So voters tend to take onboard information that confirms their previous view and to reject or discount information at odds with it.

This hypothesis of a running affective tally provides an attractively simple solution to the problem of mental bookkeeping. Citizens need remember only one thing. And the one thing they need to remember is easy to remember. To respond consistently to new information, voters need only know how they feel about a candidate. They need not be aware of—indeed, they probably do not remember—the specific reasons that led them to feel as they do.

The on-line model is welcome on another ground. It calls attention to the pivotal role of affect in the maintenance of cognitive consistency. This is a point of some importance. A distinction between cognition and affect, though well-advised for understanding some problems, is ill-advised for understanding the organization of political belief systems. Many beliefs cannot be genuinely held unless the sentiments appropriate to them are also held. In politics, this entanglement of cognition and affect is inescapable and useful. From one angle, what holds a structure of beliefs together, what makes it cohere, is precisely its affective consistency.

Yet the on-line model is cramped. The fully worked-out version of the model to date gives an account only of congruence narrowly defined—the accumulation of evaluations of political objects, one by one. To give an account of consistency of political choices over sets of choices (say, an array of social welfare policies), a consistency-generating mechanism of wider scope is required. In their most recent work, Taber, Lodge and Glathar propose "node-link *structures*" as a candidate mechanism.[10] But at this stage of their research it is not clear how much the invocation of structure explains and how much it assumes.

A second consistency-generating mechanism is predicated on the simultaneous role of social groups as objects of public opinion and public policy. In his seminal essay, Converse picked out the politics of race as one of two exceptions to the general rule of minimal constraint in mass belief systems. By way of argument, he first listed a series of public policies targeting blacks—for example, to provide job training, to increase educational opportunity, and to monitor discrimination in housing. Ordinary citizens, he then suggested, need not have detailed knowledge of these policies in order to respond consistently to them. They need only know how they feel about blacks.[11] The more they like and sympathize with black Americans, the more likely they will be to support these policies; the more they dislike and feel superior to black Americans, the more likely they will be to oppose these policies.

On this view, citizens maximize congruence between policy alternatives and affect toward social groups that are the objects of these policies. They thus can mount a coherent response to a set of policies serially, responding independently to each policy. Moreover, the politics of race are not idiosyncratic, but only an especially vivid illustration of the general principle that political choices are organized around social groups or around the connections between social groups and political parties. As the authors of *The American Voter* noted long ago, citizens can go a long way in putting together a *politically* coherent set of beliefs by knowing that labor unions, for example, are specially tied to the Democratic Party, while big business is specially tied to the Republican Party. Indeed, knowing of alliances between salient social groups and political parties, together with having pronounced feelings about them, can amount to "ideology by proxy," in the telling phrase of Campbell and his colleagues (Campbell et al. 1960).

It certainly is possible to extract a consistency story out of group likes and dislikes that is consistent with the intermittent attention ordinary citizens pay to politics. And perhaps this is the path to take. Still, we have reservations. The issue of race aside, there is not a large amount of evidence that choices over political issues are based on a group calculus. Moreover, to get consistency of choice over sets of policies dealing with diverse groups, it is necessary to rely on a premise that feelings across groups are consistently organized—and that premise is not plausible for large portions of the public.[12] In any case, what is doing the real work in generating political coherence is knowledge of partisan coalitions. Absent knowing, for example, that labor unions are allied with the Democratic Party and big business with the Republican Party, there is no basis for ideology by proxy.

A third consistency-generating mechanism, *core values,* is appealing on the grounds of both explanatory scope and simplicity. On the one side, it is not difficult to see how foundational values like liberty and equality can ground choices over large sets of specific issues. On the other side, since the number of foundational values (as compared to opinions) is small, it is not difficult to see how ordinary citizens can organize them coherently. So on both counts an account of consistency is conceivable, with citizens selecting the alternative, from among those on offer, that is most congruent with their core values.

Feldman has, more than anyone, given empirical support to the hypothesis of core values coordinating policy choices. In pioneering work, he developed candidate measures of a triad of core values—egalitarianism, economic individualism, and support for free enterprise.[13] In subsequent work with Steenbergen, Feldman has shifted focus to humanitarianism as a core value, a shift we find appealing because of its fit with recent normative rethinking of equality as an ideal of humanitarianism.

Intuitively, the appeal to core values as consistency generators is attractive. It meshes smoothly with the language in which political thinkers conceive political choices without requiring unreasonable assumptions about the capacity of ordinary citizens to be political thinkers. And empirically, it surely must be true that issue choices are grounded to a degree in basic values.

The problem is that it appears to be true only to a limited degree. If the empirical benchmark of congruence is the power of measures of core values to predict specific political choices, the conclusion to draw is that congruence is modest at most. Of course, the problem may not lie with the hypothesis of core values as consistency generators. As plausibly, the problem may be the limitation of current measures to gauge adherence to core values. Measurement of core values is still in an early stage. Methodologically, it has concentrated almost entirely on the rating of values.[14] This may prove the best approach in the end, though Jacoby has recently introduced an innovative approach involving the ranking of values.[15] Future development of ranking techniques, or indeed of rating ones, may show that substantial numbers of ordinary citizens choose among political alternatives by selecting the one most congruent with their core values. But if that is the right lesson to draw, this is not the right time to draw it.

The last set of consistency-generating mechanisms is heuristics, that is, judgmental shortcuts. The intuition here is that even comparatively well-informed citizens have a limited amount of information to work with. If they are to be able to make politically coherent judgments they need an easy-to-operate calculus. Judgmental shortcuts would seem to fit the bill.

Consider the likability heuristic introduced by Brady and Sniderman.[16] The specific task is locating the positions of strategic actors in a political landscape. Although some are concrete and immediate—men and women, for example—others are more abstract and removed—liberals and conservatives, for example. How, then, are citizens able to define correctly what liberals and conservatives stand for—that is, accurately describe their positions over an array of issues—even though they cannot accurately define liberalism and conservatism?

By following a judgmental shortcut, Brady and Sniderman suggest. To estimate *accurately* the issue commitments of any pair of competing groups, it is necessary only for citizens to know their stand on the issue and to take into account the difference in their feelings toward the two groups. So, even without knowing what liberalism and conservatism are as ideologies, citizens can know what liberals and conservatives stand for. Notice, given our interest in consistency, the qualifying condition. The heuristic only works to the degree that an individual likes one side and dislikes the other. If they do not recognize that liking liberals entails disliking conservatives, the likability heuristic fails.

The hypothesis of heuristics is frequently invoked.[17] It seems to provide a method of explaining how citizens can compensate for the limited information they have about political affairs. It is worth making plain why this way of putting things is misleading, for it throws light on a neglected problem.

It is true in one sense, but false in another, that citizens can compensate for limited information by taking advantage of a heuristic. The sense in which it is true is that even comparatively well-informed citizens are unlikely to have all the information at hand to reason through an informed decision. The sense in which it is false is that the likelihood of taking advantage of an effective judgmental shortcut itself depends on how well-informed citizens are. It takes smarts to make smart moves, if it is okay to speak plainly. It accordingly is false to suggest that the public taken as a whole can make judgments about a problem in public affairs by taking advantage of heuristics that match the judgments they would make if they were to be fully informed about it. It is only true that the better informed they are, the less they are likely to be handicapped by their absolute lack of knowledge.

The efficacy of judgmental shortcuts as a consistency mechanism is heavily conditional on political sophistication. And so, a stream of studies make plain, are the other consistency-generating mechanisms. One exception aside, it is the politically more sophisticated who benefit more from each of these mechanisms, that is, who choose more consistently in virtue of them. That applies to judgmental shortcuts like the likability heuristic, core values, and basic political orientations, and even to on-line processing, which was initially commended precisely for its simplicity of operation.[18]

How, then, should the explanatory books be balanced? On the profit side of the ledger, we have gotten better and better at giving an account of how citizens make political choices the more politically sophisticated they are. On the loss side of the ledger, however, we have gotten worse and worse at giving an account of how citizens make political choices the less sophisticated they are. Since there is not an excess of the former and no shortage of the latter, this is explanatory progress of an ironic stripe. It may be useful, therefore, to approach the problem of consistency from a different perspective.

Menu Dependence: Policy Agendas, Issue Framing, and Issue Centrality

The capacity of citizens to make consistent choices, we shall suggest, is contingent on the organization of the menu of choices presented to them. We shall explore three aspects of menu dependence for facilitating consistency of choices: first, menu dependence over sets of issues; second, for issues taken one at a time; third, for variation in consistency across issues.

We start with policy agendas. To ask how citizens manage to achieve a consistent response not merely to issues one by one but to whole sets of them assumes that a substantial part of the public is in fact capable of doing so. But in order to demonstrate that this assumption of consistency is in fact warranted, it is necessary to know with respect to what they are striving to be consistent.

What might an answer look like? To the extent citizens respond to issues separately, evaluating each on the basis of considerations unique to it, then consistency understood either as constraint or congruence is ruled out. A specific issue, just by virtue of being specific, points to a particular matter—

whether the government should increase unemployment assistance, for example, or whether it should ramp up job-training programs. And when making choices about particular matters, citizens must be able to rely on a more general view of the matter if they are to make consistent choices across issues. But what might their general view of the matter consist in? On the one side, it cannot be something as general as an ideological orientation, since that is something so general as to be out of the reach of most citizens. On the other side, it cannot be something so specific as their feelings about particular social groups, since that is not general enough. Something in between is needed, and that something, we suggest, is a policy agenda.

To illustrate what we mean by a policy agenda, we draw on the research of Carmines and Layman. Analyzing a series of National Election Surveys, they pick out a three-dimensional structure of policy preferences. One dimension is defined by issues like government support for jobs and standard of living; a second, by issues like abortion and women's rights; a third, by issues like government help for blacks and spending on programs for blacks.[19] Each attitudinal dimension thus maps on to a policy agenda. Carmines and Layman accordingly label the first the social welfare agenda; the second, the cultural agenda; the third, the racial agenda. Our concern is not whether there are three agendas or two—or four, for that matter. For our purposes, Carmines and Layman's issue analysis makes two points worth emphasizing, one negative, the other positive. The negative point is that the ideas of ordinary citizens tend to be unrelated *across* policy agendas. The positive point is that they tend to be consistent *within* them.

This distinction between consistency within and across policy agendas is pivotal. The classical studies of ideology in mass publics proceeded on the premise that the menu of issue choices has no structure, that it is not divided into distinct parts. So they took as a test of ideological thinking consistency—defined as constraint—across the full spectrum of contemporary concerns, ignoring demarcation of issues into distinct sets.[20] In turn, they drew the lesson that ordinary citizens cannot take in liberalism-conservatism as a coherent whole.

But it does not follow that because the public as a whole cannot take in liberalism-conservatism as a whole, it cannot take in their component parts coherently. Each policy agenda—social welfare, cultural, and racial—captures a component of the ideological divide in contemporary American politics. But each represents a distinct component, with each having concerns that mark it off from the others, in elite as well popular discourse. And accordingly it is perfectly possible, indeed commonly the case as Carmines and Layman's results indicate, that citizens can be liberal (or conservative) with respect to issues like abortion or women's rights without being liberal (or conservative) with respect to issues of government assistance for the poor or for those in search of jobs. Carmines and Layman's results thus underscore two points: first, that the three policy agendas are distinct in the mind of the public; and second, that each of the agendas is sufficiently bite-sized to be taken in as a coherent whole by the public as a whole. Ordinary citizens thus tend to be consistently liberal (or conservative) agenda by agenda in spite of not being consistently liberal (or conservative) across agendas.

Now think of the overall view that ordinary citizens form about a policy agenda as a latent trait—in our parlance, their general view of the matter. How do citizens go about choosing among alternatives for an issue on a particular agenda? By consulting their general view of that agenda. Just so far as their general view of the cultural agenda is conservative, they will consistently choose the conservative alternative across issues on that agenda. And just so far as their general view is liberal, they will consistently choose the liberal alternative. In this way the public as a whole, and not just the most sophisticated segment of it, can make consistently liberal and conservative choices agenda by agenda even though they cannot make consistently liberal and conservative choices across agendas.

But how do issues come to be bundled together as they are? Why do policy agendas include some issues but not others? And, still more difficult, how do some citizens achieve consistency not only within policy agendas but also between them?

Part of the answer of how consistency is achieved across agendas is well established. One characteristic of citizens as choosers, their level of political sophistication, plays a crucial role. More exactly, a double role. Political awareness facilitates consistency by facilitating a coherent set of core beliefs and expectations, generalized priors if you like, on which to base a specific choice. Additionally, political sophistication promotes consistency by facilitating recognition of the relevance of these core beliefs and expectations in making specific issue choices.[21] To this harmony of views we would add just one discordant note. As we read the research literature, the emphasis is on individuals as active information processors, imposing order and coherence on what otherwise would be, in James's enduring phrase, a blooming buzzing confusion.[22] By contrast, consistent with our view on the external organization of choice spaces, we propose that political sophistication facilitates the more modest task of recognizing rather than imposing coherence.

And that coherence is imposed, we suggest, through competition between political parties and candidates for control of government. Partly because of the commitments of their core members and partly because of their strategic alliances with interest groups, parties compete against each other agenda by agenda. And very largely because of the dynamics of electoral competition they yoke agenda to agenda.

For evidence, indirect as it is, we rely on a recent study by Layman and Carsey (2002). They show that the link between the social welfare and cultural agendas is conditional on strength of party identification and awareness of partisan differences on the two agendas. For those identifying strongly with a party and aware of the differences between them on the two agendas there is a strong link; for those identifying with a party but not aware of the differences between them on the two agendas, there is only a moderate link; for those who do not identify with a party whether or not they are aware of differences between the parties there is essentially no link.

Consider the implications of Layman and Carsey's findings. A consistency theory of substantial scope has appeared a nonstarter because there has appeared to be no way to get coherence of choice out of citizens themselves. But the consistency-generating mechanisms, their findings suggest, are institutional. Political parties provide the basis for the consistency of individuals; indeed, twice over on Layman and Carsey's results: once through the consequences of attachment to parties and once through the consequences of knowing parties' contrasting positions on issues.[23] This double role of parties testifies to the institutional organization of political choices. By facilitating consistency across policy agendas, parties help the substantial part of the public attached to them to make choices across the spectrum of contested issues on the basis of a consistently liberal or conservative view of the matter.

On our view, it is parties and candidates that do the heavy lifting necessary for consistency in public opinion. They reduce the number of alternatives open to choice to only a few—indeed, frequently to only two. They portray those alternatives as competing courses of action. The implication is that rejecting one means accepting the other. They stamp a partisan and ideological brand on the arguments offered in their favor, signaling that accepting one means rejecting the other. Political candidates, by assuming the lead of a party, can do much to determine how issues are organized into policy agendas or even how policy agendas are organized into overarching ideological orientations.[24] But at the end of the day, it is through parties that the menu of choices on offer to citizens is organized.

And much to the advantage of citizens. By structuring political choice spaces, parties facilitate citizens' reasoning consistently from basic principles. It is not possible to derive a stable and coherent structure of choices the other way around, from the power of ordinary citizens to reason about politics. Coherence at the level of individual citizens is conditional on coherence in the menu of choices presented to them to make as citizens.

The role of political parties in bundling issues into bite-sized agendas promotes consistency both within and across sets, or agendas, of issues. But parties also promote consistency issue by issue. Consider the framing and highlighting of issues. Sniderman and Theriault (chapter 5 in this volume) investigate efforts to frame or define "the essence of the problem" for an issue, that is, to make a persuasive case as to "how it should be thought about and . . . [to] recommend what (if anything) should be done."[25] They show that when respondents are confronted with competing efforts to frame an issue, rather than being confused, they are markedly more likely to select the policy alternative congruent with their general view of the matter. They embed this result in a larger story about the connection between electoral competition and electoral choice. It is just so far as parties and candidates compete over issues, they suggest, that voters are in a position to make consistent choices.

Sniderman and Theriault present their story as one about the electorate as a whole, not just the upper echelon of the politically sophisticated part of it. Indeed, in their analysis, they show that their findings hold for both less sophisticated and more sophisticated citizens. Both are more likely to choose, from among the alternatives on offer, the one most congruent with their general view of the matter when they are exposed to competing efforts to frame an issue.

This result is important in its own right, illustrating as it does how citizens can more accurately find their political bearings thanks to the clash of competing arguments. But there is an aspect of Sniderman and Theriault's results that they do not explore and that we want to call attention to here.

In one of their experiments, the effect of being exposed to arguments on both sides of an issue is conditional on the respondents' level of political awareness. Finding that political sophistication makes a difference is a standard result. But in one of their experiments, Sniderman and Theriault find the opposite of what is standardly found. Instead of finding that congruence increases as political information increases, they find that the less politically aware, not the more, benefit most from exposure to competing ways of thinking about a political issue.

As things stand, only two on-the-shelf explanations do better at accounting for the choices of the less politically sophisticated than of the more sophisticated. In the contemporary version of the nonattitudes model, the decisive consideration is the extent to which people have an approximately evenly balanced set of reasons to support or oppose a policy.[26] This certainly counts as explanation, but there is no way to extract a consistency-based account from a nonattitudes model, since the pivotal factor is precisely the extent to which people's views about an issue are inconsistent.

The second on-the-shelf account centers on group affect. It can plausibly be argued that the less politically sophisticated citizens are, the more likely they are to lack a cognitive basis for making political choices, and therefore the more likely they are to rely on an affective one. There is some evidence this is so, though less than one may think.[27] Sniderman and Theriault point to a third alternative for giving an account of the choices of the less politically aware portion of the public. It is a fact, and an important one, that they are less adept at organizing their choices just by virtue of being less aware. But so far as they can choose consistently, some external machinery for organizing their responses is specially needed. Sniderman and Theriault suggest that electoral competition supplies this machinery. Admittedly, an inverse relationship between consistency of choice and level of political sophistication holds for only one of their two experiments. So we would therefore like to pitch their results at a slightly lower level. What their results show, and not just in one of the experiments but in both, is that the less sophisticated benefit at least as much as the more sophisticated from being exposed to the clash of opposing arguments. And it is electoral competition that generates the clash of arguments.

Issue-framing effects of all varieties are illustrations of menu dependence. But they are only a selection of the ways in which menu dependence is driven by the dynamics of electoral competition. Consider differences in the partisan centrality of issues. There are issues that parties do not wish to compete on; there are others that, out of a calculation of political advantage or as a consequence of political conviction, they do wish to compete on. Political issues can accordingly be located along a continuum of partisan centrality, from those most vigorously contested to those least vigorously contested.

In broad outline, the following hypothesis is worth examination. The more central an issue is to electoral competition, the greater the effort that political actors, including political parties, will make to call the electorate's attention to them and to contrast the alternatives open for choice. The more peripheral an issue, the less attention directed to it, and the more similar the alternatives open for choice will appear. Moreover, the more central an issue is to electoral competition, the "stickier" will be the identification of issues with parties over time; the more peripheral the issue, the looser the linkage. The result: the more central the issue to partisan competition, the stronger the tendency to congruence; the more peripheral the issue, the weaker.

And what follows from this? Very briefly, the relevance of alternative public opinion models varies with the partisan centrality of a political choice. Consistency and contestation go hand in hand. The more central an issue is to electoral competition, the more likely it is that causal accounts favoring opinion consistency, whether in the form of on-line processing or more elaborately hierarchical models, will apply. Conversely, the more peripheral an issue, the more likely it is that models accentuating inconsistency—Converse's black-and-white model, Krosnick's satisficing model, and Zaller's consideration sampling model with an important qualification—will apply.

Impressionistically, this hypothesis fits to a first approximation the standard findings in public opinion research. Consistency (whether interpreted in terms of consonance with other beliefs at one moment in time or stability of the same belief over time) seems weakest for issues that are remote from established partisan battlegrounds (e.g., U.S. intervention in Nicaragua) and strongest for those that are central to them (e.g., racial policies). The hypothesis of a connection between partisan centrality and opinion consistency seems to us promising, and offers an example of external anchoring of belief, although of course further research is required to test this hypothesis ex ante as opposed to trawling through previous research ex post.

SOME ESPECIALLY OBVIOUS QUALIFICATIONS

Much of our argument should be filed under the heading of "Suggestions and Speculations." Apart from issuing this general caution, we want to post some specific warning signs.

The most conspicuous concerns the problem of belief revision. Any theory of choice that is rational under any description of rational must have a provision for updating. External circumstances change, and there must be some way of taking (some of) these changes into account. Yet consistency theories take as their principal premise that what you believe and feel now is conditional on what you believed and felt before; or still more strongly, that in forming a belief or feeling now, you aim at maximizing consistency with what you believed and felt before. But if citizens have been consistency maximizing for any extended period of time, how are they capable of substantially revising their beliefs?

One route to take is to posit an accuracy motive operating in tandem with a consistency motive. On this view, "[P]eople motivated to arrive at a particular conclusion attempt to be rational and to construct a justification of their desired conclusion *that would persuade a dispassionate observer.*"[28] Under some interpretation this surely is right. Still, it is less than reassuring for revising beliefs about politics. For one thing, the notion of a "dispassionate observer" is inherently difficult to pin down just so far as political choices turn on conflicts between incommensurable values. For another, an accuracy motive may work as a self-correcting device for fairly specific motives, for example, maintaining a positive self-evaluation. But once an internally consistent framework of beliefs, feelings, and expectations has been established, how does one stand outside it? Just so far as a framework is internally consistent, it carries with it a self-affirming warrant that this is the way the world really is, as any dispassionate observer would agree. In any case, in the absence of a theoretical basis, appealing to an accuracy motive to override a motivation to consistency is unacceptably ad hoc.

An alternative route to respond to the problem of updating is to take advantage of Bayesian models of political learning.[29] Gerber and Green have put forward a case for unbiased Bayesian updating in the public as a whole.[30] On their interpretation, the case for unbiased learning is cemented by the observation that in the aggregate, citizens identifying with opposing parties revise their prior beliefs by approximately the same amount when confronted by new experiences. This is a comforting outcome. But it is not obvious that accepting Bayesian updating comes at the price of rejecting consistency maximizing. Bartels argues in response that Gerber and Green's central result illustrates partisan bias, not unbiased updating, provided that Bayesianism is properly interpreted. Bartels's interpretation eases the tension between consistency maximizing and updating in the face of new experience (Bartels 2003).

Even so, Bayesian updating and consistency maximizing make an ill-matched couple. The whole thrust of a consistency account is to emphasize the recalcitrance of people to revising their beliefs even in the face of clear evidence that their preconceptions have failed them. And what is worse, this appears to be at least as true for those who have given more thought to a problem, at any rate when it comes to politics. Consider Tetlock's (1999) studies of theory-driven reasoning. He shows that experts cope with the interpretive complexities and ambiguities of world politics by resorting to theory-driven strategies of thinking that allow them to: (1) make confident counterfactual inferences about what would have happened had different policy paths been pursued (plausible pasts); (2) generate predictions about what might yet happen (probable futures); and (3) defend both counterfactual beliefs and conditional forecasts from potentially disconfirming data. For example, experts who were convinced in the late 1980s that the Communist Party of the Soviet Union would continue to control the levers of power in the Kremlin deep into the 1990s argue that this outcome nearly did happen (the attempted coup of August 1991), whereas experts who expected the EU currency convergence project to fail could argue that the project nearly did come undone at several junctures (again, the close-call counterfactual defense) and eventually will still collapse (the just-off-on-timing defense).

The weight of Tetlock's findings is that experts do not come close to living up to the terms of the Bayesian reputational bets they make about the relative likelihood of events. On his view, there are two basic reasons—one rooted in the human mind and the other in the structure of the political environment—why experts find it relatively easy to resist changing their minds when the unexpected occurs. Resistance is easy, in part, because experts come cognitively equipped with a complex of cause-effect schemata that allow them to portray events that were not viewed as likely ex ante as close to inevitable ex post. Resistance is also easy, in part, because historical data lend themselves to a variety of alternative causal interpretations and it is rarely possible to achieve ideological consensus on how history would have unfolded in counterfactual worlds in which alternative policy paths were pursued. When reality constraints are weak, strongly held preconceptions fill the void.

There is another problem. When it comes to political matters at the center of electoral competition, political sophistication promotes divergence, not convergence, of political choices along partisan and ideological lines. It is not obvious that divergence can be accommodated on Bayesian principles.[31]

Still, consistency maximizing without a provision for updating is a formula for irresponsible voters in a world in which things do change. How can citizens change in response to changing circumstances if they are indeed consistency maximizers?

Framing the problem of change in terms of belief revision (Bayesian or otherwise) presupposes that the question that needs an answer is how citizens on their own hook revise their beliefs in the face of new experience. But the central argument of our project is that there is much that citizens don't do *on their own hook*. Throughout our claim has been that political institutions do the heavy lifting. That is just the point of emphasizing the menu dependence of choice.

And what falls out of this focus on menu dependence is updating via another route. Partisan elites have incentives to keep the menu of basic choices fixed for extended periods of time. But to the extent their continuing hold on political power is put at risk by changing circumstances, they are under pressure to respond. They must introduce new policies or revise old ones. Sometimes they do the one, sometimes the other, sometimes under old labels, sometimes under new ones. The question of updating takes a quite different form so viewed. It is not necessarily the beliefs of citizens that get revised. It is instead the courses of action they get to choose that are revised. And so far as this is true, updating is built into the menu of alternatives on offer to citizens.

Again we think it is useful to distinguish between the characteristics of citizens as choosers and the characteristics of the choices presented to them. Yet drawing distinctions by twos risks supposing that the two are separate, as though some portion of the variance in consistency is to be attributed to characteristics of citizens and a different portion to characteristics of choices. The temptation to pronounce one or the other more fundamental appears nearly irresistible—irresistible and ironic.[32] Thus, students of legislative institutions devote themselves to analysis of the strategic choices of political elites, yet they take electoral preferences to be the most fundamental causal force. Generously reciprocating, students of mass behavior devote themselves to the investigation of public opinion, yet they take the initiatives of elites to be the most fundamental causal force.[33] It is all the more worthwhile to emphasize that public opinion and elite strategic choice are part of a single account.

Elsewhere we have written about political choice spaces.[34] A choice space is, simply enough, the menu of alternatives on offer. Alternatives are defined by political elites partly by anticipation of electoral preferences, partly by consequences of past commitments. Alternatives are chosen by mass publics partly on the basis of preferences, partly on the basis of aptitudes in connecting preferences to alternatives. Plus, there is a complicating factor on both sides of the equation. Working with just two terms, elite actions and electoral preferences, is working with two terms too few. From time to time, shocks intrude—a slump in the economy, a threat overseas. Elites in office have to respond just because their eyes are on the next election. So they draw on their respective ideologies, broadly liberal or conservative depending on which party they belong to. And apart from the demands of interest group politics, they draw on their ideologies in an effort to take advantage of their best theories of how the world actually works. The whole idea is thus to tie together elite initiatives and citizen responses through the vehicle of a choice space.

Another especially obvious point of qualification: the explanatory limits of our account. We have worked to reduce explanation of choice to the maximization of consistency, where consistency is defined as congruence between selection of a policy alternative and direction of an underlying orientation. Analyzing judgments of the political commitments of strategic political actors, Brady and Sniderman have formalized a consistency model of judgment that derives accuracy of cognitive judgments from basic likes and dislikes, coherently organized.[35] This reduction, focusing on consistency, offers gains. It brings the benefit of parsimony. It facilitates formulation of a formal model cast in maximizing form. And it generates non-obvious predictions.

Still, our account has notable gaps. One illustration will have to do for many. A key question, we remarked, was "With respect to what, exactly, are most citizens trying to be consistent?" The answer, we suggested, was their general orientation toward policy agendas, one at a time. The tone of our account certainly suggests that the organization of policy agendas is the work of political elites. Even to our eyes, this suggestion is muzzy. Political institutions do the immediate work of bundling issues. But the opinions that elites have about the shape of public opinion surely must play some role. If so, how does the process work? To answer that question it will be necessary to detail how particular policy agendas come to be organized by political activists.

There is a more general point. Only after the consistency mainspring is wound do the explanatory clocks of consistency theories start ticking. But of course this involves some fairly heavy question begging. Why do some parts of the public identify with one political party while others identify with its competitor(s), and why are some disposed to a liberal or broadly left political outlook while others are disposed to a conservative or broadly right orientation? How exactly do the major pieces of citizens' political furniture, their basic beliefs and loyalties, come to be acquired? The answers must come from studies of the acquisition of basic political beliefs and allegiances. In this sense our account of political choices is parasitic on accounts of political socialization and learning.

A FINAL WORD

Perhaps quixotically, we want to suggest that the weakest point of our hypothesis of menu dependence may prove its strongest recommendation. When in need of an unseen (explanatory) hand, we point to political institutions, political parties and electoral competition in particular. But invoking institutions presents a special problem of proof. So far as political institutions are responsible for the menu of political choices (as opposed, for example, to exogenous shocks), the basic choices tend to be fixed for extended intervals, often a generation or more. Certainly that seems the case for a political system like the American one. But to say that the menu of basic choices is fixed over time is to say it is a constant. And so far as it is a constant, then how can it be shown to constrain political choice?

We have worried about this problem for some time. Historical accounts aside, we believe the best way forward is through randomized experiments in public opinion surveys. Many features of menu dependence lend themselves to experimental manipulation—the effect of taking polar positions, the party branding of policy alternatives, and the provision of explicit alternatives, among them. This is the road we have started down. We invite others to join us.

NOTES

We gratefully acknowledge the assistance of the National Science Foundation through an Achievement-Based Award (SES-0111715) in preparation of this book. On the individual front, we are deeply grateful to James H. Kuklinski, Philip E. Tetlock, and Michael Tomz for criticism laced with encouragement.

1. We interpret constraint broadly, referring not only to the connectedness of specific beliefs but also to the connectedness of any set of idea elements at the same

level of specificity. Our usage thus conforms to Peffley and Hurwitz's (1985) concept of horizontal linkage. Accordingly, we often speak of coherence in place of constraint.

2. The notion of congruence corresponds to Peffley and Hurwitz's vertical linkages in belief systems.

3. The two classic exceptions are group-centered politics, where affect—for example, toward blacks—can assure constraint across issues dealing with blacks, and issue publics, where uncommon motivation and focused attention on a specific set of concerns can also do the trick. See Converse 1964.

4. See, for example, Sniderman, Brody, and Tetlock 1991; Zaller 1992; and Jackman and Sniderman 2001. It deserves to be emphasized that Converse first sounded this note in his seminal essay, although he qualified this by positing that only a thin slice of the public is sophisticated enough about politics to form politically coherent belief systems.

5. For the concept of menu dependence in economic analysis, see, e.g., Sen 2002.

6. For the principal difficulty, in our view, see our concluding comment on menus as explanatory constants.

7. Festinger 1957.

8. For all the obvious reasons, we omit consideration of ideology, understood as an abstract and integrated outlook on politics.

9. Hastie and Park 1986; Lodge, Steenbergen, and Brau 1985; Lodge, McGraw, and Stroh 1989.

10. Taber, Lodge, and Glathar 2001:216, italics theirs.

11. Converse 1964.

12. See the discussion below on the connection between affective coherence and levels of political sophistication.

13. Feldman 1988. Feldman has carried this on in an interesting way with humanitarianism—see Feldman and Steenbergen 2001. See also Frankfurt 1988.

14. Robinson, Shaver, and Wrightsman 1999.

15. Specifically, the procedure scores forced choices over all possible pairs of a limited set of basic values. See Jacoby 2002.

16. Brady and Sniderman 1985.

17. E.g., Popkin 1991 and Lupia 1994.

18. For the conditionality of on-line processing on political awareness, see McGraw, Lodge, and Stroh 1990.

19. Carmines and Layman 1997; Shafer and Claggett 1995.

20. Converse 1964, especially Table VII.

21. Converse 1964; Sniderman, Brody, and Tetlock 1991; Zaller 1992.

22. E.g., Taber, Lodge, and Glathar 2001:198.

23. See, specifically, Layman and Carsey 2002:798.

24. For a key argument on the contingent character of issue bundling, see Carmines and Stimson 1989.

25. For a review of previous efforts, see Nelson and Kinder 1996:1057. See also Entman 1993.

26. Zaller 1992.

27. Sniderman, Brody, and Kuklinski 1984.

28. Kunda 1990:482–83, emphasis ours. Contrary to the impression that this point of disagreement may leave, we benefited greatly from Kunda's work. Her analysis on motivated reasoning introduces a very useful distinction between motives for accuracy and for directional goals.

29. See, for example, Achen 1989, 1992; Bartels 2003; Gerber and Green 1998, 1999; Zechman 1979; and Husted, Kenny, and Morton 1995.

30. Green, Palmquist, and Schickler 2002: chap. 5; Gerber and Green 1999, 1998.

31. For the connection between convergence and Bayesian updating, see Bartels 2003; for evidence on the connection between polarization and political sophistication, see Sniderman, Brody, and Tetlock 1991.

32. We can attest to the temptation, having succumbed ourselves in earlier efforts. We are especially indebted to James Kuklinski for pointing out to us the error of our ways.

33. Zaller 1992 is the preeminent example.

34. Sniderman 2000; Jackman and Sniderman 2001.

35. It may be worth remarking that the Brady-Sniderman model has the nonintuitive property of generating accurate cognitive judgments about the political commitments of strategic actors (e.g., political parties, liberals and conservatives) from affective orientations to those actors. See Brady and Sniderman 1985.

REFERENCES

Achen, Christopher. 1989. "Prospective Voting and the Theory of Party Identification." Paper presented at the annual meeting of the American Political Science Association, Atlanta, August 30–September 3.
———. 1992. "Social Psychology, Demographic Variables, and Linear Regression: Breaking the Iron Triangle in Voting Research." *Political Behavior* 14:195–211.
Bartels, Larry M. 2003. "Beyond the Running Tally: Partisan Bias in Political Perceptions." *Political Behavior* 24:117–50.
Brady, Henry E., and Paul M. Sniderman. 1985. "Attitude Attribution: A Group Basis for Political Reasoning." *American Political Science Review* 79:1061–78.
Campbell, Angus, Philip Converse, Warren Miller, and Donald E. Stokes. 1960. *The American Voter.* New York: Wiley.
Carmines, Edward G., and Geoffrey C. Layman. 1997. "Value Priorities, Partisanship, and Electoral Choice: The Neglected Case of the United States." *Political Behavior* 19:283–316.
Carmines, Edward G., and James A. Stimson. 1989. *Issue Evolution: Race and the Transformation of American Politics.* Princeton: Princeton University Press.
Converse, Philip E. 1964. "The Nature of Belief Systems in Mass Publics." In *Ideology and Discontent,* ed. David E. Apter. New York: Free Press.
Entman, Robert M. 1993. "Framing: Toward Clarification of a Fractured Paradigm." *Journal of Communication* 43:51–58.
Feldman, Stanley. 1988. "Structure and Consistency in Public Opinion: The Role of Core Beliefs and Values." *American Journal of Political Science* 32:416–40.

Feldman, Stanley, and Marco R. Steenbergen. 2001. "The Humanitarian Foundation of Public Support for Social Welfare." *American Journal of Political Science* 45:658–77.

Festinger, Leon. 1957. *A Theory of Cognitive Dissonance.* Stanford: Stanford University Press.

Frankfurt, Harry G. 1988. *The Importance of What We Care About.* New York: Cambridge University Press.

Gerber, Alan, and Donald P. Green. 1998. "Rational Learning and Partisan Attitudes." *American Journal of Political Science* 42:794–818.

———. 1999. "Misperceptions about Perceptual Bias." *Annual Review of Political Science* 2:189–210.

Green, Donald, Bradley Palmquist, and Eric Schickler. 2002. *Partisan Hearts and Minds: Political Parties and the Social Identities of Voters.* New Haven: Yale University Press.

Hastie, Reid, and Bernadette Park. 1986. "The Relationship between Memory and Judgment Depends on Whether the Task is Memory-Based or On-Line." *Psychological Review* 93:258–68.

Husted, Thomas A., Lawrence W. Kenny, and Rebecca B. Morton. 1995. "Constituent Errors in Assessing Their Senators." *Public Choice* 83:251–71.

Jackman, Simon, and Paul M. Sniderman. 2001. "The Institutional Organization of Choice Spaces: A Political Conception of Political Psychology." In *Political Psychology,* ed. Kristen Renwick Monroe. Malwah, NJ: Lawrence Erlbaum.

Jacoby, William. 2002. "Core Values and Political Attitudes." In *Understanding Opinion,* ed. Barbara Norrander and Clyde Wilcox. 2nd ed. Washington, DC: CQ Press.

Kunda, Ziva. 1990. "The Case for Motivated Reasoning." *Psychological Bulletin* 108:480–98.

Layman, Geoffrey C., and Thomas M. Carsey. 2002. "Party Polarization and Conflict Extension in the American Electorate." *American Journal of Political Science* 46:786–802.

Lodge, Milton, Kathleen McGraw, and Pat Stroh. 1989. "An Impression-Driven Model of Candidate Formation." *American Political Science Review* 83:399–420.

Lodge, Milton, Marco R. Steenbergen, and Shawn Brau. 1995. "The Responsive Voter: Campaign Information and the Dynamics of Candidate Evaluation." *American Political Science Review* 89:309–26.

Lupia, Arthur. 1994. "Shortcuts versus Encyclopedias: Information and Voting Behavior in California Insurance Reform Elections." *American Political Science Review* 88:63–76.

McGraw, Kathleen M., Milton Lodge, and Patrick Stroh. 1990. "On-Line Processing in Candidate Evaluation: The Effects of Issue Order, Issue Importance, and Sophistication." *Political Behavior* 12:41–58.

Nelson, Thomas E., and Donald R. Kinder. 1996. "Issue Frames and Group-Centrism in American Public Opinion." *Journal of Politics* 58:1055–78.

Peffley, Mark A., and Jon Hurwitz. 1985. "A Hierarchical Model of Attitude Constraint." *American Journal of Political Science* 29:871–90.

Popkin, Samuel L. 1991. *The Reasoning Voter: Communication and Persuasion in Presidential Campaigns.* Chicago: University of Chicago Press.

Robinson, John P., Phillip R. Shaver, and Lawrence S. Wrightsman, eds. 1999. *Measures of Political Attitudes.* New York: Academic Press.

Sen, Amartya. 2002. *Rationality and Freedom.* Cambridge, MA: Belknap Press.

Shafer, Byron E., and William J. M. Claggett. 1995. *The Two Majorities: The Issue Context of Modern American Politics.* Baltimore: Johns Hopkins University Press.

Simon, Herbert A. 1985. "Human Nature in Politics: The Dialogue of Psychology with Political Science." *American Political Science Review* 79:293–304.

Sniderman, Paul M. 2000. "Taking Sides: A Fixed Choice Theory of Political Reasoning." In *Elements of Reason,* ed. Arthur Lupia, Mathew D. McCubbins, and Samuel L. Popkin. New York: Cambridge University Press.

Sniderman, Paul M., Richard A. Brody, and James H. Kuklinski. 1984. "Policy Reasoning in Political Issues: The Problem of Racial Equality." *American Journal of Political Science* 28:75–94.

Sniderman, Paul M., Richard A. Brody, and Philip E. Tetlock. 1991. *Reasoning and Choice: Explorations in Political Psychology.* New York: Cambridge University Press.

Taber, Charles S., Milton Lodge, and Jill Glathar. 2001. "The Motivated Construction of Political Judgments." In *Thinking about Political Psychology,* ed. James H. Kuklinski. New York: Cambridge University Press.

Tetlock, Philip E., 1999. "Theory-Driven Reasoning about Plausible Pasts and Probable Futures in World Politics: Are We Prisoners of Our Preconceptions?" *American Journal of Political Science* 43:335–66.

Zaller, John. 1992. *The Nature and Origins of Mass Opinion.* New York: Cambridge University Press.

Zechman, Martin. 1979. "Dynamic Models of the Voter's Decision Calculus." *Public Choice* 34:297–315.

Index

Abelson, Robert P., 9, 96, 271

abortion: ambivalence regarding, 102, 111–12, 117, 126; attitude-expressive behavior regarding, 224; voting behavior and, 195

accountability, political awareness and electoral, 7–8

Achen, Christopher H.: and measurement error and opinion instability, 4–5, 18, 22, 47, 53, 252, 319–20; research influenced by, 19; and retrospective voting, outcomes of, 203–4

affect-driven choice model, 19, 32

affirmative action, 98–100, 108–9, 125

Ajzen, Icek, 87, 315–16

Alcser, K. H., 309

Alvarez, R. Michael: on abortion, ambivalence regarding, 67, 94, 102, 112; on affirmative action, lack of ambivalence regarding, 67, 99, 109; on ambivalence, presence of, 7; on "conscious" ambivalence, 28; on measurement of ambivalence, 73, 120; on predictability of responses, ambivalence and, 97, 112; on weak opinions and ambivalence, 244

ambivalence: attitude stability and, 112–15; attitudinal, 63–64, 86–88; the Choice Questionnaire and, 328–30; of citizens, 66–68; conceptualizing/defining, 68, 95–96, 103; conscious distinguished from unconscious, 28, 30; consequences of, 70–71, 85–86, 108–12; framing effects and, 137; horizontal constraint and, 115–18; incidence of in America, 93–95, 104–8, 119–22; indicators of, 97–98; measurement of, 71–74, 103–4, 120–21, 252–53; toward policies, 6–7, 98–102, 108–12, 116–17; political psychology of, 96–97; toward presidential candidates, 6–7, 68–70, 74–77, 80–86; regarding presidential performance, 77–79; research on, 64–66; response predictability and, 108–12; types of, 71–

72; value conflict, distinguished from, 66; vertical constraint and, 118–19

Anderson, Christopher J., 173

Anderson, N. H., 40–42

Andrews, F. M., 52

attitudes: accessibility of, 228–34; defined, 63; importance of, 218–21, 227–28; multidimensional conceptualization of, 64–66; stability of (*see* stability of attitudes/opinions/responses); strength of (*see* strength of attitudes/opinions)

attitudinal ambivalence. *See* ambivalence

Bachman, J. G., 309

Bartels, Larry M., 168, 203–4, 295, 298–99, 350

Bassili, J. N., 233

Belgium, political alienation in, 273–86

belief sampling model, 21

Bell, David W., 71, 86

Berelson, Bernard R.: on citizens' attention to politics, 134; and election of 1948, study of, 179, 192; and two-stage model, 17, 19; on voting and background variables, relationship of, 30

Berent, Matthew K., 9, 223, 231

Bettman, J. R., 299

Billiet, Jaak, 10, 283

Bizer, George Y., 9–10, 47, 228, 230–34, 236

black-and-white model, 4, 18, 22, 252, 256, 319, 323, 327, 330, 348

Boninger, D. S., 231

Boynton, G. R., 38, 53

Brady, Henry E., 342, 352

Brau, Shawn, 20, 31, 89n6

Breckler, Steven J., 73, 87

Brehm, John: on abortion, ambivalence regarding, 67, 94, 102, 112; on affirmative action, lack of ambivalence regarding, 67, 99, 109; on ambivalence, presence of, 7; on "conscious" ambivalence, 28; on measurement of ambivalence, 73,